Ancient History Vol. 1

An Enthralling Guide to
Mesopotamia, Egypt, and Rome

Free limited time bonus

Stop for a moment. We have a free bonus set up for you. The problem is this: we forget 90% of everything that we read after 7 days. Crazy fact, right? Here's the solution: we've created a printable, 1-page pdf summary for this book that you're reading now. All you have to do to get your free pdf summary is to go to the following website:

https://livetolearn.lpages.co/enthrallinghistory/

Once you do, it will be intuitive. Enjoy, and thank you!

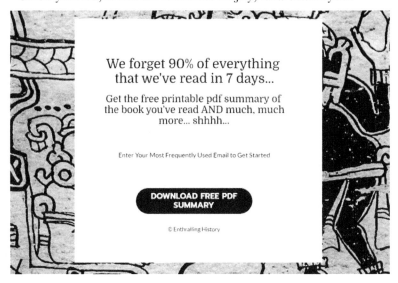

Table of Contents

Part 1: Ancient Egypt

An Enthralling Overview of Egyptian History, Starting from the Settlement of the Nile Valley through the Old, Middle, and New Kingdoms to the Death of Cleopatra VII

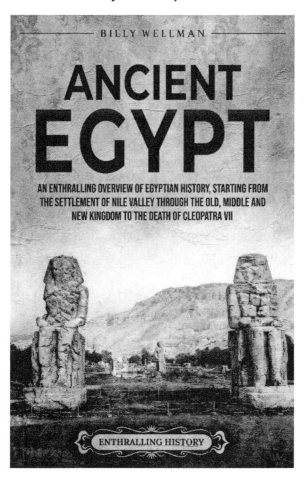

Introduction

Long before the emergence of the first pharaoh, the Great Pyramids, hieroglyphs, and the towering obelisks was a land known by its people as Kemet. Literally translated as the "Black Land," the ancient name was believed to have been derived from the fertile yet pitch-black soil along the valley left by the Nile's annual inundation. While Kemet earned its name from the black soil, the natives also had another name for the deep reddish deserts; they called them Deshret or simply the "Red Land."

It was not until the birth of the ancient city of Memphis that its people began to refer to Kemet with a new name. Within the city was a temple called Hikuptah, which was dedicated to Ptah, the ancient god of craftsmen. The temple was so grand that it caught the attention of many, especially the Greeks. Upon learning about the prominence of the temple to the people of the Nile, the Greeks began to refer to the entire city as "Aigyptos," which was Greek for Hikuptah. From there on, the name became widely used by both natives of the land and foreigners. Eventually, Aigyptos was simplified to Egypt, the English spelling that we are all so familiar with today.

For many centuries, the ancient Egyptian civilization has managed to intrigue not only Egyptologists and scholars but also an array of other professionals, including writers, artists, and even architects from all over the world. The kingdom's impressive architectural designs and techniques have been studied over and over again just so we can uncover their secrets and apply them today, though the exact building technique of the pyramids was never entirely debunked until recently. The tales of the many pharaohs and stories of their battles are forever immortalized in books and movies, while the Egyptians' knowledge of astronomy and medicine was also greatly studied and used as a foundation by modern astronomers, medical practitioners, and scientists.

Whenever Egypt is mentioned, one cannot help but imagine the sight of the bleak and dry desert surrounding the pyramids, but have the lands of the Nile always been this way? Science tells us that due to the dramatic climate change that occurred at the beginning of the 4th millennium BCE, Egypt turned into a vast land full of life. The areas close to the Nile River were filled with lush vegetation, which attracted not only various species of animals but also the very first people who eventually set up seasonal camps and took shelter in the Nile Valley. Nabta Playa, a region of the Nubian Desert, for instance, was thought to have been wetter than today and was a site where one could find one of the earliest settlements in the ancient world. It was only after 3500 BCE that the valley witnessed another climate change, which led Egypt to gradually dry out and transform into the desert that we know today.

Being one of the earliest civilizations in the ancient world, it is definitely not a surprise that Egypt had gone through numerous changes, conflicts, disasters, and wars. The first unification of the kingdom thousands of years ago led to the rise of the Old Kingdom, a prosperous era that saw the construction of the pyramids, which are known by many. Perhaps the most flourishing era of Egypt was during the reign of the powerful pharaohs of the New Kingdom, which gave birth to the many impressive temples that survived the test of time.

However, although Egypt lasted for many centuries, it could not fully escape the dark times that terrorized the lands and its people. Famine, continuous political strife, constant warfare, and foreign invasions were some of the most common events that nearly crushed the kingdom. The Egyptians, led by the mighty god-like pharaohs, managed to overcome and repel the threats that could have engulfed their kingdom whole, but freedom was never meant to linger around the valley for too long.

In this book, you will not only get an insightful look into the early inhabitants of Egypt and the daily life of its people but also an enthralling journey of how the kingdom rose to power and eventually became desired by many foreign forces around the world. Jump from one pharaoh to another, reimagine their battles with other fierce forces beyond Egypt's borders, and dive deep into the unique Egyptian beliefs and traditions that held their people together.

Chapter 1: Settlers on the Nile
I: Lower Egypt

Egypt, unsurprisingly, has its roots buried deep beneath the golden sands of the desert. The absence of written records caused scholars and historians alike to argue about when life first sprang across the Egyptian valley. After many series of excavations over the years, many agree that humans first occupied the region at least a millennium ago. Archaeologist Waldemar Chmielewski is believed to have discovered some of the oldest Egyptian structures near Wadi Halfa, a city in modern-day Sudan. These ancient structures, possibly a type of early Paleolithic dwelling, were estimated to date from 100,000 BCE. In the early 1980s, another excavation proved to be fruitful, as archaeologists discovered the Nazlet Khater skeleton, a complete set of human remains believed to have been over thirty thousand years old. With the success of the excavation and after several tests, experts could confidently conclude that Egypt had already gone through the Late Paleolithic period around 30,000 BCE.

The Nazlet Khater skeleton.

Though the traces of the past are largely visible in Egypt today, only a few of them can tell us the story of the Predynastic Period: a time when pyramids and pharaohs did not yet exist. Back then, Egypt was separated into two different lands: Lower Egypt, which was in the northern part of the Nile (the Nile runs south to north), and Upper Egypt in the south near the Sahara. Since these two separate lands had significant geographical differences, Egypt saw the birth of several different cultural eras, which were later named by experts after their respective Egyptian settlements.

Faiyum A Culture (c. 9000 BCE–6000 BCE)

During the Stone Age, Egyptians lived a rather simple life. They hunted big-game animals and collected berries and nuts. They did not even have permanent shelters. They often moved from one place to another, possibly to find better food sources and to escape from the impending dangers that nature holds. However, this lifestyle began to change as Egypt was ushered into the Late Neolithic period. The Egyptians began to resort to a semi-settled lifestyle.

With their knowledge of farming, which was acquired from the Levant, according to certain historians, the Egyptians built their new homes along the Nile, with some choosing the fertile lands of Faiyum. From what was once a barren desert basin with nothing in sight but dust and sand, Faiyum transformed into a lush oasis when the basin was filled with water from a branch of the Nile River. With new plants springing to life surrounding the oasis, several species of animals began to call Faiyum their new home, which eventually led to human beings occupying the area sometime around 9000 BCE.

The map of Lower Egypt and the location of Faiyum.

Since large cities were still thousands of years away from forming, these early Egyptians lived in small communities with only a few families. Seasonal camps with simple reed huts and mats were common in the Faiyum A culture, with the only permanent structures within their settlement being granaries and hearths. Pottery and tools of the Faiyum settlers, on the other hand, did not face any tremendous changes.

The three hundred ancient baskets, storage bins, and jars excavated from the surrounding area of this oasis town led experts to believe that Faiyum was, in fact, the birthplace of early Egyptian agriculture. Although Faiyum was not located on the banks of the Nile—the ancient town was approximately a hundred kilometers (sixty-two miles) away from Memphis (close to modern-day Cairo)—agricultural practices still thrived thanks to the river's annual flooding.

Typically, plants were cultivated in autumn, and harvests would be ready by spring. Since the crops relied heavily on the annual inundation, the harvests were not always guaranteed. The Egyptians could expect a terrible shortage of food supplies should the highlands of Ethiopia farther up the stream witness only little to zero rainfall. And so, to avoid such disaster, it could be plausible that the Egyptians moved to other locations in between the seasons, where they could hunt animals to further support their diets. However, once their crops were ready, they would return to Faiyum. These harvested crops, especially wheat and barley, were then collected in communal woven baskets, which were stored in close proximity to their settlement.

Merimde Culture (c. 5000 BCE–4200 BCE)

Over ninety years ago, the world was yet again surprised by another discovery. An expedition led by a German archaeologist named Hermann Junker uncovered another Egyptian neolithic culture up on the edge of the Western Delta. After sixteen years of excavations, the ancient settlement, also known as Merimde Beni Salama, went down in history as the earliest permanent settlement to ever exist in the Egyptian valley. Overlapping in time with the late period of the Faiyum A culture, the Merimde culture was believed to have been rather more advanced, despite sharing influences from both the people of Faiyum and the Levant. In fact, the settlement went through a total of three main cultural phases, each with its own characteristics, technology, and customs.

Like its predecessor, the early people of the Merimde culture were often described as primitive. They lived in small dwellings, which were typically flimsy and unrefined, while their ceramics were untempered; perhaps they preferred functionality over design. Occasionally, some were subtly decorated with a simple herringbone pattern. Agriculture was, of course, their main occupation from the beginning, although animal domestication and big-game hunting also played important roles in their daily lives. Goats, pigs, fish, turtles, crocodiles, and even hippopotami were some of the most common animals eaten by the Merimde people.

As Merimde entered its second cultural phase, the most evident advancement one could notice was the people's shelters. From simple huts, they evolved into sturdier dwellings with an oval-shaped ground plan. Given their larger spaces, these wooden houses often featured clay floors with hearths and a few storage jars. Even though only a little difference could be seen in their ceramic works—there were little to zero decorations—each piece appeared to be more polished and greatly refined. To sustain their diet, grain cultivation, fishing, and hunting activities continued, while animal domestication focused more on cattle.

The third and final phase, which many prefer to refer to as the Classic Merimde period, was a time when the people were beginning to take the first few steps to create a more organized community. Sticking to the previous oval-shaped ground plan, their houses were bigger and well constructed. Narrow streets occupied the spaces of the densely packed settlements. Each of the dwellings housed its own granaries, hearths, storage jars, and even grinding stones, which could possibly indicate that, in contrast to the Faiyum A culture, the families of the Merimde settlement were more independent, both socially and economically.

By the final phase of the Merimde culture, the ceramic works began to appear more intricate. The wares were often painted in a combination of deep red and black, with different types of engravings adorning the outer layers. This was also the time when human-like pottery first flourished. The cylindrical Merimde clay head, despite lacking realistic features, was believed to have been made as early as the 4th millennium BCE, thus making it the earliest known pottery representation of a human in ancient Egypt.

Without written records, it is hard for us to get a deep insight into the early beliefs and customs of the predynastic Egyptians. However, the discovery of a few grave pits could suggest that the people of Merimde practiced a simple burial tradition. Since no children's graves have ever been found surrounding the settlement, some Egyptologists conclude that only adults received a proper burial, while the remains of deceased children were simply thrown into rubbish pits. However, this has been disputed by a few scholars, as some suggest that the lack of a child's grave within the settlement was due to the annual flood, which could have possibly washed them away entirely. Nevertheless, in contrast to the later burial customs of the ancient Egyptians, the people of Merimde did not bury their deceased with any grave goods or weapons.

Merimde Clay Head.
kairoinfo4u, CC BY-SA 2.0 <https://creativecommons.org/licenses/by-sa/2.0>, via Wikimedia Commons:
https://commons.wikimedia.org/wiki/File:Merimde_clay_head,_Predynastic_Period,_Maadi_Era,_4th_millennium_BCE.jpg

El-Omari Culture (c. 4000 BCE–3100 BCE)

The El-Omari culture was named after Amim El-Omari, an Egyptian mineralogist who first discovered the site of the settlement. Located about five kilometers north of Helwan, a city on the bank of the Nile on the opposite side of Memphis, the settlement has left us with very little information about its inhabitants and their characteristics. By the time the site was discovered, Egyptologists could only find clear remnants of pits and post holes, some of which could indicate that the people of El-Omari once lived in houses made of wattle and daub. Certain pieces of tools were also found that resembled those from the Merimde culture. From the discovery of the tools, it could be concluded that the inhabitants of El-Omari focused more on fishing and agriculture rather than desert hunting. Their pottery was rather polished and decorated with a red coating.

Although we might not be able to reimagine exactly how the people of El-Omari lived their daily lives, we can get insights into how they once buried the dead. In contrast to those from the Merimde culture, the inhabitants of El-Omari buried the deceased with grave goods, though the items were not at all elaborate; they were often buried with only a single pot. While the dead were usually buried close to their shelters, their bodies were placed in a specific position. The deceased were placed in shallow pits lying on their left side with their face facing the west. The reason behind this position is uncertain, but some scholars believe that it was possibly due to the direction where the sun sets.

Though many remains found within the settlement were buried the same, with only a pot placed by their feet, one grave appeared slightly different. This particular man was buried with a staff that closely resembles an early version of the Ames Sceptre, a type of ancient weapon typically used by later Egyptian kings and perhaps, at least according to ancient Egyptians, gods. This could signify that the man was probably an important figure within the settlement; perhaps he was some sort of leader or local chief.

Maadi Culture (c. 3900 BCE–3500 BCE)

Almost similar to the inhabitants of El-Omari, the villagers of the Maadi culture preferred agricultural activities rather than desert hunting. Various animal remains discovered at this ancient settlement indicate that animal domestication was the norm, with cattle, sheep, goats, and pigs being the most common animals in the village. The people of the Maadi culture were also the earliest to have domesticated donkeys, which were often used for trade. Aside from neighboring Upper Egypt, they were believed to have traded widely with people who lived in what today comprises Palestine. Through the many trade activities, the people of Maadi were able to import various resources. Copper, oil, and resin were imported from Palestine, while greywacke cosmetic palettes were obtained from Upper Egypt.

Only little remains of their dwellings, but we know they lived in oval huts made out of wood and matting. Both rectangular and subterranean structures were common within the settlement, with some bearing similarities with those discovered in the ancient city of Beersheba (located in modern-day southern Israel). It could also be plausible that the villagers stored their supplies communally since several jars and large pits were found at the end of the settlement. Contrary to the El-Omari culture, the Maadi pottery was rarely decorated; it was only painted black or red.

When it comes to burial customs, the villagers of Maadi laid the dead to rest in simple graves located in cemeteries away from the settlement. Only children and stillborn infants were believed to have been buried within the settlement. Since their pottery was rather simple and undecorated, burying the dead with grave goods was not a must for the people of the Maadi culture. Apart from humans, the villagers also had a designated cemetery for animals. However, not all animals were given proper burials since the graves were reserved for animals used in a sacrificial ceremony for a funerary cult.

Chapter 2: Settlers on the Nile II: Upper Egypt

To say the people from the ancient world were brilliant is definitely an understatement. They were, indeed, far more advanced and ahead of their time. Nabta Playa, an archaeological site located in the Nubian Desert about a hundred kilometers away from Abu Simbel, is best known for portraying the excellent minds of the ancient people. The site contains the very first alignments of megaliths in the world. The ancient stone circle, thought to have been built at least seven thousand years ago, was accidentally discovered sometime in 1973 by a nomadic Arab guide. Believed by many to have been constructed by a group of nomadic people who once worshiped cattle, the megaliths were mainly used to determine the summer solstice and estimate the arrival of monsoons.

The reconstruction of the Nabta Playa stone circle at the Aswan Nubian Museum.
Raymbetz, CC BY-SA 3.0 <https://creativecommons.org/licenses/by-sa/3.0>, via Wikimedia Commons: https://commons.wikimedia.org/wiki/File:Calendar_aswan.JPG

Apart from the ancient megaliths, Nabta Playa was also considered one of the world's earliest settlements. Historians suggest the site welcomed its first inhabitants between eleven thousand and nine thousand years ago. Inhabited by a group of nomads, possibly of sub-Saharan African origin, the region was initially filled with only seasonal camps. As the centuries went by, Nabta Playa, like other prehistoric settlements in Egypt, witnessed gradual developments. From seasonal camps, the inhabitants began building more sophisticated huts and fire hearths, which were usually arranged in a straight line. The existence of gazelles and numerous wild plants growing around the area allowed the people to enjoy a more settled lifestyle. Later on, animal domestication became the norm; they usually raised goats and sheep.

The Badarian Culture (c. 4400 BCE–4000 BCE)

Named after its location at El-Badari, some two hundred kilometers away from the city of Thebes (modern-day Luxor), the Badarian culture mostly focused on agriculture. This settlement had the earliest evidence of agriculture in Upper Egypt. While the Badarian people often cultivated barley, wheat, herbs, and lentils to supplement their diet, they were also involved in fishing, animal domestication, and hunting, with gazelles being their main target.

Unfortunately, little is known about their dwellings, though the discovery of wooden stumps might suggest they once lived in simple and lightweight wooden huts; after all, they were semi-mobile. However, their burial practices were slightly complex, at least compared to the settlements found in Lower Egypt. In Badari, the deceased were wrapped in animal hides and placed on reed mats before getting buried in pits with their head facing west. The lack of battle wounds on the human remains discovered at the site also suggests the villagers of Badari were rather peaceful. Men were not buried with weapons, which possibly indicates that the Badarian people were not warriors.

Certain graves featured more than one grave good. Some were buried with a type of female mortuary statue, while there were also others that featured different personal items, such as shells, tools, jewelry made out of precious stones, and amulets carved in the shape of various animals, such as hippopotami and antelopes.

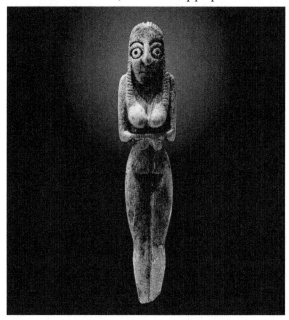

A Badarian female mortuary statue.
Louvre Museum, CC BY-SA 2.0 FR <*https://creativecommons.org/licenses/by-sa/2.0/fr/deed.en*>, *via Wikimedia Commons:*
https://commons.wikimedia.org/wiki/File:Woman-E_11887-IMG_9547-gradient.jpg

The people of this particular settlement were best known for their human-like sculptures and pottery. They were finely crafted and polished compared to the earlier periods. Some of the Badarian figurines became the foundation for later ancient Egyptian sculptures. The black-topped pottery, which made its first appearance in Nabta Playa, were commonly seen in this settlement, though they were often reserved for funerary and ritual purposes.

Historians and anthropologists have also suggested that the people of the Badarian culture were of the same racial mix as the ancient Egyptians of later dynasties. Egyptologist John Romer supported this claim by explaining the similarities of the Badarian people with the later ancient Egyptians. Their hair was either curly or straight and either light brown or black. Like the men of later periods, the Badarian people were mostly clean-shaven, while women often styled their hair in fringes and adorned it with combs made of either bone or ivory.

The Naqada Culture (c. 4000 BCE–3000 BCE)

The most important prehistoric culture of Upper Egypt is none other than the Naqada culture, which blossomed following the Badarian culture in 4500 BCE. Similar to the rest of the cultures discovered in the valley, the Naqada culture was also named after its location. This particular culture was divided into three different phases, each with its own unique characteristics and developments.

The earliest phase, Naqada I (also referred to as the Amratian phase), emerged concurrently with the Badarian culture, though it slowly replaced the latter as time passed. The people of Naqada I supplemented their diets by cultivating crops, and they lived in rather small villages. Their dwellings were more sophisticated. It is plausible that their houses featured windows and had walls made of wattle and daub. Despite appearing smaller in size, each of these villages had its own totems that represented its animal deity. The deities were possibly chosen according to their association with their clan or village.

However, the most prolific change was in terms of their sculptures and art. During this time, Naqada saw an increase in bearded male statues and sculptures of women, the latter of which were often associated with fertility. These statues were typically used for funerary purposes. Many graves of the Naqada culture featured at least one statuette, which served as company for the deceased in the underworld. This custom was practiced by later Egyptians. Food, pottery, jewelry, ornaments, weapons, and decorated palettes were some of the most popular items interred with the dead.

Sometime around 3500 BCE, the second phase of the Naqada culture happened, which is known to us today as the Naqada II culture. The people of this culture no longer hunted animals as part of their daily activities since they had mastered the art of agriculture. The discovery of artificial irrigation during this period greatly aided their agricultural activities. The people of Naqada II went from living in small villages to building bigger towns and, later on, cities, which resulted in a booming population. Their houses also faced tremendous changes. They were constructed out of sunbaked bricks, and certain dwellings even had courtyards. Not to forget the dead, their graves also witnessed major changes. They were more ornate and expensive. The best example was found in Abydos (which later developed into a necropolis or a city of the dead), which contained a great number of massive and important tombs.

With their growing skills in architecture, they constructed palaces and temples. The oldest Egyptian temple built by them was in the city of Nekhen, better known as Hierakonpolis. This temple complex had its own courtyard and several small buildings, which later became a source of inspiration for an Old Kingdom pharaoh named Djoser when he constructed his famous Step Pyramid complex.

The final phase, the Naqada III culture, also referred to as the protodynastic period or Dynasty 0, was considered the most important part of Egypt's early history since this was the very culture that shaped the future Egyptian dynasties. During this period of time, Egypt had already seen the birth of many kings and rulers who claimed their holds over the divided kingdom. These rulers were usually named after animals related to their totems and were considered the personification of their gods—a belief that no doubt made its way into dynastic Egypt. In contrast to the rulers of Lower Egypt, who wore red crowns, those in

Upper Egypt wore white crowns that resembled a bowling pin. Military campaigns were constantly launched, which eventually reduced the many city-states of Upper Egypt into only three: Thinis, Naqada, and Hierakonpolis (Nekhen).

Hieroglyphs, which simply mean "the words of god," were believed to have originated during the earliest Naqada phase, though they continued to develop during the period of Naqada III. This form of writing was initially used only on pottery and acted as nothing but decoration. However, starting from 3200 BCE, hieroglyphs were used to keep important records, but no complete sentences were ever found originating from this period. The earliest record of complete hieroglyphs dates to the Second Dynasty.

The hieroglyphs, which were composed of a combination of logographic, syllabic, and alphabetic elements, were difficult to translate. However, thanks to the discovery of the Rosetta Stone in 1799, Egyptologists and scholars were able to decipher the ancient Egyptian language. Another form of writing introduced in Naqada III was serekh, which was used as royal crests to identify a ruler's name.

One of the earliest forms of Egyptian hieroglyphs.
https://commons.wikimedia.org/wiki/File:Design_of_the_Abydos_token_glyphs_dated_to_3400-3200_BCE.jpg

The royal serekh representing the first pharaoh of Egypt, Narmer.
https://commons.wikimedia.org/wiki/File:Narmer_Palette_verso_serekh.png

Many scholars agree that Mesopotamia played a significant role in the development of Egyptian civilization. Certain sculptures, ceramics, construction techniques, tomb designs, and even the early form of the ancient Egyptian religion could be traced back to Mesopotamian influences. This was probably due to the growing trade activities that took place around the kingdom. Egypt was believed to have made constant contact with not only Mesopotamia but also Canaan and Nubia.

Chapter 3: The Early Dynastic Period and the First Pharaoh

Before the age of mortal kings and pharaohs, the Egyptians believed their land was once ruled by a mythical king known as Osiris. Born shortly after the creation of the world, Osiris was made the lord of the earth and married his sister, Isis, who was the goddess of fertility, healing, and magic. The tradition of marrying siblings was widely practiced by the ancient Egyptians, typically among pharaohs and royals.

Osiris watched over his people but grew weary of their unfortunate state; they were rather primitive and uncivilized. And so, the compassionate god bestowed culture on them and introduced laws, agricultural activities, and religious practices to them. With his gifts and just reign, Egypt blossomed into a vast paradise where crops flourished and food supplies were plentiful.

Osiris, the god of the afterlife.
Eternal Space, CC BY-SA 4.0 <https://creativecommons.org/licenses/by-sa/4.0>, via Wikimedia Commons: https://commons.wikimedia.org/wiki/File:Osiris_(God).png

Set, the god of chaos.

The Egyptians adored their king and queen since the people were treated fair and equally, no matter their status, age, wealth, or gender. While the royal pair were loved by many, one figure was hiding in the shadows, plotting to remove them from the throne and steal the crown for himself. This envious figure was Set, the god of chaos and the brother of Osiris.

Set eventually came up with a slow yet vicious plan to eradicate his brother. While hosting a grand banquet, Set presented his guests with a specially crafted chest or coffin, which he had secretly made to fit only Osiris. He then offered the intricate chest to whoever could fit into it, knowing full well that it could only fit his brother. The moment Osiris lay down in the chest, Set immediately sealed the lid and threw it into the Nile River. With the beloved king and god of Egypt gone, Set successfully realized his dreams. He was pharaoh.

Learning of her husband's terrible fate, Isis wept as the years passed by, leading to the flooding of the Nile. She managed to recover Osiris's remains; however, before she could attempt to resurrect the deceased god-king, Set arrived to put a stop to the plan. The god of chaos chopped the ice-cold remains of his brother before scattering the pieces to every corner of the world.

And so, Isis set on another journey to find and collect the pieces of Osiris so that she could bring him back to the land of the living. However, even the mightiest of gods could not escape their fate. Isis found all of Osiris's missing pieces except for one. Without the missing piece, he was only able to return to the living world for a short while. When his time was up, Osiris was left with no choice but to leave his dear wife and newborn son, Horus, to carry on with his new destiny as the lord of the underworld and judge of the dead. Heartbroken by the eternal departure of her husband and afraid of her son's future, Isis hid Horus somewhere in the isolated swampy marshland until he became old enough to fight for his right to the throne.

Golden statues of Horus (left), Osiris (middle), and Isis (right).

Under Set's reign, Egypt was plunged into mayhem, as the lands and the people were no longer united. Peace was a thing of the past. Seeing the chaos unleashed by Set and remembering his father's murder, a fully grown Horus challenged and battled Set. This struggle between the two gods was referred to as "The Contendings of Horus and Seth" (with Seth being a common variant of Set). In the end, Horus, who was proved to be the mightier warrior, successfully defeated Set. While some claimed the god of chaos was killed by his nephew, many suggest that he was, in fact, spared but driven out of the land.

With the chaos finally conquered by Horus, Egypt was reunited again. Order was restored, and the people welcomed Horus as their new king, thus marking the beginning of another prosperous era in Egypt.

Although the story of Set's demise and Horus's rise to the throne is nothing short of a myth that survived thousands of years, several researchers and Egyptologists agree that the myth was, believe it or not, created to mirror the historical unification of Egypt sometime around 3150 BCE. Since the Egyptians were a step closer to becoming more civilized, the two lands—Upper and Lower Egypt—witnessed an increasing number of wars and battles between the different settlements and villages. That was, however, until a king of Upper Egypt made a move to change the course of history and finally unite the two separate kingdoms.

Before the discovery of thousands of artifacts that tells us the story of Egypt's unification, scholars and historians depended on the *Aegyptiaca* (*History of Egypt*), a collection of three history books authored by a man known as Manetho. Nothing is known about Manetho except that he was a priest living in Sebennytos (modern-day Samannud) during Egypt's Thirtieth Dynasty. His works, which were originally commissioned by the second king of the Ptolemaic dynasty, Ptolemy II, consist of a long chronological list of the kings who once reigned over ancient Egypt, from the mythical god-kings of the earliest of times to the very first pharaoh who wore both crowns of Upper and Lower Egypt to the establishment of the New Kingdom.

According to Manetho, Egypt was united by a certain king who went by the name of Menes. Considered the first human king of Egypt by some ancient Egyptians, Menes was often credited with the successful conquest of the Nile Delta and the establishment of Memphis, the glorious city that stood on the border between Upper and Lower Egypt. He was believed to have ruled the two parts of Egypt for over sixty years until he was killed by a hippopotamus. However, whether Menes was merely a legendary figure or the first king of a unified Egypt has been disputed by many due to the lack of archaeological evidence.

This can be seen when British archaeologists James E. Quibell and Frederick W. Green discovered the Narmer Palette in the late 19th century. The palette, which had survived over five millennia in almost perfect condition, contains the earliest example of hieroglyphic inscriptions that depict the scenes of Egypt's unification. However, the inscriptions left historians and scholars with more questions rather than a clear answer; the name of the king on the palette credited with uniting Egypt was not Menes but a figure named Narmer.

Narmer was believed to have initially ruled over Upper Egypt, with his seat being in Thinis. The king, who was completely aware of the need to form a strong army for his unification campaign, gathered the many tribal leaders across his regions, thus forming a confederacy. With the tribes in tow, Narmer was able to march toward the north and launch his invasion, which resulted in the defeat of Lower Egypt. With zero opposition standing in his way, Narmer successfully united the lands of the Nile, crowning himself as the first pharaoh of Lower and Upper Egypt in the process.

The Narmer Palette, depicting Narmer in the Hedjet, the white crown of Upper Egypt subjugating his enemy.

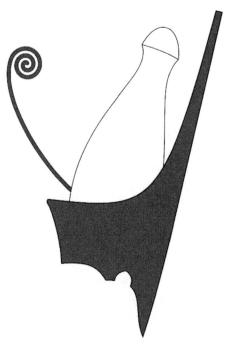

The double crown of Upper and Lower Egypt.
Jeff Dahl, CC BY-SA 4.0 <https://creativecommons.org/licenses/by-sa/4.0>, via Wikimedia Commons: https://commons.wikimedia.org/wiki/File:Double_crown.svg

For quite some time, scholars agreed that the two kings were two different individuals. Narmer was thought to have peacefully unified the two kingdoms at the end of the Predynastic Period, while Menes was his successor who continued to unify the region through conquest, thus kickstarting Egypt's Early Dynastic Period. With more archaeological evidence, however, this view began to change. The Egyptologist Flinders Petrie finally put the debate to rest by suggesting that Narmer was the name of Egypt's first pharaoh while Menes was his honorific.

Many historians agree that Narmer was married to a woman named Neithhotep, with whom he had a child. And so, when it was high time for the Egyptian throne to welcome a new ruler, his son, who went by the name of Hor-Aha, took over his father's legacy and ruled over the unified kingdom. Similar to his father, not much is known about Hor-Aha. Certain sources even claimed that Hor-Aha was, in fact, Menes himself; however, the discovery of the seals bearing his name that identified him as the second pharaoh of the dynasty contradicts the claim.

Nevertheless, we can conclude that Hor-Aha was once a religious ruler. Tablets originating from his reign seem to describe his visit to the shrine of the goddess Neith, possibly to perform a ritual or important religious activity. Aside from the tablets, the discovery of a few intricate items, such as ivory boxes, white marble, and finely carved copper axes, also suggests the quality of craftsmanship across the kingdom had greatly improved during the time of Hor-Aha. The second king of the First Dynasty was also said to have led expeditions into Nubia. However, compared to his father's rule, trade activities, especially with the southern Levant, did not fare so well under his reign.

Hor-Aha was succeeded by his son, Djer, about whom we know almost nothing. According to the inscriptions on the Palermo Stone, the king ruled for nearly forty years and was said to have launched a campaign to an unspecified land somewhere in southern Canaan. The specifics of this campaign and the rest of his reign are forever lost to us since the Palermo Stone was heavily damaged. Though not enough details survived the time that could tell us more about his reign, his death has given us great insight into ancient burial customs and traditions of the Egyptians, especially the kings. Surrounding his tomb in Abydos, archaeologists discovered at least three hundred subsidiary graves, which belonged to the members of the court, the royal family, and possibly the king's most loyal servants. They were thought to have been sacrificed and buried alongside the king. The Egyptians believed that after death, these people would rise and join their king in the next world.

After Djer's death, Egypt saw the rise of many new kings who would continue to lay the foundations of a booming civilization. Over a period of a few centuries, the Nile kingdom went through gradual changes. More local districts established new trade networks that further led to Egypt's flourishing economy. Agricultural activities were done on a larger scale than before, and the Egyptian writing system also saw tremendous growth.

Chapter 4: Pyramids, Gods, and Pharaohs: The Rise of the Old Kingdom

The Egyptian civilization continued to flourish after the unification of the lands. Settlements turned into towns, and cities began to see the birth of dozens of glorious monuments, temples, and statues. Most of them were dedicated to their pharaohs (or kings since the term "pharaoh" only began to be used in the New Kingdom) and the ancient gods and goddesses who were thought to have blessed the people with gifts and protection in life and death. Although the gods were believed by the ancient Egyptians to have had their eyes on all of their subjects, most of the time, only the mighty pharaoh could communicate with them. The first king of the Third Dynasty, Djoser, was said to have saved Egypt from famine following a conversation with a god in his dream.

The Famine Stele of Djoser.

According to the Famine Stele, the people of Egypt were terrorized by a terrible famine and drought that lasted for nearly seven consecutive years. The farmlands were left with no harvests. Grains were scarce, and kernels dried up when the annual flooding of the Nile failed to come. Hundreds of families suffered, with death and starvation becoming the norm across the valley. Some succumbed to their fate without protests, while many others began to break the laws in desperation. Farmers turned into robbers, and priests were left with no choice but to return to their homes since temples and shrines were closed down.

Seeing the chaos gradually devouring his subjects—possibly at the behest of Set, the god of destruction and chaos—Djoser grew wary and decided to consult his chancellor and the high priest of Ra, Imhotep. Since no one had even the slightest idea of how to overcome the drought, the king asked Imhotep to leave the safe walls of Memphis and go on a journey to find the ancient god who had the power to control the Nile. With haste, Imhotep traveled to Hermopolis, where he began his investigation by reading a series of archives from the city's temple. There, he discovered that the flooding of the Nile was controlled by a god named Khnum.

Imhotep returned to Memphis and presented his findings to the pharaoh, who later thanked him. Following the meeting with his chancellor, Djoser was visited by the god Khnum himself in a dream; some sources claim that it was Imhotep who dreamt of the god. Nevertheless, the kind-looking god informed the pharaoh of an abandoned temple on the island of Elephantine. Khnum claimed the Egyptians no longer respected the gods, especially the one who gave them life through the river.

Waking up from his unusual dream, Djoser consulted with Imhotep and another one of his governors, both of whom suggested that the pharaoh set sail to the island and see about the temple. Agreeing to the suggestion, Djoser traveled to the island of Elephantine. Just as his dream had foretold, the pharaoh discovered the dilapidated temple described by Khnum a few nights before. In an effort to pay his respects to the god, Djoser ordered his priests and people to restore the temple and issued a decree in which regular offerings were to be made to Khnum. When the reconstruction of the temple was completed, and the Egyptians resumed their offerings to the god, Khnum was pleased, resulting in the end of the seven-year-long drought and famine.

King Djoser: His Capital City, Expeditions, and Architectural Contributions

A limestone statue of Pharaoh Djoser.
Jon Bodsworth, Copyrighted free use, via Wikimedia Commons;
https://commons.wikimedia.org/wiki/File:Djoser_statue.jpg

Although already being hailed as the hero of Egypt by his people, Djoser continued to add more titles and honors to his name. Very little is known about his early years except that he was probably the son of the last king of the Second Dynasty, Khasekhemwy. Djoser had a wife named Hetephernebti, who was also his half-sister. The king was also known for moving the capital to Memphis.

Also referred to by the Egyptians as "Men-nefer" (which simply means "the enduring and beautiful"), Memphis was believed to have been secured by great white walls that gleamed under the scorching sun. The city was filled with monuments, markets, and grand religious temples that drew pilgrims and foreigners. Thanks to the continuous constructions and developments commissioned by Djoser and his successors, Memphis became ancient Egypt's most important cultural and commercial center. While the Egyptian cities were already beginning to blossom as early as the First Dynasty, by the reign of Djoser, they began to appear more intricate and complex.

The country learned the meaning of peace and harmony right after the unification of the two kingdoms by Narmer; however, wars were never fully resolved, especially outside of Egypt's borders. During Djoser's reign, one of his first goals was to strengthen the borders. With his country secured, the king then moved on to the next step: extending the borders of Egypt. Through carefully planned military expeditions, the king expanded his power over the region of Sinai, thus giving the Egyptians a way to mine precious minerals, such as copper and turquoise, from the area. Under the king's orders, the Egyptian military clashed swords with the Libyans and easily annexed certain parts of their land. Just like that, Djoser gained another honor to his name and was remembered by many.

However, Djoser's greatest contribution to ancient Egypt was not his successful military expeditions or even how he miraculously overcame the drought and famine. As soon as Djoser claimed the throne of Egypt, he showcased his fondness for architecture and design by commissioning the construction of a wide collection of structures and buildings in the city, including the very first pyramid of Egypt.

In Saqqara, northwest of glimmering Memphis, lies Djoser's proudest creation: the Pyramid of Djoser, which is also referred to as the Step Pyramid of Djoser. The pyramid was commissioned by the king at least 4,700 years ago in an attempt to set new standards for the burial rites of an Egyptian pharaoh. Before the pyramids, kings and royals were buried in rectangular tombs made out of mud slabs known as mastabas. These simple tombs were typically built above underground chambers and rose only six meters in height.

An example of a mastaba.
Jon Bodsworth, Copyrighted free use, via Wikimedia Commons;
https://commons.wikimedia.org/wiki/File:Mastaba-faraoun-3.jpg

Djoser's Step Pyramid, which was believed to have been Imhotep's idea (Imhotep was later deified by the ancient Egyptians and immortalized by historians), was the tallest structure to ever exist during that time. The pyramid, which consists of six mastabas stacked on top of each other, stood over sixty meters (almost two hundred feet) tall and was surrounded by a temple, courtyards, shrines, and living quarters built specifically for priests. In contrast to the earlier mastabas, this pyramid was made entirely out of limestone blocks.

Pyramid of Djoser.
Olaf Tausch, CC BY 3.0 <https://creativecommons.org/licenses/by/3.0>, via Wikimedia Commons: https://commons.wikimedia.org/wiki/File:Sakkara_01.jpg

The reason behind the pyramid's height and all of the ornate images, statues, and symbols carved on the walls and columns vary. While some suggest that it was merely for the sake of inspiring awe, others claim their purpose was to assist the soul of the deceased. In ancient Egyptian beliefs, the souls of the rulers were thought to have the ability to fly from the heavens to earth. So, it was necessary for the deceased to be buried in a significant structure so that their souls could easily recognize their resting place from high above. That way, they would be able to visit the earthly plane and watch over their people once again.

No exact details of the pyramid's construction survived, but historians and archaeologists believe that the pyramid took years to complete, even with the help of hundreds of skilled craftsmen. However, we can be sure that the pyramid was once the resting place of King Djoser. The maze of tunnels underneath the base of the pyramid was designed to confuse and discourage grave robbers from getting their hands on the precious grave goods and the king's remains. Djoser's granite burial chamber was not the only room within the pyramid; there was also a ceremonial chamber built for the deceased pharaoh's soul. Unfortunately, the complex maze tunnels did not stop the grave robbers from finding their way in since Djoser's remains have been lost, along with most of the grave goods. What remains to this day is his Step Pyramid and some of his deeds carved onto the structures around the complex, which serve as a testimony to his prosperous reign.

Sneferu and the First True Pyramid

Sneferu was the first king of the Fourth Dynasty. He ruled over the vast kingdom for nearly twenty-four years. Thought by many to have been responsible for bringing Egypt much wealth and stability, the pharaoh was popularly known for his effort in perfecting the building of pyramids. To finance his construction programs, Sneferu turned to military expeditions. The pharaoh launched campaigns into the lands of Nubia and Libya. Aside from increasing the supplies of raw materials, Sneferu also looked to increase Egypt's labor force. Sources claim that due to the success of his raids, the pharaoh managed to get his hands on a great number of captives, who would later be put to work in the construction sites of his pyramids.

A relief of Sneferu in his funerary temple of Dahshur.
Juan R. Lazaro, CC BY 2.0 <https://creativecommons.org/licenses/by/2.0>, via Wikimedia Commons: https://commons.wikimedia.org/wiki/File:Snefru_hed-seb_festival.jpg

His reign is thought to have been a period of experimentation since he had numerous builders constructing various structures using an array of techniques. The discovery of different painting techniques on the tomb walls clearly indicates the Egyptians were experimenting to find the best ways to preserve images and inscriptions.

Sneferu's first pyramid, known as the Meidum Pyramid, can be found at Dahshur. The complex featured courtyards, temples, and a cult pyramid that was used as a place of worship for the pharaoh's funerary cult. Initially designed as a step pyramid, the pharaoh had his builders transform the structure into almost a true pyramid, making it the first pyramid with straight sides.

Sneferu's second pyramid, which is known to us today as the Bent Pyramid, also stood in Dahshur. Just as its name suggests, this pyramid was unlike any other since it appeared crooked. The reason behind this design was probably accidental; the unstable and sandy ground beneath the base of the pyramid left the builders with no other choice but to improvise the slope just so they could prevent the structure from collapsing.

His third and last pyramid, also known as the Red Pyramid, was considered his best. Consisting of 160 layers of stone, the Red Pyramid was Sneferu's first successful true pyramid, complete with a full limestone casing. This pyramid also went on to become the blueprint for the Great Pyramids of Giza. It is also the fourth-tallest surviving pyramid in Egypt today.

The Meidum Pyramid.
https://commons.wikimedia.org/wiki/File:Meidoum_pyramide_003.JPG

The Bent Pyramid.
*Ivrienen at English Wikipedia, CC BY 3.0
<https://creativecommons.org/licenses/by/3.0>, via Wikimedia Commons:
https://commons.wikimedia.org/wiki/File:Snefru%27s_Bent_Pyramid_in_Dahshur.jpg*

The Red Pyramid of Sneferu.
*Hajor, CC BY-SA 1.0 <https://creativecommons.org/licenses/by-sa/1.0>, via Wikimedia
Commons: https://commons.wikimedia.org/wiki/File:Egypt.Dashur.RedPyramid.01.jpg*

The Pyramids of Giza

Perhaps following in the footsteps of his father, Khufu initiated the construction of his resting place shortly after his succession to the throne in 2575 BCE. He put his trust in his architect, Hemiunu, who told the pharaoh that he needed at least two decades to finish the pyramid. An unthinkable amount of limestone and granite was needed, and Hemiunu was also believed to have dug over six kilometers of a canal before he could even start constructing the pyramid's foundation.

The enormous building project required the energy of twenty-five thousand laborers. However, contrary to popular belief, these construction workers were not all enslaved people or captives of war. In fact, Egypt had its own labor supply; Egyptians were obligated to perform work for the government throughout the year. These builders were not only tasked to move and arrange the massive limestone blocks for ten hours every day, but they were also responsible for crafting the tools they needed for the work, as well as administrative tasks. The Egyptian government prepared houses and food for the workers. Some sources claim that those who worked on the pyramid lived a better life compared to the average citizen.

The Great Pyramid of Giza.
Nina at the Norwegian bokmål language Wikipedia, CC BY-SA 3.0
<http://creativecommons.org/licenses/by-sa/3.0/>, via Wikimedia Commons:
https://commons.wikimedia.org/wiki/File:Kheops-Pyramid.jpg

The construction process of the pyramid was rather complicated; one minor error at the base of the pyramid could result in a terrible failure at the top. Though historians and archaeologists today have discovered where the Egyptians obtained the materials needed to build the colossal structure—the stones were quarried from a site in Giza while the limestone casing was obtained from Tura, ancient Egypt's main limestone quarry right across the Nile—no one is able to determine the exact process of its construction. Upon completion, it was estimated that the pyramid was made of 2.3 million blocks of limestone, each weighing from 2.5 to 15 tons.

The remains of the limestone casing on the side of the pyramid.
Jon Bodsworth, Copyrighted free use, via Wikimedia Commons;
https://commons.wikimedia.org/wiki/File:Cheops_pyramid_02.jpg

The second pyramid of Giza was built by Khufu's son, Khafre, sometime in 2520 BCE. While Khufu's Great Pyramid was named the largest and tallest structure in Egypt at the time, the Pyramid of Khafre's most prominent feature was the mysterious limestone statue called the Sphinx. Like Khufu's pyramid, the outer part of the Pyramid of Khafre was once coated with limestone cladding, making it glimmer under the sun. On the apex of the pyramids, one could find a golden capstone, which sources claim would shine brightly even under the night sky.

About three decades after the construction of Khafre's pyramid, the complex saw the birth of the third and last tomb. The pyramid was considerably smaller than the other two and was built for Pharaoh Menkaure, Khafre's son. Despite its size, the pyramid had a more complex temple compared to both of its predecessors.

Chapter 5: The First Intermediate Period: Thebes, Memphis, and Herakleopolis

Among their many beliefs and ideologies, the ancient Egyptians believed that their rulers or pharaohs were the true embodiment of peace, justice, and divinity. (Most pharaohs were male, although there were a few female pharaohs.) Once crowned as the ruler of Egypt, the fate of the kingdom rested on their shoulders. Pharaohs had to oversee their realm with the blessings of the gods. Omens and signs were not to be taken lightly since they were considered messages from powerful deities. The rulers were expected to lead religious events and military campaigns against foreign powers beyond the borders of Egypt. They also had to oversee their subjects' welfare without rest and feed them during difficult times while ensuring justice in courts and trials.

Indeed, a pharaoh's power over the lands of the Nile was supreme, but even the divine ruler needed support to ensure Egypt never fell into chaos. Next in the hierarchy was the pharaoh's vizier, a high-ranking position within the government similar to a modern-day prime minister. Initially, the position could only be filled by a member of the royal family. However, by the Sixth Dynasty, pharaohs would typically appoint an individual based on their loyalty and attributes. Aside from being the bearer of the pharaoh's seal, viziers were also tasked with trade records, the government treasury, central granaries, state archives, and even the construction of monuments and structures across the valley. A vizier was supported by nomarchs. As king-appointed governors, the nomarchs were the ones expected to keep the Egyptian nomes or provinces under control.

Some of the government officials acted as the pharaoh's strongest supporters. Although they were given the power to oversee certain aspects of the government, they had to do so with the pharaoh's blessing. That was, however, until the decline of the Old Kingdom. Right after the death of Pepi II, Egypt saw the first signs of a decentralized government, as the nomarchs grew in power and eventually reversed Narmer's efforts. The kingdom was yet again divided.

While many would suggest that the Old Kingdom began to crumble at the end of Pepi II's reign, others claim that the signs were already visible before the pharaoh was even crowned. It started when the fourth king of the Sixth Dynasty, Pepi I, unknowingly bestowed more power and influence on the nomarchs. He first married two daughters of a nomarch and made their brother a vizier. Years later, Pepi II granted even more power to these provincial officials, perhaps because he was in need of more support due to his long years of reigning and old age. However, this move caused them to not only hold more influence over the people of the Nile but also led them to grow extremely wealthy. The nomarchs had a luxurious lifestyle, especially when they were exempted from taxes. They lived in opulent palaces, owned massive estates, and were fully protected by their own army. In death, they were put to rest in elaborate tombs.

To make matters worse, Pepi II appointed two viziers in his court instead of one. One of them was sent to Upper Egypt to oversee all official matters on the king's behalf, while the other gained power over Lower Egypt. This was a decision that no doubt contributed to the kingdom's division in the First Intermediate Period that followed.

Taking the mantle of kingship when he was just a child, Pepi II ruled Egypt for about ninety-six years—some suggest sixty-four years—making him the longest monarch to ever sit on the throne. The pharaoh died sometime in 2184 BCE and left Egypt in turmoil. His son, Merenre II, who was quite old, took the throne. However, it is plausible that his power was only limited to the capital city. By this time, many believed the kingdom was beyond saving, as the increasing power of the nomarchs had put a crack in the central government, thus shaking the pharaoh's authority.

As the kingdom entered the First Intermediate Period (an era that is classified by many as Egypt's dark age), its people continued to fear for their future since chaos or *isfet* was clearly on the horizon. The land witnessed more than one individual who claimed to be the ruler of the vast valley, which was a huge sign of instability. According to Manetho, during the Seventh Dynasty, Egypt was ruled by seventy different kings in the span of seventy years. However, this was most likely a metaphor to describe the kingdom's fragmented state.

Just like the Seventh Dynasty, the next line of rulers (the Eighth Dynasty) left us with only scarce evidence. Not much has been discovered about their reigns except that they had only little to zero power in the kingdom. The lands were almost entirely ruled by the nomarchs who, at times, would wage war among each other and coerce the inhabitants of other nomes to accept their reign. Having different overlords, the fate of the Egyptians was rather uncertain. Those who resided within a nome governed by a reckless nomarch would face multiple challenges. Those who were fortunate enough to be put under a considerate nomarch had better chances to fall asleep at night. One nomarch who went by the name of Ankhtifi was said to have cared for his nome responsibly. According to his autobiographical inscription, the nomarch was believed to have eradicated the famine that plagued his people by supplying grain to the people.

While the power-hungry nomarchs attempted to grow their power, Herakleopolis, a city in Lower Egypt, saw the emergence of an individual who proclaimed himself to be the new pharaoh of Egypt. His name was Meryibre Khety I, the founder of Egypt's Ninth Dynasty, which is also referred to as the House of Khety. Despite having the title of king, Khety was never favored by his subjects. Manetho claimed that the king was the worst of them all. Violence was his answer to everything, and those who refused to acknowledge him faced a fate even worse than death. His cruel reign was thought to be despised by the gods, as the king soon turned mad and died (he was apparently eaten by a crocodile).

The House of Khety continued to claim themselves as kings, although their power was not enough to put a stop to the ruling nomarchs. Sources claim there were also times when they struggled with those who lived within Herakleopolis. The House of Khety was said to have been forced to deal with the rise of the Tenth Dynasty for nearly a decade until they could finally suppress them once and for all, thus permanently severing their plans to take over the throne.

Outside of Herakleopolis, Ankhtifi was gaining prominence. Despite claiming to have served the king from Herakleopolis, Ankhtifi had an ambitious plan to expand his power over the kingdom, specifically the southern territories of Egypt. So, he worked to gain control over two nomes in the south before moving on to take over the cities of Thebes and Gebtu. However, his attempt was unsuccessful when the two cities formed an alliance to repel his attack. The squabble between the two factions took a couple of years. Ultimately, Ankhtifi was defeated, resulting in Thebes taking control of the nomes held by the ambitious nomarch. With the end of the conflict, Thebes saw the birth of the Eleventh Dynasty, which was founded by an individual named Intef I. By proclaiming himself as both the king of Egypt and the son of Ra, Intef officially initiated a war with the neighboring ruler of Herakleopolis.

Conflicts between the two rival kings went on for years, beginning from the reign of Intef I up until his successors, Intef II and Intef III. By the time of Theban Pharaoh Mentuhotep II's reign, Egypt was beginning to witness clear signs of unification. Although having control over both Lower and Middle Egypt, the kings of Herakleopolis soon signed their own death warrants when they damaged the royal necropolis of Abydos. Without hesitation, Mentuhotep II dispatched his troops to the north, where they laid an attack on the city of Herakleopolis itself. The Theban king and his armies swiftly defeated the enemy garrison and immediately wasted the city. Those who opposed them were slaughtered, and the many tombs belonging to the royal families were desecrated.

The fate of his rival, the king of Herakleopolis, remains a mystery, but we can be sure that Mentuhotep achieved a great victory during this battle and was made the sole ruler of Egypt, thus unifying the kingdom and kickstarted the flourishing Middle Kingdom.

A relief of Mentuhotep II.
https://commons.wikimedia.org/wiki/File:MentuhotepII.jpg

Learning from the mistakes made by the last rulers of the Old Kingdom, which led to Egypt's decentralization of power, Mentuhotep immediately reformed the kingdom's governing system. He limited the powers of the nomarchs and established a set of new government positions, which were later given to only his most loyal men. Government officials from the capital were encouraged to regularly visit the many territories of Egypt just so they could keep a close eye on the regional leaders.

Aside from launching campaigns beyond the borders of Egypt and strengthening the kingdom's name in the eyes of foreign powers, Mentuhotep II also focused on the construction of many temples throughout the valley, though few of his works survived. His biggest building project was none other than his large mortuary temple, which later became a huge inspiration for a pharaoh of the New Kingdom, Hatshepsut.

Chapter 6: Egypt Unified: Rise of the Middle Kingdom

The unification of Egypt might have been credited to Mentuhotep II, but the kingdom was not completely free from chaos; it took decades, if not centuries, and the reigns of several competent kings for Egypt to finally recover and usher in another golden age. After ruling the lands for slightly over fifty years, Mentuhotep II left the world of the living to take his seat among the gods, leaving his throne and legacy to his son, Sankhkare Mentuhotep III.

Believed to have taken the mantle at an old age, Mentuhotep III ruled over Egypt for only twelve years. Despite his short reign, he managed to permanently carve his name into the history books, mostly because of his success in his expedition to Punt— an expedition that had not been undertaken since the last rulers of the Old Kingdom. As Mentuhotep III stepped into the eighth year of his reign, the king sent at least three thousand men under the command of his most trusted steward, known as Henenu, toward the Red Sea, where they were tasked with ridding the region of any rebels and reopening the trade routes to Punt and Libya. The expedition's success rewarded Egypt with precious resources, as the troops returned to Gebtu with incense, perfumes, gum, and stones quarried from Wadi Hammamat, a major mining and quarrying region near the Nile.

Apart from expeditions, Mentuhotep III was also praised for his construction projects. The Temple of Montu, which was thought to have been built by the rulers of the Old Kingdom to honor the falcon-headed god of war, was further extended under Mentuhotep III's orders. Parts of the structure that feature a relief of the king still survive to this day and are currently on display in the Louvre.

Another temple dedicated to Montu was erected on top of Thoth Hill, the highest peak overlooking Egypt's Valley of the Kings. This mud-brick temple was destroyed, possibly due to a terrible earthquake that terrorized the land at the end of the Eleventh Dynasty. Perhaps to honor and thank his father for bestowing a nearly prosperous kingdom upon him, the king finished many of Mentuhotep II's unfinished projects at Abydos, Elkab, Armant, El-Tod, and Elephantine.

The remnants of the Temple of Montu.

Mentuhotep III died sometime around 1998 BCE—some sources claim he died earlier—and what happened after his death was not properly documented, leading to several views. The Turin Royal Canon, an ancient papyrus that contains a list of Egypt's kings, claims that after Mentuhotep III passed, the

Egyptians lived without a ruler for seven years. However, with what little evidence that was left and discovered, Egyptologists have come to the conclusion that Egypt welcomed another king, though his reign was not as great as his predecessor's.

The throne was said to have been passed to Mentuhotep III's son, who went by the name of Mentuhotep IV. His reign was even shorter than his father's; the last king of the Eleventh Dynasty ruled over Egypt for only six years. No inscriptions about his deeds survived. However, it is plausible that Mentuhotep IV was way past his glory days when he took the reins and had already predicted his demise. During his early years on the throne, the king was believed to have put his entire focus on building a perfect tomb for himself. He entrusted his vizier, Amenemhat, with an important mission. The old king ordered him to travel outside the safe walls of Thebes to search for high-quality stones that could be used to craft an intricate royal sarcophagus. Amenemhat discovered a quarry during his travels, thus completing his mission. The site exists today and features an inscription that credited Amenemhat's effort in realizing his king's wish.

When Mentuhotep IV finally died due to an unknown reason, Egypt was yet again troubled since he left neither a successor nor an heir. Amenemhat, who likely saw an opportunity to expand his power, took the mantle and claimed himself to be the new king of Egypt and the founder of the Twelfth Dynasty. How he rose to the throne remains a mystery. Some suggest that he did so peacefully, while others claim that he was the one who had secretly murdered Mentuhotep IV. We do know that his reign was not widely accepted at the beginning.

A relief depicting Amenemhat I.
Metropolitan Museum of Art, CC0, via Wikimedia Commons:
https://commons.wikimedia.org/wiki/File:Lintel_of_Amenemhat_I_and_Deities_MET_DP322055.jpg

Now referred to as Amenemhat I, the new king made a move to further strengthen his position. The king knew he had created many enemies, especially since he did not have royal blood flowing through his veins. Early on, Amenemhat was forced to face at least two rivals who also claimed the Egyptian throne. However, Amenemhat successfully removed the threat without heavy resistance. After obtaining some support from his people, who were beginning to accept him as their new ruler, Amenemhat filled his early days on the throne with sailing up and down the Nile to vanquish the rebels and those who exposed even the slightest signs of opposition.

He was indeed unpopular during the early years of his reign. He initially ruled with an iron fist, which further pushed the Egyptians away from him. One nomarch who went by the name Nehri specifically claimed that Amenemhat was so ruthless that he had to rescue his town from the king's terror. In contrast, those who willingly and faithfully bowed to the new pharaoh were greatly rewarded and saved from punishment. Many of them were even made the new nomarchs and viziers.

Eventually, Amenemhat I successfully quenched the rebellions and restored order across the kingdom. To prove to his people that his reign was nothing but the start of a new golden era, the Egyptian king commenced several construction projects, with most of them dedicated to the mightiest god, Amun. Although what remains of Amenemhat's biggest temple are only pieces, the temple was absorbed into a complex built by the rulers of the New Kingdom a few hundred years later. Today, the remnants of Amenemhat's temple can be found in the massive Karnak Temple Complex.

Thirty years into Amenemhat's reign over the vast land of the Nile, he began the construction of Amenemhat-itj-tawy (more commonly known as Itjtawy), which soon became the capital city of the Twelfth Dynasty. From the king's point of view, the city was important since it acted as a symbol of the Egyptian civilization's rebirth. Through this rebirth, Amenemhat was able to revive old traditions. The pyramid, which had last been built over two centuries before Amenemhat's reign, began to make a comeback. The king even went as far as to reuse the blocks from the Great Pyramid to construct his own pyramid, hoping it could match or perhaps surpass the standards set during the Old Kingdom.

Aside from reviving the old traditions and ordering massive construction projects, the king was also credited with restoring and strengthening Egypt's influence abroad. Ever since the chaotic rule of the Sixth Dynasty, Egypt's borders gradually waned, which led to the arrival of raiders from each corner of the kingdom's borders. The east was terrorized by the Canaanites, while the Libyans showed their fangs in the west and the Nubians in the south. Upon witnessing the uprising of the Nubians, who established their own state and gave themselves royal titles that imitated the Egyptian kings (one of them claimed to be the living son of Ra), Amenemhat launched a strategy to suppress the Nubians and secure the Egyptian borders. He first built fortresses along the frontier. During the last ten years of his reign, the king launched a full attack against Lower Nubia. The Nubian town of Buhen, which was strategically located near the Nile's Second Cataract, was captured by the Egyptians and converted into one of Egypt's greatest fortresses. With that, Egypt managed to reestablish its military influence in Nubia, thus paving the way for the kingdom to reopen and extend its trade routes.

To secure his legacy and ensure Egypt's prosperity, Amenemhat was careful not to leave the throne without a successor. Sometime during his twentieth year of rule, the king named his son, Senusret, as his successor. To show his son the ropes, Amenemhat appointed him as co-regent.

When the news of his father's sudden death reached Senusret, he did not hesitate to claim his rights to the throne. Legend has it that he was visited by his deceased father in his dreams. His dead father later explained the reason behind his death: he had been assassinated by his own bodyguards. Advised by his father not to put his complete trust in anyone, Senusret tracked down every possible rival and quickly eliminated them. His relentless advance soon reached beyond the borders of Egypt, as he successfully launched campaigns against Nubia all the way to the Third Cataract of the Nile, which rewarded Egypt with attractive supplies of gold and copper.

With the new riches he obtained after pacifying the south, Senusret followed in his father's footsteps, filling the lands with even more impressive structures. One of his most popular constructions that still stands today is the obelisk in Heliopolis, which measures at least twenty meters (sixty-five feet) in height.

The obelisk of Senusret.
https://commons.wikimedia.org/wiki/File:Heliopolis200501.JPG

Senusret ruled over Egypt for forty-five years and was succeeded by his son, Amenemhat II, who went down in Egyptian history as yet another one of the Middle Kingdom's most powerful rulers, mostly because of his successful military campaigns and trade policies. Following the tradition started by Amenemhat I, the king appointed his son, Senusret II, as co-regent and passed the mantle to him when he finally died after thirty-five years of ruling. Although Senusret II's reign was described as a period of peace, thanks to the continuous efforts of his predecessors, Senusret III has been branded as the most remembered king of the Twelfth Dynasty.

As Egypt continued to prosper, the kingdom witnessed rapid growth in its population. However, this growth troubled Senusret III since the central government began to show signs of weakening, especially when the nomarchs started to rule their respective provinces more independently. To prevent history from repeating itself and to remove any possibility of yet another civil war, Senusret III introduced a new political reform. Under the reform, the nomarchs were called back to the capital and given positions in court, thus cutting them off from overseeing the operations within their territories. By moving the nomarchs to the capital, Senusret could keep a close eye on them and easily put a stop to their plans should they show signs of opposition.

Apart from stabilizing the central government, Senusret was also credited with protecting Egyptian borders and trade routes. In the early years of his reign, the king launched a series of devastating campaigns against Nubia and emerged victorious most of the time to the point where the king was able to boast his success on a great stele erected in Semna. Senusret III claimed that, under his leadership, the campaigns led to many Nubian deaths, while women were taken as slaves, their crops destroyed, and their water sources poisoned. New fortresses were built along the frontier, which greatly helped his future campaigns.

However, Nubia was not the only region that the king paid attention to, as he also led his troops against Syria. While Senusret III aimed to expand his power, the campaign in Syria was also done to secure precious resources. Most of the plunder was directed toward the great temples in Egypt. The pharaoh ordered the reconstruction of the temples and refurbished them with loads of valuable stones, such as lapis lazuli, gold, and malachite.

Senusret III was succeeded by his son, Amenemhat III, who had served the kingdom during his father's reign as co-regent. Amenemhat resumed his father's projects. Sometime during his forty-five years on the throne, Egypt reached its peak, which was mostly owed to the king's efforts to elevate the kingdom's economic state. His work on the water system greatly benefited Egypt's farming activities, and his involvement in upgrading the facilities near the turquoise mines in Sinai was also appreciated by many. Aside from commissioning a temple for the goddess of love and fertility, Hathor, Amenemhat III's greatest achievement in architecture was the Labyrinth, an impressive, long-lost underground complex that was described by the Greek historian Herodotus.

Chapter 7: Decline of the Middle Kingdom and the Reign of the Hyksos during the Second Intermediate Period

After the death of Sobekneferu, Egyptologists are again left with only mysteries and questions since little evidence survived that could describe the events that took place in the kingdom. The Turin Royal Canon mentions a few kings who ruled over the lands after the end of the Twelfth Dynasty, but the record is damaged and far from complete. The Thirteenth Dynasty has been described by historians as rather obscure. No one has been able to determine how the first king of the Thirteenth Dynasty took over the mantle from Sobekneferu, the first female pharaoh, though most sources agree there was no bloodbath involved; instead, the throne passed to the next ruler peacefully. It is plausible that Sobekneferu, like her predecessor, did not name anyone to succeed her. Without a child of her own or even an heir from her immediate family, Egypt was left with no choice but to welcome a new ruler from a completely different family.

The identity of the first king of the Thirteenth Dynasty remains a mystery. The chronology of this period is often described by Egyptologists as confusing. Nevertheless, the unnamed king faced little to zero obstacles when he claimed the throne, as there were no signs of threats or rebellions. However, this did not mean that Egypt was going through a period of peace, as many sources claim the kingdom witnessed nearly 70 different kings in the course of 150 years. Like the First Intermediate Period, these short reigns of dozens of kings were a huge sign of political instability. This was a new era of Egypt known to history as the Second Intermediate Period.

Fortunately, the kingdom never went through major changes during the first few decades of the Thirteenth Dynasty. The rulers still even reigned from the same capital, Itjtawy, possibly due to the systematic government bureaucracy established by the great rulers of the previous dynasty. The kingdom was overseen by not only the king but also his viziers, other high officials, and civil servants. Egyptologists have even suggested that the king was merely a figurehead during this period of time. He might have only played an important role for religious reasons.

But, of course, without a highly capable ruler at the helm, the power of the central government waned. Unlike the great kings of the late Twelfth Dynasty, the rulers of the Thirteenth Dynasty barely left their throne in the capital of Itjtawy. Without the ruler's oversight, the provinces began to drift apart, and the central government gradually lost its effectiveness. During Sobekhotep IV's reign, Egypt began to see clearer signs of a collapse. Although historians and scholars agree that he was the most powerful ruler of the dynasty, the kingdom's future had been written and could not be altered. The many fortresses built along the frontiers in the south were beginning to be abandoned, with many of the guards and soldiers stationed at the garrisons choosing to defect and side with the growing power of the Nubian Kingdom of Kush. Almost the same could be said about the fortresses in Sinai and Canaan. Since there were fewer troops in the garrisons, the men were eventually disbanded or called back to the capital.

Trouble was also brewing on the eastern branch of the Nile Delta, particularly in the city of Avaris. Initially founded by

Amenemhat I of the Twelfth Dynasty, the city was mostly inhabited by immigrants who typically originated from western Asia and parts of the Levant. Some of these immigrants were sent to Egypt as slaves, although there were also those who willingly came in search of work that could reward them with enough food on the table. They could work at one of the many construction sites scattered throughout the valley.

The city of Avaris in Lower Egypt.
Ancient_Egypt_map-en.svg: Jeff Dahlderivative work: MinisterForBadTimes, CC BY-SA 3.0 <https://creativecommons.org/licenses/by-sa/3.0>, via Wikimedia Commons: https://commons.wikimedia.org/wiki/File:Lower_Egypt-en.png

Since Avaris was strategically located near the shores of the Mediterranean Sea, the city became a popular spot for traders, which eventually attracted even more immigrants, especially Canaanites. Despite retaining most of their culture, the Canaanites who called Avaris their new home were culturally Egyptianized over time. Around 1800 BCE, when the Middle Kingdom was at its peak, these Egyptianized Canaanites began to populate big cities across the kingdom. Some of those who remained in Avaris managed to secure positions within the Egyptian government, while many others grew extremely wealthy from their flourishing trade businesses.

Upon witnessing the weakening of the central government, especially when the king's power was barely present in the many provinces, these wealthy immigrants began to devise a plan of their own to further assert their power and influence in the vast kingdom. Sometime between 1750 BCE and 1700 BCE, a new dynasty was born. The Fourteenth Dynasty was mostly made up of rulers from Canaan and the Levant. The dynasty is considered even more of a mystery than the Thirteenth Dynasty. However, we do know that the rulers of this newly formed dynasty reigned from the city of Avaris. The two dynasties coexisted with each other and were believed to have had a difficult time expanding their power. The Egyptians were again faced with a famine, and both dynasties struggled to make ends meet due to the terrible economic state caused by the worsening trade businesses.

Despite having the support of the majority of the provinces in Upper Egypt, the Thirteenth Dynasty was unable to make a move and secure the territories in the Eastern Delta, which was controlled by the ruler of the Fourteenth Dynasty. The latter was also incapable of expanding his influence beyond the Nile Delta due to his state's weak military. This inadvertently opened the door for a stronger group of people to showcase their power and invade the kingdom. They came from the east and were referred to in the Egyptian tongue as *heka khasut*, more commonly known to us as the Hyksos ("rulers of foreign lands").

This was the first time Egypt was forced to bow down to a foreign power. However, how the Hyksos breached the kingdom and asserted their dominance over the vast valley remains a debate. According to Manetho, they were believed to have entered Egypt on chariots from the east while carrying compound bows and other advanced technology of the Bronze Age. Also referred to as invaders, the Hyksos took over Lower Egypt with force. Oppression was their absolute answer to ensure the Egyptians gave in. Manetho claimed that they not only sacked the rulers of the land with great aggression but also burned several Egyptian cities, destroying many of the kingdom's most sacred temples. The Egyptians who survived the brutal massacre and surrendered were far from safe. They were subjected to slavery; even women and children were not spared.

With the Egyptians—be it the nobles or the commoners—either lying lifeless on the ground or forced into slavery, the Hyksos appointed one of their own to be Egypt's new king. The king was known as Salitis, and he ruled from Memphis with an iron fist. He was succeeded by five more kings, whose combined reigns lasted for at least a century. However, Manetho's record about the Hyksos is to be taken with a grain of salt, especially since his descriptions of the event were written at least 1,400 years after the invasion and were infused with biased opinions. While Manetho claimed the Hyksos used violence to conquer the northern part of Egypt, archaeological findings suggest otherwise. Since there were no clear signs of heavy casualties and damage in most of the major cities of the Eastern Delta, including Avaris, Egyptologists arrived at the conclusion that the invasion was not a terror campaign as Manetho suggested.

Nonetheless, the Hyksos rulers had successfully expanded their influence by 1600 BCE. From initially sowing their seeds of power only in the cities scattered throughout the Eastern Delta, the invaders extended their rule as far as the region of Beni Hasan in Middle Egypt. However, while the Hyksos were occupied with expanding their grasp over half of the kingdom, another dynasty was born, this time in Thebes. Classified as the Sixteenth Dynasty, some sources claim that it was, in fact, established by what was left of the obscure Thirteenth Dynasty, whose members could have possibly sought refuge in Thebes. Others suggest that it was a completely new line of rulers founded by a Theban family. Whatever its origins might be, we can be sure that the rulers of the Sixteenth Dynasty constantly faced conflicts and obstacles. Thebes was located in the middle of the chaos; the northern regions were mostly conquered by the Hyksos, while the Egyptian fortresses in the south were under the control of the Kushites. Raids from the Hyksos, rebellions from the natives, and famine shook the dynasty and its capital.

The Hyksos and their many regions, on the other hand, were blooming. The population was steadily growing, and the economy flourished. The Hyksos rulers managed to elevate

Egypt's trade links with almost all parts of the known world. Various objects from the Levant began to emerge more often than before in the local markets, attracting even more traders. The Hyksos kings were also believed to have made contact with rulers from other kingdoms. For instance, one particular king known as Khyan had his name carved on a few artifacts that were possibly sent to different kingdoms of the ancient world. A set of bowls with an inscription of the king's name was once discovered in Hattusa, an ancient city in central Turkey, and a few other objects bearing the king's name were also found in Knossos, the capital of the Minoan civilization.

The regions under the Hyksos witnessed an increasing number of new temples, although most of them were constructed in honor of the Canaanite god of fertility, Baal, rather than the Egyptian deities. Of course, with their stability and growing power, the Hyksos rulers, specifically Apepi and Khamudi, began to work on an even bigger ambition. They planned to have all of Egypt within their grasp and remove any rivals that stood in the way.

Under King Seqenenre Tao of the Seventeenth Dynasty, Egypt finally began to oppose the Hyksos. According to Manetho, the Egyptian king was said to have been insulted by the Hyksos king, Apepi, which eventually resulted in a vicious battle. Not planning to let a foreign invader tarnish his reputation, Seqenenre Tao gathered his troops and marched out of Thebes. However, luck was not on Seqenenre's side, as the fight was won by the Hyksos. It could be plausible that Seqenenre fell in one of the skirmishes against the Hyksos since his mummy was discovered with battle wounds.

The Thebans were then led by another king of the Seventeenth Dynasty, Kamose, who was the son of Seqenenre. The Theban king had enough of the taxes imposed by the Hyksos government. He resumed his father's campaign and tried to realize his dream, which was to free the lands of Egypt from a foreign power. After spending most of his time on the throne strategizing, Kamose launched a devastating attack on Avaris and slaughtered those who stood in his way or showed support for the Hyksos. Although his inscription tells us that he successfully ravaged the fortified city of Avaris to the ground, Egyptologists agree the description of the event might include a touch of exaggeration. The Hyksos still controlled Lower Egypt after the attacks launched by Kamose.

After leading the Thebans for possibly three to five years, Kamose was succeeded by his brother, who went by the name Ahmose. Taking the mantle when he was only a child, Ahmose, like his predecessors, had the same ambition: to drive the foreign rulers out of Egypt once and for all. He spearheaded several campaigns against the last Hyksos king, Khamudi. Kamose launched multiple attacks and quelled a few rebellions that were brewing in the south. The Theban king then reconquered parts of Lower Egypt.

Sources claim that it took four attacks against Avaris before Ahmose could finally capture the fortified city. After the Hyksos were finally defeated, they retreated out of Egypt and took shelter in the town of Sharuhen, which was turned into their next stronghold. However, the Theban king was far from done with the foreign invaders, as he went on to showcase his military prowess by besieging the stronghold. After years of laying siege to Sharuhen, the Hyksos fell, thus freeing Egypt from the hands of foreign rulers. With the fall of the Hyksos, Egypt was set in motion to enter another booming era: the New Kingdom.

Chapter 8: The New Kingdom: Egypt's Most Glorious Era

If it was not for Ahmose I, Egypt might have suffered even longer under the reign of the ruthless Hyksos kings. Ahmose claimed the throne when he was barely an adult—sources claim that he was ten at the time. He did not only avenge the death of his father and free Egypt from foreign invaders, but he also founded the Eighteenth Dynasty. Although his success in driving out the Hyksos was admired and cheered for by nearly all of his subjects, Ahmose was not planning to slow down, especially since the kingdom was in dire need of restoration.

After moving the capital to Thebes, the king shifted his entire focus to the power-hungry Nubians. During his reign, Egypt was able to reassert its control over the south, specifically the Nubian territories. Their gold supplies were plundered and transferred to the Egyptian treasury. Seeing how his kingdom was still far from achieving economic stability, Ahmose reopened mines, quarries, and trade routes throughout Egypt. Many construction projects also started to take place under his rule. The temples and monuments that had been destroyed by the invaders were restored or rebuilt, and many other structures built by the Hyksos kings were destroyed in an effort to bury all traces of their power. After laying the foundations for Egypt's New Kingdom, Ahmose died after at least twenty-five years on the throne. His success was remembered by his subjects to the point where he was worshiped as a god as soon as news of his passing reached the public.

Hatshepsut, the Once Forgotten Female Pharaoh of Egypt

The act of removing evidence and contributions of prior rulers from the official accounts—later known by the Romans as *damnatio memoriae*—was not only applied to the Hyksos. Believe it or not, Hatshepsut was one of the many rulers who were subjected to the act. Her statues were destroyed, her public recognition was erased from official documents, and her contributions to many impressive constructions were never mentioned by later pharaohs and scribes. However, the reason behind the condemnation of her memory remains disputed. Some suggest the main reason was that the Egyptians were not fully accepting of a female taking the mantle of pharaoh. Others claim that her traces of power were actually erased by Thutmose III, her stepson, who possibly held a grudge toward her for taking the throne away from him.

Hatshepsut was first appointed as regent to the young Thutmose III before she claimed her spot as a fully-fledged pharaoh. Although her reign was successful, it caused many of her subjects to be dissatisfied, possibly because of her gender. Although women in ancient Egypt had almost the same rights as men (women in ancient Egypt could start their own businesses, own properties, marry and divorce their partners, and even become witnesses in court), allowing a female to be crowned as the ruler might have been a tad too much. The Egyptians believed that by placing Hatshepsut at the top of their hierarchy, they could cause a disturbance to Ma'at, the balance of the world. Having her as a ruler disrupted their centuries-long tradition of male rulers. It also contradicted their belief that a pharaoh was supposed to be the living embodiment of Horus, the male god of war.

It could be plausible that Hatshepsut was well aware of the issues that would arise if she continued to ignore her subjects' dissatisfaction. In the seventh year of her reign, she began to make some changes, especially in terms of how her reliefs and statues depicted her. She was often pictured as a male pharaoh and sometimes referred to herself as Hatshepsu, which contained a masculine ending. However, this did not completely solve her problems since her image was almost entirely erased from the kingdom following her death.

The Sphinx of Hatshepsut.
Sphinx_of_Hatshepsut.jpg: Postdlf/derivative work: JMCC1, CC BY-SA 3.0
<http://creativecommons.org/licenses/by-sa/3.0/>, via Wikimedia Commons:
https://commons.wikimedia.org/wiki/File:Sphinx_of_Hatshepsut_c.jpg

Even though she was once removed from history, Egyptologists today recognize her as one of the most notable pharaohs to rule over Egypt during the New Kingdom. Regarded as a great builder, Hatshepsut commissioned various construction projects across the kingdom. Her mortuary temple, Djeser-Djeseru, is considered one of the most impressive architectural achievements of the ancient world and is still standing today. Egypt also owed parts of its booming economy to the female pharaoh since she was the one who commandeered the successful and lavish expedition to the land of Punt, Egypt's trade partner since the Middle Kingdom. Her military campaigns mostly centered around the regions of Nubia and Syria. Her inscriptions claim that she marched alongside her army in battle. To put it simply, Hatshepsut was a capable ruler, just like some of the other male rulers of Egypt. Most of her traces might have been removed, but the remaining fragments of her reign that survived were enough to attest to her deeds.

Thutmose III and the Battle of Megiddo

It is believed that Thutmose III spent most of his youth proving he could be one of Egypt's most powerful pharaohs. He participated in a number of campaigns launched by his stepmother, Hatshepsut, giving him a chance to sharpen his military skills. He was even appointed as the head of the army by Hatshepsut the moment he reached adulthood. So, when his ruling stepmother passed away sometime in 1458 BCE, Thutmose immediately assumed the title of the sixth pharaoh of the Eighteenth Dynasty.

Although he had been left with a prosperous kingdom and well-trained military, the new pharaoh was not able to enjoy a minute of peace since he was forced to face threats imposed by the leaders of the Levant, who thought he was a weak leader. The rebels threatened to turn their backs on the kingdom or, worse, invade Egypt if he refused to step down. Being a great military strategist, Thutmose refused to bargain with the rebels and launched an attack on the ancient city of Megiddo (better known by its Greek name, Armageddon). Leading his troops at the front, Thutmose laid siege to the city. After seven to eight months, the rebels were left with no choice but to surrender, as they faced starvation.

Despite gaining a victory, Thutmose did not cause any further bloodshed within the city. Instead, he offered a deal. In return for leaving the city and the rebels almost unscathed, Thutmose demanded they sheathe their weapons and ensure there would be no more rebellions in the future, to which they agreed. However, he did strip the rebels of their positions and powers before appointing new officials who had been loyal to him. Children of the rebellion's leaders were taken as hostages and brought back to Egypt. They were treated with kindness and granted an Egyptian education. They were only allowed to return to their homeland once they came of age.

A relief at Karnak depicting Thutmose III slaying his enemy at the battle of Megiddo.
Olaf Tausch, CC BY 3.0 <https://creativecommons.org/licenses/by/3.0>, via Wikimedia Commons: https://commons.wikimedia.org/wiki/File:Karnak_Tempel_15.jpg

The success of this particular campaign no doubt increased Egypt's standing in the Near East. From this battle alone, Thutmose and his fierce military obtained lucrative spoils of war. The Battle of Megiddo was the first battle in history recorded in detail. The troops brought back 340 captives, over 20,000 sheep, 2,238 horses, nearly 1,000 cattle and chariots, 552 bows, and 200 fine pieces of armor. With this victory, Egypt easily asserted its dominance over northern Canaan. Thutmose's military achievement was celebrated not only by his loyal subjects but also by the kingdom's neighboring empires. Kings from Babylon, Assyria, and Anatolia were among the leaders who sent tributary gifts to the pharaoh following his victory.

However, Thutmose III's campaigns did not stop there. The great pharaoh soon commenced more successful campaigns to Nubia, the Kingdom of Mitanni, parts of Phoenicia, and Kadesh. With his long list of military triumphs, Thutmose III went down in history as the deadliest Egyptian pharaoh who greatly expanded the kingdom's borders.

Akhenaten, the Heretic Pharaoh

Akhenaten rose to the throne at least a century after Thutmose III. He gained a kingdom that was already at its peak largely due to previous pharaohs' successful attempts at expanding Egypt's borders. By the time he was crowned, his vast kingdom had its fingers firmly wrapped around the neighboring regions, including Palestine, Nubia, and Phoenicia.

However, Akhenaten was known by a different name when he first claimed the mantle; he was known to his subject as Amenhotep IV. It was only during his fifth year on the throne that the pharaoh changed his name to Akhenaten. The reason behind this was largely due to his decision to introduce a new religion to the kingdom. Although Akhenaten was first said to have worshiped the traditional gods of Egypt, such as Amun, Ra, and Osiris, the pharaoh chose to abandon the old gods and establish a monotheistic religion. Why exactly Akhenaten decided to defy the traditional beliefs of the ancient Egyptians remains a question, but certain sources suggested that part of it was due to the influences brought into the kingdom by foreigners settling in the land of the Nile.

Known as Atenism or the Amarna heresy, the religion centered around the sun god Aten. No clear details remain today that can tell us more about the new religion; however, we do know that, unlike the old gods, Aten was depicted in neither his animal nor human form. In fact, the new god was often represented by only a sun disk with several lines of sun ways extending downward. Since the monotheistic religion forced the Egyptians to worship only Aten, Atenism was not widely accepted by many, especially those who were not willing to neglect their centuries-old king of gods, Amun.

And so, Akhenaten resorted to closing down all of the temples that were once dedicated to the old gods—a move that forever harmed his reputation. Even the name of the great god of the afterlife, Osiris, was erased, as the Egyptians were forced to seek blessings for the dead from the one and only Aten. The capital was also moved from Thebes to a newly constructed city called Akhetaten ("Horizon of the Aten"), which is now known as Amarna.

Apart from his infamous religious reforms, the pharaoh also lost the support of his subjects when he paid little to zero interest in performing his kingship responsibilities; he paid no attention to the military and neglected the kingdom's trade and economy. Since the pharaoh chose to focus more on the newly founded religion rather than running the kingdom, local officials began to take advantage of the situation. Most of the taxes collected from the people of Egypt went directly into their pockets.

During his last years on the throne, the pharaoh was left with no choice but to deal with many of his discontent subjects, especially the army commanders and priests. It was also believed that the pharaoh even became estranged from his wife and strongest supporter, Nefertiti, during his last years. He finally died seventeen years after his rise to the throne. A few years after his burial, the pharaoh's sarcophagus was destroyed, and his city was completely abandoned—Akhenaten was indeed hated even after death. He was then succeeded by an obscure figure known by the name of Smenkhkare.

While some were certain that Smenkhkare was Akhenaten's co-regent and assumed to be his nephew, brother, or son, other sources suggest that Smenkhkare was none other than the heretic pharaoh's own wife, Nefertiti. Due to the troubles Hatshepsut faced, it would not be a surprise if Nefertiti chose to rule the kingdom under a male alias. If this, by any chance, is true, we could be sure that Nefertiti was the one who was responsible for the beginning of the kingdom's religious change. After the death of Akhenaten, the Egyptians slowly reverted to their ancient beliefs and traditions. The worship of the sun god Aten was nowhere to be seen, while the temples of Amun and the other old gods began to reappear. However, the reign of Smenkhkare (or Nefertiti) only lasted for a short while, but the next pharaoh, Tutankhamun (the son of Akhenaten), would continue to reverse his father's religious changes and erase his footsteps. It was only when the young pharaoh rose to the throne that ancient Egypt was able to fully return to its polytheistic roots.

Ramesses II and the Battle of Kadesh

The Eighteenth Dynasty ended with the death of Pharaoh Horemheb, who had no heir to succeed him. However, despite having no surviving son who could continue his legacy, Horemheb had one particular individual in mind to whom he would pass the throne. His name was Paramesse, and he once served the pharaoh as his chief vizier. The main reason behind Horemheb's decision to appoint Paramesse as his successor is uncertain. Some claim that the pharaoh completely trusted his vizier since he had long portrayed his undying loyalty to the Egyptian royals, while there are others who claim that it was possibly because Paramesse had both a son and a grandson, thus saving the kingdom from any future power struggles.

With the death of Horemheb in 1292 BCE, Paramesse rose to the throne, just as the late pharaoh had wished. He adopted the name Ramesses I and founded the Nineteenth Dynasty, which comprised some of Egypt's most successful rulers. The second king of the dynasty, Seti I, soon led Egypt to become the power center of the ancient world. His successful reign saw the expansion of the kingdom, as the pharaoh was able to reclaim the territories once lost during the reign of the heretic pharaoh Akhenaten. To prepare his son for the throne, Seti I appointed fourteen-year-old Ramesses II as prince regent. The pharaoh also introduced his son to the military by bringing him on his many campaigns. After obtaining enough skills, the teenage Ramesses was appointed as the captain of the Egyptian troops.

After eleven years on the throne, Seti I moved on from the world of the living and made his journey to the underworld, leaving his son, whom he had well prepared for the throne, to rise as the new pharaoh of Egypt. Ramesses II (later known as Ramesses the Great) no doubt possessed an extensive experience of the battlefield due to his involvement in Seti I's many campaigns. One of his two greatest military achievements happened during his second year on the throne. At the time, Egypt was continuously threatened by the Sea Peoples, who were described by the Egyptians as pirates possibly originating from

Ionia. They were called the Sherden. After receiving reports of pirates terrorizing the local populations and pillaging a great number of Egyptian vessels along the Mediterranean coast, the pharaoh ordered a retaliation.

A colossal statue of Ramesses II at Memphis.
Dominik Knippel, de:Niedernberg, CC BY-SA 3.0
<http://creativecommons.org/licenses/by-sa/3.0/>, via Wikimedia Commons:
https://commons.wikimedia.org/wiki/File:Kolosstatue_Ramses_II_Memphis.jpg

Ramesses knew going against the pirates head-on would only cause higher casualties. So, the pharaoh strategized a trap to lure the pirates into an ambush. A number of cargo-laden vessels were positioned in a specific area off the coast to act as bait. The Sherden, who took the bait, were immediately surrounded by a fleet of Egyptian warships. Within a short time, the Egyptians, led by the cunning pharaoh, successfully defeated the pirates, resulting in their capture. Those who survived the ambush were brought to the capital city of Pi-Ramesses (modern-day Qantir) and forced to serve the pharaoh as his personal bodyguards until their last breath. These bodyguards, who were often depicted wearing horned helmets and equipped with round shields and huge swords, were said to have accompanied the pharaoh in many of his battles.

A relief of Ramesses II capturing his enemies from Nubia, Libya, and Syria.
Speedster, CC BY-SA 4.0 <https://creativecommons.org/licenses/by-sa/4.0>, via Wikimedia Commons: https://commons.wikimedia.org/wiki/File:Ramses-ii-relief-from-memphis2.png

Ramesses II's most remarkable military achievement was none other than his battle with the Hittites. Known as the Battle of Kadesh, the conflict took place in 1274 BCE near an important trade city in Syria called Kadesh. The tension between the Egyptians and the Hittites had long existed; the Hittites were believed to have caused trouble in the valley, especially during the reign of Thutmose III. Ramesses II's father, Seti I, successfully captured Kadesh but not for long, as the Hittites were able to reclaim and fortify the city to ensure they could withstand any future invasion by the Egyptians. Sources claim that the strain between the two escalated when Ramesses launched his campaigns into Canaan, during which a Hittite vassal was captured. Upon hearing of the capture, the Hittite king, Muwatalli II, decided to confront the Egyptian pharaoh in battle.

Ramesses II, who was eager to capture Kadesh and benefit from its booming trade and location, gathered the Egyptian forces, which counted at least twenty thousand infantry and two thousand chariots, in preparation for the upcoming war. He then organized them into four divisions named after the Egyptian gods: Amun, Ra, Ptah, and Set. The king of the Hittites raised a greater force of almost forty thousand infantry and three thousand chariots. The Egyptian pharaoh might have been popular for his military brilliance, but many forgot that he, too, was a human being. Ramesses II was thought to have made his first mistake by marching with the Amun division too fast, thus leaving the rest far behind.

After moving through the Gaza Strip, he set up camp about eleven kilometers away from Kadesh. The pharaoh and his forces stumbled upon a couple of tribal nomads, who informed the Egyptian king of Muwatalli's location: he was said to be camping in the land of Aleppo, some two hundred kilometers away from Kadesh. This, however, turned out to be false information; the nomads were actually hired by the Hittites to purposely confuse the Egyptians. Ramesses II was afterward presented with two Hittite prisoners who were brought back by one of his scouts. The captives were tortured and finally revealed the real location of the Hittite king. Muwatalli and his troops were camped right on the other side of Kadesh.

Ramesses II in his chariot attacking the Hittites.

Muwatalli II and his troops hastily charged toward the Ra division, which had been left behind by the Amun division. The Hittites then moved on to round up Ramesses and his Amun division, causing havoc. The pharaoh himself claimed that his forces panicked and scrambled from the battlefield, leaving him to deal with the enemies alone. Whether or not his claim was true, we do know that the pharaoh, along with the remaining charioteers and infantrymen of the Amun division, launched a counterattack against the Hittites. After regrouping, Muwatalli II planned another attack against Ramesses, but his plan was cut short upon the Ptah division's arrival from the south.

The battle resumed the following day. The Hittites were forced to retreat, allowing Ramesses II to advance on the city of Kadesh. However, the Egyptians were unable to recapture the city, possibly due to their inability to lay a long siege on a fully fortified city. Having no other choice, Ramesses II led his troops back to Egypt. The Battle of Kadesh was a stalemate, but the conflicts between the two sides continued for years to come. Due to the rising Assyrian threat to the east, the new Hittite king, Hattusili III, decided to halt any further attacks against Egypt. About fifteen years after the great battle, a peace treaty was signed by Ramesses II and Hattusili III. With the Egyptian-Hittite peace treaty, sometimes known as the Treaty of Kadesh (the earliest surviving peace treaty), Egypt and the Hittite Empire put down their weapons and ended their centuries of bloodshed.

Chapter 9: The Third Intermediate Period: The Kushite Empire

The ancient Egyptians, like the other ancient civilizations, believed in polytheism. Ra, Osiris, Horus, Set, Ptah, Anubis, and Hathor are some of the most popular deities often worshiped by the Egyptians. The gods were believed to be the creators and sustainers of all life, so honoring and pleasing them would be one of the few ways to ensure blessings in one's life, be it in the form of health, wealth, or even peace.

However, by the start of the New Kingdom, another god came to prominence. This particular god went from being a local deity during the Old Kingdom to the patron god of the pharaohs centuries later. He was referred to as Amun, whose name can be translated as the "Hidden One" due to its association with the wind. First gaining popularity in Thebes, Amun was believed to be the god who created all things, including himself.

The ancient Egyptian god of Amun.

In the beginning, the god was worshiped alongside the falcon-headed Ra as two different divine entities. It was only sometime around the 16th century BCE that the two powerful gods were fused together to become Amun-Ra, the chief of the Egyptian pantheon. For centuries, Amun's influence greatly expanded, with his high priests typically placed at the top of the hierarchy, second only to the kings since pharaohs were considered Egypt's

"First Priest." The high priests of Amun were thought to have been blessed with a special relation to the god and were expected to tend to his needs. If a certain unfortunate event took place in the Nile Valley, such as famine, plague, and even poverty, the priests were responsible for finding out the reason behind the god's wrath and looking for ways to mend the problem.

Over time, the priests of Amun gained so much influence and power over the land that they owned even more land compared to the pharaoh. Their prominence waned during the reign of Akhenaten, the pharaoh who worshiped the sun god Aten and attempted to convert Egypt into a monotheistic kingdom. However, the priests managed to regain their influence after the pharaoh's death and were at their height during the reign of Ramesses XI, the last king of the Twentieth Dynasty.

The Division of Power in Egypt

Egypt was again heading toward chaos and instability under Ramesses XI. The kingdom was believed to have witnessed another division in power between the pharaohs and the Theban high priests of Amun. It began when High Priest Amenhotep clashed swords with Panehesy, the viceroy of Kush. The priest was not a favorite among the Egyptians, possibly because of his hunger for power. He was ousted from office by his people, but his appeal to Ramesses was successful since he was reinstated to his former position. Unbeknownst to the priest, despite granting him the position, the pharaoh was also cooking up another plan to suppress his power. Ramesses XI requested Panehesy and his Nubian troops to march into Thebes, which eventually led to a siege of the priest's fortified temple of Medinet Habu.

Amenhotep's fate remains a mystery; it is unsure whether he survived the attack or if he simply retreated. However, the outcome of the battle was not what Ramesses XI had pictured mind since Panehesy went on to claim himself the de facto ruler of Lower Egypt. Ramesses XI sent an army led by another viceroy of Kush named Piankh against Panehesy. Despite successfully sacking the ancient city of Hardai (better known as Cynopolis) in Middle Egypt, Panehesy's forces were eventually defeated by Piankh and his army. He was then forced to retreat back to Nubia sometime around 1080 BCE. Ironically, after

Panehesy's retreat, Piankh assumed the title of the high priest of Amun, thus starting wehem mesut, a period where high priests held power over Upper and Middle Egypt.

Ramesses XI was succeeded by Smendes, who founded the Twenty-first Dynasty, marking the beginning of Egypt's Third Intermediate Period—an era often described by many as the kingdom's darkest age since Egypt never fully recovered from this period. Much of Smendes's origins are unknown. Some suggest that he was once a governor in Lower Egypt under Ramesses XI, while others claim that he was somehow related to Herihor, the ruling high priest of Thebes. Nonetheless, Manetho stated that the first pharaoh of the Twenty-first Dynasty actively reigned over a divided kingdom (particularly Lower Egypt) from Tanis for twenty-six years. He died sometime in 1052 BCE and was succeeded by six more pharaohs, with Psusennes II being the last ruler of the Twenty-first Dynasty.

During the Twenty-second Dynasty, the highest power in Egypt was again passed to a foreigner, though all of them were pretty much culturally Egyptian. This time around, the throne belonged to rulers from the land of Tjemehu, better known to us today as Libya. Also referred to as the Bubastite dynasty (due to their main residence being at a location along the Nile called Bubastis), the very first ruler was believed to have ascended to the throne with little to no struggle. However, despite not facing tremendous opposition from the Egyptians, the king, Shoshenq I (who scholars claim to be the same person as Shishak from the Hebrew Bible), did not accept the responsibilities of a ruler empty-handed. He was an accomplished warrior and the head of the Libyan mercenary tribe called the Meshwesh. The king was exceptionally fluent in military skills and strategies. His most popular military campaign was the one in Palestine; inscriptions of his success and exploits can be found carved on the wall of the Bubastite Portal at the Temple of Karnak.

However, military prowess alone was not enough to ensure the kingdom operated without problems. Given how vast Egypt's territories were, Shoshenq I knew right away that he had to delegate his power to several of his most trusted people. So, the king sent his sons to different regions of Egypt to serve as governors. Although referred to as governors, their roles varied, with some even becoming priests of Amun in Thebes. As for Shoshenq I, he reigned for at least twenty-one years, passing the mantle to his son, Osorkon I, whose deeds mostly focused on the many construction projects across the valley, though most of them are forever lost to us.

Many other kings rose to the throne and claimed their rights over the kingdom, while the seat of the high priest changed hands fairly often. Under the reign of Shoshenq III, the royal house was split into two. While rulers of the Twenty-second Dynasty continued to assert their power from Bubastis, the kingdom was introduced to the Twenty-third Dynasty, which gradually grew its influence in several regions of the Nile Delta. Although the two dynasties initially ruled together, they were soon caught up in conflicts, with the main reason being issues of succession. The many civil wars exploding across the valley resulted in an even more fragmented kingdom. There were separate monarchies ruling from different cities, such as Herakleopolis, Tanis, Hermopolis, Thebes, Memphis, and Sais. The political instability greatly weakened Egypt's borders, which allowed the Nubians in Kush to plan their next steps.

The Rise of the Kushite Empire

Nubia had come a long way since the end of the New Kingdom. Its power had been gradually increasing until the Kingdom of Kush was eventually formed. The kingdom was based in the capital city of Napata. However, the Nubians never had a chance to expand their grasp over Egypt due to the constant fights happening between the many tribes that existed within the kingdom. But everything changed when Egypt began to lose its grip, especially when the state was already divided.

Although known to have been involved in numerous battles and conflicts with Egypt, the Nubians admired the colorful Egyptian culture and tradition; even the Nubian king Kashta was believed to have mirrored Egyptian customs and religious beliefs during his reign. When the king's daughter was appointed as the god's wife of Amun, the highest-ranking priestess of the cult of Amun, Kashta began to plot his moves to further expand his influence. Through his daughter's significant position, Kashta was able to assert his power with minimal effort. He eventually took control of Thebes and, later on, parts of Upper Egypt.

However, the Kushites' power was strengthened under the reign of Kashta's son, Piye. The new king of Kush was described by many to be a religious man who believed that he was chosen by the chief god Amun to rectify Egypt's corruption. When he learned that a particular Libyan prince named Tefnakht had proclaimed himself the sole ruler of Egypt after driving the last king of the Twenty-second Dynasty out of Memphis and forming a union with rulers of several nomes in the Nile Delta, Piye decided that it was high time for him to act. He first set his eyes on Thebes.

The Kushite king sent his army up the Nile, where they were faced with ships carrying dozens of soldiers, each equipped with weapons meant for war. Without haste, the Kushites bravely advanced and emerged victorious. The Kushites were able to resume their initial plan, which was to enter Thebes. The troops continued on land with hopes of reaching the city of Herakleopolis. Nearing the city, the Kushites were yet again entangled in a battle involving Tefnakht's united forces. Although well prepared for war, the Kushites were stunned upon discovering Nimlot's participation in the battle. Nimlot, the ruler of Hermopolis, had initially sworn his allegiance with the Kushites, so his betrayal no doubt angered Piye. Nevertheless, according to Piye's victory stele, the Kushites massacred the coalition of Delta rulers, except for Nimlot, who managed to escape.

When the news of Nimlot's betrayal and escape reached Piye, the king did not waste any time to leave his seat of power in Kush and march into Egypt with his personal army in tow. Under his command, the Kushite king laid siege to Hermopolis for several months. Sensing his defeat on the horizon, Nimlot was said to have sent his wife to negotiate with Piye. No details survived that explain the negotiations between the two factions; however, we can be sure that Hermopolis submitted to the king after the siege, with Piye granting Nimlot forgiveness for his betrayal. With the fall of Hermopolis, other cities soon bowed down to the Kushite king, with some even offering tributes.

Piye proceeded to shift his focus to Memphis. Wishing to avoid more unnecessary bloodshed, the king offered the ancient city peace if it surrendered. However, the generous offer was declined, which led to another battle. This time, Piye faced an elite army of eight thousand men led by none other than Tefnakht himself. But luck was clearly shining on the Kushite king, as his forces emerged victorious and successfully captured Memphis. As for Tefnakht, he was said to have set out on another campaign against Piye to no avail. He was then left with no choice but to surrender and swear an oath of loyalty to the king.

Being a pious man, Piye immediately began the process of purifying the city. He sent guards to protect the Temple of Ptah and tended to the many shrines of the Egyptian gods. The king might have gone to the Temple of Ptah, where he was purified and anointed as the ruler of Egypt. With Memphis securely in his grasp, Piye soon received tributes from the remaining cities across the valley and the submission of a few other rulers.

After his successful conquest, Piye left Egypt and sailed back to his homeland, never to return again. He started Egypt's Twenty-fifth Dynasty; however, the control of Egypt was left in the hands of his vassals while he remained on the throne of Kush, ruling his own booming empire until his very last breath.

Chapter 10: Egypt under Assyrian Occupation

Gone were the eras of native Egyptians claiming the throne. Ever since the start of the Third Intermediate Period, Egypt was under the control of numerous foreign kings who claimed to be the living embodiment of the ancient gods. First came the Libyans, whose rule led to the kingdom's division. Soon after, Egypt witnessed the rise of the Kushites, who eventually ended a series of civil wars that had long plagued the valley.

Indeed, the campaigns launched by Piye resulted in many deaths and bloodshed, but the outcome was not all unfortunate. Shabaka, Piye's brother who succeeded him, was said to have admired and respected Egyptian culture just as much as his predecessors to the point where he preserved almost all of the Egyptian traditions during his reign. Aware of the close ties between the Egyptians and their religious beliefs, Shabaka appointed his own son as the high priest of Amun at Thebes. He would also be responsible for many reconstruction projects. To put it simply, Kushite Egypt flourished.

However, that was the case until a Kushite pharaoh named Shebitku came into conflict with the Assyrians. Egypt openly provided safe sanctuary to the rebels of Judah, who had revolted against their Assyrian overlords. Egypt's Twenty-fifth Dynasty never failed to provide support to the rebelling kingdom, which eventually led to a set of wars that were first launched by the Assyrian king, Esarhaddon.

Esarhaddon's rise to power was far from peaceful. When his father, Sennacherib, died at the hands of his two sons, Esarhaddon embarked on a six-week-long civil war against his brothers. After he eradicated his father's murderers—including their associates and family members—he finally sat on the throne, just as Sennacherib had envisioned. And so, after having a crown placed on his head and successfully restoring Babylon and securing the empire's borders, Esarhaddon set his eyes on Egypt, which was always seen as a nuisance to the Assyrian Empire.

The Assyrian king launched a campaign against Egypt in 673 BCE. During this time, Taharqa ruled the Nile kingdom. Hoping to defeat Egypt in one fell swoop, Esarhaddon marched his troops quickly. This advance was described by historians as his greatest mistake; his army was exhausted from the march, causing them to lose focus on the battlefield. Because of that, Esarhaddon's forces were easily defeated by Taharqa right outside of the city of Ashkelon. The Assyrian king was left with no other choice but to return to his capital, Nineveh.

It took at least two years before Esarhaddon could finally breach the borders of Egypt. Sometime around early 671 BCE, the Assyrian king, after learning from his mistake of his past invasion attempt, marched his large army toward Egypt at a much slower pace. While passing through the city of Harran (a major Mesopotamian cultural and religious center), Esarhaddon supposedly received a prophecy involving his successful campaign against Egypt. The prophecy, combined with the great state of his army, could have possibly elevated the king's confidence. The Assyrians soon emerged victorious over Egypt.

Esarhaddon then led his army to the kingdom's ancient capital, Memphis. The Assyrian king did not hold back, as he sacked the city as soon as he arrived. He ordered the capture of the royal family who called Memphis their home. Taharqa's wife and children were among the captives sent to Nineveh as hostages. As for Taharqa himself, the pharaoh managed to slip out of the city and make his escape to the south in one piece.

Esarhaddon did not pursue Taharqa right away. Instead, he focused on consolidating his position in Egypt. After sacking Memphis and capturing most of the royal family, the Assyrian king came up with a political reform for the northern regions of Egypt. Those who had been extremely loyal to Esarhaddon were chosen to be the governors of his newly conquered territories. An individual known as Necho I was named Egypt's new king, who ruled from his seat of power in Sais; however, some sources claim Necho I was nothing more than a puppet ruler.

With the riches that Esarhaddon had obtained from his successful campaign, he prepared for his return to the Assyrian capital. There, he erected a victory stele, which featured an image of Taharqa's son in chains. Statues of Taharqa were also brought back to Nineveh as trophies and placed at the entrance of the palace.

The Victory Stele of Esarhaddon.
Richard Mortel from Riyadh, Saudi Arabia, CC BY 2.0
<https://creativecommons.org/licenses/by/2.0>, via Wikimedia Commons:
https://commons.wikimedia.org/wiki/File:Victory_stele_of_Esarhaddon.jpg

Egypt, led by Pharaoh Taharqa, who had managed to evade the Assyrians, was not ready to submit to the Assyrians. So, in 669 BCE, another revolt led by the Twenty-fifth Dynasty pharaoh exploded just as soon as Esarhaddon left the kingdom. The news of this revolt reached the Assyrian king and immediately infuriated him. The king readied his army yet again and embarked on another campaign to quell the rebellion. Despite the king's strong will to defeat the rebels and finally put an end to Taharqa, the campaign was brought to a halt following the sudden death of Esarhaddon while he was still en route to Egypt. His death no doubt caused a stir in the Assyrian Empire, but this did not mean Egypt was safe from the Assyrians. Esarhaddon was succeeded by his son, Ashurbanipal, who would soon resume his late father's mission.

The state of the new Assyrian king's empire made it impossible for him to leave Nineveh. The empire constantly faced threats from the ancient Iranians (the Medes, Cimmerians, and Scythians). However, this did not stop the king from dispatching his troops to Egypt. The Assyrians clashed swords with Taharqa's forces near Memphis. The Kushite pharaoh faced defeat but yet again escaped to the south and found refuge in Thebes.

While pursuing the pharaoh, the Assyrians discovered that a few of the empire's appointed vassals who ruled Lower Egypt—including Necho I—were plotting to betray them. With haste, the conspirators were ordered to be captured. Some of the people over which they ruled were massacred; some were put in chains and deported to Nineveh. However, much to everyone's surprise, Necho I was pardoned and reinstated as the king of Egypt, while his son, Psamtik, was appointed as the mayor of Athribis, an ancient city in Lower Egypt. Taharqa fled to the Kushite capital of Napata, where he remained until his death. The Kushite kingdom was passed to possibly Taharqa's cousin, a man known as Tantamani.

Taharqa's death slightly calmed the conflict between Egypt and the Assyrian Empire but not for long. Tantamani, the new ruler of the Kushite kingdom, had only one wish: he wanted to restore his family to the Egyptian throne. Knowing that the Assyrian troops had returned to their capital, Tantamani grabbed the opportunity to march down the Nile and regain the territories lost to the Assyrians. He first reoccupied Aswan before advancing to Thebes and, finally, Memphis, where he killed Necho I.

Necho I's death angered Ashurbanipal, which led to a renewal of the violent conflict. The Assyrian king, assisted by Psamtik I's army, which consisted of strong mercenaries from Caria, launched a massive attack against Tantamani in northern Memphis. The battle resulted in Tantamani's terrible defeat. Seeing no other way out, he fled to the south. The Assyrians chose to do the unthinkable: they marched to Thebes and sacked the city. Its inhabitants were put in chains and deported, the city's riches and gold were seized, and horses and two towering obelisks were brought back to Assyria. The Assyrians gained control of Egypt, with Tantamani's reign only limited to Napata. His death in 656 BCE ended both the Twenty-fifth Dynasty and the Nubian domination of Egypt.

The Twenty-sixth Dynasty began with Pharaoh Psamtik I, who succeeded to the throne after the death of his father, Necho I. Ruling the kingdom from Sais, the pharaoh was believed to have created a foundation for Egypt to bloom yet again. In an effort to unify the kingdom, the pharaoh formed an alliance with Gyges, the king of Lydia in Asia Minor, and raised an army that was made up of reliable Greek and Carian mercenaries. He then went on to deal with the unruly vassals and princes in the Nile Delta. To further consolidate his power, Psamtik I shifted his attention to Thebes, the holy city of Amun. He arranged the adoption of his daughter, Nitocris I, to Shepenupet II, the current god's wife of Amun. With his daughter next in line as the god's wife, Psamtik I expanded his power over the vast valley and held the state together. The pharaoh also gained popularity due to his encouragement of the revival of the Old Kingdom's religion and art.

Sometime in 653 BCE, Psamtik I gained even more autonomy, which was largely owed to Assyria's internal strife. He took this opportunity to break away from the Assyrians' hold, thus making him the sole ruler of Egypt. However, some sources claim that despite the Egyptian kingdom's detachment from Assyria, the pharaoh maintained a friendly relationship with the waning empire. For instance, Psamtik sent reinforcements to Assyria to repel the Babylonian attacks.

With Egypt completely in his hands, Psamtik I went on to bring Egypt back to its feet. He oversaw a great number of construction projects and was also responsible for the expansion of the Serapeum of Saqqara and the construction of fortresses at Daphnae, Naukratis, and Elephantine.

After over five decades, the mantle was passed to Psamtik's son, Necho II, who would soon be in the middle of Assyria's continuous conflicts. The declining empire had already lost its capital, Nineveh, in 612 BCE to the hands of a combined force of Babylonians, Medes, Persians, and Scythians. To retaliate, the Assyrians requested the help of the Egyptians, which Necho II granted. While marching toward the battlefield, the Egyptians likely met King Josiah of Judah's forces. Josiah had formed an alliance with Babylon. The king of Judah's plan to block the Egyptians' advance failed, as he was killed in Megiddo. With the path cleared, the Egyptians joined the Assyrians in Haran. However, they were swiftly defeated. The Egyptians retreated into northern Syria.

The fight, however, did not stop there, as they were left with no choice but to face the Babylonian army led by Nebuchadnezzar II (also known as Nebuchadnezzar the Great). This battle resulted in the defeat of the combined forces of Egypt and Assyria, with the latter ceasing to exist as an independent state. Despite Necho II's defeat against the Babylonian king, he continued to rule over Egypt and left a few great contributions to the kingdom. The pharaoh initiated the construction of a canal (also known as Necho's Canal), which later on became the blueprint for the Suez Canal. Necho II also recruited a great number of Ionian Greeks and formed an Egyptian navy, thus increasing the kingdom's shipbuilding activities, especially triremes.

After ruling over the valley for fifteen years, Necho II was succeeded by his son, Psamtik II. Psamtik II ruled Egypt for only six years, but he accomplished some significant achievements. To secure the valley from any possible invasion from the Kushites, Psamtik II launched an expedition into Nubia. He marched his troops as far as the city of Kerma and the Kushite capital of Napata; both cities were destroyed. With their capital city reduced to only ashes and rubble, the Kushites were left with no choice but to move their capital farther south toward the city of Meroe.

The following year, after Psamtik II's successful expedition against the Kush, he made a move to display his support for Zedekiah, the king of Judah, who was preparing a revolt against the Babylonians. Although Zedekiah received reinforcements from Egypt, the revolt failed terribly, as Nebuchadnezzar II laid siege on the city for two years.

Psamtik II died sometime in 525 BCE, and the throne was passed down to his son, Apries. Like his father, the pharaoh became entangled in Palestinian affairs. He sent reinforcements to Jerusalem, hoping to assist the city in repelling the Babylonian forces under the command of Nebuchadnezzar II. Unfortunately, after an eighteen-month siege, Jerusalem fell. This resulted in the capture of the Jews. The nobles were held in captivity and sent to Babylon, while those who managed to escape migrated to Egypt.

Apries was also plagued with several more internal conflicts that eventually led to his own demise. While dealing with a civil war that broke out between the native soldiers and the foreign mercenaries, the pharaoh was forced to deal with his own general, Ahmose II, who was proclaimed by the Egyptian troops as the next king of Egypt.

When the news of the military coup reached Apries, the pharaoh fled to Babylon to seek support. He returned to Egypt in 567 BCE with an army of Babylonians to reclaim the throne. However, his advance failed. Apries was killed in battle, leaving the throne to none other than Ahmose II.

To further strengthen his position as the new ruler of Egypt, Ahmose II married one of Apries's daughters. Ahmose II, who was officially crowned as pharaoh, brought Egypt to its zenith. He built and restored numerous temples and structures across the valley, oversaw Egypt's agricultural growth, cultivated a close relationship with the Greek world, and defeated an invasion by the Babylonians in 567 BCE. He is regarded as one of the most powerful pharaohs of his time. But before his death, the pharaoh witnessed the early threats imposed by the rising Persian Empire.

Chapter 11: The Persian Conquest

The Persian Empire (known as the Achaemenid Empire at this point in time) owed its glory to none other than Cyrus the Great. Claiming the throne at the ripe age of only twenty-one, Cyrus was believed to have freed his city from the grasp of the Median Empire by orchestrating a successful revolt sometime in 549 BCE. However, his triumph over the king of the Medes was only the beginning of his conquests. He soon expanded his empire by launching campaigns in Lydia, which rewarded him and his empire with tremendous wealth. Cyrus later marched into Mesopotamia and conquered its surrounding regions.

In 539 BCE, the king was able to assert his power over the ancient city of Babylon without a single drop of blood being shed. The Babylonians were said to have welcomed Cyrus peacefully, as the king was not only popular for his military brilliance but was also a man of mercy; those who yielded were promised no harm and were allowed to practice their religious customs and traditions. He even liberated nearly forty thousand Jews, some of whom had been held in captivity for around fifty years.

An illustration of Cyrus the Great.

It could be plausible that the great Persian king once sought to expand his power as far as Egypt, possibly because of the valley's invaluable economic resources. However, Cyrus never set foot in Egypt, as the king met his fate about a decade after his conquest of Babylon. Cyrus the Great was believed to have died in battle during his campaign against the defiant nomadic tribe known as the Massagetae. However, Egypt was not forgotten for long, as the valley would soon be forced to bow down to Cyrus's son and successor, Cambyses II.

The main reason for the first confrontation between Egypt and Persia is uncertain, but according to the Greek historian Herodotus, it all began during the reign of Ahmose II, a pharaoh from the Twenty-sixth Dynasty. Cambyses II was said to have requested for an Egyptian physician—some said he specifically asked for an ophthalmologist—to serve in his empire. Choosing to comply with the Persian king, possibly to avoid any tensions, the pharaoh forcefully ordered an Egyptian physician to move to Persia, thus leaving the doctor with no choice but to leave his wife and children behind. This no doubt angered the physician, who later planned to take down the pharaoh from afar. He established a good relationship with the Persian king before slowly injecting his malicious agenda. The physician suggested that the king ask the Egyptian pharaoh for his daughter's hand in marriage, which he claimed could result in a firm relationship with the Egyptians.

Upon learning of Cambyses's proposal to tie the knot with one of his daughters, the pharaoh grew wary. He refused to see his daughter as a concubine to a foreign king, but at the same time, the pharaoh wished to avoid any possible battle that could take place should he decline the Persian king's offer. And so, instead of sending his daughter, Ahmose II sent Nitetis, the daughter of his predecessor, Apries, who, according to Herodotus, was tall and beautiful. However, Ahmose's deception did not last long, as Nitetis chose to betray the pharaoh and informed Cambyses of her true lineage. The revelation angered the Persian king, which eventually led to his careful plans to invade the Egyptian kingdom.

Whether Herodotus's description of the story has any truth at all remains unknown. Nevertheless, Cambyses II spent years preparing for the Egyptian conquest. The way into the valley was indeed rough, and finding the best route proved to be rather difficult. However, thanks to Phanes of Halicarnassus, a mercenary and a wise tactician serving under Ahmose, the Persian king was able to perfect his strategy. Herodotus told us the mercenary was once loyal to the pharaoh until, for reasons unknown, he fell out of favor with Ahmose II and decided to leave Egypt for Persia. After successfully escaping his captivity that had been ordered by the anxious pharaoh who suspected his betrayal, Phanes of Halicarnassus arrived in Persia, where he eventually spoke with Cambyses II, who was in the midst of preparing the conquest. The mercenary made use of his knowledge of Egypt and advised Cambyses of the best way to enter the valley. He suggested the Persian king negotiate with the Arabian kings so that they would grant him safe passage to the

Nile kingdom.

Holding hatred toward Ahmose, the Arabs gladly complied with the king's request and even supplied the Persians with fresh water and more troops. With a safe passage secured and aid from the Arabs, Cambyses II finally launched his campaign. However, his battle was not against Ahmose II since the pharaoh died six months before the Persian king could even set foot in the desert. Instead, Cambyses's rival was the new king of Egypt, Psamtik III, the son of Ahmose II.

Legend has it that a few days after the coronation of Psamtik III, the holy city of Thebes witnessed a sudden rainfall. It was a rare occurrence, and it was interpreted as a bad omen by the Egyptians. Perhaps it was a warning to the new pharaoh about the incoming attack from the Persians led by the vengeful Cambyses II. When news of the invasion reached Psamtik III, the young pharaoh immediately mounted a defense and spent days and nights preparing for the battle. Psamtik likely lacked enough experience on the battlefield, as he relied on the help of allies. He first sent his admiral, Udjahorresnet, to the Mediterranean coast to fend off the Phoenician fleet sent by Cambyses. Unfortunately, the admiral chose to turn his back on the young pharaoh and sided with the Persians. The same could also be said of his other ally, Polycrates of Samos; instead of supplying mercenaries to the Egyptians, Polycrates sent his men to join the ranks of Cambyses instead.

Despite having to face the betrayals of his allies, Psamtik III carried on with his defense strategy. The pharaoh held his ground at Pelusium, a major city on the easternmost branch of the Nile, and fortified his capital city, Memphis, hoping it could withstand a possible siege. Psamtik was said to have been quite confident about the battle, as, initially, his troops were able to hold back the Persians. However, the tide soon changed when the battle erupted at Pelusium. Cambyses, who had learned all about the Egyptians' customs and religious beliefs, especially their veneration for cats—cats were considered sacred to the Egyptians; they were often associated with the goddess Bastet—ordered his troops to paint their shields with an image of Bastet. Some sources even claimed that the Persians brought cats and other sacred animals onto the battlefield. Upon seeing the images of their goddess on the shields of their enemy and the sight of their sacred animals, the Egyptians sheathed their swords and attempted to retreat.

The meeting of Psamtik III and Cambyses II.
https://commons.wikimedia.org/wiki/File:Meeting_Between_Cambyses_II_and_Psam metichus_III.jpg

Herodotus claimed that despite the surrender, many Egyptians were massacred on the battlefield. Historians suggest that nearly fifty thousand Egyptians perished during the battle, while the Persians only lost seven thousand lives. Any of the Egyptians who survived the battle immediately retreated to Memphis; the young pharaoh was one of the survivors. However, the Persians were far from done, as they laid a siege on Memphis shortly after the Egyptian retreat. Psamtik III was taken prisoner following the successful siege. The pharaoh was said to have been treated fairly despite being a prisoner but was later executed when it was discovered that he was planning a revolt against the Persians.

Cambyses continued his campaign and marched his army throughout the valley. By 525 BCE, the Persians had conquered all of Egypt, with the neighboring Libyan tribes voluntarily submitting to the triumphant king. With the vast valley officially becoming a satrapy to the Persian Empire, Cambyses proceeded to Sais, where he finally crowned himself the new pharaoh of Egypt.

Adopting the pharaoh name of Mesuti Ra, Cambyses II founded the Twenty-seventh Dynasty of Egypt. However, according to Herodotus, the Persian king was the complete opposite of his father. While Cyrus the Great's greatest value was his mercy, Cambyses II was known for his cruelty. The Greek historian even went to the extent of describing him as a stereotypical mad king.

Since the conflict between Egypt and Persia started during Ahmose II's reign, the Persian king was believed to have held grudges against him. When the pharaoh died before he could even arrive in Egypt, Cambyses decided to seek his revenge on Ahmose's preserved body. He trespassed in the pharaoh's tomb, stole his mummy, and burned it to ashes. Herodotus's most famous accusation of the Persian king was the slaying of the sacred Apis bull of Memphis.

CAMBYSES KILLING THE APIS.

Cambyses II slaying the Apis Bull.
https://commons.wikimedia.org/wiki/File:Cambyses_killing_the_Apis.jpg

Whether or not Cambyses did all those atrocious acts remains a debate, though most contemporary evidence suggests otherwise. The Persian pharaoh seems to have never dreamed of erasing Egyptian culture. His image might have been tarnished by the priests since the Persian king was not at all favored by them, possibly due to one of his opinions; in contrast to the native rulers of Egypt, Cambyses II thought that it was unnecessary for the kingdom to collect taxes from its subject just to support the temples.

The Persian pharaoh faced several revolts by the Egyptians during the first few years after the conquest. Other than Psamtik III, Cambyses was also forced to take down a resistance led by an individual named Petubastis IV sometime in 522 BCE. Upon learning of the revolt, Cambyses immediately sent his troops to quiet it down. The outcome of this battle is a mystery. Herodotus suggests that Cambyses's forces were defeated by Petubastis IV, but to cover up the failure, Cambyses claimed the troops were lost in a terrible sandstorm while marching toward the battlefield. Regardless of the outcome, the Egyptians never gained authority, and their kingdom continued to be governed by the Persians.

After Cambyses's death in 522 BCE, Egypt was reigned by the next Persian king, Darius I, who ruled for over thirty-five years. Despite having to experience numerous revolts across the Nile Valley, Darius was best known for his architectural contributions. Historians believe that, like the rest of the Persian pharaohs, Darius never sought to remove the unique cultures of Egypt. In fact, he worked on integrating Persian culture into the Egyptian culture. Under Darius I, the valley was introduced to the Persian water systems, which were more advanced compared to the ones familiar to the native Egyptians.

A relief of Darius I (also known as Darius the Great).
Surenae, CC BY-SA 4.0 <https://creativecommons.org/licenses/by-sa/4.0>, via Wikimedia Commons: https://commons.wikimedia.org/wiki/File:Darius_I_(The_Great).jpg

Darius I was succeeded by Xerxes I upon his death in 486 BCE. Xerxes I, who ruled for slightly over two decades, is best remembered for his attempt to annex Greece. He was assassinated by his own allies in court. The throne was left to his son, Artaxerxes I. During his reign, the Twenty-seventh Dynasty began to witness its first signs of decline. Artaxerxes's biggest challenge was Inaros, an Egyptian rebel who had formed an alliance with the Athenians.

To quell the rebellion, Artaxerxes dispatched an army commanded by the satrap Achaemenes. Perhaps luck was not on the Persians' side, as they were swiftly defeated by the rebels. The Egyptians regained their power over certain parts of the valley, although the Persians remained within the fortified walls of

Memphis. However, six years later, the Persians gained the upper hand and defeated Inaros and his Athenian allies, resulting in Egypt falling back into the hands of the Persians.

Another rebellion soon broke out during the reign of Darius II, the last pharaoh of the Twenty-seventh Dynasty. The rebellion was led by an Egyptian who went by the name of Amyrtaeus. He and his followers successfully removed the Persian pharaoh from the throne and returned Egypt to the hands of native rulers. Darius II's successor in Persia, Artaxerxes II, likely made a move to restore the Persian occupation in the valley, but his efforts were cut short since he was forced to face a series of uprisings and revolts imposed by the angry Egyptians. Thus, the Egyptians managed to free themselves from the grasp of foreign rulers, ending the first period of Persian Egypt. However, this only lasted for a century since the Persians would return stronger than ever.

The second period of Persian occupation began after the reign of Pharaoh Nectanebo II. During the first years of his rule, Egypt prospered. The pharaoh also successfully protected his kingdom from numerous invasion attempts by the Persians with the help of his army and Greek mercenaries. However, things changed when the pharaoh was betrayed by a Greek mercenary named Mentor of Rhodes, who brought his men into the ranks of the Persian king, Artaxerxes III. With the support of a few Greek cities (except Athens and Sparta, which peacefully declined to go against Egypt) and Mentor's mercenaries, Artaxerxes III ultimately crushed Nectanebo II's forces in 342 BCE. After his victory, the Persian king marched to Memphis and installed a new satrap. Nectanebo II fled to Nubia and made plans to reclaim the throne, though his attempt was unsuccessful.

With Nectanebo II removed from the throne, Egypt was yet again put under the control of the Persians for the next decade. Artaxerxes III ruled until his death and was succeeded by Artaxerxes IV Arses and then Darius III, who would soon face Alexander the Great and witness the fall of the Persian Empire.

Chapter 12: Alexander the Great and the Ptolemaic Kingdom

Brilliant, diplomatic, charismatic, ruthless, hungry for power, and bloodthirsty—these are some of the words often used to describe Alexander the Great. The young conqueror was said to have never been alone, be it during the short times of peace or constant warfare. He was always accompanied by his loyal men who swore to follow him anywhere he ventured.

Before permanently carving his name into the history books as one of the greatest military minds of the ancient world, Alexander, like many other powerful historical figures, was born into a highly esteemed royal family. While some believe that he was the son of Zeus, the mighty king of the Greek gods, historians prefer another version. In 356 BCE, he was born to King Philip II of Macedonia and his wife, Queen Olympias. Although brilliance and prowess are not always inherited through the bloodline, it was a different case with Alexander. His father was an impressive ruler. Despite being left with a feeble country at the beginning of his reign, Philip II proved his exceptional commanding skills by molding his ineffective army into a formidable force. His determination to lift the kingdom out of its terrible state eventually came to fruition, as he subjugated most of

Greece and transformed Macedonia into a force to be reckoned with.

Perhaps his father's victories sparked young Alexander's determination to display his vigor and bravery. In fact, the young conqueror shared the same fantasy as his father, which was to conquer the Persian Empire. At the age of twelve, Alexander proved his gift by taming Bucephalus, an enormous and furious stallion that many believed could be ridden by no one. The stallion soon became Alexander's most loyal companion in countless battles and wars.

At thirteen, Alexander began to absorb crucial knowledge from Aristotle. Three years later, he was temporarily left in charge of Macedonia when his father rode into battle. Before he was twenty, Alexander joined his father on the battlefield against the Sacred Band of Thebes, an elite force of the Theban army consisting of 150 pairs of male lovers. Some sources claim that Alexander's cavalry unit decimated the enemy troops and brought Macedonia another glorious victory.

Alexander the Great at the tomb of Cyrus the Great.
https://commons.wikimedia.org/wiki/File:Valenciennes,_Pierre-Henri_de_-_Alexander_at_the_Tomb_of_Cyrus_the_Great_-_1796.jpg

Two years after the victory, Alexander received news of his father's assassination at the hands of his bodyguard, Pausanias. With the passing of the forty-six-year-old king, Alexander rose to the throne as Macedonia's new ruler. After squashing his rivals, Alexander began to make a move on realizing his goal: to continue Macedonia's world domination plan and overthrow the Persian Empire once and for all.

Throughout the course of his vicious battles with the Persians, Alexander had one aim: eliminate the empire's ruler, King Darius III. Only three years after claiming the throne, Alexander had the pleasure of going into yet another battle and facing the Persian king for the first time. King Darius III could breathe easy when he realized that Alexander was outnumbered by his tens of thousands of troops. His relief, however, was cut short when he witnessed the Macedonians' determination to take him down. Alexander was believed to have seriously injured his thigh, but his wound never slowed his advance. Darius III went from being confident of emerging victorious over the young conqueror to fleeing the battlefield in his chariot before switching to a horse.

Alexander the Great facing King Darius III at the Battle of Issus.
momo from Hong Kong, CC BY 2.0 <https://creativecommons.org/licenses/by/2.0>, via Wikimedia Commons:
https://commons.wikimedia.org/wiki/File:Alexander_the_Great_fighting_at_the_battle_of_Issus_against_Darius_III_of_Persia_(5886504798).jpg

Sources claim that Alexander went on to pursue the fleeing king until the sky darkened, but not even his tracks were found. The young conqueror only found the Persian king's mother, wife, and two daughters in Darius's private tent. As ruthless as Alexander could be, the Macedonian king refused to harm the women. Instead, he informed them of Darius's escape and promised them their safety since he was only after the dominion of Persia. Sisygambis, the mother of the Persian king, was deeply disappointed by her son's cowardice, which led her to plead her allegiance to the young Macedonian king. It is also believed the two unlikely allies formed a strong bond to the point where Alexander would refer to Sisygambis as his "mother."

King Darius III wished to regain his family and end the war peacefully, but his peace offering was immediately declined by Alexander. Alexander continued his campaign in Egypt, where he was left with no choice but to endure the time-consuming siege of Gaza. At the time, the city was protected by high walls reaching over sixty feet in height. Alexander and his men attempted three times before they could finally find a way to breach the walls and capture the city. Although the Persian commander of Gaza, Batis, had been terribly defeated, he refused to surrender to the young conqueror, which resulted in a terrible death. —the commander was dragged alive by a chariot around the city until he died.

The success of the siege left a door open for Alexander to enter Egypt and assert his power with little to no resistance. Witnessing the Persians' fall at the hands of the young Macedonian king, the Egyptians celebrated his arrival with open arms. At Memphis, Alexander was crowned with the double crown, symbolizing his power over Upper and Lower Egypt, thus making him the pharaoh of the kingdom. Under Egyptian tradition and belief, the new pharaoh was deified as the son of Ra and worshiped by most of his subjects.

While Alexander was said to have respected Egyptian culture and customs—he even went as far as to publicly honor the main Egyptian gods—the young conqueror was also aware of the riches of the Nile. He knew the exploitation of Egypt's resources could play an important role in his upcoming campaigns, especially his plans to track down King Darius III. Alexander initially chose Pharos as the site of his new city, then shifted his focus to another location on the edge of Egypt, which could be used to control trade between Egypt and the Mediterranean. Delighted with the location and after encountering good omens, the conqueror founded the city of Alexandria. Even though Alexander never lived to see the completion of the city, Alexandria soon turned into the center of Hellenistic culture.

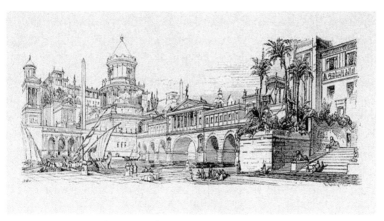

A drawing of the ancient city of Alexandria.

Gnauth, Adolf, CC BY-SA 2.5 <https://creativecommons.org/licenses/by-sa/2.5>, via Wikimedia Commons: https://commons.wikimedia.org/wiki/File:Ancient_Alexandria_(1878)_-_TIMEA.jpg

Historians suggest that Alexander spent only six months in Egypt and brought the country back to its feet before embarking on another campaign. With Mesopotamia as his next destination, the conqueror finally clashed swords for the second time with King Darius III. Overwhelmed yet again, Darius fled the battlefield. However, his fate was already sealed, as his own troops assassinated him. Alexander replaced Darius as the new king of Persia and expanded his dominion. He marched to India in 327 BCE. Four years later, he planned his next move to invade Arabia, although this campaign did not come to fruition. The mighty conqueror died in June 323 BCE at the ripe age of thirty-two. Some believe that he died of malaria, while others claim he was poisoned. Nevertheless, Alexander the Great left no successors to inherit his vast empire, which included Egypt.

Ptolemy I Soter, Founder of the Ptolemaic Dynasty

Ptolemy was one of the successors of Alexander the Great and the founder of Egypt's Ptolemaic dynasty, which would thrive until the conquest of the Roman Empire. He was born sometime in 366 BCE, but not much is known about his early life; not even his family line was ever confirmed. While historians suggest that Ptolemy was born to a well-respected Macedonian nobleman known as Lagus, others also believe that he was the illegitimate son of King Philip II. However, this is nothing but a rumor, especially since scholars claim that Ptolemy was fond of exaggerations and would use such propaganda to further strengthen his position. Nevertheless, Ptolemy was, no doubt, a Macedonian general who was more or less important during the entire course of Alexander's conquests.

Despite being older than Alexander and the other generals who marched into Persia alongside him, Ptolemy received a full education and was tutored by Aristotle. It is safe to assume that he was close to the young conqueror even before he claimed the throne. Ptolemy participated in a number of battles, especially those against the Persians. Later on, Ptolemy, who was already serving as the young king's advisor, was given the honor of being Alexander's personal bodyguard.

Alexander was said to have clearly expressed his anger upon discovering the sudden death of King Darius III. When the identity of the assassin was revealed—Darius's second-in-command named Bessus—Alexander ordered Ptolemy to travel to a certain village where Bessus was about to be extradited by his officers. Following the king's orders, Ptolemy returned with Bessus, who was tied up and stripped naked. The assassin was flogged in public before having his ears and nose chopped off—a punishment common among the Persians. To end his misery, Bessus was sent to the ancient city of Ecbatana, where he was executed in front of Darius III's brother.

After the successful conquest of the Persians, Ptolemy continued to march alongside the young king. During the campaign in India, Ptolemy was said to have been seriously injured by a poisoned arrow. He was almost at death's door until Alexander saved his life by using a special brew made up of a combination of several native herbs. This might have been one of the reasons behind Ptolemy's loyalty to Alexander. However, after the death of Alexander in Babylon, Ptolemy and the other generals began to fight each other in hopes of securing power over the many lands within the vast empire.

A marble bust of Ptolemy I Soter.
Gary Todd from Xinzheng, China, CC0, via Wikimedia Commons:
https://commons.wikimedia.org/wiki/File:Marble_Bust_of_Ptolemy_I_%22Soter,%22
Founder_of_Ptolemaic_Dynasty_of_Egypt,_c._3rd_C._BC_(28018907870).jpg

When Ptolemy accompanied Alexander to Egypt several years prior, the general was taken aback by the kingdom's rich resources. He saw the potential that Egypt had to become one of the most powerful nations in the world. When the self-proclaimed regent of the Macedonian Empire, Perdiccas, suggested they wait for the birth of Alexander IV (the son of Alexander the Great and his wife, Roxana) before they named the next ruler, Ptolemy was quick to portray his objections. After leading a campaign to divide the empire among the generals, Ptolemy managed to get his hands on Egypt. However, this was only the beginning of the Wars of the Diadochi, a conflict fought by Alexander the Great's main generals.

Although Ptolemy had already been named the governor of Egypt, he could not rest easy, as he knew that he was being watched by Perdiccas. So, he began plotting a grand theft. In the eyes of the Macedonians, the remains of Alexander the Great were more than just a cold, lifeless body; they were the talisman of authority and legitimacy. Whoever had his remains held the true power of the empire. Ptolemy attempted to steal the king's body when his elaborate funeral cart left Babylon to head to Macedonia. After successfully bribing the escort, Ptolemy diverted the cart to Egypt. Alexander was laid to rest in Memphis, the governing center of Egypt at the time.

Perdiccas, whose power was severely tarnished without Alexander's body in his possession, soon planned an attack against Ptolemy in Egypt—a move that resulted in his demise. The majority of the Macedonian troops swarmed to fill the ranks of Ptolemy's army. With his plan a success, Ptolemy was finally free from Perdiccas, although he was soon involved in yet another set of wars between the rest of Alexander's power-hungry generals and successors. In 305 BCE, Ptolemy proclaimed himself the pharaoh of Egypt, and a year later, he gained the title "Soter" or "Savior" after defending the inhabitants of Rhodes from one of Alexander's generals, Demetrius I.

After the defeat of Antigonus, another one of Alexander's generals and the founder of the Antigonid dynasty, at the Battle of Ipsus, Ptolemy was finally able to shift his entire focus to Egypt. His first step was to move the capital of the kingdom to Alexandria, the golden city envisioned by Alexander the Great before his passing. Given the city's strategic location at the mouth of the Nile, a new trade route was established, which hugely benefited Egypt's economy. More Greeks began to flock to the city, thus making Greek the official language of the government and commerce.

Although Ptolemy did not learn the Egyptian language and spoke only Greek, he never abandoned the traditions and customs of his subjects. Priests were allowed to resume their daily religious activities, and temples that had been demolished by the Persians were reconstructed. In an attempt to assimilate Greek influences into the Egyptian religion, Ptolemy founded a new cult centered around Serapis, a deity born from both Egyptian and Greek beliefs.

Ptolemy also sought to transform Alexandria into the intellectual capital of the Hellenistic world. He commissioned the construction of a museum and the famous Library of Alexandria, which housed stacks upon stacks of papyrus scrolls and books of various precious knowledge. The king of Egypt was also responsible for the foundation of the Lighthouse of Alexandria, which was later completed by his son and earned its place on the list of the Seven Wonders of the Ancient World. The Pyramids of Giza also made it on the list.

Ptolemy founded a new dynasty and placed Egypt on the right track. The land prospered, with its wealth growing continuously. Its trade and economy flourished, and its borders were secure. The kingdom soon became desirable by many forces of the ancient world. After the king's death in 282 BCE, his direct descendants would continue to rule over the rich kingdom for nearly three centuries. But, of course, no kingdom was ever free from struggles for too long. Civil wars soon plagued the land, which eventually gave way for the Romans to gradually assert their power. Egypt was brought to its glory again under Cleopatra, but peace and independence were not meant to last in Egypt for much longer.

Cleopatra, the Last Ruler of the Ptolemaic Dynasty

Many are likely familiar with the name Cleopatra. She was one of the few queens of Egypt whose name is well known today. As one of the most controversial figures in ancient history, Cleopatra is often depicted as a power-hungry ruler who would do anything to secure her throne. However, contemporary evidence suggests that the queen of the Nile was one of the most powerful pharaohs of the dynasty.

Cleopatra spent most of her youth learning about the world. It is believed Cleopatra could speak at least six different languages, and she was the only Ptolemaic pharaoh who could speak Egyptian. She aided her father during his reign, so it should not come as too much of a surprise that the queen managed to bring Egypt into yet another era of prosperity.

Cleopatra's legendary meeting with Julius Caesar.
Jean-Léon Gérôme, oil on canvas, 1866., CC BY-SA 4.0

However, her journey to claim the throne was not without its obstacles. When her father, Ptolemy XII, died, the mantle was passed to Cleopatra and her husband-brother, Ptolemy XIII. (Although there is no firm proof they married, it is likely they were since it was traditional for the Egyptian royals to marry their sibling.) Since Ptolemy XIII was merely a child when he rose to the throne, Cleopatra led the people. She even went to the extent of having only her face minted on the kingdom's currency. Only her name would be signed on official documents. This, no doubt, angered the young Ptolemy XIII; he claimed that Cleopatra was nothing more than a power-hungry ruler who sought to have the kingdom all to herself. And so, after gathering enough support,

Ptolemy XIII successfully drove his sister-wife out of her homeland. Stripped of power by her own flesh and blood, Cleopatra sought refuge in Syria until an opportunity arose that could potentially assist in her mission to reclaim the throne.

A Roman civil war exploded between two Roman generals: Julius Caesar and Pompey. The war eventually brought the future queen of Egypt back to her feet. Pompey was killed upon Ptolemy XIII's orders. Caesar sailed to Egypt to confront Pompey and was mortified to learn that the great general had died in such a way. Caesar stayed in Egypt, hoping to use the civil war in Egypt to his own advantage.

Upon learning of Caesar's stay in Alexandria, Cleopatra planned for her grand but discreet entrance, hoping she could earn the Roman general's support and pave the way for her to reclaim the crown. According to legend, the future queen hid in a sack and sailed to the fortified city of Alexandria. Once they docked, Apollodorus carried the queen—who was still hiding in a sack—on his shoulder and made his way to the palace where Julius Caesar stayed. Cleopatra revealed herself to the Roman general and easily caught Caesar's attention and won his heart.

Cleopatra was able to reclaim the throne with the support of her new lover, despite her brother-husband's clear disapproval. It was said that the young pharaoh stomped his feet in anger upon finding Cleopatra in Caesar's chamber. However, Cleopatra was not one to let her enemies remain close to her. Ptolemy XIII soon died when he launched a war against Caesar.

The Egyptian throne now belonged to her alone. Cleopatra did marry another one of her brothers, Ptolemy XIV, but it was agreed that she would be the one responsible for state matters. Egypt flourished yet again. The kingdom was stabilized, and corruption was widely minimized. When drought and famine terrorized the valley, the queen fed her subjects food from her royal granary. Under Cleopatra, the kingdom rarely saw rebellions. Before another civil war could possibly happen, Cleopatra ruthlessly removed all of her siblings who displayed even the slightest signs of revolt.

However, things began to change when Caesar was assassinated in Rome. The queen, who was believed to have been in Rome during the incident, made haste to Egypt the moment news of the general's death reached her ears. A series of wars broke out in the Roman Republic. Taking the opportunity to solidify her position and relationship with Rome, the queen forged a relationship with Mark Antony, one of the Roman Republic's greatest generals and a close ally of Julius Caesar. However, this move marked the beginning of her demise. According to several ancient Roman historians, Antony was becoming more Egyptian than Roman, which further fueled his rivalry with the future Roman emperor, Octavian (later known as Augustus).

The Romans believed the Egyptian queen had corrupted Antony with her wiles. So, the Romans declared war against Egypt. In the Battle of Actium, Cleopatra's and Antony's forces faced Octavian's troops in the Ionian Sea near the city of Actium. The naval battle, which took place in 31 BCE, resulted in the defeat of both Cleopatra and Mark Antony. Sensing their deaths were around the corner should they remain in battle, the two retreated to Alexandria. Octavian, who was insistent on ending the decades-long rivalry with Antony and removing Cleopatra from power, pursued them to the city and defeated the remaining Alexandrian troops.

A scene of the Battle of Actium.
https://commons.wikimedia.org/wiki/File:Castro_Battle_of_Actium.jpg

Seeing that victory was far from reach, Cleopatra committed suicide in August 30 BCE; Antony had already died beforehand due to a self-inflicted wound upon hearing a rumor of the queen's death. With the death of the last Ptolemaic queen, Egypt could no longer taste complete freedom, as the kingdom was annexed into the Roman Empire, which was formed by Augustus. This is considered the end of ancient Egypt. Egypt would be a part of Rome for over six centuries.

Chapter 13: Old Kingdom Art: Mummies, Figures, Temples, Reliefs, and Murals

An Egyptian man was preparing to leave his place of work and return to his home, where his wife and children were patiently waiting. However, the man's expression quickly changed when he was approached by his assistant, who informed him of the arrival of yet another dead body that required his immediate attention. The man, who had spent most of his life working as an embalmer, was left with no choice but to extend his working hours to tend to the poor body.

Working late was not uncommon for the ancient Egyptians, especially embalmers. Death was not a rare occasion in the kingdom of the Nile. After receiving the body, the embalmer began the early process of mummification. The corpse was placed on a low embalming table, with the person lying on their bare back. With the embalmer's assistant at his side, the embalmer cut an incision on the deceased's lower left abdomen. The embalmer then inserted his arm into the incision up to his elbow as he reached for the internal organs. He would first reach for the intestines and draw them out of the corpse before dropping them into a large pottery bowl. The bowl full of guts would be filled with natron, a type of preservative agent typically found in dry lake beds. Natron was the most important agent in the process of mummification since it was necessary to desiccate the corpse and its organs, preventing decomposition.

After the intestines, the embalmer moved on the liver; he would carefully jab and slice anything that held the liver together in the stomach before pulling it out and dropping it in another pottery vessel filled with natron. The same procedure was used when he moved on to retrieve the lungs. The only organ left inside the body was the heart. The ancient Egyptians believed the heart was the nucleus of a person's physical self, intelligence, and emotion. So, it was of the utmost importance to leave the heart untouched, though it might have been difficult to pull the heart out without damaging it.

The brain was seen as nothing more than a space filler in the skull. To remove the brain, the embalmer had to insert an iron hook into the nostrils until he could feel the soft surface of the brain itself. With the hook, he would then work to break the brain into tiny pieces and pull them out through the nostrils. Again, the embalmer would insert the iron hook through the corpse's nose and mash up the remaining parts of the brain until he could finally feel the hard walls of the skull. With the help of his assistant, the embalmer flipped the corpse over so that he could slap the back of its head to flush out the mashed brain, which would have turned into a thick liquid. Afterward, the embalmer poured tree resin into the skull to avoid further decomposition.

Once the body was free from all internal organs that could rapidly decay—aside from the heart, of course—the embalmer would then clean the rest of the corpse before moving it into a large jar filled with heaps of natron. The inside of the body was also filled with packets of natron to ensure thorough desiccation. The corpse was left entirely covered in natron for at least forty days. As for the internal organs that had been removed from the body, they were stored in separate limestone jars sealed with lids, each featuring the carvings of the four sons of Horus—Duamutef guarded the stomach, Hapi the lungs, Imsety the liver, and Qebehsenuef the intestines. These four jars would be interred along with the mummified corpse in its tomb.

Canopic jars representing the four sons of Horus.
https://commons.wikimedia.org/wiki/File:Canopic_jars_BM_4SoH.jpg

Forty days later, the embalmer would return to resume his work on the corpse. He would wash away the natron covering the body before stuffing linen rags into the incision to make the deceased appear more lifelike and fuller. False eyes were also added to ensure the corpse looked like how the person did while still alive. Now that the body was removed from all moisture and completely dried out, the embalmer would proceed to the final stage of mummification: wrapping the deceased. Using hundreds of yards of linen, he would carefully wrap the linen strips around the corpse while a priest recited prayers and spells for the soul of the deceased.

Anubis or a priest attending the mummy of the deceased.
https://commons.wikimedia.org/wiki/File:Anubis_attending_the_mummy_of_Sennedjem.jpg

The priests wore masks that resembled the god Anubis and would oversee the entire process to ensure a flawless mummification. When the mummy was finally completed, a mask would be placed over its wrapped head. The type of masks varied depending on the status of the deceased. Death masks belonging to a wealthy family were often covered in gold and exquisite paints, while those who were less fortunate could only afford simple masks with unembellished details. The same could be said for amulets; the rich would be interred with many amulets made out of precious stones, while the poor could only have a few amulets made of much cheaper materials.

An example of a mummy mask.

The entire mummification process took seventy days. Once done, the mummy would be ready to be interred within their tombs, which had been built and designed beforehand. Elaborate burial practices took place to ready the deceased to move on to their next life. Most of the time, the mummy was placed inside a sarcophagus before getting interred in their burial chamber. The entrance would then be sealed.

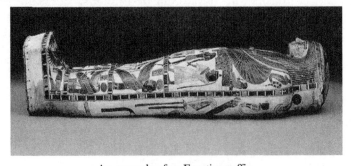

An example of an Egyptian coffin.

The interior of an Egyptian coffin.

Figures and Statues

The Egyptians of the Old Kingdom were undoubtedly ahead of their time, especially when it came to sculptures. The Great Sphinx of Giza is the greatest example of their extraordinary work. Believe it or not, the ancient Egyptians never once referred to the great sculpture as the Sphinx. It actually owes its name to the Greek travelers who thought the sculpture resembled a mythical being, the female-headed Sphinx. This was possibly due to its body resembling a lion and the Nemes on its head (a stripped linen headcloth worn by pharaohs), which was mistakenly thought to be the hair of a woman. It was only referred to by the Egyptians of the Old Kingdom as *shepsepankh* (which simply means "living image"), although people in the New Kingdom called it Horemakhet ("Horus in the horizon").

The Great Sphinx of Giza.
English: Taken by the uploader, w:es:Usuario:BarcexEspañol: Tomada por w:es:Usuario:Barcex, CC BY-SA 3.0 <http://creativecommons.org/licenses/by-sa/3.0/>, via Wikimedia Commons: https://commons.wikimedia.org/wiki/File:Great_Sphinx_of_Giza_-_20080716a.jpg

The reason behind the construction of this magnificent structure remains debated by scholars. However, many agree that it was somehow erected to honor the pharaoh Khafre because the Sphinx's head closely resembles the pharaoh. Certain parts, particularly the features on the face of the Sphinx, are no longer perfect, but through careful observations and studies, Egyptologists managed to reimagine the sculpture back to when it was at its utmost glory. From the stone fragments scattered between the Sphinx's paws, it is plausible that the sculpture once had a beard—the one typically seen on a pharaoh's statue. There were also traces of paint behind the ears, which might indicate the Sphinx was initially adorned with paint on its face. Last but not least, it is safe to assume the sculpture sports a Nemes, the blue and gold striped linen headdress worn by the pharaohs.

Why Khafre wanted his image combined with the body of a lion remains a mystery. Since felines, especially cats, were considered sacred animals by the ancient Egyptians, it is plausible that the great pharaoh wished to be seen as a divine entity, perhaps just like the gods themselves. Nevertheless, it is the construction of the Sphinx that intrigues us the most. Scholars have long agreed that besides being master builders, the Egyptians were amazing geologists. They knew how to exploit their surroundings to their advantage, and the Sphinx was a great example of that. Instead of building the Sphinx's body above the ground, archaeologists believe that the Egyptians actually dug trenches into the bedrock, thus exposing the layers of limestone underneath. From there, wooden wedges were used to separate the layers and carve out the rough shape of the Sphinx. The spoils of the limestone layers were then recycled and used to build surrounding temples. The stonemasons then worked their magic. With their copper chisels, they added the details of the pharaoh's face and carved the lion's body.

However, the many elaborate statues and figures scattered throughout the lands of the Nile did not always serve as decorations or signs of power. More often than not, they played a role in the ancient Egyptian religion. A ka statue, for instance, was crucial for the souls of the deceased. The Egyptians believed that, upon dying, the soul was released from the body, allowing it to roam the world. However, the soul needed its own permanent physical body to return to after roaming the world of the living. Ka statues were created for this very purpose. To ensure the spirit or *ka* recognized their resting place, wooden or stone statues were erected with the likeness of the deceased. Ka statues of a pharaoh usually featured a Nemes. The statue of a pharaoh also had a false beard, which signified their status as a living god. Since ka statues are classified as funerary art, they were often found in burial tombs.

An example of a ka statue.
Jon Bodsworth, Copyrighted free use, via Wikimedia Commons;
https://commons.wikimedia.org/wiki/File:Ka_Statue_of_horawibra.jpg

While ka statues were reserved especially for the pharaohs, the royals, and the rich, the tombs of those belonging to non-royals often featured a type of sculpture referred to as reserve heads. In contrast to the ka statues, reserve heads were rather simple and plain. These busts featured neither hair nor a specific headdress. Despite being considered a ka statue for the commoners, the true purpose of the reserve heads remains uncertain; some scholars claim that they merely served as portraits.

Egyptian Stelae

Unlike the Greeks and the Romans, Egyptian stelae could often be seen on the walls of a temple or tomb. The earliest appearance of an Egyptian stele can be traced back to the First Dynasty at Abydos. In contrast to those in later periods, stelae from the First Dynasty were rather simple; they featured only the title and name of the tomb owner. By the time of the Second Dynasty, these stelae began to appear more complex. One of them had an image of an individual sitting on a chair surrounded by various offerings. One of the reasons the Egyptians included a stele within a tomb was to keep the memories of the deceased alive.

Stele of the scribe Iry.

During the Old Kingdom, false door stelae were the norm. These carved false doors were believed to have been used by the souls of the dead as a passageway to the living world. Through this door, the dead would be able to access the offerings left by those who were still breathing.

A common false door in an Egyptian tomb.
Louvre Museum, CC BY-SA 3.0 <https://creativecommons.org/licenses/by-sa/3.0>, via Wikimedia Commons: https://commons.wikimedia.org/wiki/File:Louvres-antiquites-egyptiennes-img_2947_cropped.jpg

As time passed by, stelae evolved into not only serving as a form of decoration in a tomb or a passageway for the souls of the dead but were also used to commemorate a specific event or victory.

The Sun Temple

The sun god Ra had always been one of ancient Egypt's most important deities, but he gained tremendous popularity during the Old Kingdom. During this time, Ra was seen as the state deity. Due to Ra's rising importance, the Old Kingdom pharaohs commissioned the construction of temples to honor the sun god. Although Egyptologists believe more than a dozen sun temples were built in the valley, only two survived the test of time, with one of them being in Abu Gorab, just north of Abusir.

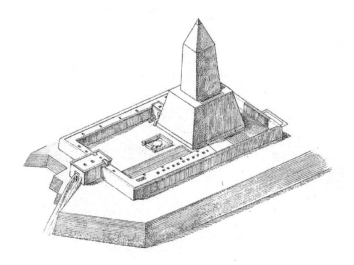

A drawing of the Niuserra's sun temple.
https://commons.wikimedia.org/wiki/File:Temple-solaire-abousir.jpg

Built sometime around 2430 BCE, the temple was also known as the Sun Temple of Niuserra. Based on the ruins, archaeologists can confirm that the temple once had three different sections, with one of them being the upper temple, complete with a 36-meter-tall obelisk, a four-sided square-based structure topped with a triangular pyramid. Obelisks were a symbol of the sun god. Directly in front of the tall structure was an altar, which was made out of white alabaster blocks. Purposely placed to be exposed to the sun, the altar was arranged to form a particular symbol that meant "Ra is satisfied."

Apart from the structures, various reliefs were carved onto the walls of the temple. One of them explained Ra's main role as the giver of life, while two other reliefs known as the "Chamber of the Seasons" depicted the changing seasons of inundation and harvest. However, these two reliefs are no longer at Abu Gorab, as they were removed and put on display in a museum in Berlin.

A mural on the wall of the temple depicting an agricultural scene of ancient Egypt.
Osama Shukir Muhammed Amin FRCP(Glasg), CC BY-SA 4.0
<https://creativecommons.org/licenses/by-sa/4.0>, via Wikimedia Commons:
https://commons.wikimedia.org/wiki/File:Fowling_with_a_dragnet,_agricultural_scene,
and_handling_ducks._Wall_fragment_from_the_Sun_Temple_of_Nyuserre_Ini_at
Abu_Gurob,_Egypt._c._2430_BCE._Neues_Museum.jpg

Due to unknown reasons, the temple was destroyed several times, possibly by Mother Nature. Fortunately, it was restored by Ramses II during his reign in the New Kingdom era.

Chapter 14: Middle Kingdom Art and Customs: Life, Death, and Beyond

We know the ancient Egyptians were obsessed with life in all its forms; to them, even death was a new form of life. However, death was far from being merciful enough to end one's peril and troubles. In death, the Egyptians were expected to go through a journey filled with obstacles and threats before they could finally achieve peace or, rather, the Field of Reeds, where their needs would always be met.

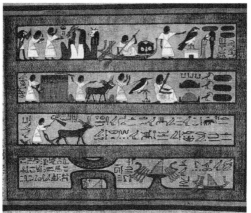

A depiction of the Field of Reeds on a papyrus.
https://commons.wikimedia.org/wiki/File:Bookofthedead-fieldofreeds.jpg

Legend has it that in order to reach eternity, the Egyptians needed some help to navigate the paths of the underworld. Back in the Third Dynasty, they believed that only their kings and pharaohs had the ability to ascend toward the heavens. To guide their deceased ruler and protect them from the impending dangers on their path, the Egyptians often included many spells and incantations on the pharaoh's sarcophagus and on the walls of his pyramid. These religious texts are more popularly known as the Pyramid Texts.

Sometime toward the beginning of the First Intermediate Period, this exclusivity began to fade away. The Egyptians began to believe that the afterlife was no longer only limited to the royals; even commoners were allowed to ascend to the next life. And so, the Pyramid Texts began to evolve into what we know today as the Coffin Texts. Since ordinary individuals were now thought to be worthy of a continued existence, it was a must for them to have their own coffins to ensure they were buried with spells and incantations that could save them in the netherworld. The number of spells varied, and the inscriptions were not only limited to coffins, as they were also written on tomb walls, stelae, and sometimes the deceased's death mask.

The Coffin Texts painted on the interior of a coffin.
British Museum, Copyrighted free use, via Wikimedia Commons;
https://commons.wikimedia.org/wiki/File:Coffin_of_Gua.jpg

The Egyptian beliefs about life after death varied slightly as the kingdom progressed into the Middle Kingdom era. However, their burial customs underwent some changes. During the Eleventh Dynasty, it was common for the Egyptians—typically those belonging to wealthy families—to build their tombs within the mountains of Thebes and as close as possible to their pharaoh's tomb. Thebes was the main location for burials since it was the city of the Eleventh Dynasty kings. By the Twelfth Dynasty, the people had begun to change their preferred burial sites. The Egyptians, especially those who served in the pharaoh's office, were interred in mastabas located in Lisht, which was in close proximity to the capital of Itjtawy. The Pyramid of Senusret can still be found in Lisht today, though it has been severely damaged over the years.

What remains of the Pyramid of Senusret in Lisht today.
https://commons.wikimedia.org/wiki/File:Licht-senwsPyramids_01.jpg

As for those who belonged neither to the royal family nor the rich, their tombs appeared rather simple. Some were mummified and wrapped entirely in linen, while others were only wrapped but not mummified. The bodies of commoners were covered by cartonnage mummy masks, which were made out of layers of linen and plaster. Unlike the royals and high officials, who had the privilege of being interred in intricate sarcophagi gilded in gold, ordinary individuals could only afford to be buried in simple wooden coffins.

Since the Egyptians believed in life after death, it was not unusual for them to include different types of food items and even weapons in the tombs of the dead. Bread, a leg of beef, and beer were among the most common offerings found within the Egyptian tombs. Wooden models, such as boats, scribes, and soldiers, were also buried with the dead. Shabti, a type of figurine, was also commonly buried with the deceased; they were believed to be able to serve the deceased in the afterlife. This custom somehow mirrored the ancient Egyptian retainer sacrifices, when servants were sacrificed following a pharaoh's death to ensure they could serve their king in the next life. These sacrifices were only widely practiced during the First Dynasty and were eventually replaced with the shabti.

Examples of shabti figurine.
Metropolitan Museum of Art, CC0, via Wikimedia Commons:
https://commons.wikimedia.org/wiki/File:Shabti_of_Khabekhnet_and_Iineferty_MET_DT202025.jpg

The most popular item was a piece of jewelry or amulet called the heart scarab. However, it must be noted that jewelry was rarely included in the tombs of commoners. Just as its name suggests, the heart scarab was a type of amulet in the shape of a scarab, which is part of the beetle family. The heart scarab represented Khepri, the ancient god who could renew life. The funerary amulet was usually placed on a mummy's chest, and its purpose was to protect the heart of the deceased.

A heart scarab with inscriptions.
Brooklyn Museum, CC BY-SA 2.5 <https://creativecommons.org/licenses/by-sa/2.5>,
via Wikimedia Commons:
https://commons.wikimedia.org/wiki/File:WLA_brooklynmuseum_Heart_Scarab_late
9_to_early_8th_century_BCE.jpg

Since the heart was considered the seat of a human's intelligence and emotions, it was a must for the Egyptians to ensure the once-beating organ remained unscathed until they finally passed through the Hall of Judgment, where their heart would be weighed against the feather of Ma'at. If their heart were damaged during the process of mummification, the heart scarab would act as a stand-in and be weighed against the feather. The amulet also played an important role during the final test in the Duat (the realm of the dead). Since the heart scarab was inscribed with a specific spell, it could prevent the heart from speaking against the soul of the deceased before the divine judges.

Architecture

The flourishing era of the pyramids might have belonged to the rulers of the Old Kingdom. However, when the Old Kingdom ended shortly after the death of Pepi II, with Egypt being ushered into its first dark era, the construction of pyramids started to become a thing of the past. The First Intermediate Period was so chaotic that the Egyptians saw a decreasing number of new pyramids being built in the valley.

By the time of the Middle Kingdom's Twelfth Dynasty, Egypt witnessed the resurgence of pyramids that resembled those from the Old Kingdom. However, the quality of these structures was, of course, average, especially compared to the magnificent pyramids at Giza. The pyramids of the Middle Kingdom were constructed with materials of lower quality. Instead of limestone blocks, many of the structures built during this time were made out of mudbricks, which explains the destruction of the pyramids in Lisht.

Amenemhat I was the first pharaoh who initiated the construction of a pyramid during the Middle Kingdom. He commissioned his pyramid complex in the necropolis of Lisht, which was not far from his seat of power in Itjtawy. Measuring at least 54 meters (177 feet) tall, the pyramid of Amenemhat I was built using a mixture of limestone blocks, mudbricks, and stones recycled from older pyramids. The entire structure was coated with limestone cladding to help sustain the unpredictable weather.

Inspired by the designs of the Sixth Dynasty, Amenemhat I had the entrance to the inner chambers built in the northern section of the pyramid, where one could find the offering hall. A tunnel that descended to an antechamber right underneath the apex of the pyramid was also built. From the antechamber was a vertical shaft that led straight down into the burial chamber, which is now submerged underwater due to the rising groundwater level. It is believed that the pyramid housed twenty-two burial shafts with at least four mastabas.

Unfortunately, the pyramid of Amenemhat I became a target for desperate grave robbers. Combined with the unpredictable weather of Egypt, what is left of the pyramid today is nothing more than ruins.

The Black Pyramid, commissioned by Pharaoh Amenemhat III, is another example of Middle Kingdom architecture. The pyramid got its name from the dark color of the exposed mudbrick core and was said to have been the first of its kind to house both the pharaoh and his queens. (The commoners often had monogamous marriages, while the pharaohs often had multiple wives to strengthen Egypt's diplomatic relations.) The pyramid also had complex interconnected passageways, which are believed to have been built to confuse tomb robbers. Some also suggest that the design had a ritual significance.

Nevertheless, like the pyramid of Amenemhat I, the Black Pyramid is in a poor state today, although its poor state is due to multiple errors made during its construction. The ground where the pyramid's foundations stood was unstable, and due to its location close to the edge of the Nile, parts of the pyramid flooded after the construction was completed.

What remains of Amenemhat III's Black Pyramid today.

Perhaps the most remarkable piece of architecture from the Middle Kingdom was another one of Amenemhat III's pyramids. Although the pyramid at Hawara failed to withstand the test of time—it currently resembles nothing but a huge mound—it was once a massive temple complex that gained the attention of many. Dubbed the Labyrinth, the ancient Greek historian Herodotus said the complex was awe-inspiring, largely because of its maze of rooms and winding passages. Unfortunately, like the pyramid itself, the temple complex was destroyed, leaving us with nothing but only small remnants.

Statues

Statues and sculptures no doubt reached new heights of technical perfection when Egypt was ushered into the flourishing period of the Middle Kingdom, particularly during the reign of Pharaoh Senusret III. Senusret III is often acknowledged as one of Egypt's most powerful pharaohs of the Twelfth Dynasty. He was popular for his supreme military prowess, but he was also known for his sculpture. The pharaoh's sculpture, which was made out of red granite, was unlike the ones carved during the reigns of his predecessors. Instead of sporting a youthful and vigorous appearance, the pharaoh had his sculpture capture his striking features as an aging king—a portrayal that deviated from the standard way of representing reigning Egyptian kings. Scholars have interpreted this portrayal as a way to symbolize the burden of kingship.

Statues of Senusret III.

Colossal statues also began to be widely used during the Middle Kingdom. These types of statues were often erected in pairs and used to flank the main entrances of Egypt's many grand temples. The colossal statues were thought to have served as guardians of sacred temples and complexes. The best example of a colossal statue built during this period is the Seated Statue of a Pharaoh. The colossal statue, which was carved out of granodiorite, is believed to have represented either King Amenemhat II or Senusret II.

Many innovations in creating sculptures were introduced during the Middle Kingdom. The most prominent example of their flourishing art is the block statue, which managed to maintain its popularity until the Ptolemaic dynasty two thousand years later. This type of sculpture often featured a man sitting on flat ground with both of his knees drawn up to his chest. His two hands were folded and rested on top of his knees. To create the block-like shape, these sculptures wore a simple yet wide cloak, which at times covered their feet. While the shape of the statue's body appeared rather simple, the head of the sculpture included fine details.

These statues were mostly used as funerary monuments for important individuals. The reason behind the creation of block statues varies. Some suggest that the statue simply portrayed a man resting, while others claim that it had a deeper religious meaning involving the process of rebirth.

The colossal seated statue of Amenemhat II.
Juan R. Lazaro, CC BY 2.0 <https://creativecommons.org/licenses/by/2.0>, via Wikimedia Commons: https://commons.wikimedia.org/wiki/File:Amenemhat_II.jpg

Literature

The Middle Kingdom also witnessed the birth of the Egyptian formal writing system, which was often used in religious scripts, administrative documents, and literary works. One of the types of text used during this era was known as hieratic. Historians describe this form of writing to be some sort of cursive Middle Egyptian hieroglyphs. This language writing system was believed to be much simpler compared to the normal hieroglyphs that we are familiar with today, and writing in Hieratic was also faster, which was useful for producing larger works of literature.

Perhaps the most impressive literary work ever produced in the Middle Kingdom was the "Tale of Sinuhe," whose author remains a mystery, though he was probably considered the "Shakespeare" of ancient Egypt. It tells the story of Sinuhe, an assistant of Pharaoh Amenemhat I. Upon the king's death, Sinuhe was said to have been shrouded with fear and decided to flee from Egypt and start a new life somewhere near Syria, where he joined a tribe called the Bedouins.

The tale gives its readers a unique insight into the afterlife, as well as the details of the cultural differences between Egypt and the Near East. After imposing a self-exile and living as a Bedouin, Sinuhe grew a beard and had long hair, which was not acceptable according to Egyptian standards, as the elites were expected to be clean-shaven and neat. The tale also explores the main character's life journey, from when he first fit into a new tribe, his challenges with the warriors, and his longing to return to his place of origin, the kingdom of the Nile.

The "Tale of Sinuhe" has been studied by many scholars all over the world, and it is still unsure whether the tale tells the story of a real individual or is strictly fiction, though the locations, rulers, and cultural details described in the text are accurate for the time period. Nevertheless, this tale is agreed to be one of the oldest written forms of storytelling, as it was produced nearly four thousand years ago.

Chapter 15: New Kingdom Art: Innovations and Alterations

While civil wars, famine, plagues, and drought were some of the most common unfortunate events that terrorized the kingdom, the ancient Egyptians also had to deal with one particular crime: tomb robbing. Although tomb robbing had long been recognized as ancient Egypt's number one crime—tomb robbers already existed in the kingdom as early as the Predynastic Period—by the Second Intermediate Period, it had gotten even worse. The most targeted tombs were, of course, the pyramids belonging to the pharaohs and their royal family. The rulers of the kingdom tried to discourage the robbers by constructing confusing mazes and passageways in their pyramids or scattering debris all over the chambers, but these efforts failed to curb the crime. Many tombs were successfully broken into, and all of their precious treasures were looted, including the mummies of the pharaohs themselves.

As Egypt ushered in the booming era of the New Kingdom, the third ruling pharaoh of the Eighteenth Dynasty, Thutmose I, decided to change the funerary tradition for the pharaohs and the royal family. Instead of burying the deceased in a massive pyramid visible to the eyes of many from far away, the rulers of Egypt were interred in hidden tombs carved in the crags of the mountains of western Thebes. This burial site is known to us today as the Valley of the Kings.

The Valley of the Kings.
Fotograf/Photographer: Peter J. Bubenik (1995), CC BY-SA 2.0
<https://creativecommons.org/licenses/by-sa/2.0>, via Wikimedia Commons:
https://commons.wikimedia.org/wiki/File:Luxor,_Tal_der_K%C3%B6nige_(1995,_860x605).jpg

The reason behind its location was never confirmed; however, it could be plausible that the pharaoh chose this site as the new necropolis due to the highest peak of the Theban hills, El Qorn, which resembled the pyramids built by his predecessors. Others have suggested that it was because of the land's condition, as the area had always been barren. Not a single plant could be seen emerging from the ground. Because of this, the land would remain isolated. No one would ever think of establishing a new settlement nearby.

The peak of El Qorn.
Marie Thérèse Hébert & Jean Robert Thibault from Québec, Canada, CC BY-SA 2.0
<https://creativecommons.org/licenses/by-sa/2.0>, via Wikimedia Commons:
https://commons.wikimedia.org/wiki/File:%C3%89gypte,_Vall%C3%A9e_des_Rois,_N%C3%A9cropole_th%C3%A9baine,_El-
Qurn_(la_Corne)_montagne_pyramidale_dominant_la_vall%C3%A9e_(49834286528).jpg

With the perfect location in mind, Thutmose laid out his idea of a secret underground tomb to one of Egypt's renowned architects at that time, Ineni. He was believed to be responsible for many major construction projects from the reign of Amenhotep I until Hatshepsut and Thutmose III. According to the architect's own tomb inscription, he claimed that he oversaw the construction of Thutmose's hidden tomb alone. However, sources suggest he used foreign captives to work on the tomb. Once the construction was finished, they were killed so that the location of the pharaoh's tomb remained a secret.

Nevertheless, Thutmose's plan to secure his tomb and possessions was a success. The necropolis had only one entrance, so it was impossible for tomb robbers to enter the valley unseen. With that, Thutmose I successfully made a great change in terms of the burial traditions of the Egyptian rulers. Their tombs were rarely broken into, and their precious possessions remained by their side. This can be seen in Tutankhamun's tomb, which was discovered by archaeologists in near-perfect condition.

Although his tomb is considered by many to be evidence of ancient Egypt's vast wealth, with his near-perfect mummy gifting Egyptologists with a clear insight into the mummification process, Tutankhamun (more famously known as King Tut) was not the most remarkable pharaoh. He rose to the throne at the age of nine, and shortly after his succession, he changed his name from Tutankhaten to Tutankhamun. This was largely due to his well-known reformation of Egypt's religious traditions.

With the crown on his head, the young pharaoh erased his father's, Akhenaten's, footsteps. King Tut encouraged his people to abandon Aten, the sun god introduced by his father, and revived the worship of Amun, thus bringing back the centuries-old religious traditions of Egypt. Despite being revered by the Egyptians for restoring their religious beliefs, his name was almost completely forgotten the moment he died ten years after his succession. King Tut was a frail pharaoh. He suffered from multiple diseases all his life, possibly caused by inbreeding.

Although Tutankhamun was forgotten, his name soon became widely known throughout the world in 1922 when his tomb was discovered by the British Egyptologist Howard Carter. However, certain sources claim a twelve-year-old boy named Hussein Abdul Rasul accidentally stumbled upon the tomb's entrance while he was fetching water for the archaeologists. Nevertheless, when words of the tomb's discovery hit the public, the world was astonished.

Within the tomb are four separate chambers, with all of its precious contents and murals intact. The antechamber contained all of Tutankhamun's prized possessions, including some of the items he possibly used on a daily basis, such as three intricately crafted golden animal couches and a paper fan. There was also the burial chamber, where the young, sickly king was laid to rest. His intact mummy was accompanied by two statues of Anubis, the god of funerary rites and the fierce guardian of tombs and graves. The walls surrounding his sarcophagus were painted with different scenes of the young pharaoh interacting with the Egyptian gods.

Although the size of Tutankhamun's tomb was noticeably smaller compared to those belonging to other pharaohs before him, the large number of untouched treasures discovered within all four chambers of the tomb surely stunned many archaeologists. Over five thousand artifacts were found, most of which were made out of gold. To the ancient Egyptians, these treasures were stored within the tomb to accompany the soul of the deceased pharaoh in the afterlife, but for us today, they serve as a guide for us to journey back in time.

The interior of Tutankhamun's tomb.

The Book of the Dead

The tradition of burying the dead with everyday items had long been practiced by the Egyptians, and it continued even when the kingdom entered a whole new era. Sandals, pottery, weapons, furniture, and cosmetic objects were some of the most common grave goods included in the tombs of the ancient Egyptians. However, in contrast to the Second Intermediate Period, the grave goods became even more elaborate during the New Kingdom, possibly due to the kingdom's growing wealth after centuries of disarray. Aside from precious jewelry, the Egyptians, typically those belonging to the elite classes, included a particular item in their tombs that served as a guide for them to continue their life after death and safely reach the Field of Reeds.

Known as the Book of the Dead, this funerary text was written on a long piece of papyrus and contained a set of unique spells that had the ability to protect and navigate the deceased through the Duat. With this book, one could get a detailed insight into what to expect after death and how to pass each test posed by the gods who were waiting to judge their deeds.

The Book of the Dead was prepared by the Egyptian scribes after being commissioned by the relatives of the deceased. However, this was not always the case, as there were many who would commission the funerary text in advance to prepare for their own funeral. Although the Book of the Dead was considered vital to ensure a smooth journey in the Duat, not everyone had the privilege to have one interred in their tomb. The production of the funerary text was rather expensive. Laborers had to save almost half of their annual pay to afford the scroll, which was why the Book of the Dead was often only included in the tombs of the rich.

The contents and magic spells in the scroll—typically written in cursive hieroglyphs—varied from one person to another. As of today, historians have discovered 192 different spells, which were used for a wide range of purposes. The best-preserved Book of the Dead is the Papyrus of Ani. It granted Egyptologists a great detail of information on ancient Egyptian beliefs of the afterlife.

Spell written in the scribe Ani's Book of the Dead.
https://commons.wikimedia.org/wiki/File:Bookofthedeadspell17.jpg

The seventy-eight-foot scroll was believed to have been prepared for Ani, a scribe who once called the ancient city of Thebes his home. According to the manuscript, the journey through the Duat was daunting. The deceased must first pass through a series of dark caverns, lakes of fire, and magical gates guarded by nothing but the most fearsome of beasts, including Apep (Apophis), the mythical demon serpent that lurks in the darkness waiting to devour the souls who pass in front of him. Ani was saved from these threats since he had specifically customized his scroll to fit his spirit's needs. With incantations, prayers, and spells, the Egyptians believed Ani was able to repel the dangers scattered on his way and arrived at the Hall of Judgment. At this particular hall, Ani had to stand before forty-two gods who would assess his life on earth.

A depiction of the weighing of the heart.
https://commons.wikimedia.org/wiki/File:Egypt_dauingevekten.jpg

Ammit, the devourer of the heart.
https://commons.wikimedia.org/wiki/File:Ammit_BD.jpg

After proclaiming his good deeds and convincing the gods of his righteous ways, Ani then moved on to the weighing of the heart. This trial was one of the most daunting parts of the underworld. If his heart weighed heavier than Ma'at's feather—signifying his many wrongdoings—then it would be devoured by Ammit, a terrifying beast with the head of a crocodile and the body of a leopard and hippopotamus, thus ending his existence forever. However, thanks to Ani's righteous deeds, he passed the judgment and was granted passage to meet Osiris, who later gave him his approval to enter the Field of Reeds, a realm without pain, sadness, and anger.

The Temple of Hatshepsut: One of the Most Elaborate Temples of the New Kingdom

Despite the hatred of some Egyptians, Hatshepsut led Egypt into a prosperous period. Her expedition to Punt was the success that she was most proud of, but her biggest contribution is still visible today: her mortuary temple in Thebes. The pharaoh sought to immortalize the story of her life and power and was said to have commissioned the construction of her temple shortly after her ascension to the throne. The design and grand layout of the temple were Senenmut's ideas. Senenmut was Hatshepsut's steward and is also believed by certain historians to have been her lover.

Inspired by the Mortuary Temple of Mentuhotep II, which was also located in Thebes, Hatshepsut's grand temple had a massive stone ramp that connected the first courtyard to the second and third levels. The two temples portrayed numerous similarities, but Hatshepsut's was even more elaborate and surpassed the grandeur of any other temple built before.

The Mortuary Temple of Hatshepsut.
Marc Ryckaert, CC BY-SA 4.0 <https://creativecommons.org/licenses/by-sa/4.0>, via Wikimedia Commons: https://commons.wikimedia.org/wiki/File:Hatshepsut_Temple_R01.jpg

Back in ancient Egypt, the courtyard featured a lush garden, which visitors had to walk past before being welcomed by a set of two lion statues flanking the entrance of the central ramp. Upon reaching the second level, visitors continued to feast their eyes on the impressive sights of the reflective pools and statues of sphinxes lining the pathway that led to yet another ramp to the third level. While the complex was adorned with dozens of murals and reliefs, one could also find a tomb belonging to Senenmut.

Hatshepsut believed she had a special connection with Hathor and did not forget to include a temple to honor the goddess. On the opposite side of the Temple of Hathor was the Temple of Anubis, which was a common feature of a mortuary temple.

The entrance to Hathor's temple.

Olaf Tausch, CC BY 3.0 <https://creativecommons.org/licenses/by/3.0>, via Wikimedia Commons:

https://commons.wikimedia.org/wiki/File:Totentempel_Hatschepsut_Hathorkapelle_12.jpg

Perhaps the most impressive part of the temple was the two colonnades standing on each side of the ramp leading to the third level. Located on the right side of the ramp was the Birth Colonnade, which featured a story of Hatshepsut's divine birth. Inscriptions on the walls of this colonnade claimed she was born after the god Amun had a sexual relationship with her mother. While the Birth Colonnade was built to tell her subjects of her divine birth origins, the Punt Colonnade on the left side of the ramp focused on her popular expedition to the land of Punt. According to the inscriptions, this expedition was not only welcomed by the people of Punt but also rewarded Egypt with exceptional wealth. Hatshepsut claimed that no king before her had ever brought the kingdom as much fortune as she did.

The Hypostyle Hall at Karnak, an Architectural Wonder Filled with Records of History

The Karnak Temple Complex was thought to have been developed during the Middle Kingdom. The complex was initially commissioned to be smaller; however, as Thebes gained more importance among the Egyptians, many kings began to leave their marks on the complex and instructed several great temples to honor the king of the gods, Amun-Ra—his temple was said to have been the earthly dwelling place for the god—and the gods Mut and Montu. As time went on, Karnak transformed into a wondrous complex complete with Egypt's most elaborate temples, a sacred lake, and other additional structures often used by priests, such as workshops and kitchens.

The central column of the Great Hypostyle Hall.

However, out of all the magnificent structures located within the vast complex, the Great Hypostyle Hall attracted the most visitors. The hall was initiated by Pharaoh Seti I. It was not difficult to spot the hall since it consisted of 134 massive stone columns, with twelve of them towering over twenty meters high. Judging from the traces of paint that survived on certain parts of the columns, it is plausible that the hall was once painted in vibrant colors.

Apart from being an architectural wonder, the hall also served as a historical record. In the northern part of the hall, one can find the reliefs that depict the battles fought by Seti I. The southern section of the hall was completed by Ramesses II, so his contributions to the kingdom were carved on the walls. This included the Egyptian-Hittite treaty that the king signed during his reign. Seti I and Ramesses II were not the only ones who had their successes recorded on the hall's walls, as later pharaohs would engrave their victories on the surfaces of the great hall as well.

Abu Simbel, Ramesses II's Proudest Construction Project

Rediscovered in 1813 after being covered by desert sands, Abu Simbel is one of the world's most impressive temples built by humans. The temple was constructed by Ramesses II to commemorate his victory at the Battle of Kadesh. Within the complex, one can find two different temples. The Great Temple, which took nearly twenty years to complete, was built to honor the pharaoh and the gods Amun, Ra, and Ptah. The second and smaller temple was constructed for the pharaoh's wife, Nefertari, and to honor the goddess Hathor. The most prominent feature of this temple is its entrance; the rock-cut gateway is flanked by four colossal seated statues of Ramesses II.

The entrance of the temple flanked by four statues of Ramesses II.
https://commons.wikimedia.org/wiki/File:Abu_Simbel_Temple_May_30_2007.jpg

The entrance to the smaller temple of Nefertari.
https://commons.wikimedia.org/wiki/File:Nefertari_Temple_Abu_Simbel_May_30_2007.jpg

Apart from the impressive architectural design, the temple also served as a great example of the ancient Egyptians' expertise in mathematics and astronomy. The site and position of the temple were chosen for a specific reason; the ancient Egyptians had perfectly positioned the temple to align with the sun so that the light would illuminate a particular chamber within the Great Temple on certain dates. Within the central chamber, one can find the statue of Ramesses II sitting alongside the gods Amun, Ra, and Ptah. Due to the temple's alignment with the sun, light only shines on the statues of the pharaoh, Amun, and Ra—Ptah's statue remains in the shadows since he is the god of darkness. This only happens twice a year: on February 21st, which was the date of Ramesses's coronation, and October 21st, which was the pharaoh's birthday. Throughout the rest of the year, the chamber is dark. This bi-annual event is known as the Sun Festival and continues to be celebrated today.

However, due to the rising water of the Nile, the temples recently had to be relocated. The painstaking relocation project took place in 1968 and was completed five years later. The temple and all of its structures were carefully dismantled and relocated about 180 meters away from its original site. Because of the change in its location, the dates of the Sun Festival have been moved to a day later. Today, visitors can witness the sun illuminating the chamber every February 22nd and October 22nd.

The relocation of the temple.
https://commons.wikimedia.org/wiki/File:Abusimbel.jpg

The sun illuminating the statues of Ramesses II, Amun, and Ra.
Diego Delso, CC BY-SA 4.0 <https://creativecommons.org/licenses/by-sa/4.0>, via Wikimedia Commons:
https://commons.wikimedia.org/wiki/File:Templo_de_Rams%C3%A9s_II,_Abu_Simb el,_Egipto,_2022-04-02,_DD_26-28_HDR.jpg

Chapter 16: Ptolemaic Art

After driving the Persians out of Egypt and peacefully proclaiming himself as the new king, Alexander the Great was thought to have immediately shifted his focus toward constructing his own city. The city of Alexandria turned into one of the most visited Mediterranean cities. It was filled with an array of architectural wonders, most of which were unfortunately destroyed and lost to us forever.

The most prominent structure built during the Ptolemaic era was the Lighthouse of Alexandria, which was built by the first ruler of the Ptolemaic dynasty, Ptolemy I Soter. Named one of the Seven Wonders of the Ancient World, the lighthouse once proudly stood on the small island of Pharos, which faced the city's harbor. The lighthouse towered over a hundred meters (over three hundred feet) above sea level and was considered one of the tallest structures ever built in the ancient world, second only to the Great Pyramids of Giza. Just like any other lighthouse, the Lighthouse of Alexandria was built with the intention of guiding sailors across the vast Mediterranean Sea. The Egyptian coast was dangerous; it had sent many ships to the bottom of the sea. Thus, the lighthouse was necessary to warn sailors of shallow waters or even submerged rocks.

Besides serving as a navigational aid, some sources suggest that the colossal lighthouse was also constructed to honor the ancient gods, particularly Zeus or Poseidon. Ancient descriptions tell us that the lighthouse once featured a statue at the top, which many historians believed to have been the statue of the mighty Zeus.

A drawing of the Lighthouse of Alexandria.
https://commons.wikimedia.org/wiki/File:Lighthouse_-_Thiersch.png

But none of the ancient writings that survived describe the exact design of the lighthouse. By piecing together all of the vague descriptions, it is safe to assume that the lighthouse had three different levels. The base was rectangular in shape, while the middle was octagonal, and the top was round. When night came, a fire would be lit at the top of the lighthouse. Ancient descriptions claimed that in order to make the fire visible to sailors from a distance, the Egyptians used a burnished bronze mirror to reflect the blazing flame.

The great lighthouse witnessed a few disasters and went through several reconstruction projects and repairs, but it stood on the small island for at least 1,600 years. In the 14th century CE, the lighthouse was no longer mentioned in the historical record. The Lighthouse of Alexandria was presumably destroyed sometime in the 1330s CE, although it has continued to leave its mark on us today.

The only remnants of the lighthouse found in the Mediterranean Sea.
*Roland Unger, CC BY-SA 3.0 <https://creativecommons.org/licenses/by-sa/3.0>, via
Wikimedia Commons: https://commons.wikimedia.org/wiki/File:AlexLighthouse01.jpg*

The Library of Alexandria

Being a student of Aristotle himself, it is not surprising to learn that Alexander the Great was very fond of knowledge. He wanted his city to become not only a center for trade and commerce but also for all knowledge of the world. Although he was never given a chance to see the completion of Alexandria, his dreams were eventually realized by his loyal general, Ptolemy I. Named the cultural and intellectual center of the Hellenistic world, the city welcomed countless visitors from all over the globe, particularly those from the Mediterranean. The greatest of Greek minds flocked to the city for one reason: to visit the Library of Alexandria.

An illustration of scholars studying in the Library of Alexandria.
https://commons.wikimedia.org/wiki/File:Ancientlibraryalex.jpg

146

The library was believed to have been nestled in the royal district of the city and integrated both Greek and native Egyptian cultures in its design. Grand Hellenistic columns might have been its most prominent features and were possibly accompanied by a great number of Egyptian statues. Unfortunately, no sources survived that give us an idea of the great library's exceptional design. We do know that inside the library were several lecture halls, classrooms, laboratories, meeting halls, gardens, and perhaps even a zoo. The library had rows of shelves, each filled with thousands of scrolls containing the world's most precious knowledge.

In the beginning, the shelves contained only Greek and Egyptian scrolls. The rulers of the Ptolemaic dynasty then began to actively invite many scholars to the city, which eventually resulted in the contribution of many more manuscripts. However, even this was not enough in the eyes of the Ptolemaic rulers, as they wished to own a copy of every book in the world. So, the rulers took advantage of Alexandria's port, which was bustling due to trade. A new policy was introduced that stipulated all ships that docked in Alexandria had to hand over their books for copying. This responsibility was given to the library's scribes, who would spend their day duplicating the texts. The original copy of the manuscript was stored in the library, while the duplicated version was returned to the ships. Book hunters were also hired to travel the world in search of new books and writings. Ultimately, hundreds of thousands of scrolls and manuscripts were housed in the Library of Alexandria.

Of course, like many other structures of the ancient world, the Library of Alexandria failed to withstand the ravages of time. The library witnessed destruction in 48 BCE when Julius Caesar laid siege to the city. However, some sources suggest that only parts of the library were destroyed. Regardless of how much of the library was destroyed, it was restored and continued to be the hub of knowledge for years to come. We do not know when the library finally crumbled to the ground, but many claimed that its popularity began to decline during the Roman Empire.

Serapeum of Alexandria

After welcoming the reign of yet another dynasty, the Egyptians saw the birth of a new cult that soon gained popularity: the cult of Serapis. Scholars agree Ptolemy I made an effort to further integrate the ancient religion of the Egyptians with that of the Greeks. Ptolemy was well aware that it was nearly impossible for the Egyptians to accept a new and foreign deity into their traditional religion. So, he combined the two most popular Egyptian deities at the time—the lord of the underworld, Osiris, and Apis, who had been gaining popularity among the Greeks since the Twenty-sixth Dynasty—with the Greek god of lightning, Zeus. With the creation of the new god, Ptolemy began another rigorous building program. He commissioned the construction of the Serapeum, which would later be continued by his son and successor, Ptolemy II.

A marble bust of Serapis.
https://commons.wikimedia.org/wiki/File:Serapis_Pio-Clementino_Inv689_n2.jpg

Considered by many to be one of the grandest and most beautiful temples in Alexandria, the Serapeum was situated in the southwest of the city, right on a hill overlooking the sea. The temple was also referred to as the "Daughter Library," possibly because of its large collection of books. The Serapeum of Alexandria was believed to have been so big that visitors were required to climb hundreds of steps just to reach its magnificent courtyard. Its porticoes never failed to impress visitors, as they were beautifully adorned with gold and gilded bronze. However, the inner temple became the main highlight of the structure, as this was the very place where one could find the colossal statue of Serapis himself.

Since the Greeks were never fond of animal-headed gods, Serapis was always depicted as a bearded man dressed in a robe. His statue in the Serapeum was accompanied by Cerberus, the three-headed dog that guarded the gates of the Greek underworld. The god's right hand rested on the beast while his other hand held an upraised scepter.

Despite being worshiped after the Roman conquest of Egypt, Serapis was gradually abandoned when Christianity emerged. The Serapeum of Alexandria was destroyed by the Romans sometime in 391 CE. All we can see of this once-grand temple are broken ruins.

The ruins of the Serapeum of Alexandria.
Daniel Mayer, CC BY-SA 4.0 <https://creativecommons.org/licenses/by-sa/4.0>, via Wikimedia Commons: https://commons.wikimedia.org/wiki/File:Alexandria_-_Pompey%27s_Pillar_-_view_of_ruins.JPG

Temple of Edfu

The Ptolemaic dynasty contributed to the construction of numerous extravagant temples, including the Temple of Kom Ombo, the Dendera Temple Complex, and the Temple of Esna. However, the best-preserved temple from this dynasty was located on the western bank of the Nile. Known as the Temple of Edfu, this particular temple had a huge difference compared to the ones often found in the Ptolemaic ruler's capital city: it had only little to zero Hellenistic influences. This massive temple surprisingly remained intact.

The Temple of Edfu had a few significances that made it important to the Egyptians. In terms of religious significance, the temple was constructed in honor of Horus and his beloved wife, Hathor, who was the ancient Egyptian goddess of fertility and love. After the temple's completion, it was believed that it immediately became the center of various ceremonies and celebrations involving the two divine entities.

The main entrance of the Temple of Edfu.
Patrick.reb, CC BY-SA 3.0 <https://creativecommons.org/licenses/by-sa/3.0>, via Wikimedia Commons: https://commons.wikimedia.org/wiki/File:Temple_Edfou_Egypte.jpg

The temple is also known for its series of hieroglyphs. One can take a step into the temple and feel as if they were transported into a book filled with thousands of writings telling different stories of the beliefs and myths from the Hellenistic period. Carvings of Egyptian writings adorned every corner of the temple, from the flat walls to the dozens of columns, chambers, and sculptures. These hieroglyphs are known as the Edfu Texts, and most of them tell the story of the creation of the world. From these texts, we know the ancient Egyptians believed the world started as an island created by the gods who descended from the skies. They also believed the gods built the first temple in the world, which soon became a blueprint for every temple that ever existed, especially the ones in the Nile Valley. Apart from the creation myth, the temple also featured texts describing the legendary feud between Horus and Set.

The Temple of Edfu fell into disuse when pagan and non-Christian worship was banned by the Roman Empire. The temple witnessed a series of destructions, which were typically perpetrated by the Christians who dominated the valley. We can see some of it today, such as the blackened ceiling of the temple's Hypostyle Hall. Centuries later, the temple was completely abandoned until it was eventually buried beneath the sands. However, this played a big role in the temple's near-perfect preservation.

Sculptures and Statues

Historians believe the artistic styles during the Ptolemaic era varied, especially during the reign of the dynasty's first few pharaohs. Perhaps due to political reasons, the sculptures of the early Ptolemaic pharaohs almost resembled those from the Thirtieth Dynasty; sometimes, the pieces from the two periods had so many similarities that Egyptologists faced difficulties distinguishing between them.

However, as time went by, the Ptolemaic statues began to abandon the old style of the previous dynasties and incorporate a hint of Greek influence. Despite still being depicted in an Egyptian pose (either seated or standing with their left foot forward), statues of the elite began to appear with curly hair, which was often seen in Greek-style art, and a full garment instead of a bare torso. Beards were also a common feature; the best example can be found on the statues of Serapis, the god of healing and fertility.

A statue of Serapis currently in the Vatican Museum.
Immanuelle, CC BY-SA 4.0 <https://creativecommons.org/licenses/by-sa/4.0>, via Wikimedia Commons: https://commons.wikimedia.org/wiki/File:The_Nile_Vatican_Statue.jpg

The statues of the Ptolemaic era were also finely carved and appeared to be more realistic compared to the typical Egyptian statues, which preferred a stiff and idealistic look. The Egyptians did not strive to achieve likeness when it came to statues and sculptures. But the Ptolemies were heavily influenced by the Greeks, so their sculptures emphasized the face more. Each feature was carved to be as realistic as possible, and the subjects were often portrayed with a smile that gave the statues a more reserved expression.

A bust of Ptolemy wearing a smile.
Stella, CC BY-SA 4.0 <https://creativecommons.org/licenses/by-sa/4.0>, via Wikimedia Commons: https://commons.wikimedia.org/wiki/File:British_Museum_Egypt_-_Tolomeo_I.png

However, the most prominent change in Ptolemaic art was the reappearance of female statues, a form of art that had been abandoned since the Twenty-sixth Dynasty. The reason behind this was uncertain, but historians believe it was probably due to the rising importance of women during the Ptolemaic dynasty. Several female royals held important positions in the kingdom, with many becoming co-regents to the ruling pharaohs and some rising to the throne themselves. Although statues of women were rarely portrayed with the same realism as male statues, they still appeared with a hint of Greek influence. Arsinoe II (the wife of Ptolemy II) was often portrayed as Aphrodite, the Greek goddess of love. To infuse some Egyptian influence, her statue wore the traditional crown of Lower Egypt, the feathers of an ostrich (the symbol of the goddess Ma'at), or other traditional Egyptian headdresses and garments indicating royalty or a divine being.

Head of a statue of Arsinoe II.
Metropolitan Museum of Art, CC0, via Wikimedia Commons:
https://commons.wikimedia.org/wiki/File:Head_Attributed_to_Arsinoe_II_MET_DT10849.jpg

The Ptolemaic period also saw the birth of a statue that depicted a younger version of the god Horus, though some sources claim the statue made its appearance during the Late

Period (the last era of native Egyptian rulers). Known as Harpocrates (a Hellenization of the Egyptian name Har-pa-khered, which simply means "Horus the Child"), the god was often represented as a young, nude boy with a sidelock of hair. He typically held one of his fingers up to his mouth—a realization of the Egyptian hieroglyph for the word "child," which was later mistaken by the Romans to be a symbol of silence and secrecy. To signify his divinity, the statue also wore a crown featuring a uraeus, a rearing Egyptian cobra.

A silver statuette of Harpocrates.
Patrick Clenet, CC BY-SA 3.0 <http://creativecommons.org/licenses/by-sa/3.0/>, via Wikimedia Commons: https://commons.wikimedia.org/wiki/File:Harpocrates_gulb_082006.JPG

Conclusion

With the shocking death of Cleopatra and her lover, Mark Antony, in 30 BCE, Egypt was left without a ruler. Its borders were soon breached by the future Roman emperor Augustus, who rode with his troops and claimed the vast kingdom. Before taking her own life, the last Ptolemaic queen was believed to have sent Caesarion, her only son with Julius Caesar, away from the dangers of the war, hoping he could survive and one day claim the Egyptian throne.

However, Cleopatra's wish was cut short, as Augustus ordered Caesarion's assassination to remove any future threat. Cleopatra's children with Mark Antony were spared by Augustus and sent to Rome, where they were left in the care of Augustus's sister, Octavia. Although the emperor tried to erase the traces of the two figures, he did grant them a proper burial. Cleopatra wished to be buried right next to Antony. However, the location of their tombs remains a mystery.

Egypt was immediately annexed into the Roman Republic after the defeat of Cleopatra. Although the kingdom's immense wealth was absorbed and eventually became the emperor's possession, Augustus was wise enough not to disturb the ancient Egyptians' old way of life, including their religious beliefs and traditional customs. The most prosperous periods of Egypt might have been a thing of the past, but Egypt no doubt managed to maintain its presence and spread its influence to every corner of the world, something it continues to do today.

Architecture and construction skills aside, the ancient Egyptians were renowned for their mastery of medical science; even the Persians agreed with this statement, as they once requested an Egyptian physician to move to their empire and share his knowledge. Many Egyptian medical texts have been discovered, each describing various medical information and surgery procedures in great detail. They were responsible for the invention of toothpaste. Back in ancient Egypt, dental issues were common. To curb the problem, the Egyptians experimented and developed several recipes for a substance to clean their teeth. One of the texts that survived the time tells us the ancient Egyptians made toothpaste using rock salt, mint, dried iris petals, and pepper. Surely, their methods and techniques had flaws, but the Egyptians were the precursors to modern medicine. Once a center of knowledge and education, it is not surprising to discover that the ancient Egyptians also laid the foundations for various other fields, such as language, astronomy, and mathematics.

Of course, ancient Egypt's most prominent influence on the world is its art and architecture. Several of the kingdom's most impressive buildings and colossal statues still stand today, and their ability to survive thousands of years amazes almost everyone. The pyramids inspired many contemporary and modern architectural works; the Louvre in Paris features a glass and stainless-steel pyramid that is heavily inspired by the Great Pyramid of Giza, while Harrods' Egyptian Hall in England is filled with the recreations of the pyramids, the Sphinx, and Egyptian columns, complete with the complex carvings of hieroglyphs and texts.

The age of ancient Egypt might have ended thousands of years ago, but everyone agrees that its presence is still in the air. Due to the remaining carvings and written documents of the events, stories, and legends that took place within the kingdom, it is certain that ancient Egypt will never be forgotten.

Part 2: Ancient Rome

An Enthralling Overview of Roman History, Starting From the Romulus and Remus Myth through the Republic to the Fall of the Roman Empire

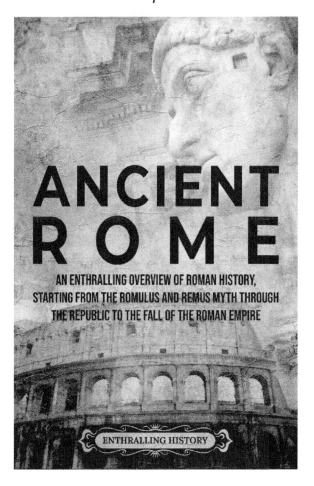

Introduction

He was supposed to kill the babies. That had been the king's order - *throw the babies in.* Instead, the guard left them in the basket and nudged it into the swollen river.

"Let the gods decide," he breathed, watching the churning Tiber carry the basket out of sight.

Miraculously, the twins survived their voyage down the raging river, and one established the great city of Rome, with an astonishing history that now spans 28 centuries. Called the *Eternal City* by the poet Tibullus, Rome grew into a massive empire stretching from Britain to the Middle East and south to Africa. Rome's culture and institutions profoundly influenced the territories it ruled, leaving an enduring legacy of religion, language, governmental structure, law, philosophy, architecture, and art that continues to impact civilizations around the world.

In this history of Rome, we will unwrap the intriguing myths of the twins and their ancestors and then explore Rome's earliest recorded accounts. Was the founder a feral wolf-child? Who was the mastermind of Rome's unique senatorial system, and how did it function? What propelled the city's rise to supremacy over parts of three continents? Were some emperors genuinely psychotic? Did Nero murder two of his wives and marry a boy? What was the *Pax Romana,* and why was it so important? Which factors influenced the Roman Empire's ultimate fall?

The second temple of Hera, also called the Poseidon temple, in Paestum, Campania, Italy, provides an example of Doric columns.

Norbert Nagel, CC BY-SA 3.0 <https://creativecommons.org/licenses/by-sa/3.0>, via Wikimedia Commons https://commons.wikimedia.org/wiki/File:Hera_temple_II_-Paestum_-_Poseidonia_-_July_13th_2013_-_08.jpg

This extensive and comprehensive examination of Ancient Rome will reveal how all the drama, politics, and empire-building unfolded. It will describe the distinguishing pillars of this awe-inspiring empire, what made it extraordinary, and how the Roman culture continues to influence today's society. Readers will acquire an in-depth understanding of how Rome influenced judiciary systems and left its mark on the culture and languages of Europe. We will explore how the Latin language, the empire's vast and excellent road system, and the *Pax Romana* enhanced the spread of Christianity – even while the emperors were feeding Christians to the lions.

With all the volumes written about Ancient Rome, why write another one? This enthralling overview is remarkably comprehensive, covering the essential information on this compelling civilization. This fascinating and easy-to-understand account will keep the reader turning pages; rather than dry facts, this history provides the captivating stories of the people who built Rome and made it what it was. Some of these individuals were exemplary and ingenious, while others were chaotically destructive. Still, they all played a part in the intrigue and internecine conflict that defined Rome.

Understanding history has multiple benefits. We require an accurate understanding of the past to wisely decide for our present and future. Valuable lessons can be gleaned from the rise and fall of extraordinary civilizations. How have they contributed to who we are today? Some stories inspire and motivate us, and others serve as cautionary tales.

An excellent grasp of Rome's history will help readers understand how today's political systems originated and how the Greco-Roman polytheism developed and influenced Rome until a carpenter and several fishermen transformed the empire and the world. Readers will discover how safe, efficient transportation influences trade, wealth, information, religion, and cultural blending. Through investigating the leaders and emperors of Rome, we can appreciate the heights that good leaders can take a civilization and the depths into which poor leaders can plunge them.

Aeneas fleeing Troy, carrying his father on his back, accompanied by his wife and son.
Pottery circa 510-500 BC
https://commons.wikimedia.org/wiki/File:Aineias_Ankhises_Louvre_F118.jpg

Now, let's take sneak peeks into what lies ahead! This overview of Ancient Rome is divided into four sections. Part one explores the mythological foundations of Rome, picking up with Aeneas as he fled the burning Troy, carrying his father on his back. We will follow the Trojan survivors' long trek over land and sea to Italy. How did a Vestal Virgin mysteriously become pregnant, and why were her baby sons, heirs to the throne, fed to the river? We will discover how Rome was established initially as a monarchy, how abuse of power by tyrannical kings led to a democratic republic, and how they finally ended up with an autocracy led by emperors.

When unwrapping these ancient Roman myths, we should remember that myth isn't fantasy. In pre-literate societies or when written accounts are lost through a catastrophe, the oral transmission of ancient incidents may acquire mythological qualities over time. Historical accounts often transform into myths as the stories are retold and embellished. Real people, especially great war heroes and exemplary leaders, become mythologized over the centuries, transitioning into gods or demi-gods.

Dionysius of Halicarnassus wrote "Roman Antiquities," a collection of 20 books that narrated Rome's history from Aeneas to the First Punic War.
https://commons.wikimedia.org/wiki/File:Dionigi_di_Alicarnasso.jpg

As we examine the origin myths of Rome – the stories of Aeneas, Remus, and Romulus – our primary ancient sources are *The Aeneid* by Virgil (first century BC), *Roman Antiquities* by Dionysius of Halicarnassus (first century BC), *Moralia: Fortuna Romanorum* by Plutarch (first century AD), and *Roman History* by Cassius Dio (third century AD). Virgil, Dionysius, Plutarch, and Dio all based their works on oral tradition and older manuscripts available in their day.

Our three oldest sources include the *Hymn to Aphrodite* (seventh century BC), an account of Aeneas's conception, Homer's *Iliad* (eighth century BC), which tells of Aeneas's exploits in the Trojan War, and several pieces of ancient artwork and pottery depicting Aeneas carrying his father out of Troy, dating to the sixth century BC.

Part Two, the Roman Republic, focuses on the new Republic's establishment, immense expansion, and internal unrest. We will investigate how Rome conquered nearby city-states and then was invaded and sacked by the Celts. How did Rome rise from the ashes to reassert its dominant power in the region, then face off against war elephants in the Pyrrhic War? We will follow the Roman conquerors through the incredible Punic Wars against ancient Carthage's Phoenicians when Rome gained territory on the Mediterranean coast, the Adriatic Sea, and northern Africa. We will analyze how Rome's successful wars in Greece enabled the empire's ascendency over the Macedonian kingdom and Corinth's Achaean League. Finally, we will delve into the brutal civil wars and social unrest in Rome, the great slave revolt under Spartacus, the First Triumvirate, and Caesar's dictatorship and assassination.

Part Three, the Principate, begins with Octavianus amassing great power and transforming the Republic into a far-reaching empire, leading to his title of *Augustus*. During his reign, a baby was born in the Roman province of Judaea who would transfigure Rome and the world. Augustus was followed by Rome's more notorious emperors, such as the unhinged Caligula, who made his horse a priest, and Caligula's nephew Nero, who lit his garden with Christians turned into human torches. What did Rome do about the Great Jewish Revolt? Which canny strategies led to the conquest of Britain, and how did the five good emperors lift

Rome to its peak of power and prosperity? What factors contributed to Rome's decline in the Severan Dynasty.

Part Four surveys ancient Rome's final years – how the Roman Empire split and eventually collapsed. How did wars, internal chaos, barbarian invasions, and peasant rebellions weaken Rome until it was divided into four emperors? We will see how Constantine the Great rose to dominance, becoming sole emperor, breaking the persecution of Christians, and receiving baptism on his deathbed. What contributed to Christianity's expansion throughout the empire? We will discuss why the empire split into eastern and western factions and how the repeated invasions of Visigoths, Vandals, Huns, and Saxons brought Rome to its knees, ending with Romulus' abdication in AD 476.

Now, let's travel back through the distant shadows of time to when a goddess desired a humble shepherd and gave birth to Aeneas, the great champion of Troy whose descendants founded the vast and breathtaking Roman Empire.

SECTION ONE: ROMAN FOUNDATIONS AND MONARCHY (753 to 509 BC)

Chapter 1: The First Roman Myths

Aphrodite, the goddess of love and lover of smiles, was mischievously causing the gods to fall in love with mortal women, so Zeus retaliated by filling her with desire for the handsome Anchises, who was herding his cattle on Mount Ida's peak. Burning with lust, Aphrodite wrapped herself in golden finery and came to Anchises as he was playing his lyre.

Overwhelmed by her beauty, Anchises vowed that neither man nor god could keep him from taking her at once. Pretending to be a virgin and a mortal, Aphrodite permitted him to make love to her. From this liaison, Aphrodite conceived, giving birth to Aeneas. When the boy was five, Aphrodite brought him to his father Anchises to raise him in Troy.

The *Iliad* relates how Aeneas fought bravely in the Trojan War as the principal lieutenant to his cousin Hector, the oldest son of King Priam. His goddess mother intently watched over the battle, occasionally intervening to save him from death. Even the gods supporting the Greeks gave him aid, recognizing he would be a king of the Trojans. A king of Trojans but not a king of Troy, as Troy would soon go up in flames.

"Aeneas! Wake up! Wake up now!"

Aeneas awakened to the gruesome ghost of his cousin Prince Hector, covered with blood after his death at the hands of

Achilles. "Get up now, Aeneas! The Greeks are storming the city. Escape now – with your family! There's nothing you can do. King Priam and Troy are lost. But you can make a new Troy. You need to leave now! Build a city elsewhere!"

Aeneas initially reached for his weapons and dashed out to defend Troy. He fought with zeal, but witnessing King Priam's death, he realized it was a losing battle. Finally, he hurried home to save his family. Carrying his father Anchises on his back, holding his son Ascanius' hand, and his wife Creusa following behind, Aeneas and his family narrowly escaped the Greek warriors overrunning the streets of Troy. After running out of the city gates, Aeneas looked back and was horrified to see his wife wasn't there. She had fallen behind! He rushed back into the city and met Creusa's ghost – she had been killed by the Greek warriors.

The ghost of Creusa guided Aeneas. Giuseppe Maria Mitelli, from Carracci's frescoed frieze in Palazzo Fava, Bologna.
https://commons.wikimedia.org/wiki/File:Enea_e_1%27ombra_di_Creusa.jpg

"Hurry! Escape to Italy!" Creusa urged him. "You have a long journey ahead, but in Italy, you will be a king and married to royalty."

Weeping, Aeneas stumbled out of the burning city, narrowly eluding the Greeks, to rejoin his father and son and the other survivors who had escaped from the city in time. As dawn arrived, Aeneas led the refugees to the summit of Mount Ida. They looked down to see black smoke rising from their beloved city Troy. Where would they go from here?

The Trojans built a fleet of 20 ships and set sail, crossing the Aegean Sea and landing in Thrace, where they built a settlement named Aeneadae. One day, Aeneas found the body of Prince Polydorus, son of King Priam of Troy. Polydorus's ghost warned Aeneas, "Leave this place! The king of Thrace murdered me! He's shifted his alliances to the Greeks. You're not safe here."

After giving Polydorus proper funeral rites, the Trojans set sail again, reaching the island of Delos, where they discovered a temple to Apollo. Needing direction, Aeneas prayed to Apollo, asking where they should go. Apollo cryptically told him, "Seek the land of your forefathers – of your ancient mother."

Aeneas interpreted this to mean the isle of Crete, the birthplace of Teucer, Troy's first king. Sailing to Crete, they built a city named Pergamum, but then a plague hit the exiles, decimating the Trojans and even killing their crops. Aeneas was confused; he was so sure Crete would be their new home. That night, the *Penates* – the household gods they had brought from Troy – came to Aeneas in a dream, saying, "Crete is the wrong place! This isn't where Apollo meant you to go."

Aeneas discussed his vision with his father Anchises, who reminded him of his wife Creusa's forgotten prophecy: "Go to Italy!"

A Harpy was a predatory monster with a woman's head and body with bird wings and claws.
https://commons.wikimedia.org/wiki/File:Harpi.PNG

Aeneas and the Trojans set sail from Crete. A raging storm engulfed them for three cataclysmic days until they found harbor in the Strophades island group. Seeing a herd of cattle, the hungry Trojans slaughtered them to eat, when suddenly Harpies attacked them. The Harpy Celaeno ordered them, "Leave my island! Go look for Italy. When you reach your destination, you will be so famished you will eat your tables!"

Eat their tables? At this odd but alarming omen, the Trojans quickly fled the island and sailed on. Arriving in Buthrotum (in present-day Albania), they joyfully reunited with another son of King Priam, Prince Helenus, who was a prophet. He was ruling with his sister-in-law Andromache, who was still grieving her husband, Prince Hector.

Helenus advised Aeneas of their upcoming challenges: "Be careful to avoid the sea monster Scylla and the Charybdis whirlpool! You should consult the Sibyl [priestess] of Cumae." Helenus then prophesied, "When you find a white sow with 30 piglets, that's the place! Establish your city there. In that place, your descendants will prosper and go on to rule the entire known world."

After exchanging gifts and bidding their old friends farewell, Aeneas and his fellow Trojans sailed to Sicily, where Mount Etna was spewing fire and smoke. A man in tattered clothing ran up to them; he was Achaemenidës, and he came from Odysseus's ship, who had been their enemy in the Trojan War. Achaemenidës had accidentally been left behind when his crewmates were fleeing the one-eyed Cyclops. "Please! I beg you. Kill me now, or take me with you! My life hiding out from these Cyclopes is unbearable!"

Achaemenidës begs for either death or protection from the Cyclopes. Engraving by Giuseppe Zocchi.

https://commons.wikimedia.org/wiki/File:Achaemenides_and_Polyphemus.jpg

Just then, the Cyclopes appeared, and the Trojans rushed to their ships, bringing Achaemenidës with them. Sailing around the coast of Sicily, they came to Drepanum, where Anchises died. After mourning his father, Aeneas sailed toward the mainland of Italy. But once again, they were thrown off course by a fierce storm that drove them away from Italy and south to northern Africa. Finally, they arrived on a peaceful beach. Aeneas scouted the area, hopeful that the 12 ships lost in the storm had found their way to these shores, but he found no trace of them.

The next day, while exploring more of the coast, Aeneas encountered men busily building a new city, reminding him of a hive of bees. Aeneas learned they had recently arrived from Tyre (in Lebanon). They were fleeing their queen's brother, Pygmalion, who had usurped her throne and killed her husband, Sychaeus. Their queen's name was Dido, and they were building the city of Carthage.

Aeneas described the Fall of Troy and their wanderings to Queen Dido. By Jacopo Amigoni.
https://commons.wikimedia.org/wiki/File:Jacopo_Amigoni_(c.1682-1752)_-_Aeneas_and_Achates_Wafted_in_a_Cloud_before_Dido,_Queen_of_Carthage,_with_Cupid_at_Her_Feet_-_772276_-_National_Trust.jpg

Wandering through the city, Aeneas entered a newly built temple to Juno and wept when he saw a mural depicting the Trojan War, showing the death of his friend Hector. At that moment, Queen Dido walked in, inviting Aeneas and his companions to join her for a feast that night. Aeneas told her how moved he was by the mural, and the queen recalled the shared history of Troy and Tyre. She told Aeneas he and his refugees were welcome to settle with her people in the new city of Carthage.

Leaving the temple, Aeneas was ecstatic to see his lost ships sailing into the harbor. They had made it! Ilioneus, one of his pilots, reminded Aeneas of their quest to reach Italy, saying he intended to head that way soon. At the feast that night, Aeneas told Dido all about their travels from Troy. Enchanted with Aeneas, the queen repeated her invitation to settle in Carthage. The attractive Dido mesmerized Aeneas, who was rapidly forgetting his mission to build a kingdom in Italy.

One day, they were hunting together when a storm broke, forcing them to quickly take shelter in a nearby cave, where they made love. Dido felt this meant they were married, and Aeneas was happy to stay in Africa with the beautiful queen. The Trojans worked alongside the people of Tyre to build Carthage. Finally, the god Jupiter sent Mercury to remind Aeneas of his foreordained destiny to become a ruler in Italy.

Aeneas couldn't bear the thought of leaving Dido, but he didn't dare disobey the gods. When Dido saw Aeneas's people preparing their ships for departure, she was shattered, vowing suicide if Aeneas left. Aeneas's ships slipped out before dawn, and Queen Dido awakened to discover him gone. She ordered a funeral pyre built, lay down on it, and stabbed herself after prophesying unending strife between Aeneas's people and Carthage.

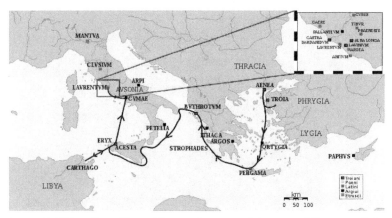

Aeneas fled Troy, first sailing to Thrace, then around the coast of Greece to Sicily, then to Carthage in Africa, back to Sicily, and finally Italy.

As the Trojan fleet sailed toward Italy, Aeneas's navigator, Palinurus, pointed to black clouds in the distance. Another storm! They changed course toward Sicily to avoid the storm on the open seas. In honor of the anniversary of his father's death, Aeneas called for a celebration of Anchises's life. But while the men were enjoying themselves with games, the women were plotting trouble.

What were the ladies up to? They were fed up with endless wandering, storms at sea, Harpies, Cyclopes, and volcanoes. They were ready to settle down for good, right where they were. They felt the best way to make that happen was to get rid of the ships, so they set them on fire. Aeneas rushed toward the harbor, praying to Jupiter, and a sudden downpour quenched the fire. Aeneas announced that whoever wanted to settle in Sicily could stay behind. That night, his father's ghost came to him, telling Aeneas to visit him in the underworld before going to Latium.

Finally! After sailing across the Tyrrhenian Sea, the Trojans arrived in Cumae, on Italy's western coast. Aeneas sought the Sibyl (priestess) in the caves, who prophesied, "Aeneas! You and your fellow Trojans will face great adversities in Latium. You will experience another war like the Trojan War."

Aeneas and the Sibyl of Cumae enter the underworld. Drawing by Giovanni Francesco Romanelli.

Giovanni Francesco Romanelli, CC0, via Wikimedia Commons
https://commons.wikimedia.org/wiki/File:Aeneas_and_the_Cumaean_Sibyl_Entering_t
he_Infernal_Regions_MET_DP811379.jpg

Aeneas pressured the Sibyl to guide him to the underworld. He saw Queen Dido in the land of fallen lovers, but she glared at him coldly. In the land of fallen warriors, he saw both Greek and Trojan warriors from the Trojan War. In the green fields of Elysium, Aeneas was reunited with his father, Anchises. His father showed him a line of souls waiting to return to earth.

"Look, Aeneas! These men will be your descendants! They will be reincarnated as the rulers of your city. There! That's Silvius – he will be your son. And this is Romulus; he will be the founder of Rome. That's Pompey the Great – he will transform your kingdom into an empire. Over there is Augustus Caesar and Julius Caesar – they will be great emperors."

Eventually, the Sibyl led Aeneas back to the land of the living, and the Trojans continued sailing north along Italy's shoreline. Reaching the river Tiber, they sailed upstream. These were King Latinus's lands; he had no sons, but he had one beautiful daughter with many suitors. While performing sacrifices, Latinus received a prophecy: he should marry his daughter, Lavinia, to a foreigner – this man would make the Latin name famous.

Meanwhile, Aeneas's fleet laid anchor off Laurentum, where they set up their tents on the beach and gathered fruit to eat. Before sitting down, they placed wild parsley and dry wheat cakes on the sand to keep the fruit clean. They were ravenous, so after eating the fruit, they nibbled on the parsley and wheat cakes until somebody exclaimed, "Look, everyone! We even ate our table!"

The prophecy of the Harpy Celaeno had been fulfilled! And it wasn't as horrible as they expected. They laughed and shouted with joy – they had reached their destination! Aeneas announced a sacrifice to the gods. Dancing and singing, they brought their idols out of the ship and prepared to sacrifice a pig. The large white sow suddenly broke free, running into the forest. Remembering the prophecy of Helenus, Aeneas followed the pig from a distance until she threw herself down in exhaustion on a hilltop.

When Aeneas (with his son Ascanius) found the white sow with 30 piglets, he knew he had arrived at his destination

Looking around him, Aeneas felt the area was an unlikely spot to build a great city. It was a little too far from the sea and close to an immense swamp. But the next morning, the sow gave birth to 30 piglets, fulfilling Helenus's prophecy. This was the place! This was where the Trojans would build their city.

They set out to explore and came to the city of Latium. Aeneas sent envoys into the city with gifts and assurances to King Latinus that the Trojans came in peace. They told the king about the Trojan War, vowing that if he permitted them to live in his kingdom, they would work for him and help protect the kingdom. Remembering the prophecy about his daughter Lavinia marrying a foreigner, King Latinus welcomed Aeneas and made a treaty: the Trojans could have land for a city, and in return, they would help the Latins fight any enemies.

With the treaty settled, the Trojans built a city on the land where the sow had given birth to 30 piglets. The Latins helped build the town, which Aeneas named Lavinium after Lavinia, who King Latinus had promised to him in marriage. When Queen Amata heard Latinus was planning to marry her daughter to a stranger, she implored her husband not to force this marriage, but Latinus was adamant. Amata flew into a rage. She shared her indignation with the other women, inciting an uproar, then hustled Lavinia off to hide her in the mountains.

Queen Amata was not the only one distraught over Latinus's plans. King Turnus of the Rutuli kingdom had been planning to marry Lavinia. Upon hearing Latinus had promised her to another man, he declared war on the Trojans. Meanwhile, Aeneas's son Ascanius was hunting in the woods and wounded a stag. He didn't realize the deer was a pet of a Latin herdsman. The stag staggered home before dying, enraging the Latins.

The Latin herdsmen attacked Ascanius, and the Trojans rushed to his aid, killing many Latins. The grieving shepherds carried their dead to the palace and laid them at King Latinus's feet, pleading with him to evict the Trojans from their land. Latinus did not want to engage in battle with the Trojans - they'd just made a treaty! But everyone cried out for war, and the loudest proponents were Queen Amata and the women. Unable to calm his people - and sensing the destiny of the gods - the king retreated to his rooms.

Meanwhile, Turnus had amassed a huge army that was marching toward the Trojans, who were in a tight spot. They weren't strong enough to resist the Rutuli on their own, and even though they had made a treaty with the Latins, these people were declaring war against them. Aeneas quickly set about making allies with Turnus's enemies. King Evander (a Greek from Arcadia who had recently settled in Italy) offered aid against their common enemy and sent armies led by his son, Prince Pallas.

King Evander also rallied the friendly neighboring kingdoms, and they marched toward Latium.

An epic war ensued between the Trojans and their allies against King Turnus and the Latins. Aeneas and Prince Pallas become close friends in the struggle. Pallas was a great warrior and killed every man he encountered until Turnus impaled Pallas with his spear, ripping off his belt as a trophy. Hearing of the death of his friend Pallas, Aeneas flew into a rage, vowing vengeance. He killed many of their enemies, but Turnus jumped into the river Tiber and escaped.

The Latins suffered a great loss of their people in the war. They built pyres to burn their dead, wailing and lamenting, cursing Turnus and the war. King Latinus reminded his people how misguided it was to fight the Trojans; they should have honored the treaty they had made.

The next day, King Latinus, King Turnus, Aeneas, and his son Ascanius rode out to the battleground. Aeneas swore an oath: if Turnus were victorious, the Trojans would leave Italy. If Aeneas were victorious, the Trojans would live together peacefully with the Latins. King Latinus renewed his treaty with Aeneas. Turnus suggested they end the war with a duel between him and Aeneas to spare the lives of the other warriors.

King Turnus pleads for his life from Aeneus. By Luca Giordano, 17ᵗʰ century, Palazzo Corsini, Florence.
https://commons.wikimedia.org/wiki/File:Aeneas_and_Turnus.jpg

The two men faced off alone. Turnus grabbed an enormous rock, hurling it at Aeneas, but missed. Aeneas threw his spear, which pierced through Turnus's shield and into his thigh. Turnus fell to the ground, and as Aeneas stood over him, Turnus begged for mercy, telling Aeneas he could have Lavinia. Aeneas paused for a moment, considering, then saw the belt of his friend Pallas on Turnus's waist. Enraged, Aeneas thrust his sword into Turnus's heart, ending the war.

Peace at last! The Trojans and Latins joined as one. Lavinia and Aeneas married, and the Trojans took the language and customs of the Latins. They freely intermarried until the people of Troy no longer called themselves Trojans but Latins.

Two years later, King Latinus died, and Aeneas became king of the Latins. After ruling for three years, Aeneas disappeared during a battle against the Rutuli. No one knew what happened to him, but everyone assumed he must have died. He left behind his wife, Lavinia, pregnant with their first child.

Aeneas was succeeded by his oldest son, Ascanius. Thirty years after arriving in Italy, King Ascanius built a new city, which he called *Alba Longa* (long white town), between a towering mountain and a deep lake offering protection on both sides. In the plains below the city lay fertile land for growing the best wine and fruit in all of Italy.

Chapter 2: Alba Longa, Rome's Ancestral City

Lavinia was in a dilemma. Her husband, King Aeneas, had disappeared while fighting King Mezentius of the Etruscans. Some said he was dead. But where was his body? Others said he had become a god; indeed, he was half-god already. It was all a mystery, but now she was due to give birth any day, with no husband to be found. The city needed a ruler, and her stepson Ascanius, her husband's son from his first wife, had assumed the throne.

What would happen to her now? More importantly, what would happen to her unborn child? Would her stepson give her protection? Or would he fear her power and lineage? How did he feel about this child about to be born? Would he perceive the child as a contender for the throne against his sons? The more she considered the situation, the more alarmed she felt.

She confided her fears to Tyrrhenus, one of her father's most trusted friends and the lead herdsman for the royal swine. The herdsmen had no great love for the Trojans, and especially not for Ascanius – they still carried a grudge that he'd killed their pet stag. As she explained her fears, Tyrrhenus nodded. "My lady, we have no idea what these Trojans will do. The wisest course of action is to go into hiding. I will help you and protect you until it is safe for you and your child."

The next day, Tyrrhenus spirited Lavinia out of the city, dressed in commoner's clothing. No one gave her a second look. He led her into the forest and up into the mountains, where he built a house for her; only a trusted few knew about it. Lavinia gave birth to a boy, and Tyrrhenus named him Silvius – for the forest in which he was born. Tyrrhenus helped rear the boy, and when Silvius was old enough, he joined the king's herdsmen. Few knew his identity. For 38 years, Silvius lived in the forest with his mother.

Meanwhile, his older half-brother Ascanius was facing his own crisis as the new king of Lavinium. King Mezentius of the Etruscans, the Latins' perennial enemy, was pressing his advantage against the inexperienced king and marching toward Lavinium! Within days, Mezentius had surrounded the city with his forces. The people of Lavinium were quickly running out of food and fresh water. In desperate straits, Ascanius had no choice but to surrender to Mezentius, agreeing to pay a yearly tribute.

Many years later, Ascanius broke free from the Etruscan overlords. Ascanius fell upon King Mezentius and his army, taking them unaware. He killed Lausus, son of Mezentius, and vanquished the Etruscan army. Now the tables were turned, and Mezentius had to pay tribute to Ascanius. But that day would be a long time coming.

For now, Ascanius stood on the wall of Lavinium, built by his father on a hill five years earlier. He gazed at the dense laurel forest to the north – the Silva Laurentina – with no inkling his younger brother was hidden away there. Ascanius turned to the south, where the wetlands of the Pontine Marshes lay. He slapped a mosquito and frowned. The *miasmas* (vapors) arising from the stagnant waters caused intermittent fevers among his people, killing one in five. He cursed the *malus aria* (bad air) of the place. He cursed the great white sow who had given birth on this hill, impelling his father to build a city in an unhealthy, unfertile place.

Ex-voto statues in Lavinium.

What would Ascanius have thought if he knew Lavinium would endure with no significant break in habitation right through the next three thousand years? Today, the town is known as *Pratica di Mare* and still has a Roman gate and sits surrounded by the ruins of the ancient city. Over the millennia, attempts were made to drain and fill in the malarial wetland; those endeavors were completed by the engineers of Benito Mussolini in 1939, making the Pontine Marshes the Pontine Fields.

During the 38 years that Ascanius reigned, Lavinium's population continued to grow quickly, but the city lacked arable land to feed a large population. The Latins scorned the mosquito-infested marshlands, so Ascanius established a new capital in a better location. He built the new city on the slope of *Mons Albanus* (Mount Alba), about 12 miles southeast of present-day Rome, and resettled 600 families in 1151 BC. Some say the city's name Alba Longa (*long white*) was after the large, white sow Aeneas had found. Others say it was because of the long, narrow ridge with white walls and houses which ran along between the mountain and the lake.

On the left side of this silver denarius coin struck in Rome in 106 BC are the Penates gods. The reverse depicts the white sow of the prophecy.

A curious incident happened after Ascanius built Alba Longa. When his family had escaped from Troy, his grandfather Anchises was clinging to the household gods (*Penates*). They were the guardians of Trojan culture and family life and an embodiment of the past. When the ghost of Prince Hector had come to Aeneas to warn him to escape Troy, he'd told him to take his family and the Penates.

These idols had spoken to Aeneas in a dream, redirecting him to Italy. Aeneas had carried them with him throughout his wanderings until he arrived in Lavinium. According to Dionysius, Aeneas built a shrine for them at the highest point of Lavinium's hill, implying that they were no longer just family idols, but gods for the whole Trojan remnant. By bringing them to Italy, they aligned Aeneas' new city with Troy and his ancestors' traditions.

Twenty-five years after Aeneas supposedly died, Ascanius moved the Penates to the newly built city of Alba Longa. One morning, he woke up to find the images gone. Who would have taken them? And then he received the baffling news that the Penates were back in Lavinium! He brought the household gods back to Alba Longa, and the same thing happened – they returned to Lavinium, apparently by themselves.

After that, the Penates were left in Lavinium, in their shrine built by Aeneas. Although Alba Longa became the political capital, Lavinium continued as a sacred religious center, even after Alba Longa fell to Rome. According to the fourth-century Roman writer, Symmachus, Lavinium continued as a municipal town as late as AD 391, where new Roman praetors and consuls customarily came to offer sacrifices to the Penates and Vesta when they entered their new offices. This indicates the importance of the Penates in linking the Romans to their Trojan ancestors; they were preserved for at least 1500 years.

The worship of Vesta began in Lavinium (brought from Troy) and continued in Alba Longa after it was built. Vesta was the virgin goddess of the hearth and family. She rarely had idols or images depicting her; she was represented by the fire in her temple. The worship of Vesta was one of the longest-lived pagan cults of Rome, enduring into AD 391 when her temple was closed and her sacred flame extinguished by Emperor Theodosius I.

Vesta was considered the purest of the Roman gods, not engaging in quarreling and drama with the others; she had very few myths about her. Her temple could only be entered by the Vestal Virgins, her white-robed priestesses, who remained celibate and kept the eternal flame burning. Besides the shrine for Vesta that Aeneas erected in Lavinium, Ascanius also built a temple to Vesta in Alba Longa.

Ascanius built a shrine to Jupiter on Mount Alban's peak, overlooking Alba Longa. Each year, he invited all the cities that belonged to the Latin League to gather in Alba Longa to worship Jupiter, sacrificing and eating a white bull. Jupiter, the god of the sky and thunder, was king of the gods in Latin, Greek, and Roman mythology. He was often associated with an eagle holding a thunderbolt in its claws. The eagle became an emblem of the Roman military.

All that is left of Alba Longa today are the remnants of the ancient walls. It was built on a ridge running out from Mount Alban's base and extending north. The side of the ridge facing the lake was steep, offering good natural protection. Peperino, a volcanic stone, was the primary building material. One can still see the ancient quarries in the valley between Alba and Marino.

After ruling for 38 years from Lavinium (and later from Alba Longa), Ascanius died. Who would succeed him? Many assumed it would be Iulus, Ascanius's oldest son. But the Latins asked what had happened to Queen Lavinia, daughter of King Latinus and wife of Aeneas. No one had seen her since Ascanius had succeeded his father's throne. And wasn't she pregnant when Aeneas disappeared? Where was that baby? If that child were a boy, wouldn't he have a greater claim to the throne as a son of both the Latin and Trojan royal lines?

Everyone made a big fuss about finding Lavinia. Rumors circulated that Ascanius had murdered his stepmother and her child. Finally, the herder Tyrrhenus came forward and explained what he had done and that Queen Lavinia and her son, Prince Silvius, were unharmed. They had hidden in the forest all these years. He brought them out of the forest and to Alba Longa.

Prince Iulus, the oldest son of King Ascanius, contested Silvius' right to the throne. But the Latins had an election, and Silvius won the vote. He was double-royal, grandson of King Latinus of the Latins and son of King Aeneas of the Trojans. His mother, Lavinia, was heiress to the Latin kingdom, as King Latinus had no sons. Silvius represented both the Latins and Trojans of the kingdom.

After living in the forest for 38 years as a herder, Silvius assumed the throne of Alba Longa, ruling over the Latins and Trojans for 29 years. He appointed his mother as the queen of Lavinium, the city named after Lavinia by her late husband. Silvius named his son Aeneas, after his grandfather, and he ruled the Latins for 31 years.

Ascanius' other son Iulus (or Julus), nephew to Silvius, became a priest. His clan became known as the *Gens Julia* (or Julians), one of the most important patrician families in Ancient Rome, from whom Julius Caesar descended. Dionysius said this family was relocated to Rome after the third Roman king, Tullus Hostilius, destroyed Alba Longa. However, some Julians were living in Rome from its inception, as Senator Proculus Julius announced that Romulus had become the god Quirinus.

Aeneas's descendants, through his youngest son Silvius, ruled Alba Longa for the rest of its history, with Silvius becoming the family surname. One of his descendants, Romulus Silvius (also known as Aremulus or Alladius), was notorious for his tyranny and arrogance. He made himself odious to the gods by forcing the people to worship him as a deity and by using technology to imitate lightning and the sounds of thunderclaps to terrify his people. Finally, the gods had enough of the pretender and sent rain and lightning down on his palace in Alba Longa. The lake rose higher than it ever had, flooding the palace, killing everyone inside, and permanently submerging it. Even today, if the lake is clear and still, the ruins of ancient porticoes appear in the depths.

Tiberinus' grandson, King Proca, had two sons: Numitor and Amulius. And with Numitor's daughter, we move from the history of the Latins in Lavinium and Alba Longa to the birth of Rome. When King Proca died, his oldest son Numitor succeeded the throne, but his younger brother Amulius was plotting to usurp the throne. First, while on a hunting expedition, there was a "tragic accident" in which Numitor's only son Aegestes was killed. With the male heir gone, Amulius organized a coup d'état and stole the throne from his brother. He didn't kill Numitor, just sent him into exile. But Amulius was worried about his brother's daughter, Rhea Silvia.

What if Rhea Silvia got married and had a son? Could that son claim the throne he'd stolen from Numitor? And there was something else – an oracle. He'd received a prophecy he would be killed by a descendent of Numitor. He'd gotten Aegestes out of the way, and he didn't think Rhea Silvia would kill him. But she might have a son who would.

To prevent that, Amulius forced his niece to become a vestal virgin – a priestess of the goddess Vesta. The vestals pledged virginity for 30 years; if they had sexual relations with a man, they were stoned to death or buried alive, and any man that dishonored a vestal was beaten to death. Now, Silvia Rhea would remain childless, and Numitor would have no descendants to challenge Amulius' throne or kill him. Or would he?

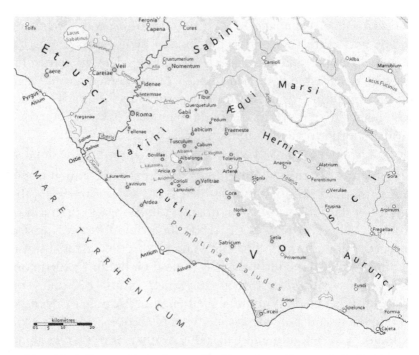

Map of Latin League cities and towns. To the north, on the coast, is the Etruscan (Estruci) nation, long-time enemies of the Latins. To the south, on the coast, is the Rutulian nation (Rutili), who, led by Turnus, fought with the Latins against the Trojans but were defeated. South of Rutili is the Volsci (the tribe of the woman warrior Camilla), who allied with the Latins but later were fierce enemies of Rome. Alba Longa is on the lake northeast of Rutili, and Laurentum and Lavinium are nearer the coast. The towns surrounding Alba Longa – Lanuvium, Aricia, Bovillae, Tusculum, Tiber (to north on the river), Cora (to south), and Ardea on the coast – were some of the 30 towns and cities that joined the Latin League.

For now, let's explore the Latin Confederation or Latin League. During the 500 years that Aeneas's descendants ruled the Latins and Trojans, they formed the Latin League, probably in the seventh century BC. The Latin League was a confederation of about 30 cities and towns in the region of Latium, Lavinium, and Alba Longa. Most towns belonged to the Latin tribes or Latin-Trojans but included Cora and Pometia, which Livy said were Volscian towns, and Ardea, which is described in the Aeneid as the capital of the Rutuli.

The Latin League was a multi-ethnic, multi-tribal confederation formed for mutual defense against their common enemies – mostly the Etruscans. The leading city of the Latin League was Alba Longa, which would host annual celebrations for all the towns and cities to gather to worship Jupiter and feast together, which created a strong bond between the cities.

The Latin League also held conferences at the sacred grove of the goddess Ferentina, at the springs in the scenic valley between Lake Albano (where Alba Longa lay) and Marino. The tribes would assemble to resolve disputes between league members, deal with common problems that arose, and strategize against their enemies.

When Rome was just a fledgling city, it allied with the Latin League, still led by Alba Longa. These relations became shaky as Rome surged in power, a growing threat to the Latins. Around 534 BC, Tarquinius Superbus, the last king of Rome, called the Latin leaders together to persuade them to renew the alliance between the Latin League and Rome.

However, Turnus Herdonius, a leading Latin citizen and stateman, warned the League not to trust Tarquinius. To get rid of him, Tarquinius bribed Turnus' servant to stockpile swords in Turnus' tent and then charged Turnus with staging a coup. When everyone saw the "proof" of the swords, they executed him by drowning. The meeting resumed, and the Latins agreed that their troops would unite as a military force with the Roman troops.

In 509 BC, the Romans revolted against their monarchy, sent King Tarquinius into exile, and began self-rule as a republic. The Latin League allied with the exiled King Tarquinius against Rome in the Battle of Lake Regillus. The Romans won the battle, and in 493 BC, Rome and the 30 Latin-League cities established a treaty (the *Foedus Cassianum*), stipulating peace between the two powers, a Roman-Latin troop coalition against common enemies, and a two-way split of plunder from battles they fought together. Roman generals would command joint military campaigns.

Together, the Latin League and Roman coalition repelled the Aequi and Volsci tribes of the Apennine Mountains, defeated the Etruscans, and deflected the Celts invading from Gaul. However, the Latins and Romans often quarreled, mostly disputing over the spoils of joint battles. Rome combatted individual Latin cities and sometimes even the entire Latin League. The Latin cities felt increasingly threatened by Rome's soaring power.

The Latin War broke out in 343 BC between the Latins and Rome. Rome won the victory, dissolving the Latin League in 338 BC. The Latin cities came under the full control of Rome as colonies of the Roman Republic. The Latin people were considered Roman citizens but without voting rights. But all of that was still in the future. For now, we will return to Silva Rhea, priestess of Vesta, and discover what happened to her babies.

Chapter 3: From the Founding of Rome to the Last King

The vestal virgin – Princess Rhea Silvia – was pregnant. By whom? The story was she'd gone out to draw water, and in the momentary darkness of a solar eclipse, was raped by the god Mars. Her uncle, King Amulius, ordered his servant to kill the babies, remembering an oracle: he would be killed by his brother's descendent. And so, the infants were floated in a basket down the river Tiber.

Romulus and Remus were suckled by a wolf.
*Trougnouf, CC BY 4.0 <https://creativecommons.org/licenses/by/4.0>, via Wikimedia Commons
https://commons.wikimedia.org/wiki/File:Maison_de_la_Louve_(DSC_0377).jpg*

Eventually, the basket bumped against the shore, and a she-wolf heard their cries. Her pups had died, and her teats were painfully swollen with milk. Lifting the babies from their basket, she nursed them. A shepherd named Faustulus came across this bizarre scene. As the wolf slunk into the underbrush, he scooped up the babies and carried them to his wife, who had just lost her own baby. She took them to her breast and raised them.

Romulus and Remus grew up unaware of their royal origins, tending flocks with their foster father. One day, they got into a conflict and killed some of Numitor's shepherds. Numitor arrested Remus, and Romulus rushed to tell Faustulus. Faustulus came to Numitor and told him the peculiar story of finding the twin boys with the wolf by the riverbank 18 years before. Numitor realized the twin boys had been found shortly after his daughter had given birth. These must be his grandsons!

After an emotional reunion with his long-lost grandsons, Numitor related how his ruthless brother Amulius had usurped the throne. The boys killed Amulius, fulfilling the prophecy, and restored their grandfather to his throne. Then, Romulus and Remus traveled back to the seven hills, about 12 miles north, planning to build their city where Faustulus had found them as infants. But they disagreed about where to build and who would be the ultimate sovereign. In a rage, Romulus killed his twin brother.

Romulus built the city on the Palatine Hill, beginning with fortifications. With only a small group of followers, he welcomed everyone from the surrounding regions to be citizens of the new city – including former slaves and those from the lower classes.

Settlements already existed in the seven hills area. Dionysius, Virgil, and Ovid all recorded that Evander of Arcadia (who had allied with Aeneas against Turnus) led his fellow Greeks to found the city of Pallantium centuries earlier, bringing the Greek gods, laws, and alphabet to Italy. Virgil said the Roman citizens were a mixture of Latins and Trojans from Alba Longa with Greeks from Pallantium. The Sabines and Etruscans also lived in the immediate area; the Etruscans were an especially powerful people that at one time were the overlords of the Latins and Trojans until Ascanius had overthrown them and made them a tributary to Alba Longa.

After Romulus called a council to determine their government, the citizens put Romulus at the helm with a 100-person Senate. A *gen (clan)* was an extended-family group led by a *pater* (father) – the patriarch of the clan. The first senators were the *patres* – or family leaders of the gens. The descendants of these patres became the patrician class that formed the Senate.

What did the Senate do? Their key responsibility was electing new kings. When a king died, the Senate became the temporary ruling power while a new king was nominated and elected. The second most important task was serving as the king's advisory council. The Senate also served as a legislative body representing Rome's people. The king was the only one who could make laws, but he did so in close consultation with the Senate.

When Romulus first founded Rome, he had a problem – a shortage of women. Rome had about 3000 unmarried men who needed wives to sustain the new city. His new city was scorned by its neighbors, who refused to offer their daughters as wives to Rome's citizens. Romulus decided on another tactic to gain wives for his men.

The Romans abduct the Sabine women to be their wives. Painting by Nicolas Poussin.
https://commons.wikimedia.org/wiki/File:The_Abduction_of_the_Sabine_Women.jpg

The Romans invited the neighboring Sabine tribe to celebrate a religious festival with them. At the feast, the Romans drank diluted wine but gave the Sabine men full-strength liquor. The

Romans pretended to get inebriated, and then when the Sabines had drunk themselves under the table, the Romans captured all the unmarried female guests to be their wives. When the Sabines sobered up and demanded their young women be returned, Romulus refused.

Outraged, two Sabine towns attacked almost immediately, attempting to recapture their young women, but the Romans defeated them. Finally, the Sabines mustered a united force led by King Tatius and attacked Rome. As the Romans and Sabines were drawn up in two opposing forces, the Sabine women, many pregnant by this point, ran into the space between the armies, shouting to the Sabines, "Why do you do this, fathers? Why do you do this, brothers?"

They then turned to the Romans, "Why do you do this, husbands? When will you stop fighting?"

Turning back to the Sabines, the women cried, "Spare your grandchildren! If not, then kill us since we're the reason you're fighting!"

Deeply moved, the warriors on both sides broke down weeping, put away their weapons, and held a peace conference. They joined into a united kingdom, with both Romulus and Tatius serving as co-rulers. King Tatius was mysteriously assassinated in Lavinium five years later, making Romulus the sole king of both the Latins and Sabines.

Rome also warred with the Etruscans, ancient enemies of the Latins and exiled Trojans. During Romulus' reign, the Fidenates, an Etruscan clan, attempted to obliterate Rome, considering it a future threat. Romulus marched out to their city, but rather than confront them directly, he set an ambush – hiding most of his men in the thickets while sending a small company of soldiers to the city gates to lure the Etruscans out. When the Fidenates stormed out in pursuit, the Romans leaped out, catching them by surprise and vanquishing them.

This worried the Etruscan citizens of nearby Veii. They launched a preemptive strike into Roman territory and quickly hurried home with their spoils of war. But Romulus led his men in hot pursuit, catching up with the Veientes just as they got back to their city. Rather than besieging the city, they ravaged their lands until the Veientes surrendered, made a 100-year peace treaty, gave Rome some of their lands.

When Rome's third king Tullus reigned, the Fidenates and Veientes launched a coordinated attack on Rome. By this point, Rome had joined the Latin League, so King Tullus called on King Mettius of Alba Longa to ally with him. Mettius and the Alban army arrived, unwillingly and slowly, but the Etruscans fled, nevertheless.

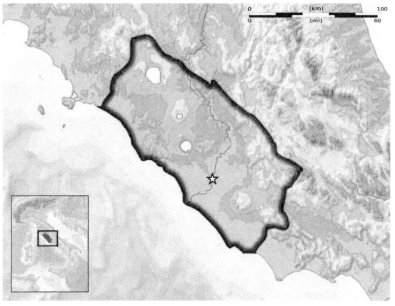

This map depicts the expansion of Roman territory in the late Roman monarchy period.

© Sémhur / Wikimedia Commons
https://commons.wikimedia.org/wiki/File:Late_Roman_kingdom_map-blank.svg

Romulus and his descendants expanded Rome's borders by first allying with the Latin League to conquer common enemies, such as the Etruscans, then later conquering the Latin League, subjugating Latin cities to Rome. By kidnapping the Sabine women, they merged with the Sabine people in a joint rule. Gradually, Rome expanded its power base through central Italy.

Romulus was an astute warrior – but a poor politician. He was harsh and tyrannical with the Senate and haughty with his citizens. Dio recorded that the exasperated senators grew so incensed that they exploded in a frenzy, tearing him limb from limb. Just at that moment, a solar eclipse (like during his conception) and a violent windstorm occurred. The senators quickly hid the body and spread the tale that the windstorm had carried him away.

While the citizens were frantically searching for Romulus, his killers in the senate were in a quandary. They couldn't elect a new king unless Romulus was dead, but they didn't want to reveal their guilt. Finally, one senator rushed into the midst of the people, crying, "Don't grieve! I just saw Romulus ascending into the sky! He's become the god Quirinus. He said to elect a new king without delay."

Everyone believed him and stopped worrying about Romulus. They built a temple for him and moved on to who would be their next king.

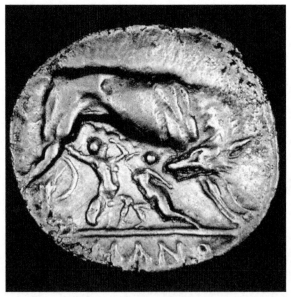

This silver didrachm Roman coin, dating to 269 BC, depicts the she-wolf suckling Romulus and Remus.
Curtius, CC BY-SA 3.0 <http://creativecommons.org/licenses/by-sa/3.0/>, via Wikimedia Commons https://commons.wikimedia.org/wiki/File:Cr_20-1-Reverse.jpg

Was Romulus a real person? The Roman historian Marcus Terentius Varro (first century BC) said his tomb was located under the Forum. In November 2019, archeologists unearthed a sixth-century tomb beneath the steps of the Curia in the northwest corner of the Forum with a votive altar believed to be dedicated to Romulus. The stone sarcophagus is empty, but they didn't exactly have a body to bury – he was either torn to pieces or ascended bodily into the sky. Along with the bronze Capitoline Wolf sculpture in Rome that dates to the fifth century BC, numerous Roman coins dating to at least 269 BC show the she-wolf suckling the twins.

The Roman king was not hereditary but elected for life (or until he suddenly became a god). Now that Romulus was gone, the Sabines reminded everyone that a Sabine king was supposed to co-rule with a Roman king, and since King Tatius had been assassinated decades earlier and never replaced, it was their turn for a Sabine to rule over Rome. The Romans argued about this with the Sabines for a full year. With no king to rule, the Senate stepped in during this gap year (the *interregnum*), and each of the most distinguished senators ruled for five days in rotation.

Finally, the Sabines got their way, and Numa Pompilius was elected. He brought law and order to Rome and secured peace with the surrounding states. He lived a disciplined and simple life with few luxuries. Numa is known for implementing a 12-month calendar and naming January as the first month – after Janus, the god with two faces – one representing the past and the other the future.

The next king was Tullus Hostilius, a violent man of war who sneered at the gods. During his reign, he marched against Alba Longa, the mother city of Rome, but neither side wanted a long war against their kinsmen. After negotiations, they agreed to come under a common leadership – but who would lead? Alba Longa or Rome?

To decide, they held a small battle. Each side had a set of triplets who became the champions for the two sides – three against three. They battled each other until all three of the Albans were wounded and two of the Romans were dead. The surviving Roman, Horatius, didn't like the odds of three to one, so he ran away from the battleground, with the Albans chasing him, spreading out as they ran, slowed by their injuries. One by one, he turned and quickly killed the first, the second, and then the third, making Rome the ruler of Alba Longa.

Although the Albans were now allied with Rome, they feigned obedience to their overlords. Later, when King Tullus called them to help fight the Etruscans, they hung back, intending to fight with the Etruscans against Rome. Rome won the battle anyway, but Tullus executed their king, Mettius, and demolished Alba Longa for their duplicity.

Another Sabine, Ancus Marcius, was elected as Rome's fourth king. Like his grandfather, King Numa, he was peaceable but realized he was forced to engage in what he called "war as a means of peace." He fought against the Latins who were pillaging the Roman settlements, capturing their cities, and resettling many in Rome. He laid siege to the Etruscan Fidenates, long-time enemies of Rome, and subdued the Sabines. Marcius built the first bridge over the river Tiber and extended Rome's territory to the sea, giving them a port.

The fifth king of Rome, Lucius Tarquinius Priscus, was an outsider. His father was an exile from Corinth who had settled in Tarquinii, an Etruscan city, and married an Etruscan woman. Tarquinius grew up with great wealth, but being half-Greek, his political ambitions in Tarquinii went unrealized. He headed to Rome, hoping for a more promising future.

In Rome, his generosity, intelligence, and versatility won the admiration of influential people, especially King Marcius. Tarquinius would readily offer to help anyone needing assistance, never said or did anything unkind, and was quick to forgive others. Marcius was so impressed that he enrolled Tarquinius as a patrician, made him a senator, trusted him with the supervision of his children, and made him second in the kingdom. Through his cleverness and reputation of wisdom and honor, Tarquinius dominated Marcius and the senators.

When King Marcius died, the senators were planning to elect one (or both) of Marcius' sons to the throne. Tarquinius suggested himself as the temporary monarch until Marcius' sons came of age. He was so well-liked that virtually everyone agreed this was a splendid idea.

Tarquinius built the Circus Maximus for racing horses and chariots, gladiator confrontations, and games.

Tarquinius expanded Rome's territory through the successful conquest of the Latins, Etruscans, and Sabines. He celebrated his military triumphs by riding in a golden chariot wearing a purple toga with gold embroidery and a crown of gold with precious stones. These persevered as symbols of Roman kings and emperors. He built the great stadium known as the *Circus Maximus* for games, chariot racing, and gladiator fights. He drained the marshy low-lying areas of Rome and provided waste removal with one of the world's first sewer systems – the *Cloaca Maxima.*

Tarquinius was a successful king, but the two sons of Marcius, who never received the promised crown, were plotting against him. Tarquinius made Servius Tullius (probably his illegitimate son) second-in-command and promoted him as his heir, which wasn't well-received: Tullius was the son of a slave – not of the patrician class. The sons of Marcius conspired with some patricians and sent two men into the palace who murdered Tarquinius with axes and sickles.

The paternity of the sixth Roman king, Servius Tullius, was a mystery. His mother was Ocrisia, a Latin slave-woman to Tarquinius' wife, Tanaquil. One story was that a man rose from the hearth flames as Ocrisia was offering sacrifices of food and wine. Frightened, Ocrisia ran to her mistress, and Queen Tanaquil, deciding he must be a god, dressed Ocrisia in wedding finery, sent her back into the room, and shut the door. Ocrisia conceived, and Tullius' half-god identity occasionally manifested by fire leaping from his head. The more probable story was that he was Tarquinius' illegitimate son since the king elevated him so highly, promoting him as his heir.

And now we come to Tullius' bizarre accession to the throne. Tarquinius had been assassinated, but Queen Tanaquil schemed to retain power by pretending he was still alive. She called to the people from the palace balcony, "My husband survived the attack! You'll see him shortly. He asks that Tullius take over his affairs while he is healing."

The citizens believed their queen, and Tullius took over as if he were receiving orders from Tarquinius. The murderers were arrested, executed, and Queen Tanaquil pretended to be tending to her husband, having agreed with Tullius he would be regent until her sons came of age. Fearful of being implicated in Tarquinius' assassination, King Marcius' sons fled to the Volsci kingdom.

With no other serious contenders for the throne, Tullius and Tanaquil revealed the sad news that Tarquinius had succumbed to his wounds. Tullius continued as the regent while Tarquinius' sons were growing up. He groomed the citizens to accept him as king – assigning them land (so they could vote – for him, of course). He also planned to free the slaves and give them citizenship, perhaps because his mother was a slave.

This last plan incensed the patricians. Not only would they lose labor, but the freed slaves would support Tullius. They circulated charges that Tullius was ruling without the Senate's sanction. Tullius gathered the people and gave a stirring oration of all the reasons he was their best choice for king. Immediately, the citizens of Rome voted him in as their monarch.

Tullius took the first census of Rome, which had about 80,000 citizens. He gave his daughters in marriage to the two sons of Tarquinius, still promising to restore the monarchy to them when the time was right. The oldest son, Tarquin, realizing his father-in-law would never relinquish the throne, plotted a takeover. When his younger brother refused to cooperate, he gave poison to his sister-in-law to kill him. When his wife criticized his plot, he poisoned her as well, then married his sister-in-law. His new wife happily plotted with him against her father.

Lucius gathered a group of patricians and senators unhappy with King Tullius, lauding the stellar leadership of his father Tarquinius while ridiculing Tullius. Hearing of this, Tullius hurried to the Senate but only blurted out a few words before Tarquin forced him out of the building, throwing him down the stairs. The bewildered king sat on the pavement, amazed that no one came to assist him.

After congratulating her husband on his successful coup d'état, Tullia ran her chariot over her father's body. Painting by Jean Bardin.
https://commons.wikimedia.org/wiki/File:Bardin_Tullia.jpg

The Senate took an immediate vote to elect Tarquin as their king. His first act was ordering the death of Tullius, who was stumbling home, abandoned by his guards. Tarquin's wife congratulated her husband with an embrace, saluted him as her king, then charged off in her chariot, driving over the body of her father as he lay in the street.

When Lucius Tarquinius Superbus succeeded to the throne, he surrounded himself with bodyguards, fearful of what had happened to his father. Desiring to rid himself of any senators who would question the murder of Tullius or his right to the throne, he decimated their numbers: executing those against whom he could bring plausible charges, secretly murdering some, and banishing others.

He didn't stop with Tullius' followers; he even killed his close friends who had conspired with him, fearful they would turn against him later. He didn't appoint new senators to replace the dead ones, desiring to render the Senate powerless. He ran the state's affairs with only his sons to assist him, not wanting anyone else to rise in power. He was inaccessible to both citizens and senators, displaying shocking brutality and arrogance. Besides killing his brother and first wife, Tarquin also killed his sister's husband and son. The second son of Tarquin's sister, Lucius Junius Brutus, feigned intellectual disability to survive.

Tarquin expanded Rome's borders and power through canny negotiations with the Latins, triumphant conquest of the Volsci, and subterfuge with the city of Gabii. He achieved peace with the Aequi and renewed Rome's treaty with the Etruscans and Sabines. He also continued his father's construction projects on the stadium and the sewers.

Tarquin's downfall came from a coup d'état led by his nephew Brutus, the one who pretended to be cognitively challenged. It all started when Tarquin's son Sextus raped Lucretia, the beautiful wife of a distinguished senator. Afterward, Lucretia told her husband and father what had happened, asking them to avenge her, then pulled a dagger from under her pillow and killed herself.

This spurred an uproar against the tyrannical rule of the Tarquin family. Brutus persuaded the military to join him in the revolt. King Tarquin and his sons fled Rome, where he rallied some Etruscan and Latin cities to his support and attempted to retake Rome three times, but he lost and died in exile. After Tarquin was deposed, the citizens of Rome established the Roman Republic in 509 BC, with magistrates elected each year, representative assemblies, separation of powers, and a constitution that mandated a system of checks and balances.

SECTION TWO:
THE ROMAN REPUBLIC
(509 to 27 BC)

Chapter 4: The Republic's Establishment

The Roman Republic, lasting five centuries, led Rome's stunning metamorphosis from a modest city-state to a far-reaching domain stretching around the Mediterranean. The Romans had an incredible ability to assimilate organizational methods, knowledge, and technique from other powers they encountered and put that into play as their borders swiftly extended and their governmental system evolved.

The Roman Republic left an impressive legacy that markedly influenced the organization of new governments around the world – like the United States – two millennia later. Officially called the *Senate and People of Rome (Senatus Populusque Romanus),* the Republic ushered in a rule of the people in 509 BC when they expelled the tyrannical King Tarquinius Superbus. The Romans realized they didn't need a king – they would run things on their own. And they did, until 27 BC when Octavian (Augustus Caesar) became the first Roman emperor.

This involved a learning curve; they had to figure out just how to run a republic because that hadn't been done before – by anybody. Greece was working out something called a democracy, but their system was different; the Greek ideal was the rule of the many (regular people) over the few (rich aristocrats), and the Roman Republic, at least initially, was the rule of the elite

Patricians over the Plebeian masses of common people.

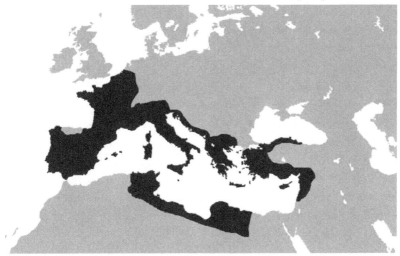

This map shows the extent of the areas conquered by Rome by 44 BC – close to the end of the Republic era. In this map, the seas are white – so you can see how much of the Mediterranean Sea (in the middle) was controlled by Rome.

english wikipedia, CC BY-SA 3.0 <http://creativecommons.org/licenses/by-sa/3.0/>, via
Wikimedia Commons https://commons.wikimedia.org/wiki/File:Roman_Republic-44BC.png

The Romans had to employ a great deal of ingenuity and flexibility – just when they thought they had the republican system mastered, something would happen. What should they do with all these people they were conquering. How would the Republic form of government work for them? And, what about these Plebeian commoners having the audacity to demand equal representation? As if that weren't enough, the slaves revolted! The Roman Republic was constantly evolving and adapting to one crisis after another.

Their biggest challenge was the internal conflict that had cursed Rome from the day Romulus murdered his twin brother. The wealth and power Rome was accumulating did not mitigate the destructive discord that spelled the collapse of Rome's Republic. But to their credit, they held it together spectacularly for five centuries, all the while conquering much of the known world.

The rape of virtuous Lucretia sparked a revolution, overturning the monarchy that had ruled Rome since its inception. The ensuing constitutional reforms launched Rome into a new era with a stronger constitution. They'd had unwritten guidelines – and the constitution was still unwritten, but now they had innovations like term limits, separation of powers, checks and balances, impeachments, quorum requirements, filibusters, vetoes, and regularly scheduled elections. The constitution was continuously evolving, based on precedent, and driven by conflict between commoners and aristocrats.

Two men serving together – called consuls – replaced the former kings. Instead of serving for life, they were elected for a one-year term by the military Centuriate Assembly. The Romans reasoned that two heads of state were better than one because if one made disastrous decisions, the other could use his veto power to keep him in check. A consul could be prosecuted at the end of his one-year term if he abused his powers.

The two consuls wore white togas with a broad purple border, indicating their position and power to command as the highest judicial power in the Republic. The consuls appointed new senators (during the early Republic) and exercised supreme authority in military and civil affairs. One led the Centuriate Assembly, and the other led the Assembly of Tribes. When on military campaigns, they would each command an army with nearly absolute power.

The idea of having two men lead the country assisted by a Senate was quickly picked up by Carthage in North Africa. After becoming a Republic in 509 BC, Rome established a treaty with Carthage, which controlled North Africa and the Western Mediterranean with its powerful navy. Like Rome, Carthage established a Senate of 300 affluent citizens with two heads of state they called *Suffetes* or judges.

"The Oath of Brutus," by François-Joseph Navez, depicts Brutus' vow to avenge Lucretia.

The first two consuls of the Roman Republic were Lucius Junius Brutus and Lucius Tarquinius Collatinus, the revolutionaries who overthrew the monarchy. Brutus was the grandson of King Lucius Tarquinius Priscus and the nephew of Rome's last king, Tarquinius Superbus. The men carried Lucretia's body to the Forum, where Brutus shouted, "Act like men and Romans and take up arms against our insolent foes!"

Brutus was the one who'd been pretending to be mentally deficient so his uncle – the king – wouldn't kill him. Now he had to explain to the crowd he had faked disability because his evil uncle had killed his father and brother. He proposed banishing the king and forming a republic form of government. Moved by the sight of Lucretia's bloody body, a vote was taken: the king was out, and the Republic was in.

The other first consul, Lucius Tarquinius Collatinus, was Lucretia's husband, the nephew of King Lucius Tarquinius Priscus. He was a cousin of both Brutus and Sextus Tarquinius, his wife's rapist. Ironically, these two men who instigated the revolt and served as the first consuls belonged to the royal family they overthrew. When the dust settled, the people murmured about Collatinus' connection to the Tarquin tyrants, so he abdicated his position as consul.

Oddly enough, though more closely related to the former royal family than Collatinus, Brutus did not receive such suspicion, perhaps because he resolutely executed his own two sons when he discovered they were part of a conspiracy to restore Tarquin as king. Brutus died before the end of his one-year term when he and his first cousin Arruns (son of Tarquin) killed each other at the Battle of Silva Arsia.

In emergencies – such as a military or internal crisis – one consul could nominate a temporary dictator, following the Senate's recommendation, who would be confirmed by the Comitia Curiata. The dictator was expected to relinquish his powers once the crisis was abated – or at the end of six months – whichever came first. In the later years of the Republic, the Plebs gained the power to nullify the dictator's executive actions, which reduced his power to act swiftly in times of crisis; by 202 BC, this position was no longer utilized.

Under the consuls were the censors and the praetors. The censors oversaw the census and maintained public morality (from which we get the English word *censor* for an official who suppresses any behaviors, communications, or objects considered obscene, politically unacceptable, or a threat to security).

Marcus Claudius Marcellus was elected as consul five times and celebrated for killing King Viridomarus, commander of the Gauls, in hand-to-hand combat in 222 BC.
https://commons.wikimedia.org/wiki/File:Print_Marcus_Claudius_Marcellus_Roman_Consul_Elect_Statue_Spolia_Opima_Rome.jpg

Rome's elected praetors served as judges of Roman law and as army generals. As Rome conquered more territory, the praetors served as governors of the provinces. When the two consuls were away on military campaigns, the Praetor Urbanus became the senior official over the city of Rome. He couldn't leave Rome if the consuls were not there, except for very brief periods. He could call the Senate together and command a defense if the city were attacked. Each year, the Praetor Urbanus issued an Edict that legislated the rights and dues of people.

The people living in Rome during the Republic era weren't automatically citizens – and even if they were, there were distinct levels of citizenship. People over 15 who descended from the original 35 tribes of Rome had the right of citizenship – unless they were a slave, a former slave, or a woman. Women could own property, run a business, and get a divorce, but they couldn't vote or hold a position in government. Slaves weren't even considered people. Freedmen (former slaves) eventually won limited citizenship. The tribes of Rome weren't ethnic or family groups but based on geographic location – something like a congressional district.

Men with full citizenship with all the accompanying political and legal rights proudly wore white togas to display their status as *Optimo Jure* (optimum rights). Each full citizen belonged to one of the three voting or legislative assemblies. During the monarchy period, Romans had only one voting assembly – the *Comitia Curiata* (Curiate Assembly) – but most of the political powers of this assembly were transferred to the Comitia Centuriata (Assembly of Centuries) for the military men and the Comitia Tributa (Tribal Assembly) for those of the patrician ruling class. These assemblies were each led by one of the two consuls. In 494 BC, the Concilium Plebis (Plebeian Assembly) was organized for the common people (called Plebs or Plebeians).

Each citizen had the right to elect the leaders of their respective assemblies. Their assembly leaders elected the magistrates, passed laws, and held capital trials. The military assembly (Centuriate Assembly) was the only power that could declare war and ratify a census. It also served as a Supreme Court of Appeals for certain cases.

The tribunes filled several offices, most notably the *Tribuni Plebis* and the *Tribuni Militum*. The Tribuni Plebis, which numbered from two to ten elected tribunes, presided over the Plebeian Assembly, organizing legislation for the vote and vetoing legislation from the Senate that disfavored the common people. Using the commoners as a political weapon, the Tribuni Plebis exercised great control over Rome.

The Military Tribunes took care of organizing command among the ranks, supervising logistics, and leading legions to battle. They had senior rank in the Roman army and had to serve for at least five years. Other tribunes included the *Tribuni Aerarii,* who served in the treasury, collecting taxes and distributing the funds – mostly to the Roman legions.

The magistrates were elected officials with extensive authority in the public sphere and the military. The two consuls were the lead magistrates, and the most influential aristocratic families (*gentes)* dominated the most powerful magistrate positions. Each magistrate had a *provincia* – a scope of authority over a geographic region or a specific responsibility. The Patricians – and later the Plebeians – voted for their magistrates, so it was a form of representation by the people. Magistrates maintained the peace and could sentence people for crimes with the power of *coercitio* (coercion). They were also supposed to keep an eye out for omens, which the Romans took seriously.

Just like they had two consuls in top leadership, most of the magisterial offices had two people for the same position – called the *Collega* (collegiality) – which checked abuse of power. Roman citizens were protected from abuse of the coercion power through *provocation* (due process). Magistrates served one-year terms and had to wait ten years before they could hold that office again.

The Senate continued into the Republic but in a different capacity. In the Republic, the Senate's main responsibilities were electing new kings and advising the king. In the Republic, the Senate passed *Senatus Consulta* to the magistrates, which meant *senator's advice,* but the magistrates followed it as more of a decree. The Senate placed most of their focus on foreign policy, particularly as they were constantly adding in new provinces throughout Italy and eventually around the Mediterranean. The Senate also had explicit power over the state budget, which translated to power over the military and many other entities. The Senate's influence grew immensely over time and began passing laws as the legislative assemblies' strength faded.

In the early years of the Republic, the Senators were appointed by the two consuls, and of course, they selected men who would support them politically. Around 312 BC, the Plebeian Assembly successfully gave the Roman censors the power to appoint the new senators (for life) from a pool of newly-elected magistrates, bringing the Senate out from under the power of the consuls. In emergencies – war or civil unrest – the new senators were selected by the temporary dictator or by the current senators.

The Via Appia, (Apian Way) Rome's first major road, was built 312–264 BC and stretched 150 miles from Rome to Benevento. Photo by Paul Vlaar.

At the beginning of the Republic, the Senate had 100 men. After 312 BC, when the censors got to appoint senators, Appius Claudius Caecus raised the number of senators to 300 and included Plebs and descendants of freed slaves, which the Patricians considered a scandalous plummet into the abyss. During his one-year term as censor, Caecus launched the construction of the Aqua Appia – the first Roman aqueduct – and the Apian Way – the first major Roman road, traveling 150 miles from Rome to Benevento in the south. As the Roman Republic was nearing its end, the number of senators increased to 900 under Sulla and 1000 under Julius Caesar.

Rome had three classes of people. At the bottom were slaves, who had no power or representation in government. At the top were the Patricians – wealthy, upper-class citizens from noble families, who were successful businessmen or large landholders. The Plebeians were everyone else – the working class.

In the early years of the Republic, the Patricians dominated politics and society, monopolizing the priesthood, important military posts, and prestigious magistracies. The original Patricians were an exclusive group of 50 distinguished extended families called *gentes,* of whom the most eminent was the Cornelii gens. Other esteemed gentes of the Republic era included the Aemilii, Valerii, Fabii, and Claudii families – recognized for their massive landholdings, wealth, and patronage of their *clients.* Clients were usually commoners for whom the Patrician patrons took responsibility: providing legal representation in court, financial assistance, marriage arrangements, and other favors.

The Plebeians or Plebs formed the backbone of Rome: the farmers, artisans, merchants, and other workers. Initially, they had little political power. Their influence quickly grew as they developed an internal social organization and legislative assembly, passing their own laws and holding the power of veto over the Senate.

Higher positions in the priesthood and politics were off-limits to Plebians. One grievance of the Plebs was that the Patricians would pass laws, not inform the Plebs, and then prosecute them for breaking laws they didn't know existed. Another grievance was beating and imprisoning debtors unable to repay their debts.

If the Patricians got too outrageous, the Plebeians would go on strike in a *Secessio Plebis* (Plebeian withdrawal). They would close shop, put down their tools, and walk out of the city, heading to a nearby mountain to enjoy a little vacation time, leaving the Patricians to fend for themselves. After a few days with no shops to buy food or goods, no construction workers, no bodyguards, no soldiers, and none of the other services the Plebs provided, the Patricians were ready to come to the negotiating table.

Gaius Gracchus represented the Plebeians, advocating for great reforms until his suicide in 121 BC.

https://commons.wikimedia.org/wiki/File:Gaius_Gracchus_Tribune_of_the_People.jpg

Various strikes resulted in the easing of debt punishments, access to new laws, and acquiring their own legislative assembly and tribunes. Little by little, the Plebs achieved political equality with the upper classes. The tribunes safeguarded the Plebeians from abuse and could exercise *intercession*, or veto the Senate's laws and actions, and block any magistrate or even a fellow tribune failing to consider the Plebs' best interest. In the late Republic era, tribunes could be Senate members, which gave them great sway over legislation; they acquired a reputation of being revolutionaries within the system.

The veto (*intercessio*) was a powerful tool created by the Romans that still regulates many government systems today. Each of the two consuls could veto the actions of the other. The tribunes could veto the Senate's decrees or magistrates' actions, especially protecting the common citizens from unfair domination by the aristocracy. The Senate could still pass a bill, but it was impotent if vetoed.

In 385 BC, Marcus Manlius Capitolinus, who provided heroic defense for Rome amid the sacking of the Gauls, was troubled by the devastating effect the invasion had on the Plebs. Losing their livelihoods – their shops, farms, and tools – plunged them into nightmarish debt to the Patricians. Manlius watched as a centurion, who had defended Rome from the Gauls, was led to prison for debts he could not pay. Manlius suddenly leaped forward, offering to pay the man's debt himself, and the centurion walked home a free man.

A Patrician himself, Manlius became a champion for the Plebeian class, even selling off his estate to pay off their debts. He relentlessly advocated for the Plebs, charging the Senate with embezzling public funds that could relieve the horrific misery of the common workers who contributed so much to the city. His efforts at social reform were not well received by the Patricians, who threw him to his death from the Tarpeian Rock.

The menacing unrest continued in rollercoaster fashion between the Patricians and Plebs: the Plebs made gains and then lost them again as their rights were suppressed. In 366 BC, Dictator Camillus resolved the crisis by a compromise – the Plebians got their own consul, while the Patricians had a monopoly over the offices of praetor and *curule aediles* (formal magistrates). Once they got their own censor, it wasn't long before the positions of censor and dictator were filled by Plebs. Gaius Marcius Rutilus, a Plebeian, served as consul four times, then dictator, and finally as censor.

As the Plebeians accomplished striking advances in politics and society, they were experiencing an internal separation of classes. Some of the Plebs were becoming affluent elitists who, like the Patricians, were exploiting the poorer Plebs to their advantage. They had grown out of touch with the working class and were failing to represent their issues. The Patricians' loss of power led to many prominent gentes fading away, supplanted by the self-made new aristocrats – twenty families of Plebeians – joining the dozen or so remaining Patrician gentes to form the new class known as *Nobilitas.*

Chapter 5: The Wars of Central Italy

From the Republic's inception in 509 BC, Rome endured almost perpetual warfare. The first 200 years of conquest and defense solidified Roman power in central Italy and parts of southern Italy. The wars of this era began with the Tarquinian Conspiracy, then the Celtic invasion, and the Sack of Rome, followed by war with the Apennine Mountain Samnites. Throughout epic battles, the Romans demonstrated astounding resilience, overcoming catastrophic losses.

Tarquinius Superbus' insidious attempts to regain the throne swept the Romans, Etruscans, and Latins into the intrigue known as the Tarquinian Conspiracy. Having brazenly murdered his wife, brother, and father-in-law to gain the throne, Tarquinius was now seeking any means possible to recapture it. He began by sending ambassadors to the Senate requesting the return of the royal family's personal belongings. While the Senate was debating their request, Tarquin's ambassadors were secretly instigating a coup d'état, recruiting even Brutus' two sons and his wife's two brothers (of the Vitelii family) as chief conspirators, along with the Aquillii family.

These young men met at the Aquillii house, where Tarquin's ambassadors were staying, swearing a dreadful oath sealed by pouring out the blood of a man they'd killed and touching his entrails. A slave named Vindicius happened to walk into the darkened room, unnoticed by the others. Observing the horrific scene and hearing their plans to kill the two consuls, Vindicius stole out of the house and alerted the consuls. The conspirators were hustled to the Forum; because their letters to King Tarquin were discovered, their guilt was undisputed. Brutus called out to his sons, "Come, Titus, come Tiberius, why aren't you defending yourselves against these charges?"

Three times Brutus demanded an answer, but they remained silent. Brutus resolutely turned to the guards, "Do what you must do."

Brutus watched with an expression of stern wrath as his sons were seized, stripped of their togas, and beaten with rods. When they were thrown to the ground and beheaded, a groan escaped Brutus, stoic up to this point. He silently rose and walked out, leaving the rest of the conspirators to be judged and executed.

The guards return the bodies of Lucas' sons.
https://commons.wikimedia.org/wiki/File:David_Brutus.jpg

Unwilling to admit defeat, Tarquinius rallied the Etruscans of Veii and his ancestral city of Tarquinii, confronting Rome in the fierce Battle of Silva Arsia. His son, Arruns, and the Roman consul, Brutus, were killed when the cousins simultaneously impaled each other with their spears. Having lost that battle, Tarquinius next allied with Lars Porsena, the king of the powerful Etruscan city of Clusium.

In 508 BC, King Porsena marched on Rome, approaching the Pons Sublicius bridge over the Tiber. Three fearless young men

– Horatius, Herminius, and Lartius – dashed across the bridge to valiantly hold off the Etruscans while the Romans frantically destroyed the bridge behind them. Herminius and Lartius ran back just as the bridge collapsed, while Horatius jumped off the bridge as it fell, swimming back under a hail of Etruscan arrows and spears.

King Porsena lay siege to Rome, blocked river transportation, and raided the surrounding farms. One night, an extraordinary young man named Gaius Mucius snuck into the Etruscan camp, intending to assassinate Porsena, but mistakenly killed the king's scribe instead. Captured, he boldly declared to King Porsena why he was there. "You'll never stop us! I'm only the first of 300 Roman youths who will do the same!"

Thrusting his hand into the flames of a nearby brazier, he cried, "Look! See how cheap our bodies are to men whose focus is great glory!"

Gaius confronts the Etruscan king Porsena after his failed assassination attempt.
https://commons.wikimedia.org/wiki/File:Matthias_Stomer_-
Mucius_Scaevola_in_the_presence_of_Lars_Porsenna_-_Google_Art_Project.jpg

Horrified yet admiring the young man's brazen courage, King Porsena released Gaius and sent his ambassadors to negotiate peace with Rome. The Romans staunchly refused his request for Tarquinius' restoration as king, yet they did return the land to the Veientes they had taken earlier. Shortly after, many Etruscans came to Rome to live and were granted their own district.

Around 496 BC, Tarquinius Superbus, leading the Latin League, waged the Battle of Lake Regillus against Rome in a last-ditch attempt to regain the crown. Rome appointed Aulus Postumius Albus as temporary dictator. The Volsci had allied with the Latins, but the Romans rushed out so quickly, enraged by the sight of their former king, they won the battle before the Volsci arrived.

In the 483 BC Fabian War, Veii took advantage of Rome's internal unrest and an invasion by the Aequi (a tribe to the east) and marched on Rome. Rome's Fabii clan asked and received permission to deal with the Veientes, and 309 soldiers of their gens marched north, demolishing the Veii territory. However, the Veientes ambushed and annihilated all the Fabii men. Rome sent a second army against the Veientes and lost once again. The following year, the Veientes allied with the Sabines against Rome. This time the Romans allied with the Latins and were triumphant, and a truce was declared with the Etruscans paying tribute to Rome.

The 458 BC Battle of Mount Algidus was fought against the Aequi, who attacked Rome's territories at an inopportune time: Rome's slaves were revolting, the Patricians and Plebs were deadlocked in toxic politics, and one of their consuls had just died. Despite their internal woes, Rome defeated the Aequi, but the following year the Aequi attacked again. Cincinnatus, nominated as a temporary dictator, vanquished the Aequi so swiftly that he was able to resign his dictatorship in only 16 days.

The Aequi and Volsci allied against Rome in the 446 BC Battle of Corbio, outnumbering the Roman forces. The Romans divided into two armies, taking on the Aequi-Volsci coalition from two sides. The Aequi retreated – technically a victory for Rome – but with at least 6000 Roman casualties. In a little over 60 years, the Roman Republic had gained ascendancy over their nearest neighbors – the Etruscans and Latins – and were preparing to deal with the threatening Apennine hill tribes when an unexpected foe suddenly invaded.

The Senones were a Gallic tribe of the Celtic people from the Seine basin in northern France. As their population grew, part of this tribe crossed the Alps, invading northern Italy and founding what is now Milan. In 387 BC, these Celtic people collided with Rome. The Senones had learned about central Italy's rich farmland from a young man named Aruns who lived in the Etruscan city of Clusium. When the king's son seduced his wife, the bitter Aruns left his city to sell wine, figs, and olives in northern Italy, where he encountered the Senones. The Gauls were fascinated with his products, and Aruns saw an avenue for revenge. He told them he came from a fertile land, sparsely populated with inept fighters. They could easily take the land for their own and enjoy this wine and food every day.

So, the Gauls marched on Clusium, who desperately asked Rome for aide. Rome sent three ambassadors – the Fabii brothers – who cautioned the Senone people not to attack Clusium unless they wanted to fight Rome. A scuffle broke out, and one ambassador killed a Senone chieftain, breaking the *Law of Nations* that ambassadors couldn't engage in violence.

The Senones sent ambassadors to Rome, demanding Rome hand over the three Fabii brothers in payment for their chieftain. The Senate didn't want to offend the Gauls, but the Fabii gens was so powerful that the three brothers had just been elected as military tribunes. Outraged, the Gallic ambassadors took word of this back to Clusium, and the Senones marched on Rome.

The Romans were thunderstruck when the Senones swiftly marched against them in the Battle of the Allia (around 387 BC), led by their Celtic chieftain Brennes. Rome was unprepared and outnumbered. Rome's army marched out, crossed the Tiber, and met the Celts about ten miles north of Rome.

The army positioned themselves with two flanks, with the most inexperienced warriors on the hill to the right flank. The Senone chieftain, Brennus, put his strongest men on the side facing the hill. When the two forces collided, the weaker Roman flank on the hill was pushed back, and the flank on the left was pinned against the river. The Gauls charged the sparse middle ranks of the Romans, dividing the army in two.

In a panic, both flanks of the Roman army retreated in a disorderly flight. The panic-stricken left flank attempted to swim across the river, but the inexperienced swimmers or those with heavy armor were drowned. The survivors fled to Veii as the remnants of the right flank fled back to Rome. At least half of the Roman army perished, while the Senones suffered few casualties.

The Celts were astonished by their swift, extraordinary victory. They spent two days looting the Roman camp and then set off for Rome. Reaching the city just before sunset, they were startled to see the city gates open and unarmed. Not wanting to battle at night in unfamiliar territory, they set up camp near Rome.

The men in Veii thought they were the only survivors and that Rome was lost. In the city, meanwhile, the people were in hysterics, thinking that most of their army had been wiped out. They didn't know part of their army was sheltering in Veii. The remnant of the army, any able-bodied men, and their leaders headed up the Capitoline Hill with weapons and food and as many valuables and sacred items as they could carry. Fencing off the hill, they hunkered down.

The common people grabbed what provisions they could, barricaded their houses and streets, and bolted. When the Gauls arrived two days later, most of the city had emptied. But many priests and the elderly men who had served as consuls stayed. Dressing in their ceremonial robes, they swept into the Forum and sat in their ivory chairs, waiting.

The Senone Gauls were amazed by the aged Roman priests and statesmen sitting stoically in their ivory chairs.

On the third day, the Senones arrived, entering the open gate tentatively, fearing an ambush. Finding no one around, they plundered the city. Arriving at the Forum, they found the ancient priests and former consuls in their magnificent robes, sitting majestically on their ivory thrones. The Gauls stood in reverence, not sure what to do, wondering if the men were gods. Finally, one stroked the beard of an aged Patrician, who indignantly smacked him on the head with his ivory staff. At that provocation, Gauls slaughtered the aged men in the Forum and anyone else they found in the city.

The Gauls looted and burned the city, destroying valuable documents of Roman history and holding Rome for seven months. They could not take the Capitoline Hill – it was so steep that the small force at the summit held them off. Meanwhile, the Roman soldiers who had fled to Veii were regrouping and stockpiling arms.

The Senones were raiding the surrounding countryside and towns for food and made the unfortunate mistake of raiding the farms near the town of Ardea. A former Roman dictator, Camillus, lived in Ardea, exiled by his political enemies. Learning that the Gauls were prone to getting drunk at night, Camillus and the men of Ardea attacked the Celtic camp at night, killing many men.

The Romans who had fled to towns and villages of the area asked Camillus to be their leader. He insisted it be official, so a young man snuck back to Rome, scaled the steepest part of the Capitoline Hill, and got approval from the senators for Camillus to be appointed dictator again. As official dictator, Camillus then mustered a 12,000-man army of the remaining Roman soldiers, the men of Ardea, and allies from Veii and other cities.

Back in Rome, the Senones noticed the places where rocks and plants had been torn away as the young Roman had scaled the Capitoline hill. That night, a group followed the same path up the hill, unheard by the sleeping guards at the top. But the sacred geese of Juno's temple on the summit awakened and charged the Gauls, honking, pecking, and flapping their wings. The clamor woke the Romans, who fended off the Senones.

The Romans on the Capitoline hill had run out of food. They were comforted to learn that part of the army was alive and well in Veii but had no idea how long it would be for Camillus to muster an army. The Senones were also in a bad way, surrounded by the corpses of the Romans they had killed but not buried, suffering from the heat, and decimated by malaria and dysentery. Their chieftain Brennus and the Roman military tribune Sulpicius met together; the Romans agreed to pay one thousand pounds in gold for the Gauls to immediately vacate the city and surrounding country.

When the Romans weighed out the gold, they felt cheated by the Senone's scale. With an evil laugh, Brennus stripped off his sword belt, and threw his sword and belt on the scale, adding to the weight. "Woe to the vanquished!" he smirked.

Just at that moment, Camillus arrived with his thousands of soldiers, marching right up to where the confrontation over the gold was taking place. Lifting the gold from the scales, he handed it to his attendants, then ordered the Gauls to take their scale and leave. "Rome will be delivered by iron, not gold!"

The Roman Consul Camillus confronts the Gallic Chieftain Brennus over the gold.
https://commons.wikimedia.org/wiki/File:Sebastiano_Ricci_-_Camillus_Rescuing_Rome_from_Brennus_-_27.537_-_Detroit_Institute_of_Arts.jpg

Brennus sputtered in outrage, but Camillus asserted the contract was not legally binding: as the elected dictator of Rome, it was made without his agreement. After a small skirmish,

Brennus and his men abandoned Rome and camped about eight miles away. The following day, Camillus' army attacked; according to Livy, the Gauls were slaughtered, with not even a messenger to report the great massacre.

Samnite soldiers march to war, as depicted in a fourth century BC tomb frieze in Nola, Campania.
https://commons.wikimedia.org/wiki/File:Samnite_soldiers_from_a_tomb_frieze_in_N ola_4th_century_BCE.jpg

After rebuilding its city and population, Rome was embroiled in three wars with the Samnite tribe of the Apennine Mountains from 343 to 290 BC. The struggle for control of central and southern Italy also involved the Etruscans, Senones, Umbri, Picentes, and more. Rome ultimately defeated all the Etruscan and Latin tribes and consolidated dominion over the area.

The first war began when the Samnites attacked Campania, who asked Rome for help. The Campanians wanted a treaty, but Rome couldn't, as they already had a treaty with the Samnites. So, the Campanians surrendered, making themselves a possession of Rome. Rome then sent envoys to the Samnites, asking them not to harass Campania as this was now Roman territory. Defiantly, the Samnites ordered their armies to immediately march against Campania and raze it. When further negotiations failed, Rome declared war on the Samnites and won three battles, ending the first war.

In 328 BC, Rome founded a settlement at Fregellae on the ruins of a Volsci town the Samnites had destroyed. The nearby

Volscian towns of Fabrateria and Luca asked Rome to be their overlords in exchange for protection from the Samnites. This instigated the Second Samnite War. As tensions between the Samnites and Rome flared for several years, Rome assiduously formed alliances with the surrounding tribes, such as the Lucanians and the Apulians in the southernmost part of Italy. Meanwhile, the Samnites had allied with the Vestini.

In 321 BC, the Samnites spread the rumor they were preparing to attack the city of Lucera, a Roman ally. A Roman army quickly marched that way, taking the fastest route through the Caudine Forks in the Apennine Mountains, where they had to pass through a narrow ravine. Before they arrived, the Samnites blocked the furthest end of the ravine with tree trunks and boulders. Once the Romans entered the ravine, they blocked the other end, trapping the Roman army in the ravine.

Gaius, the Samnite commander, ordered the Romans to surrender, evacuate their territory, and pull out from their new colonies. The Romans were forced to surrender, passing under the humiliating "yoke" of one spear resting on two others, where they had to bow, one by one. Following this, Rome determined the treaty was invalid because it hadn't been made by the consuls, so the war resumed. Rome defiantly established colonies in Samnite areas, which did not go well for the colonists – the Samnites killed most of them.

In 312 BC, the Etruscans took advantage of Rome's preoccupation with Samnium and mobilized their forces against cities allied with Rome. In one battle, Rome prevailed, and the Etruscans fled into the dark and fearful Ciminian Forest, which Romans dreaded entering. The consul's brother, Marcus Fabius, spoke Etruscan and volunteered to enter the forest posing as an Etruscan shepherd. He came to the town of Camerinum in Umbria, where the locals provided him with soldiers and supplies to fight the Etruscans. Together they crossed the forest and decimated the Cimian Mountain region.

The enraged Etruscans mustered their largest army in history, marching against the forces of Quintus Fabius (Marcus' brother). Quintus launched a surprise attack on the Etruscans at dawn, routing the Etruscans. Three Etruscan cities – Perusia, Cortona, and Arretium – agreed to a 30-year truce with Rome. Despite great losses, the Romans won a decisive victory against the Etruscans in the ferocious, drawn-out Battle of Lake Vadimo, thwarting the Etruscan strength. The entire Etruscan army sued for peace, agreeing to a one-year truce and offering a tribute of two tunics and one year's pay to every Roman soldier.

Now Rome gave its full focus to the Samnites. In 305 BC, both consuls marched on Samnium. Together, in a series of savage battles, their armies brilliantly vanquished the Samnites, who negotiated for peace. At the end of this war, Rome took over the regions of the Hernici and Aequi people, most of whom had allied with Samnium, and parts of Volsci and Sabine territory. But peace only lasted several years.

The Third Samnite War raged from 298 to 290 BC. The Etruscans were momentarily distracted by an invasion of the Gauls, but they bribed them to leave so they could assault Rome. As rumors floated that both the Samnites and Etruscans were raising colossal armies, Rome allied with the tribes surrounding Samnium. The Samnites allied with the Etruscans and hired the Gauls as mercenaries, but they were no match for Rome. With 15,000 troops and 12,000 allies, Rome marched on Etruria and routed their army, killing 8000 soldiers.

Meanwhile, the Samnites were raiding Roman colonies in Campania. In the Battle of Sentinum in 295 BC, Rome took on the combined forces of Samnites, Etruscans, Umbrians, and Gauls. In this deadly confrontation, Rome lost 8700 men but killed 20,000 of the coalition enemies. In the next few years, the Samnites rallied new forces but were defeated in daring attacks by the two Roman consuls, sealing the doom of the Samnites. Rome then turned to the Sabines, crushing them and annexing their territory. Rome conquered or allied with the remaining Latin tribes. The Roman war machine was now fixated on conquering the Mediterranean.

Chapter 6: Expansion to the South

Everyone enjoys victories, big or small, but a *pyrrhic victory* costs so much to win that the hard-fought triumph seems meaningless. That's what happened to Pyrrhus, King of Epirus, remembered as the ruler who defeated Rome and Carthage in multiple battles yet reportedly said, "If we win another such battle against the Romans, we will be completely lost."

The series of battles known as the Pyrrhic War (280-275 BC) involved Rome, the Greek states of Italy, Epirus, Egypt, Sicily, Carthage, and the tribes of central and southern Italy – mainly the Samnites and Etruscans.

The war started when Rome violated a naval agreement with the city of Tarentum. Rome controlled part of southern Italy, but Tarentum (in the heel of Italy's boot) was the most important city of the *Magna Graecia* (Greater Greece) colonies. Founded by the Spartans, Tarentum was a cultural and economic center – the primary commercial port for southern Italy. With about 300,000 people, it was among the most populated cities in the world at that time.

Rome's increasing power was worrying the Tarentines, especially after the Samnites – their former allies – were defeated. With the most powerful navy in Italy, Tarentum quickly formed an agreement with Rome prohibiting Roman ships from entering the Gulf of Taranto.

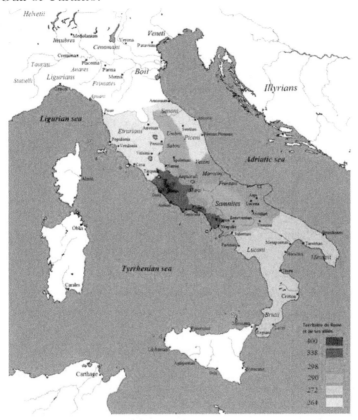

This map shows Rome's expansion of power over the Italian peninsula from 400 BC to
shortly after the end of the Pyrrhic War.
User:Javierfv1212, CC0, via Wikimedia Commons
https://en.wikipedia.org/wiki/Pyrrhic_War#/media/File:Conqu%C3%AAte_romaine_de_l'Italie_(400-264).png

In 282 BC, a Roman fleet was transporting troops to their
garrison in Thurii, on the far side of the Gulf of Taranto from
Tarentum; technically, Rome had broken the agreement even
before a tempest blew ten ships toward Tarentum's shores. The
infuriated Tarentines believed this was an intentional, aggressive
act violating their pact, so they promptly sunk four Roman ships
and captured another. The Tarentine navy then sailed across the
gulf to Thurii, aided that city's democrats to overcome and exile
the aristocrats, and forced the Roman garrison in Thurii to
withdraw.

Rome sent their diplomats to work things out with Tarentum, but the hostile Tarentines broke off the peace talks and insulted Rome's ambassador. In retaliation, the Roman Senate declared war on the Tarentines, who called on an old ally who owed them a favor. Pyrrhus was the king of Epirus (now mostly Albania), just across the Ionian Sea from Italy's heel. Tarentum had aided King Pyrrhus in conquering the island of Corcyra (Corfu), so now it was his turn to help them. Pyrrhus agreed to help Tarentum, mainly because he was keenly interested in gaining a foothold in Italy - he had ambitions for his own empire like his cousin Alexander the Great.

After borrowing warriors, funding, horses, and elephants from his brother-in-law Ptolemy II, Pharoah of Egypt, Pyrrhus set sail across the Strait of Otranto toward Italy. He arrived in the Gulf of Taranto in 280 BC, with 25,000 soldiers, including 3000 elite soldiers and 20 war elephants (guided by their Indian mahouts). Pyrrhus sent envoys to Rome, letting them know he had arrived in Italy and was eager to help them mediate their dispute with Tarentum.

The Romans scoffed at this, mobilizing eight legions (about 80,000 soldiers) divided into four armies. They sent two armies to Vanusia and Etruria to engage the Samnites, Lucanians, and Etruscans, preventing them from assisting Pyrrhus. The third army stayed home to protect Rome, while the last army of 30,000 men, led by Publius Valerius Laevinus, marched toward Tarentum, plundering Lucania on the way.

This terracotta doll from Tarentum dates to the third century BC, about the time of the Pyrrhic War.

Before charging into battle against the Romans, it became glaringly apparent to Pyrrhus that the Tarentines he had come to rescue were incapable of saving themselves. Plutarch said they were happy to let Pyrrhus go to war on their behalf while they stayed behind enjoying their baths and festivals and defending their city through valiant speeches. Pyrrhus sternly forbade frivolities as inappropriate during wartime: he closed their gymnasia and parks and outlawed drunkenness, festivals, and any revelry. He then called up all the able-bodied men for service in the military. Unaccustomed to being ordered about, many men left the city, considering it slavery not to live as they pleased.

When Pyrrhus received word that the Roman consul Laevinus was swiftly marching south with a huge army, he was irritated that his expected allied forces had not yet arrived. He decided not to wait on them because any delay would give time for the Romans to advance even further. He sent another envoy to the Romans, offering his services as an arbiter for the Greek states in Italy. Laevinus answered that they didn't need a mediator with the Greeks, nor did they fear him.

Pyrrhus had no choice but to march forward, setting up camp on the opposite side of the river Siris from the Romans. He rode up a bluff overlooking the river, where he could view the Roman camp. The Greeks used the word *bárbaros* (barbarian) to designate anyone who wasn't Greek – who lacked what they considered civilized ways. After observing the Romans' discipline and order, he remarked, "These barbarians aren't barbarous; we shall see what they amount to."

The first battle took place in Heraclea (in the arch of Italy's boot), about halfway between Thurii and Tarentum. With his Tarentine allies, Pyrrhus had 35,000 troops positioned on the left bank of the Siris river, which the Romans had to cross before the battle. He intended to begin with a charge of his 3000 men on horseback and 20 elephants.

As the Romans crossed the river at dawn, Pyrrhus' calvary successfully broke up their lines. Yet Pyrrhus met an army that was stronger and more disciplined than any he'd ever encountered. In the heat of the ferocious battle, Pyrrhus fearfully switched his armor with one of his lieutenants, so he wouldn't be recognized and targeted. The man wearing his armor became the focus of the Roman forces, who killed him. His men believed the dead man was their king and panicked, forcing Pyrrhus to take off his helmet, so they could recognize his face. The Greeks cheered and pressed on with the battle.

Pyrrhus sends out his secret weapon – war elephants!
https://commons.wikimedia.org/w/index.php?curid=32722047

Finally, Pyrrhus released the mighty war elephants. The Romans had never encountered elephants in battle before; their foot soldiers staggered at the sight of the massive animals while their terrified horses stampeded away. Pyrrhus then sent his cavalry charging into the Roman forces, routing them and winning the victory for the Greeks. However, one of Pyrrhus's elephants was wounded, and the panicked animal charged, crushing a segment of Pyrrhus' own army.

The casualties were colossal for both sides, even though reports differed on how many died that day: ranging from 7000 to 15,000 Romans and 4000 to 13,000 Greeks. The Romans lost more men, but they still had three other armies ready to move into place. For Pyrrhus, replacing thousands of troops would be almost impossible. Fortunately for him, several Italic tribes – the Lucanians, Messapians, and Bruttians – joined forces with him, as did two Greek cities in southern Italy – Croton and Locri. Advancing north, he allied with the Samnites, Rome's former enemy.

Once again, Pyrrhus offered to make peace with Rome, and once again, Rome rejected the offer. Pyrrhus then tried to conquer Campania, but by that time, the Romans had reinforced their army in that region. Brazenly, he even attempted to take Rome but found its fortifications too strong. Meanwhile, the Romans had allied with the Etruscans and had sent word to the other consul Curuncanius. Pyrrhus realized three armies were rapidly closing in on him: Rome's garrisons, Consul Laevinus from the south, and Curuncanius from the north. He quickly withdrew from the area and wintered in Tarentum.

King Pyrrhus spent the winter rebuilding his forces, calling in troops from Macedonia and his allies on the Ionian Peninsula. In the spring of 279 BC, Pyrrhus set out once again to dominate Italy with a 40,000-man army confronting Rome's forces on the opposite banks of a river. Cassius Dio said the river's strong current made it difficult to ford. The Romans politely asked Pyrrhus if he preferred to cross over to their side for the battle. If so, they promised to back off and not interfere with his troops while they crossed. Pyrrhus said they could cross over to his side unmolested, as he had great faith that his elephants would win the day.

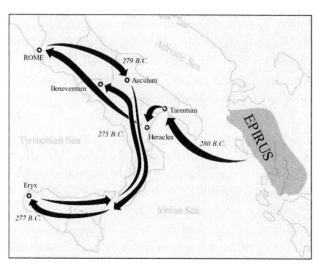

This map traces Pyrrhus' battles in the Pyrrhic War: Heraclea, Rome, Asculum, and finally Maleventum (renamed Beneventum).

For two days, the Romans and Greeks fought at a place called Asculum. This time, the Romans were prepared for the elephants. First, the Romans fought in forested terrain on uneven ground, which deterred the charging elephants and horses. Second, they had devised ingenious ox-drawn wagons, with tall iron beams that had spears attached, bristling in all directions; lined up, they blocked the elephants from advancing. Using small catapults, they could shoot fiery projectiles and other ammunition from their 300 anti-elephant wagons.

At the beginning of the battle, the Romans prevailed over the Greeks, slowly but firmly forcing them back. The fighting was fierce, and many were killed or wounded before nightfall interrupted the battle. In the morning, Pyrrhus brought the elephants out but had them enter the battlefield at each end, avoiding the wagons. The sight of the elephants terrified the Romans' horses even before they drew close, and once again, the Roman cavalry broke up as the frantic horses stampeded. However, the undaunted Roman foot soldiers held firm.

At the end of the battle, between 6000 to 8000 Romans lay dead or wounded on the field, but it seemed to Pyrrhus that Rome replenished their forces like a gushing fountain, remaining resolute and courageous. Even though the Greek casualties were lighter – around 3500 – Pyrrhus was exhausted and unnerved by the savage battle. Just as the fighting was winding down at sunset, the Romans destroyed his camp as they were retreating, and he was pierced by a javelin. Most of his commanders were dead, and his Italian allies were hesitant and ambiguous – fearing the wrath of Rome should Pyrrhus lose. "One more victory like that, and we're finished!"

Pyrrhus requested more funds and military forces, preparing for his next assault. While the Romans were likewise regrouping, a man named Nicias, who had been among the allies supporting Pyrrhus, approached the Roman consul Fabricius, offering to assassinate King Pyrrhus. Fabricius found this an outrageous affront to Roman honor, taking pride in defeating the enemy through valor, military strength, and strategy. He sent envoys to Pyrrhus, alerting him of the plot.

Astonished, Pyrrhus released his Roman prisoners of war, sending them back to Rome with renewed offers of peace. For his treachery, Nicias was executed and flayed – straps formed from his skin were made into a chair. Rome replied to offers of peace by requesting Pyrrhus leave Italy. Rome also renewed their alliance with Carthage due to mutual concerns about Pyrrhus' potential involvement in Sicily, which might jeopardize Carthage's colonies there. This alliance was a blow to Pyrrhus, who had hoped to pit one nation against the other, distracting them from his schemes for Italy and Sicily.

Pyrrhus sailed to Sicily when Syracuse and other Greek cities on the island offered him rule over them in exchange for defending them from Carthage and ridding them of tyrants. The Macedonians also sent him an offer – the throne of their country – their king had just been captured and beheaded by the Gauls. Pyrrhus liked Sicily better: it was closer to Africa, and he had his sights set on eventually conquering Carthage.

Pyrrhus' abrupt departure from Italy aggravated the Tarentines, who had grown weary of his tyrannical rule over their city. They demanded he either continue fighting Rome or leave Italy for good. The Romans were amazed Pyrrhus suddenly interrupted the war but pleased for the opportunity to bring the

Samnites back in line and gain control over the Lucanians and Bruttians who had thrown their lot in with Pyrrhus.

The Romans immediately set to work, conquering Croton and Lokrami – Greek cities that had allied with Pyrrhus. Tarentum and Regi alone remained as independent city-states. The Roman consuls Junius and Rufinus invaded Samnium, devastating the rural farms and taking over some deserted forts. While Junius remained in Samnium to continue wreaking havoc, Rufinus moved on to harass the Lucanians and Bruttians.

This ancient Greek theater in Syracuse, Sicily, built from 450 to 400 BC, was standing when Pyrrhus arrived.

Arriving in Sicily in 278 BC, Pyrrhus found Syracuse already under attack by Carthage. The Carthaginians realized that Pyrrhus' forces were modest in size and not especially strong, so they ruthlessly attacked his army repeatedly, attempting to drive him out of Sicily. Pyrrhus did capture two Sicilian cities – Panormus and Eryx – but eventually left the island after three years due to the Carthaginians' constant harassment. No sooner did he sail away than Panormus and Eryx overthrew his rule.

Pyrrhus arrived back in southern Italy, met by the irate Tarentines disgusted with him for pulling out in the middle of things and leaving the Samnites and Lucanians vulnerable to Rome. Most of the resentful Samnites had no future interest in allying with him against Rome. He had only 20,000 troops left, but he was determined to gain a foothold in Italy. He devised a strategy for his third and final attack.

Pyrrhus divided his army into two divisions – each would fight one army of the two Roman consuls: Cornelius Lentulus and Manius Curius. Pyrrhus led one division toward Maleventum (meaning *bad arrival* or *evil omen*), where Curius was stationed, marching through the night in hopes of a surprise attack before Lentulus could come to his aid. This tactic did not go well for Pyrrhus and his men.

Rather than taking the main road, Pyrrhus chose a longer route through the woods where they would be unseen and able to preserve the element of surprise. But after a few hours, their torches burnt out, and they got lost navigating through unfamiliar territory in the dark. They wandered off the paths used by people and mistakenly followed goat-paths that veered here and there, up steep crags of rock and down into deep ravines.

The troops got separated from each other, and by the time they finally staggered into Maleventum, it was an ominously bad arrival: they were weak and fatigued, overcome with thirst, and the elephants were jittery. To make matters worse, they stumbled out of the woods at dawn on the top of a hill, easily seen from miles around by Curius' troops assembled in the valley below, ruining all hopes of a surprise attack.

Within moments, Curius led a charge from their camp against Pyrrhus and his army, even capturing some elephants. The battle moved down toward the level ground of the plain, where Curius routed some of Pyrrhus' exhausted troops. Then an elephant charge forced the Romans to retreat to their camp, but the camp guards on the ramparts threw their javelins at the elephants, who turned around and charged off. The Romans had finally learned how to deal with war elephants by spearing their sides, a tactic they later used against Carthage. The out-of-control elephants charged back through Pyrrhus' ranks, crushing men and throwing the troops into pandemonium. The battle was disastrous for Pyrrhus. He so desperately needed a victory, but instead of even a pyrrhic victory, he suffered a humiliating loss to the Romans at Maleventum.

Then the Samnites demanded his aid. They had stuck their necks out for him, and now the Romans were making their lives miserable. When Pyrrhus arrived to assist the Samnites in the battle against the Romans, an adolescent elephant was wounded. Shaking off his Indian mahout (driver), he charged off trumpeting for his mother. Hearing him, the agitated mother elephant stirred up the other elephants, and soon everything was in confusion – another catastrophe. The Romans scored an extraordinary victory, capturing eight elephants, killing many soldiers, and occupying the Samnite's entrenchments.

Pyrrhus escaped to Tarentum with only a few horsemen and quickly sailed to Epirus, leaving behind a small detachment in Tarentum. His victories in Italy and Sicily were fruitless; he returned home with nothing to show for it. The Tarentines who had invited him much hoped he would stay away, as their situation was much worse than before he came to their aid. As a parting gift, Pyrrhus left the Tarentines the chair made from Nicias' skin.

Pyrrhus never returned to Italy, although he vowed he would. Three years later, while engaged in battle in Argos in southern Greece, an old lady on a rooftop threw a tile down at him, which hit him in the neck and knocked him from his horse. He lay paralyzed in the street until a Macedonian soldier cut off his head. When word of this traveled back to Italy, the Tarentines surrendered to Rome, continuing as a self-ruled city, but with Roman laws and a Roman garrison. The Greek city-states in Italy quickly followed.

Dogged perseverance had won the day for Rome. The Romans celebrated their victory over Pyrrhus by renaming the city of Maleventum (*bad arrival* or *evil omen*) to Beneventum (*welcome* or *good omen*). Soon, the Appian Way would connect the town to Rome. By 272 BC, the Latins, Etruscans, Samnites, and other Italic tribes came under complete submission, making Rome the established ruler of Italy, except for the Gauls to the far north.

Rome was now poised to go forward and conquer the civilizations surrounding the western Mediterranean Sea. Their only plausible contender was Carthage.

Chapter 7: The Punic Wars

In an enthralling struggle for supremacy, Rome and Carthage clashed in three epic wars spanning eight decades from 264 to 146 BC. The legendary feats of the Punic Wars included the Romans building 120 ships in 60 days, Hannibal crossing the Alps with his war elephants, and Scipio ingeniously deflecting an elephant charge back toward the Carthaginians, crushing their ranks. Both Rome and Carthage suffered horrific casualties, and the outcome affected the Western world for centuries to come.

Why were they called *Punic* Wars? *Punicus* is Latin for Phoenician - the people of Tyre who fled with Queen Dido to North Africa, where they built the new city of Carthage. When a tempest blew Aeneas's ships to her shores, a passionate romance ignited - until Aeneas abandoned Dido to sail to Italy. Just before Dido committed suicide, she prophesied unending wars between their descendants, and now those wars were happening.

It all started with Messana (Messina) in Sicily, just across the Strait of Messina from the toe of Italy's boot. The city had given refuge to the Mamertines - Italian mercenaries - who returned the kindness by attacking and killing the entire population, sparing only the younger women to be their wives. These desperados transformed the peaceful Messana into the hub of their pirate raids on land and sea.

After the Mamertine pirates ravaged Sicily's coast for 20 years, an exasperated Hiero II, king of Syracuse - 100 miles down the coast from Messana - resolved to rid Sicily of the marauders. Marching north, he successfully dispatched most of the Mamertines forces, then closed in on Messana. As it happened, a fleet from Carthage was harboring in Messana, and the Mamertines called on them for assistance. Unwilling to get involved with Carthage, Hiero withdrew.

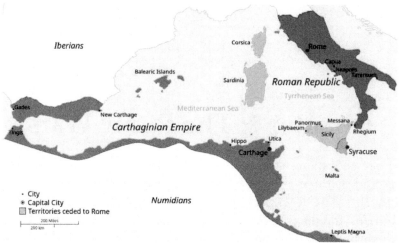

This map depicts Rome and Carthage's territory just before the First Punic War.
GalaxMaps, CC BY-SA 4.0 <https://creativecommons.org/licenses/by-sa/4.0>, via Wikimedia Commons https://commons.wikimedia.org/wiki/File:First_Punic_War_237_BC.png

The Mamertines expected the Carthaginians to leave, but instead, they established a garrison in Messana. The Mamertines weren't too happy with that state of affairs - it infringed on their pirating escapades. Four years later, Hiero attacked again; this time, the Mamertines appealed to Rome for protection. Rome was wary of the pirates but didn't want Carthage to expand its power in Messana, only six miles across the Strait of Messina from the toe of Italy's boot. Rome agreed to ally with the Mamertines, who then convinced the Carthaginian garrison to leave.

Rome deployed 16,000 men to Sicily - the first time their military had ever left the Italian peninsula. Alarmed, Syracuse approached Carthage for protection. Hanno, commander of the Carthaginian forces, first crucified the garrison commander who left Messana without orders. Next, the allied Syracusan and Carthaginian armies marched to Messana, where the Romans brutally defeated them.

Rome then attacked Syracuse. Hieron surrendered and allied with Rome, allowing him to remain in power. In 262 BC, Carthage sent new forces to Acragas (Agrigento) in southeastern Sicily. Both Roman consuls leading four legions savagely attacked Acragas and sacked the city, selling the population into slavery. This eye-opener influenced Segesta, in northeast Sicily, to revolt against Carthage and ally with Rome, swaying other cities to likewise defect from Carthage.

After several engagements with the Carthaginian navy – the greatest in the world at that time – Rome realized it needed a substantial naval force to take on Carthage's war machine. At manic speed, Rome astonishingly built a fleet of 100 heavy warships in only two months, using a shipwrecked Carthaginian quinquereme as a guide. The oar-powered, 50-meter-long quinqueremes could carry 420 sailors and soldiers, providing power, speed, and reasonable maneuverability in marine battles. They also built 20 smaller triremes propelled by oars and sails.

As novice sailors, Rome could not compete with the experienced Carthaginian marine tactics, so they had to devise an ingenious way to bring their superior combat skills into play. They developed an 11-meter-long *corvus* – a gangplank that could hook onto the enemy's ship – allowing the Romans to board and engage in the hand-to-hand combat in which they excelled. The ships also carried catapults for flinging missiles (often burning) that pummeled the enemy ships.

This Roman mosaic from Tunisia shows a trireme vessel during the Roman Empire.
Mathiasrex, CC BY-SA 3.0 <http://creativecommons.org/licenses/by-sa/3.0/>, via Wikimedia Commons https://commons.wikimedia.org/wiki/File:Romtrireme.jpg

The brilliant corvus boarding tactic ushered in immediate victory over Carthage's 130 ships in the 260 BC Battle of Mylae (Milazzo) and again in the 258 BC Battle of Sulci, where the Carthaginians crucified the losing commander. Bolstered by these extraordinary successes, the Romans sailed from Italy toward Africa to attack Carthage itself, having increased their fleet to 330 ships carrying 140,000 men.

The Carthaginians mustered 350 ships, intercepting the Romans off the coast of Sicily in the unforgettable Battle of Cape Ecnomus – the largest naval battle in history, with 680 ships and 300,000 men in the two navies. After a long day of confounding conflict, the Romans won a decisive victory over Carthage, sinking 30 of their ships and capturing 64, while losing 24 Roman ships. About 10,000 Romans were killed, compared to three to four times as many Carthaginians.

Having scored a stunning naval victory, the Romans confidently sailed on to Africa, winning a land battle only 10 miles south of Carthage, where the rough terrain impeded their enemies' elephants. Unfortunately for the Romans, Carthaginians counterattacked, led by the Spartan general Xanthippus, with 100 elephants and 4000 soldiers, surrounding and wiping out 12,000 Romans and capturing 500. The 2000 Romans who escaped the massacre were picked up by the Roman fleet that had just returned from Italy, but another disaster loomed ahead. When they were out to sea, a violent storm sunk all but 80 of their 400 ships and drowned up to 100,000 men – the greatest loss of life in a single shipwreck incident in history.

Returning to Sicily, the indomitable Romans rallied, capturing Panormus (Palermo) in 254 BC, enslaving everyone except any citizens who could pay a 200-drachmas fee. Meanwhile, Carthage overcame and razed Acragas. Rome suffered another crushing loss when 150 more ships were sunk in a storm as they were returning from a raid in North Africa. Two Carthaginian attacks on Sicily in 251 and 250 BC failed – in the second, the Romans even captured their elephants, shipping them back to Rome to entertain the citizens.

But Carthage won a sea battle the following year, capturing 93 of Rome's 120 ships. The Romans blamed their consul Claudius

Pulcher for bringing bad luck – he had thrown his sacred chickens overboard when they failed to give him a good omen and was put on trial for impiety when he returned to Rome. Then another disastrous storm sunk 800 Roman supply ships. By now, both sides were running out of supplies, ships, and men. The Egyptian Pharoah Ptolemy II declined Carthage's request to help with 2000 talents.

Hamilcar (Hannibal's father) was promoted as Carthage's remarkable new fleet commander. He brutally raided Italy's coast, then headed to Sicily in 244 BC to harass the Roman forces, earning the nickname *Barca* (lightning) for his swift guerrilla tactics that enabled him to capture Eryx, making it his base. Within two years, however, Rome had rebuilt their fleet to 200 ships, which they sensationally used to defeat the Carthaginian fleet, sinking 50 ships, capturing 70, and taking 10,000 prisoners of war. After two decades of war, a humiliated Carthage was forced to sue for peace in 241 BC – withdrawing completely from Sicily and paying Rome 3200 talents of silver. Thus, Sicily became Rome's first offshore province.

This win affected the large island of Sardinia, east of Italy, which had been settled by the sea-faring Phoenicians of Lebanon about the same time they were founding Carthage. Later, Carthage had taken control of these colonies and built new ones. When the First Punic War ended, these colonies revolted, allowing Rome to occupy the entire island without resistance.

This map depicts Rome and Carthage's territory immediately before the Second Punic War.

The Second Punic War began in Spain, where Carthage had been establishing colonies for several hundred years. The champion Hamilcar Barka victoriously extended Carthage's control to about half of the Iberian Peninsula, and his son Hannibal became Iberia's supreme commander in 221 BC. Following Rome's advice, the city of Saguntum on Spain's eastern coast resisted Carthage's control. Hannibal viciously retaliated in 219 BC by laying siege to Saguntum while Rome was distracted with an Illyrian revolt. Despite a serious javelin wound, Hannibal overcame Saguntum in eight months, killing every adult in the city.

Infuriated, Rome declared war. The Second Punic War – or the Hannibalic War – was a struggle between Carthage's formidable commander Hannibal and his nemesis – Rome's great general Scipio – who received the agnomen (honorable nickname) *Africanus* for his stunning North African military triumphs.

As Hannibal astutely anticipated, Rome sent 60 warships under Scipio's command to Spain – but by the time they arrived, Hannibal was executing his unbelievable surprise move far north of Spain. With 90,000 foot-soldiers, 12,000 cavalrymen, and 37 elephants, he marched up Spain's coast, fighting off local tribes, crossed the 11,000-foot-high Pyrenees into Gaul (France), and advanced toward the Alps.

Hannibal approached the Rhone River, knowing a tribe of Gauls was waiting to attack him on the other side. He diverted his lieutenant Hanno to cross the Rhone 25 miles upstream. Hanno then marched downstream, sneaking up behind the Gauls whose full attention was on Hannibal's men, boats, and especially the elephants – creatures the mountain people had never seen. The Gauls were riveted by the sight, ready to attack Hannibal as he crossed with his fleet of boats and rafts. Suddenly, Hanno's men launched a surprise rear attack, routing the Gauls so Hannibal's army could cross the river unmolested.

Now it was time to conquer the 13,000-foot-high Isère region of the Alps before the winter snows began. Depending on which route he took – and scholars are still arguing about that – the pass through the Alps would have been from 6500 to 9500 feet high.

As the men, horses, and elephants labored up the steep slopes, fierce mountain tribes dropped boulders on them.

This is a potential site of the landslide on the Col de la Traversette pass, which reaches 3,000 meters above sea level.

Hannibal's descent down the Alps on Italy's side was free of human attack, but steeper and treacherous, with deep snow and a narrow, icy path along the edge of the mountains – one misstep would send man or animal hurtling to the rocks a mile below. At one point, a landslide blocked the path. Hannibal attempted a detour, but the heavy snow was impassable. Finally, they cleared the rocks from the mountainside to make a level path and got the men, horses, and pack mules down to the tree line beyond the snow. It took another three days to get the starved elephants down.

Hannibal unexpectedly descended into Italy with the remnant of his army – 20,000 foot-soldiers, 6000 soldiers, and an unknown number of elephants. The Gauls of northern Italy, eager for another opportunity to take on Rome, joined Hannibal and the Carthaginians. Hannibal took swift advantage of Rome's lack of preparedness, overcoming the Romans in two disastrous battles in northern Italy in December 218 and in a third battle in June 217 at Lake Trasimene in central Italy – in that horrific battle, 15,000 Romans were killed and 10,000 captured.

The unstoppable Hannibal fought a spectacular campaign in August 216 against a much larger Roman army of 80,000 soldiers versus 50,000 Carthaginians in Cannae – in the heel of Italy's boot; 50,000 Romans were slaughtered compared to 5700 casualties (mostly Gauls). This influenced most of southern Italy's city-states to defect to Carthage, while the Latins and other tribes of central Italy stayed loyal to Rome.

Rome realized Hannibal's innovative strategies in battle made him indomitable, so their new strategy was to wear him down by using their navy to cut off access to new supplies and manpower. Meanwhile, in 209 BC, General Scipio Africanus scored a staggering win in Spain, capturing Carthage's treasury and supply base.

Elected as consul in 205 BC, the enterprising Scipio turned his attention to Africa. With 440 ships and 30,000 soldiers, he sailed to Tunisia, while Carthage mustered a force of 30,000 foot-soldiers and 3000 cavalrymen led by General Gisgo. Attacking in the dead of night with two divisions of Romans surging in from opposite sides, Scipio devastated the Carthaginians forces. Carthage rallied with reinforcements of African Numidians (a Berber tribe) who were outflanked and overwhelmed by Scipio's outstanding calvary.

Predicting that Rome would win the conflict, the shrewd Numidian King Masinissa defected to Rome, putting Carthage in grave danger from their former allies. Hannibal hurried to Carthage from Italy to defend his homeland, facing off against Scipio in the decisive final Battle of Zama in 202 BC.

Both the Romans and Carthaginians had to fend off the charging war elephants at the Battle of Zama

Although outnumbered, Hannibal's troops fought fiercely for their city, but Scipio deftly channeled Carthage's 80 war elephants through his ranks with minimal harm, then herded them back in a charge that laid havoc to Hannibal's men. While the Carthaginians were distracted with corralling the elephants, the Roman and Numidian horsemen circled round to the rear of Hannibal's forces, sandwiching them between Rome's foot-soldiers at the fore.

Rome won the day; 20,000 Carthaginians perished in the bloodbath, compared to 5000 Roman fatalities. Carthage conceded defeat; the terms of surrender included dismantling its navy, agreeing not to war against anyone without authorization from Rome, and paying a 50-year annual tribute to Rome of 200 talents of gold in war reparations.

Hannibal slipped away to exile in Ephesus, and Carthage paid its war debt for 50 years, maintaining friendly terms with Rome – even allying with Rome in several foreign military campaigns. But they chafed against Rome, forbidding them to war against the Numidians – who had been steadily capturing the territory surrounding Carthage under their King Masinissa. After half their territory had been taken, they sent 31,000 men in 150 BC to unsuccessfully defend the city of Oroscopa; most of these men were slaughtered by the Numidians.

Roman felt this act of aggression without permission – against Rome's ally – breached the treaty, even when Carthage explained their side of the story. Cato, one of Rome's censors, had been part of a senatorial embassy that visited Carthage in 152 BC to negotiate peace with the city and King Masinissa. The Second Punic War veteran was shocked at the wealth Carthage had accumulated – since they were no longer spending all their manpower and funding on conquering other lands, Carthage had been growing its economy.

Cato considered the city a great threat to Rome. "Carthago delendam est!" he cried out. "Carthage must be destroyed!" Repeatedly, Cato had been denouncing Carthage, ending all his speeches – even on unrelated topics – with "Carthago delendam est!" – "Carthage must be destroyed!"

At first, the Senate resisted Cato's demands for Carthage's destruction. The powerful Senator Corculum, the son-in-law of Scipio Africanus, argued that fear of Carthage preserved Roman unity. He ended all his speeches with, "Carthago sevanda est!" "Carthage must be saved!" However, once Carthage attacked King Masinissa and the Numidians, the senatorial debate swung to Cato's side. Carthage had gone to war without permission, and worse yet, against an ally of Rome.

The Senate sent an embassy to Carthage with their ultimatum: dismantle their army, surrender their arms, leave Carthage, and resettle inland. Carthage rejected Rome's terms, and the Third Punic War began with Rome sailing to North Africa with 80,000 foot-soldiers and 4000 cavalrymen, laying siege to the city of 200,000 for three years.

Initially, Carthage held up well with 21 miles of massive walls surrounding and protecting their city along with the sea on two sides and moats surrounding the rest. The Roman forces failed to block all the supplies coming into the city. Carthage counterattacked with fire-ships – older ships set on fire and quickly abandoned by the crew, which sailed into the Roman fleet, setting it on fire. The surrounding cities weren't capitulating as quickly as Rome had hoped. Despite sustained attacks, the Carthaginian city of Hippacra would not surrender to Rome. The Numidians' new king Bithyas sent 800 cavalrymen to assist

Carthage. Then, to the Carthaginians' glee, the Romans were hit by an epidemic in the 148 BC summer's heat.

This bronze statue found on the Quirinal in Rome is believed to be Scipio Aemilianus.
Carole Raddato from FRANKFURT, Germany, CC BY-SA 2.0
<https://creativecommons.org/licenses/by-sa/2.0>, via Wikimedia Commons
https://commons.wikimedia.org/wiki/File:Bronze_statue_of_a_Hellenistic_prince,_1st_half_of_2nd_century_BC,_found_on_the_Quirinal_in_Rome,_Palazzo_Massimo_alle_Terme,_Rome_(31479801364).jpg

This wasn't turning out to be the quick and easy war Rome was expecting. What could they do to turn things around? Step one was to elect Scipio Africanus' capable grandson Scipio Aemilianus as the new consul and commander of the Roman forces. He was about five years too young to meet the minimum age requirement of 41 for consul, but Rome disregarded the age limit, certain he would carry the day as his grandfather had in the past war.

Scipio Aemilianus set to work immediately, building an improved siege wall and a mole (breakwater) on the south side, blocking access to Carthage's harbors. The Carthaginians secretly built 50 new warships inside their walls, then opened a second harbor entrance and sailed them out against the Roman fleet. The Romans prevailed against the new fleet and successfully kept supply ships from entering the new passageway. Scipio then relentlessly attacked the walls, concentrating on the harbor. At night, the Carthaginians would silently swim across the harbor and set fire to the catapults and other siegeworks.

Finally, after three years, Rome broke through Carthage's walls in 146 BC, and soldiers poured into the city, fighting street by street and house by house against the citizens, who fiercely defended their city and homes. After a week of brutal hand-to-hand combat, Carthage was overcome. The 50,000 remaining citizens were sold into slavery, and Carthage was plundered and burned to the ground. Polybius wrote that Scipio wept as he watched the city burn, remembering the Fall of Troy and perhaps wondering if the same fate eventually awaited Rome.

The Fall of Carthage brought an end to that great city and its Phoenician civilization. Apart from a short-lived Roman colony soon after the war, the ruins were abandoned for a century until it was rebuilt as a Roman city by Julius Caesar and Caesar Augustus. With no more competition from Carthage, Rome now controlled the western Mediterranean, developing into a powerhouse of trade and military expansion, dominating much of the known world.

Chapter 8: Rome versus Greece

While embroiled with Hannibal in the Second Punic War, Rome was simultaneously engaged in intense wars with the Macedonian Kingdom, the Seleucid Empire, and the Achaean League in Corinth. Rome's struggles with these Greek empires, driven by complicated politics, continued until the same year that Carthage fell at the end of the Third Punic War.

When the Ptolemaic Empire of Egypt tottered, the Macedonian and Seleucid Empires surged forward to grasp power, prompting several Greek city-states to seek Rome's protection. Rome's involvement with these eastern empires wasn't so much a long-term plan of expansion but short-term goals in an unpredictable situation that affected Rome's alliances and provinces. Rome fought on Greece's mainland for the first time in the Macedonian wars.

The First Macedonian War (214-205 BC) began while Hannibal was wreaking havoc in Italy – pursuing a scorched-earth strategy of destroying anything that could sustain Rome's military machine: food stores, water sources, weapon manufacturing, and transportation venues. King Philip V of Macedonia entered into a treaty with Hannibal because Rome's increasing interference with Illyria and Epirus was disturbing Philip's empire-building schemes.

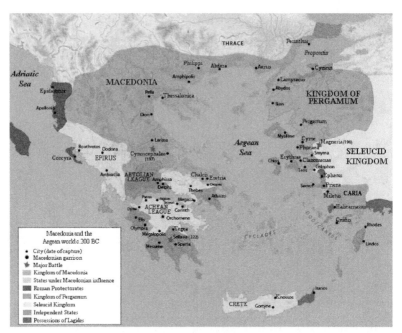

This map depicts Macedonia and the Aegean world just before the First Macedonian War.

Philip capitalized on Rome's crisis with Hannibal by targeting Rome's allies on the Adriatic coast. His treaty with Carthage stipulated mutual support – each would be the enemy of the other's enemies – the chief enemy being Rome. Philip's envoys had snuck into Italy to negotiate the treaty with Hannibal; on their way out, they were captured by the Romans, who seized the treaty document. The Romans weren't especially concerned about the alliance but determined to keep a short leash on Philip.

In 214 BC, Philip initiated a siege on Apollonia – a city in Illyria on the Adriatic Sea; Rome sent reinforcements to Apollonia, forcing Philip to retreat. The following year, Philip captured two strategic fortresses in Illyria. Rome needed an ally in the area, and the Aetolian League – a Greek tribal confederation on the Corinthian Gulf already hostile to Philip – seemed the best candidate. King Attalus of Pergamum (eastern Turkey) agreed to assist the League. Rome supplied 25 warships, while the Aetolians provided soldiers.

While Philip was off campaigning on his northern borders, the Aetolian League invaded Acarnania – Philip's ally in Greece's mainland. The Acarnanians hurried their women and children off to Epirus, swearing they would defeat the invaders or die trying. They prevailed over their menacing invaders until Rome's navy got involved, capturing the cities of Nasus, Oeniadae, and Zacynthus – which Rome handed over to the League.

In 211 BC, the joint forces of Rome and the Aetolian League captured Anticyra on the Gulf of Corinth. Rome sold the population into slavery, but Philip recaptured the territory. Philip then campaigned to drive the Aetolian League from Thessaly (on Greece's western coast), allying with Bithynia (northern Turkey). Sparta (in southernmost Greece) entered the war, siding with Rome and the Aetolian League, creating chaos for Philip.

Philip's formidable Macedonian-Bithynian forces successfully defeated the Aetolian-Spartan coalition in Greece's southern Peloponnese peninsula in 209 BC – convincing the Aetolian League to enter peace negotiations, which broke down when Rome's commander Sulpicius sailed in with a Roman fleet. However, Philip brilliantly defeated the Romans, taking Sicyon in the Peloponnese before he had to hurry home to defend against an invasion from Dardania on Macedonia's northern border.

In 208 BC, the fleets of Rome and Attalus patrolled the Aegean Sea, but Philip's forces nearly captured Attalus after slipping through the Thermopylae Pass – the "gates of fire" – a narrow passage with hot sulfur springs between Mount Kallidromo and the Gulf of Malia. Then Bithynia invaded Pergamum, compelling Attalus to withdraw completely from the war to fight off the invaders. Rome's fleet harbored on the island of Aegina, leaving the Corinthian Gulf undefended against Philip's campaigns; he captured several cities, then headed to the Peloponnese to fight the Spartans.

This didrachm of Philip V of Macedon is on display at the British Museum.
https://commons.wikimedia.org/wiki/File:Philip_V_of_Macedon_BM.jpg

Rome withdrew from the Aegean Sea, concentrating on protecting Illyria's coast on the Adriatic, their primary objective all along. With Attalus pulling out and Rome retreating to the Adriatic, the Aetolians and the Spartans were the only challengers to Philip and his Greek allies. Captain Philopoemen of Megalopolis in the Peloponnese defeated the Spartans, killing their commander Machanidas. Now the Aetolians were wide open for Philip's ferocious attacks – he drove them out of Thessaly and the Ionian Islands and sacked Thermum – their federation capital.

Pummeled by Philip and with no support from Rome, the Aetolian League sued for peace, stirring Rome to send an army of 10,000 foot-soldiers and 1000 cavalrymen to Illyria, but the League refused to join with Rome against Philip. Realizing that Carthage was losing the Second Punic War, Philip determined it was in his best interest to end his war before that happened – while he was ahead.

The Macedonians, Aetolians, and Romans formed the Peace of Phoenice Treaty in 205, ending the First Macedonian War. Philip had expanded his power to Greece's mainland and inland Illyria, while Rome was satisfied the Illyrian coast was no longer threatened. The treaty held for five years, until Rome finally conquered Hannibal, ending the Second Punic War.

A secret pact instigated the Second Macedonian War (200-197 BC). King Ptolemy IV of Egypt died in 204 BC, succeeded by his six-year-old son Ptolemy V. This led to chaos over who would be regent while the boy was growing up. Philip V of Macedonia plotted with Antiochus the Great of the Seleucid Empire to conquer Egypt's empire in its vulnerable state. If successful, Philip would get Cyrene and the Aegean Sea territories, and Antiochus would claim Egypt and Cyprus.

Before taking on Egypt, Philip wanted to subdue the Greek colonies bordering Macedonia in Thrace and near the Dardanelles Strait. His masterly conquest of Chios in the Aegean Sea disturbed nearby Rhodes and Pergamon – they had been eying Chios for themselves. Meanwhile, Antiochus was plowing through Coele-Syria, taking Damascus, Sidon, and Samaria. Alarmed, the Aetolian League solicited Rome's help against Philip and Antiochus, but Rome initially ignored their pleas.

Antiochus III (The Great), the ruler of the Seleucid Empire, plotted with Philip V to divide the Egyptian empire.
Photo: Bruckmann, CC0, via Wikimedia Commons
https://commons.wikimedia.org/wiki/File:Greece_from_the_Coming_of_the_Hellenes_to_AD._14,_page_287,_Antiochus_III.jpg

In 201 BC, Philip laid siege to the island of Samos, Egypt's marine base, and conquered the island of Miletus – both in the Aegean Sea. Meanwhile, Antiochus defeated the Anatolians in the Battle of Panium at the Jordan River's headwaters, ending the Egyptian Ptolemaic rule in Judea. The Jews opened the gates of Jerusalem to Antiochus - preferring Seleucid rule over Egyptian. Little did they know that his son, Antiochus *Epiphanes* (*God manifest*) - but called by his haters Antiochus *Epimames* (*the madman*) - would place an idol to Zeus and sacrifice a pig in Jerusalem's holy temple - defiling it and leading to the Maccabean Revolt.

By now, Rome had wrapped up their final, victorious war against Carthage. They still didn't think Philip and Antiochus threatened their interests, but they sent Commander Laevinus to investigate if there was cause for a "just war." Eventually, Rome sent Philip an ultimatum - he could keep Macedonia and Thrace, but he had to withdraw from Greece and stop aggressions in other places - especially Egypt.

Philip ignored Rome's ultimatum, which he received while laying siege to Abydos - the crossing point between Europe and Asia - in the Dardanelles. He warned Abydos the walls would be stormed in three days; anyone who wanted to surrender or commit suicide needed to do so by then. The citizens killed their women and children, threw their gold and jewels into the sea, then fought Philip's army until the city fell.

At this point, the Roman Senate, finally swayed by their new Consul Sulpicius, voted for war against Philip. Sulpicius mustered his troops - many who had just returned from fighting Carthage in Africa - and sailed across the Adriatic. Philip and Sulpicius faced off in 200 BC in the Dassaretae territory, but after a couple of skirmishes, Philip received word that the Dardanians were invading Macedonia, so he and his men slipped away at night to defend his borders.

The Romans were surprised to wake up the next morning to find Philip's troops gone. Sulpicius chased after Philip, ravaging his land on the way. Philip sent half of his army to the north to fight Dardania and led the other half south to meet Sulpicius. But by this time, Sulpicius had turned back and was back on his fleet launching attacks on Macedonian military bases.

Meanwhile, in Rome, elections were held for the next two consuls. Consul Villius was sent to Corcyra to replace Sulpicius.

When he arrived, Villius encountered 2000 disgruntled veterans of the Third Punic War, resentful that they'd been given no break between wars. Villius spent most of his one-year term sorting out the Roman military, then two new consuls were voted in.

The newly-elected Titus Quinctius Flamininus, only 31 years old (much younger than the age requirement of 41 for consuls), won the lottery for Macedonia. He speedily drove Philip out of most of Greece, and then confronted Philip in the Battle of Aous in Albania. The Macedonian army was in an impregnable position behind a pass, but a shepherd showed the Romans a secret path that led to the rear of their position, allowing them to launch a surprise attack with 2000 Macedonian casualties.

Flamininus' term was ending, but he was performing so well that Rome appointed him as proconsul, granting him authority to continue fighting Philip. In the 197 BC Battle of Cynoscephalae, fought against Philip in Thessaly, Flamininus had 20 of his own war elephants! At dawn, no one could see anything due to heavy fog that covered the hills and valley where the two armies met. But the elephants routed the Macedonian phalanx, and at least 8000 Macedonians were killed. Philip sued for peace, forced to abandon the Greek territories he had acquired and to stay within his borders.

This map depicts the Seleucid Empire in 200 BC, just before the war with Rome.
Thomas Lessman (Contact!), CC BY-SA 3.0 <https://creativecommons.org/licenses/by-sa/3.0>, via Wikimedia Commons, https://commons.wikimedia.org/w/index.php?curid=4079843

With Philip subdued, Rome turned its attention to his co-conspirator, Antiochus the Great of the Seleucid Empire. Rome had no problem with Antiochus retaining his previous empire, along with Egypt, but they wanted him out of Thrace. Antiochus felt Thrace belonged to him – for a brief window of time, it had belonged to his ancestors.

The Aetolian League in Greece, former allies of Rome, were now hostile to Rome and allied with Antiochus. They invited Sparta and Macedonia to join them. King Nabis of Sparta, resentful that Rome had taken his coastal cities, happily joined forces with the Aetolians. King Philip V didn't dare incur Rome's wrath again; instead, he assisted Rome against Antiochus.

In 192 BC, Nabis of Sparta won back several of his coastal towns. However, General Philopoemen of the Achaean League (Greek city-states in the southern Peloponnese peninsula) overpowered him, chasing him back to Sparta. Nabis appealed to the Aetolian League. In a heinous act of betrayal, they sent 1000 foot soldiers and 300 cavalrymen to Sparta, seemingly to aid the king, but assassinated him instead.

Meanwhile, Antiochus marshaled his forces and sailed to Greece with 10,000 troops, 500 cavalrymen, and six elephants, landing in Demetrius and taking on the Achaean League. Rome immediately sent two legions and ran Antiochus out of Greece within six months.

The war now shifted to Asia Minor, where Rome, allied with Pergamum and Rhodes, sent their imposing forces commanded by Lucius Scipio and his brother Scipio Africanus (hero of the Second Punic War). Hannibal had gambled on fighting for Antiochus; now, he commanded the striking new Seleucid fleet he had constructed in Phoenicia. However, the Rhodian fleet intercepted and defeated Hannibal, leaving only Antiochus' main fleet in Ephesus.

In the ensuing marine battle, Antiochus lost half his fleet – sunk or captured by the fleets of Rome and Rhodes. The final clash between Antiochus and Rome climaxed in Magnesia, Thessaly, where half of the Seleucid army was destroyed. Antiochus agreed in 188 BC to hand over his cities in Asia Minor to Rome and pay a war debt of 15,000 talents to Rome and 4000 talents to Pergamum. Despite this defeat, Antiochus was still the powerful king of the Seleucid Empire, spanning from Egypt east to Persia (Iran) and north to the Taurus Mountains of modern-day Turkey.

In 171 BC, Rome entangled once again in the Third Macedonian War. Philip had died, leaving his ruthless and enterprising son Perseus as King of Macedonia. Perseus was never meant to be king – he was the son of a concubine, and his brother Demetrius, son of Philip's wife, was the legal heir. But Rome had taken Demetrius hostage while only a small child – part of the peace deal ending the Second Macedonian War.

Perseus expected to ascend to the throne, but five years later, Rome returned Demetrius to his father. When Demetrius grew up, Philip sent him as his ambassador to Rome's Senate. The Romans were fond of Demetrius, and he won great esteem from the Senate. Insanely jealous of his half-brother's soaring diplomatic accomplishments, Perseus knew Demetrius would likely be the next king. How could he get rid of him?

Perseus attempted to ruin Demetrius through deplorable intrigues; when that failed, he falsely accused Demetrius of trying to kill him. When no one believed him, he manipulated Philip's General Didas to accuse Demetrius of treason with Rome against Macedonia – showing "evidence" of a forged letter from Flamininus. Philip fell for this ruse, putting Demetrius into Didas' custody. Perseus then deceived Didas into believing Philip had ordered Demetrius' death – which he conducted secretly.

Now Demetrius was dead, Philip was dead, and Perseus was king – and he hated Rome. King Perseus strategically allied with the Seleucid Empire by marrying King Seleucus' daughter Laodice. He arranged a marriage for his sister Apame IV to their cousin, Prusias II of Bithynia –Macedonia's ally in the First Macedonian War.

Unexpectantly, King Abrupolis of Thrace attacked Macedonia, devastating the country and capturing its gold mines. Perseus fought back and drove Abrupolis out of Macedonia. Although Perseus was rightfully defending his own country, Rome was offended because he trounced their ally.

Perseus enlarged his military and allied with King Cotys IV, ruler of Thrace's largest state. He circulated propaganda he could reform Greece, restoring its legendary wealth and power. His generosity to the Greek states and cities influenced their support; they visualized him as one of their own, a revolutionary who wanted freedom from Rome.

Meanwhile, King Eumenes II of Pergamum (Macedonia's neighbor to the east) was in Rome, triggering hostilities against Perseus – astutely pointing out his influence, marriage alliances, and how he was stockpiling weapons for war. Perseus determined to get his revenge by assassinating Eumenes. His plot to kill Eumenes failed, but Rome got wind of it, declaring Perseus public enemy number one and voting for war against Macedonia.

In 171 BC, Perseus triumphantly seized all the primary cities in northern Thessaly. Meanwhile, the Roman commander Publius Licinius led his troops in an intense march from Epirus through treacherous mountains to Thessaly's capital city of Larissa. Eumenes of Pergamon joined him, bringing 4000 foot-soldiers and 1000 cavalrymen. In the Battle of Callinicus, Perseus withdrew from the Roman forces but declared a Macedonian victory because Rome lost 2000 men compared to 400 Macedonian casualties.

A little later, most of the Romans had left their camp to harvest the ripening grain in the region. Catching them off-guard, Perseus raided their camp, capturing supplies and 600 men. Publius Licinius rushed to the area with his men and elephants, attacking Perseus and trapping his heavy infantry in a narrow passage. In this deadly battle, 8000 Macedonians died, and 4000 Romans perished.

In the decisive 168 BC Battle of Pydna on Macedonia's coast, Perseus suffered a crushing defeat at the hands of the talented new Roman commander Aemilius Paullus. The cowardly Perseus abandoned the battle early on, leaving the Romans to kill 20,000 of his men and capture 11,000. Pydna's plunder was so valuable that the exhilarated Roman citizens got a massive tax break. The Romans then hunted Perseus down to the island of Samothrace. The islanders handed him over, and Perseus was hauled to Rome in chains.

Following great military victories, Rome would host a "triumph" – a grand procession through the streets displaying the captives and plunder, with the victors wearing crowns of laurel.

The triumph (celebration of a military victory) in Rome was the most magnificent the Romans had ever seen – lasting three days, displaying Perseus led in chains and trophies of the war, including Perseus' chariot accompanied by exuberant soldiers wearing laurels. Rome's spectacular victory spelled the end of the Antigonid Dynasty in Macedonia; Rome divided the kingdom into four republics under Rome's control.

In 146 BC, the Achaean League declared war against Rome – a suicidal act, considering Rome's recent triumphs over Carthage and Macedonia. Although former allies, the Achaean Greeks held a bitter grudge against Rome for taking many of their citizens as hostages in the Third Macedonian War. The Achaeans also grappled with Rome over their desire to expand, while Rome wanted them to shrink back to their original states.

Led by their generals Critolaos and Diaeus, the Achaeans desperately fought two Roman armies led by Praetor Metellus and Consul Mummius. Caught off-guard by Mummius' astounding maneuvers, the main Achaean force led by Critolaos fled to Scarpheia, where the ones who didn't commit suicide were killed or captured by the Romans. Critolaos disappeared, never to be seen again. The Achaean League panicked, and many towns surrendered immediately.

Part of the League, especially Corinth, rallied around Diaeus as the massive Roman forces led by Mummius advanced on Corinth. Within a few hours, the Achaean troops who didn't escape were captured or killed. Diaeus fled to Arcadia, where he committed suicide. Most of the Corinthians slipped out of the city before the Romans – suspicious of an ambush – entered three days later. The Romans massacred all the remaining men, enslaved the women and children, then sacked the city, plundering her precious works of art to carry home to Rome; many valuable pieces were damaged or destroyed in the chaos.

The Achaean League dissolved, and the weakened foundations of Greece crumbled before Rome. For the next century, the city-states and kingdoms of Greece and the rest of the eastern Mediterranean constantly shifted alliances, no longer the unparalleled world powers they once had been. However, in the realms of religion, philosophy, literature, and art, Greece exerted a paramount influence over Rome for centuries to come.

Chapter 9: The Civil Wars

In his tirade on civil war in the *City of God*, Augustine mockingly asked why Rome erected a Temple of Concord following Gaius Gracchus' murder. "Why didn't they build a Temple of Discord instead?" Ancient Rome engaged in epic wars of conquest during its Republic era, but the vicious bloodbaths that strikingly transformed Rome were those fought against itself.

Social unrest in Rome swirled around land ownership. The *ager publicus* (public land) Rome acquired through conquering new territories was usually distributed to aristocrats, who also confiscated lands the peasants were working – forming large plantations farmed by slaves. This left the hapless peasants with no means of support. They couldn't join the military because they weren't landholders, yet the military desperately needed more men.

The Gracchi brothers, Tiberius and Gaius, struggled for social reform – they advocated for limiting the public lands an individual could hold to about 325 acres and redistributing the rest of the land to the displaced peasants and war veterans whose land was often stolen while they were fighting abroad. Tiberius was elected Tribune of the Plebs in 133 BC, but the aristocratic senators, fearful of losing their lands, stirred up a brutal mob who clubbed Tiberius and 300 of his supporters to death.

Ten years later, Gaius was elected Tribune, and once again, the insidious senators raised a mob to kill him – but he

committed suicide first. The brothers' deaths were not in vain –
their cause would be championed by forward-thinking politicians
in the coming decades.

Gaius Marius, Roman war hero and statesman, was elected as consul seven times.
*Diego Delso, CC BY-SA 3.0 <https://creativecommons.org/licenses/by-sa/3.0>, via
Wikimedia Commons*
*https://commons.wikimedia.org/wiki/File:Glyptothek,_M%C3%BAnich,_Alemania,_20
13-02-02,_DD_19.JPG*

Gaius Marius – a rising star in Roman politics – began his
brilliant career as a plebeian military tribune, married to Julia,
Julius Caesar's aunt. After Jugurtha violently usurped the throne
of Rome's ally Numidia (now Algeria in Africa), Rome engaged
the pretender in war. Marius enabled a sensational victory after
Jugurtha cut the Romans off from the river – their water supply –
and split them into small groups in the desert. Marius formed a
unified column of 2000 soldiers who broke through the
Numidians, causing them to withdraw.

Elected as Consul in 107 BC, Marius needed more soldiers
for his army but found Rome's military reserves depleted
because only landholders could serve. Marius convinced the

Senate to exempt his army from the land requirements. With his new troops, Marius marched across the African desert, relentlessly pressing Jugurtha southwest into Mauritania. Marius's shrewd cavalry commander – Lucius Cornelius Sulla – cunningly convinced King Bocchus of Mauritania to turn Jugurtha over to Rome, which Bocchus did, annexing Numidia to Mauritania.

While Marius was in Africa, aggressive tribes from Denmark and Germany – the Cimbri, Teutones, and Ambrones – arrived in the Rhone valley, pillaging settlements at Italy's northern border. Elected as consul again in 104 BC, Marius returned from Africa in triumph, with Jugurtha in chains, then headed to the Italian Alps with Sulla to drive out the savage Germanic tribes.

The legendary Battle of Aquae Sextiae began accidentally when the Romans, fetching water, encountered the Ambrones bathing in the same stream. In a spontaneous battle, the Romans killed 30,000 Ambrones. A combined force of Teutones and Ambrones counterattacked the following day, and 37,000 well-trained Romans butchered at least 100,000 of the Germanic tribes. Marius then bombarded the Cimbri, winning a decisive victory in the Battle of Vercellae, slaughtering 120,000 Cimbri and enslaving the rest. With a great triumph, Rome proclaimed Marius as the "third founder of Rome."

Rome's Senate passed the unpopular *Licinia Mucia* decree in 95 BC, expelling all non-citizens from Rome. In 91 BC, the Plebeian Tribune and reformer Drusus zealously advocated for greater distribution of state lands, enlarging the Senate, and granting citizenship for all of Italy. Drusus was assassinated, leading to a revolt of the Italian states – particularly the Marsi and Samnites – in the Social War of 91-87 BC.

Marius was called up to quell the rebel states. With Sulla, he killed 6000 rebels and captured 7000 before illness forced him to withdraw. To end the war, Rome decreed that all free people in Italy's mainland who were loyal to Rome would become citizens, receiving the right to vote. This led to the Romanization of Italy, as the Italic tribes integrated into Roman culture, abandoning their languages for Latin.

Tetradrachm of King Mithridates VI of Pontus, who fought with Rome in three wars.
© *Marie-Lan Nguyen / Wikimedia Commons*
https://commons.wikimedia.org/wiki/File:Tetradrachm_of_Mithridates_VI_CM_SNG_BM_1038.jpg

While concluding the Social War, Rome's attention fixated on the determined King Mithridates VI of Pontus on the Black Sea. Mithridates had invaded Cappadocia – Rome's ally – on his southern border. The First Mithridatic War (89-85 BC) began when Rome sent troops to Cappadocia. King Mithridates ordered the horrific extermination of all Romans living in Asia Minor – even women and children – killing 80,000 Romans as his forces savagely conquered one Roman city after another all the way to Greece.

In 87 BC, Consul Lucius Sulla – Marius's chief lieutenant in two wars but now his bitter rival – landed in Greece, recovered Athens and southern Greece for Rome, then headed north to crush Mithridates' army in the shattering Battle of Chaeronea (86 BC), despite being outnumbered. Continuing to score land and sea victories, Sulla forced Mithridates to accept a humiliating peace treaty in 85 BC, abandoning all lands except Pontus.

Leaving his general Murena to maintain stability, Sulla hurried back to Rome to confront the civil war roaring on in his absence. In 83 BC, the Second Mithridatic War was initiated when Murena heard rumors that Mithridates was building up his army again. Not waiting for Sulla's permission, Murena impetuously launched a preemptive strike on Mithridates, who swiftly defeated him at the River Halys. Sulla angrily ordered Murena to withdraw, ending the war indecisively.

The politician-generals Marius and Sulla both had razor-sharp fighting instincts that empowered joint success on the battlefield. But by 88 BC, they were engaged in a savage rivalry that plunged Rome into brutal civil war when Marius circumvented Sulla – consul for that year – by stealing his command of the Roman forces against King Mithridates.

Enraged, Sulla marched on Rome with his forces – an unprecedented and forbidden move for a Roman general and consul. Marius desperately rounded up gladiators to counter Sulla, but they were no match for his ferocity. Marius narrowly escaped to Africa, while Sulla consolidated his command of the forces heading to Greece, then set sail to pummel Mithridates.

In his absence, Rome erupted into a vicious civil war between the Plebeian *Populares* and the Patrician *Optimates*. Marius slipped back from Africa, clandestinely organized an army, and marched into Rome in 87 BC, taking control of the city. He murdered his political enemies, displaying their heads on spikes, and manipulated his election as consul for the seventh time in 86 BC. But within two weeks, he suddenly died – apparently of pleurisy.

In 83 BC, Sulla wrapped up the war with Mithridates and crossed the Adriatic to Italy. Rome dispatched two armies to stop him; Sulla swept aside the first army, and the second army defected to his side. Marching on Rome once again, Sulla fought and won a fierce battle just outside Rome's walls and was quickly appointed dictator by the Senate.

Sulla exercised total control over Rome for two years before voluntarily resigning one year before he died in 78 BC. Blood flowed as he executed everyone considered an enemy of the state – 80 the first day, 220 the next day – the purge continued for months. One target was the teenage Julius Caesar, who fled Rome.

As a Patrician Optimate, Sulla was contemptuous of the Gracchian reforms championed by the Plebeian Populares. He empowered the aristocracy, strengthening the Senate over the Plebeian Council. He prevented the Plebeian tribunes from initiating new laws and vetoing Senate acts. Sullied increased the number of senators from 300 to 600, and extended Rome's sacred boundary - the *Pomerium* - which had not been moved since the monarchy period.

Rome and the rest of Italy had slaves - many slaves - captured from conquered cities and provinces. One intrepid slave from Thrace, named Spartacus, was sold to a gladiator school. Spartacus and 78 other gladiators succeeded in a daring escape one night in 73 BC, armed with cleavers and spits stolen from the kitchen. At least one gladiatrix escaped (yes, Rome had a few female fighters) - Spartacus' wife, also from Thrace. She was a prophetess of the god Dionysus and would occasionally be possessed by him. Once, Spartacus awakened, horrified, with a snake coiled on his face; his wife prophesied it was a sign of the formidable power that would drive him to greatness but kill him in the end.

The gladiators hiked to Mount Vesuvius, which was in a quiet stage at that time, joined by other slaves, raiding the area for weapons and provisions. The praetor Clodius besieged the mountain with 3000 soldiers, thinking the slaves were trapped on Vesuvius, where they'd run out of food. But the enterprising slaves wove vines into strong rope ladders, long enough to reach from the cliffs to the valley below, and they all escaped. The vagabonds roamed through Italy, ambushing Roman units, appropriating supplies, and freeing the rural slaves - as their numbers mushroomed to about 10,000.

The exasperated Senate sent both consuls and thousands of troops after the escaped slaves. The escapees divided into two groups - one remained in southern Italy with Crixus - spelling their doom - while the rest joined Spartacus in a long hike north toward the Alps. Spartacus planned to cross out of Italy, and everyone could then escape back to their respective countries, but some of the escaped slaves were growing over-confident and wanted to stay in Italy as desperados or revolutionaries.

One Roman army captured and killed Crixus and most of his rebel force, then marched north, entrapping Spartacus' group between the other Roman army. What the Romans didn't anticipate were horses! Spartacus had been building a cavalry; he unexpectedly charged the Romans, routing them and stealing their baggage. Spartacus reached the base of the Alps but inexplicably didn't cross over – perhaps the steep peaks proved too daunting.

The audacious new plan was to head south, cross over to Sicily, rekindle the slave revolt of 50 years earlier, and take over the island. Reaching the straits between Italy and Sicily, they hired pirates to sail them across but made the blunder of paying them in advance. The pirates sailed off with their money but without them, shattering their hopes of escaping Italy.

Spartacus and his band encamped at Rhegium, at the toe of Italy's boot, with the Roman commander Crassus closing in, whose strategy was to entrap the slaves and starve them out. Crassus built a 37-mile-long ditch across the peninsula from sea to sea – 15 feet wide and 15 feet deep – which filled with seawater. Then he built a wall along the canal. But the resourceful slaves waited until one stormy winter night, built a dam across the canal with dirt and trees, and crossed over.

General Crassus panicked, thinking they'd head to Rome and sack it. He was relieved to discover the volatile slaves had quarreled and divided into smaller groups. Crassus chased Spartacus' band up a mountain, but the slaves suddenly whirled around to fight, catching the Romans off-guard and routing them. The reckless slaves now felt invincible. Spartacus couldn't stop them from challenging the Romans.

Realizing a full-on battle was inevitable due to his men's overconfidence, Spartacus dismounted and killed his horse – saying if he won, he'd steal a horse from the Romans, but if he were killed, he wouldn't need the horse. In the blood-soaked struggle, Spartacus and most of his fellow slaves perished on the battlefield, but 6000 were captured and crucified, their crosses lining the Apian Way from Rome to Capua.

Crassus' triumph over Spartacus got him elected as consul in 70 BC, along with Gnaeus Pompeius (Pompey) Magnus. Pompey had just scored an impressive victory in Spain against Marius' supporter Sertorius, who was conducting guerilla warfare against the Roman Hispania provinces. On his overland route to Spain, Pompey forged a new route through the Alps, leaving a bloody swathe of carnage among the fierce mountain tribes. He spent five years in Spain in heated battles until the rebel forces lost morale and conspired to murder Sertorius.

Pompey's next challenge was to cripple the Cilician pirates raiding Italy's coast – a long-term and growing threat. In 67 BC, Pompey commanded 500 ships to vanquish the havoc wreaked by the pirates in the eastern Mediterranean. In only three months, he overcame the pirates based in Cilicia (southern Turkey), then rounded up marauding pirates in the Mediterranean, rehabilitating them by resettling them as farmers.

Immediately, Pompey turned his attention to King Mithridates in Pontus, who was stirring up trouble again. Rome gave Pompey supreme command in the east, and in 66 BC, he sailed to Asia Minor, marching through Bithynia to Pontus with eight experienced legions. Outnumbered, Mithridates put up a fierce resistance near the town of Dastira, but Pompey crushed his forces – later renaming the town *Nicopolis* (Victory City). Mithridates abandoned his kingdom, escaping to Armenia with the remnants of his army, where his son-in-law King Tigranes refused him refuge. Mithridates fled to Crimea, fruitlessly plotting his come-back until he committed suicide in 62 BC.

Once he'd defeated Mithridates, Pompey consolidated and reorganized the frontier kingdoms into Roman provinces. Amenia became a client state of Rome, with King Tigranes keeping his crown. Pompey then turned to Syria – once the heart of Antiochus III's grand Seleucid empire. After Antiochus' death, Syria had destabilized. The 163 BC Maccabean Revolt triggered by his son Antiochus IV's defilement of the Jerusalem temple made Judea semi-independent. The Parthians conquered Iran and took Babylon in 139 BC, reducing the Seleucid Empire to a small territory of Syria. Pompey conquered Syrian strongholds and cities until he reached Damascus, completing Syria's takeover and making it a Roman province.

He then turned to Judea, embroiled in a civil war between two royal brothers. Aristobulus II had usurped his brother Hyrcanus II's throne, and then, egged on by the wily Antipater – an Idumean – Hyrcanus had allied with the Arabian King Aretas to retake the throne. Pompey's General Scaurus came on the scene and kicked Aretas out of Judea. When Pompey arrived shortly after, he brought Judea under Roman control. Later, in 47 BC,

Julius Caesar appointed Antipater as the first Roman Procurator. His son, Herod the Great, was notorious for ordering the massacre of all baby boys under two in Bethlehem following the birth of Jesus.

While Pompey was restoring order in Asia, the devious and deadly senator Lucius Sergius Catilina had his sights set on ruling Rome. During Sulla's bloodbath, he had decapitated his brother-in-law, then murdered his wife and son to marry the beautiful daughter of Consul Orestes. He bribed his way to acquittal at his trial. Incensed that the murder accusations prevented him from standing for consul election, he plotted to assassinate both consuls.

That conspiracy fizzled, but in 64 BC, Catiline ran for consul again, was defeated by Cicero and Hybrida, and defeated again the following year. Unable to rule legally, he conspired with disgruntled Patricians and veterans to overthrow the Roman Republic - planning to incite a slave revolt, burn Rome, then murder Cicero and the unsupportive Senators in the chaos. Cicero got wind of the plot and exposed Catiline, who fled Rome, but several other conspirators were arrested and, without trial, executed by strangling, despite Julius Caesar's forceful protest. Catiline and his men were later killed by the Roman army.

Rome's First Triumvirate was an alliance of Gnaeus Pompeius Magnus, Marcus Licinius Crassus, and Gaius Julius Caesar.
Mary Harrsch, CC BY-SA 4.0 <https://creativecommons.org/licenses/by-sa/4.0>, via Wikimedia Commons
https://commons.wikimedia.org/wiki/File:The_First_Triumvirate_of_the_Roman_Rep ublic_720X480.jpg

Rome's First Triumvirate formed as an alliance between its three most powerful men, all popular war heroes: Julius Caesar, Crassus, and Pompey. Pompey was aggravated when the senators balked at providing farmland for his war veterans and ratifying the treaties Pompey had made in the east. Caesar had just returned from a brilliant military campaign in Spain; supported by Pompey and Crassus (the richest man in Rome), he won the election as consul in 59 BC, then used his influence to secure Pompey's treaties and land for his men.

After serving as consul, the Senate posted Caesar to Roman Gaul as proconsul. He conquered Gallic tribes beyond Rome's province, expanding Rome's territories to all of today's France and Belgium, protecting Rome from Gallic invasions. He slaughtered two-thirds of the ferocious Helvetii warriors of the Swiss plateau. His 55 BC massacre of the Germanic Usipetes and Tencteri tribes, including women and children – prompted Cato to demand Caesar be turned over to the barbarians. In 55 BC and 54 BC, Caesar made daring expeditions to Britain, where he penetrated to what is now London.

Julia – Pompeii's wife and Caesar's daughter – died in childbirth, the first stage of failure for the Triumvirate. The following year, Crassus died on the battlefield. In 50 BC, the Senate ordered Caesar to return home – telling him to first dissolve his army. Caesar brazenly crossed the Rubicon River from Roman Gaul into Italy in January 49 BC – without disbanding his army – he came with one legion (about 5000 men), quoting Athens' playwright Menander: "The die is cast."

Pompey ordered the senators to evacuate to southern Italy. Caesar walked into Rome unhindered, helped himself to the treasury, then set out after Pompey. Before Caesar could catch up to him, Pompey sailed to Macedonia. Rather than chasing after Pompey, Caesar headed to Spain, where Pompey's army was stationed. "I'm going to fight an army without a leader, so I can later fight a leader without an army." Without much of a fight, Pompey's forces capitulated to Caesar.

Meanwhile, Pompey was busily assembling an army of his friends and allies throughout the East, commanding a fleet of 300 ships. Caesar had only a few ships – not even enough to get all his army to Greece. He left half of his army behind, waiting until Mark Antony could join him months later with four more legions – causing Pompey to withdraw quickly. But then Pompey's son sailed into the Adriatic with an Egyptian fleet and sank or captured virtually all Caesar's ships. Pompey won the Battle of Dyrrachium but failed to pursue Caesar's army, causing Caesar to remark, "The enemy would have won the war today if they had a commander who knew how to use a victory."

Pompey then risked a battle with Caesar on Thessaly's plains. Following their victory in Dyrrachium, Pompey's men foolishly assumed triumph was theirs. Despite being outnumbered, Caesar's seasoned military, following his innovative tactics, outmaneuvered Pompey's army, putting them to flight. Pompey fled by horseback to the coast. Caesar pardoned all who surrendered to him, including Marcus Junius Brutus, who would one day be his undoing. Pompey sailed to Egypt, but instead of finding refuge, the Egyptians murdered him, sending his head to Caesar.

Julius Caesar and Cleopatra VII became lovers while Caesar was in Egypt. By Jean-Léon Gérôme
https://commons.wikimedia.org/w/index.php?curid=1399233

Caesar headed to Egypt to avenge the death of his former ally and rival Pompey, where he became entangled in a civil war between the 12-year-old Pharaoh Ptolemy XIII and his sister (and wife) Cleopatra VII. Dazzled by Cleopatra's exotic charms, Caesar became her lover, forcing Ptolemy out and restoring the throne to Cleopatra. The following year, Cleopatra gave birth to Caesarion – Caesar's only biological son. Caesarion became Pharaoh at age three, ruling with his mother until he was executed as a teen by Caesar's adopted son Octavius.

Caesar served as consul in 48 BC, and again from 46 to 44. He was dictator for several short-term periods and then appointed dictator for life in 44 BC – but his life was cut short that very year. As consul and dictator, Caesar implemented major reforms: alleviating debt and unemployment, revising the calendar, and initiating massive building projects in Rome, eager to match the grandeur of Alexandria. Caesar forgave his political enemies – extending *clementia* (mercy) – rather than reap revenge. But they had not forgiven him.

Fearing Caesar planned to crown himself king, at least 60 Senators had formed a conspiracy led by Marcus Junius Brutus, Gaius Cassius Longinus, and Decimus Junius Brutus. Desperate to retain the Republic form of government, even though many approved of Caesar's reforms, they plotted his murder. It was to take place in the Senate on March 15, 44 BC – the Ides of March. But when the senators assembled, Caesar didn't show up. Where was he?

Julius Caesar was assassinated by a Senate conspiracy, stabbed 23 times.
https://commons.wikimedia.org/wiki/File:Death_of_Julius_Caesar_2.png

Early that morning, Caesar's wife Calpurnia woke up screaming from a nightmare of Caesar's body flowing with blood. She begged her husband to stay home. Caesar, remembering a recent prophecy that his life would end by the Ides of March, sent Mark Antony to dismiss the Senate. One conspirator – Decimus Brutus – came to Caesar's house, mocking him for listening to a woman, and Caesar accompanied him to the Senate. Within moments of walking in, the senators surrounded Caesar, stabbing him repeatedly – 23 times.

Caesar's murderers hoped his death would preserve the Roman Republic, but the opposite happened. The people of Rome could no longer trust their senators and became openly hostile toward them. Two days after Caesar's murder, Mark Antony – Caesar's right-hand man and consul for 44 BC – convinced the Senate to accept a compromise: amnesty for the conspirators in exchange for Caesar's laws remaining in effect.

Two days later, the reading of Caesar's will revealed he had named his grandnephew and adopted son Gaius Octavianus as his heir. At that time, 19-year-old Octavian was stationed with Caesar's army in Macedonia, waiting for Caesar to come to lead them against the Parthians. On March 20, Mark Antony gave the eulogy at Caesar's funeral, stirring the citizens into a riot as he held up Caesar's bloodstained toga.

Most conspirators fled the country, leaving Mark Antony as the primary leader for the remainder of the year. Marcus Lepidus, Caesar's Master of the Horse, was named *Pontifex Maximus* (high priest), and Antony and Lepidus arranged an engagement between Antony's daughter and Lepidus' son.

Gaius Octavianus returned to Rome in May, claiming his inheritance. Even though Caesar's will left his fortune to Octavian, Mark Antony refused to release the funds. Octavian borrowed heavily to honor Caesar's will that left money to every citizen of Rome. Friction between Mark Antony and Octavian escalated, with the Romans preferring Octavian over Antony. Cicero gave speeches depicting Antony as a threat to Rome. Two of Antony's legions defected to Octavian, but as a private citizen, he couldn't legally command them.

Antony's one-year term as consul was ending. Customarily, when consuls completed their term, Rome appointed them to govern a province. The Senate assigned Antony to Macedonia, but he wanted Cisalpine Gaul in northern Italy instead, which had been assigned to Decimus Brutus – Caesar's assassin. Antony marched north to take the province by force, while the fiery Cicero led the Senate to declare Antony an outlaw. They gave Octavian legal command over his forces and sent him with Rome's two new consuls to defeat Antony. Both consuls were killed in the battle, but Octavian prevailed, and Antony fled over the Alps into Transalpine Gaul (northern France), where his friend Lepidus was the new governor.

With Antony gone, the devious Senate felt the time was ripe to reassert their power – but they needed to get rid of Octavian, Caesar's heir, and the rest of Caesar's supporters. They put Caesar's assassin Decimus Brutus in charge of Rome's legions and Pompey's son Sextus over Rome's fleet. Octavian realized the only way he'd survive was to join forces with the man he'd just chased over the Alps. He initiated secret negotiations with Antony and Lepidus. Fortunately, Octavian's legions – who had been led by Caesar before – remained loyal to Octavian, refusing to be led by Caesar's assassin.

Octavian boldly marched on Rome with his legions in August 43, took the city, proclaimed himself consul, and put Caesar's assassins on trial, convicting them *in absentia.* In November, he traveled to northern Italy to meet with Antony and Lepidus. Together, they negotiated a three-man dictatorship – the Second Triumvirate – officially ending the Roman Republic.

They split up the available provinces among themselves: Octavian got Africa, Lepidus got Spain, and Antony took Gaul. They would have to fight their enemies for the rest of the Rome provinces: Sextus Pompey controlled the Mediterranean islands with his fleet, and Brutus and Cassius held the eastern Mediterranean provinces with the remainder of Rome's forces.

The Triumvirate first concentrated on avenging Caesar's death on the conspirators who had stayed in Rome or returned – executing one-third of the Senate, including Cicero, and confiscating their lands and fortunes to replenish Rome's treasury. Then they sailed to Macedonia to retake the Mediterranean from Brutus and Cassius, first breaking the blockade of Sextus' fleet.

In the first Battle of Philippi, Antony and Octavian attacked Brutus and Cassius from two directions. Antony scored a profound victory over Cassius' troops, and Cassius committed suicide. With Octavian ill and unable to lead, his troops lost to Brutus' forces, but 20 days later, Brutus lost the second Battle of Philippi and committed suicide. Now the triumvirs held control of all Rome's land forces and only had Sextus Pompey's fleet to conquer.

The Triumvirate had more provinces to divide among themselves. Antony got the lion's share, keeping Gaul and adding all the eastern provinces. Octavian and Lepidus traded – now Octavian had Spain and Lepidus ruled Africa. They technically ruled over Italy together, but Antony remained in the East, ruling the extensive Roman provinces from Ephesus.

In 41 BC, Antony asked Cleopatra for a meeting in Tarsus to iron out the alliance between Rome and Egypt. She had been living in Caesar's villa in Rome with their son Caesarion but had returned to Egypt after Caesar's murder. Cleopatra sailed up the river in a magnificent boat with silver oars, purple sails, and a golden prow – dressed as Aphrodite. The alliance was not only renewed, but Antony deliriously fell under Cleopatra's enchantment, living with her in Alexandria through the winter. Cleopatra gave birth to their twins – Alexander Helios and Cleopatra Selene – in 40 BC.

While Antony was frolicking with Cleopatra, Octavian was distributing land to Caesar's war veterans – until he ran out of land. Wanting to keep on the soldiers' good side, he confiscated land belonging to Roman citizens, even whole towns. Egged on by Fulvia – Antony's rich and powerful wife – the Senate opposed Octavian's land grants, which led to Octavian divorcing Fulvia's daughter Claudia (from Fulvia's first marriage). Octavian had married Claudia when she was only thirteen to seal the Second Triumvirate; two years later, he sent her back to her mother, saying the marriage had not been consummated.

The outraged Fulvia, the most powerful woman in Rome, allied with Mark Antony's younger brother Lucius Antonius – Rome's consul that year – in a war against Octavian. Some whispered her war was a ruse to draw her husband Antony away from Cleopatra and back to Rome. Octavian besieged Lucius's legions in Perugia – starving them out – while they waited desperately and futilely for Antony's return.

Finally, Lucius surrendered and was sent by Octavian on an appointment to Spain. Fulvia fled to Greece, meeting up with her annoyed husband Antony, who rebuked her for the war; she died of a sudden illness shortly after. Antony returned to Rome, smoothed things over with Octavian, and married Octavian's sister Octavia within weeks of Fulvia's death.

Sextus Pompeius still had control of the fleet and was blocking shipments of grain and supplies coming into Italy. In exchange for lifting the blockade, Octavian granted him control of Sicily, Sardinia, Corsica, and the Peloponnese. Octavian had married Scribonia, a relative of Pompeius, after divorcing Claudia. After two years, he divorced Scribonia on the very day she gave birth to his only biological child, Julia (he adopted four sons of his wives). That stirred up trouble with Pompeius again.

Octavian agreed with Antony to send 20,000 legionaries for Antony to fight Parthia in exchange for 120 ships to fight Pompeius. Antony kept his side of the deal, but Octavian only sent 10,000 legionaries. Fighting together, Octavian and Lepidus destroyed most of Pompeius' fleet. Lepidus then tried to claim Sicily, unsuccessfully, which got him kicked out of the Triumvirate.

Meanwhile, because Octavian had reneged on his end of the deal, Antony's shortage of manpower turned his Parthian expedition into a catastrophe. Cleopatra could replenish his army, so he resumed his affair with her, sending Octavia back to Rome and angering Octavian. Giving Cleopatra the title *Queen of Kings*, Antony awarded the province of Armenia to their son Alexander Helios. In 36 BC, they had another son – Ptolemy Philadelphus.

Acting on information from a defector from Antony, Octavian raided the Vestal Virgins' temple where Antony's secret will was hidden. It revealed Antony's plan to give away more of Rome's provinces to his sons and stipulated Antony was to be buried in Alexandria with his "Queen" Cleopatra. Antony also declared Caesarion to be Caesar's legitimate son and heir – a great threat to Octavian who was Caesar's son by adoption. With this information, the Senate revoked Antony's powers and declared war on Cleopatra in 32 BC; however, a third of the Senate and both consuls defected to Antony

In 31 BC, Octavian faced off against Antony and Cleopatra in the naval Battle of Actium. Octavian's General Agrippa outmaneuvered Cleopatra's fleet, and the two lovers fled with 60 ships to Egypt, which Octavian successfully invaded a year later. Antony fell on his sword, dying in Cleopatra's arms. Realizing she would be paraded through Rome in chains, she committed suicide from a snakebite. Octavian honored her request to be buried next to Antony, but he killed 16-year-old Caesarion – her son from Caesar. After parading the children of Antony and Cleopatra in gold chains in the streets of Rome in his Triumph, Octavian gave Cleopatra's children from Antony to his sister Octavia (Antony's former wife) to raise.

The Republic of Rome, which had expanded exponentially and adapted to many changes in five centuries of existence, was crumbling. Rome would survive, but its semi-democratic government would die – the victim of incessant civil wars and internal strife. A new imperial political structure would now rise to lead the Roman Empire for the next four centuries.

SECTION THREE:
THE PRINCIPATE
(27 BC – AD 235)

Chapter 10: The Julio – Claudian Dynasty

If someone asked you to name a famous Roman emperor, perhaps you'd think of Julius Caesar and "Et Tu, Brute?" ("You too, Brutus?") Or maybe Nero leaps to mind, playing his lyre while Rome burned. In this chapter, we'll learn what led to Julius Caesar's assassination and Brutus' betrayal, and why Nero didn't mind that Rome burned.

Some of the best-known and notorious emperors piloted Rome through the next two centuries. Rome enjoyed its pinnacle of wealth, power, literature, and arts, but its Golden Age was marred by debauchery, cruelty, paranoia, and conspiracies. In 27 BC, the Roman Republic transitioned to the Roman Empire, led by the five emperors of the Julio-Claudian dynasty: Augustus (Octavian), Tiberius, Caligula, Claudius, and Nero.

Following the suicide of Antony and Cleopatra, Octavian returned to Rome, intending to gradually become the sole ruler without anyone realizing his aspirations. On the surface, he supported Rome's Republic and its senators. Elected as consul shortly after his return, his first objectives were to restore stability and, temporarily, the traditional legal and political system. He handed full power back to the Senate, giving up his command of Rome's armies and provinces.

Octavian was still running the show through delegated power from the Senate, his monumental wealth, and the relationships he had courted throughout the Roman world. He put his fortune to work buying the hearts of the people – for instance, privately funding Italy's road system. Because most of the empire's provinces were in chaos, the Senate asked him to resume his control over them for the next ten years, to which he agreed, pretending reluctance. Of course, commanding the provinces gave him control of most of the military.

This sculpture of Octavian (Caesar Augustus) was made shortly after he became Princeps.
Stephencdickson, CC BY-SA 4.0 <https://creativecommons.org/licenses/by-sa/4.0>, via Wikimedia Commons https://commons.wikimedia.org/wiki/File:Augustus_Caesar.png

In January 27 BC, in the *First Settlement*, the Senate gave Octavian two new titles: *Augustus (illustrious one,* implying religious authority) and *Princeps Senatus / Princeps Civitatis (first in the Senate, first among the citizens)*. In the past, the *Princeps* title designated the leader of the Senate, but with Octavian, it acquired the meaning of first in the land – a pseudonym for emperor – which he refused to be called. Taking *Caesar* as his family name from Julius Caesar, his adopted father, he was now known as Caesar Augustus. He refused to wear the tokens of supreme power that Julius Caesar had worn – the purple toga and gold crown – but he continued as consul for several years, despite the position ordinarily being limited to one year.

In 23 BC, the Senate granted a *Second Settlement,* giving Augustus the power of tribune and censor – meaning he could call a meeting of the Senate, present business to the Senate, veto Senate actions, speak first at Senate meetings, supervise public morality, and hold a census. He was granted *sole imperium* – authority over all armed forces within the city of Rome, and *imperium proconsulare maius* – power over the governors of the provinces. Although he refused the title of emperor, he gradually acquired all the powers an emperor would hold.

Augustus used his powers productively. He restored law and order to Rome and the empire, enabling Rome to press forward. He reorganized the economic system, so the empire prospered financially, embarked on massive building projects of marble to beautify Rome, and established the Roman postal service, police and fire departments, and the Praetorian Guard.

He nearly doubled the size of the empire – conquering and consolidating northern Spain, Portugal, Switzerland, Bavaria, Austria, Slovenia, Albania, Croatia, Hungary, Serbia, and other points in western Asia and the Middle East. He expanded provinces in Africa to the south and east – forming an extensive trading network. He integrated a census and taxation system and a road system for the entire empire.

This map depicts the extent of the Roman Empire at the end of Augustus' reign.

Homoatrox, CC BY-SA 4.0 <https://creativecommons.org/licenses/by-sa/4.0>, via Wikimedia Commons https://commons.wikimedia.org/wiki/File:Roman_empire_14_AD_(provinces)_en.png

Despite three marriages, Augustus had only one child – Julia. His third wife, Livia, had two sons from her first husband – Tiberius and Drusus (the latter born about three months after she married Augustus). Drusus married Augustus' niece – Antonia – and their son Claudius became the fourth emperor of the Julio-Claudian dynasty.

Livia's older son Tiberius married Vipsania Agrippina, and they had a son: Drusus Julius Caesar. Romans had a habit of naming their sons after their brothers, which can get confusing. After eight years of happy marriage with Vipsania, Augustus asked Tiberius to divorce his wife and marry Augustus' daughter Julia – Tiberius' stepsister. That marriage was a disaster. Tiberius was still in love with Vipsania; Julia had been unfaithful to her previous husband, and she was unfaithful to Tiberius. Finally, Augustus charged his daughter with adultery and treason, declared her marriage to Tiberius void, and exiled her to a tiny island in the Tyrrhenian Sea. However, Augustus adopted two of her five children – Gaius Caesar and Lucius Caesar – as small children.

This left the question – who would be the next emperor? One of Augustus' biological grandsons? Or Tiberius – his stepson and former son-in-law? Augustus had all three educated and trained to succeed him – keeping his options open. Perhaps Tiberius assumed his stepfather would choose one of the grandsons, or perhaps he fell into one of his depressive episodes, but suddenly, after a promising political and military career, Tiberius dropped out of everything and retired to Rhodes.

After several years, both Gaius and Lucius died – leaving Tiberius as the only successor. Augustus legally adopted Tiberius in AD 4, and Tiberius adopted his nephew Germanicus. With his biological son Drusus and adopted son Germanicus, Tiberius now had two potential successors to the throne. Tiberius returned to Rome, picking up his political career. In AD 13, Tiberius became co-Princeps with Augustus – with equal powers – so Rome would have an uninterrupted rule whenever Augustus died.

Caesar Augustus died a year later in AD 14 and was promptly pronounced a god. The Senate met and validated Tiberius' position as Princeps (emperor). Tiberius deferred most decisions to the Senate, with little interest in the affairs of state – yet Rome mostly enjoyed peace and prosperity during his reign.

This bust of Tiberius was found in the ancient Roman city of Termes (in present-day Montejo de Tiermes, Province of Soria, Spain)
Luis García, CC BY-SA 3.0 <http://creativecommons.org/licenses/by-sa/3.0/>, via Wikimedia Commons https://commons.wikimedia.org/wiki/File:Tiberius_(M.A.N._Madrid)_01.jpg

Tiberius suffered from crushing and debilitating bouts of depression, not helped by his life's circumstances being – well, depressing. A dejected and disinterested leader, he only dipped into the state coffers for necessary things. On a high note, his lack of extravagance enabled him to leave an economic surplus to his successor.

Tiberius' nephew and adopted son Germanicus was highly popular, displaying brilliance in his military and political career; in AD 18, Tiberius gave him control over the Empire's eastern half - implying he would be Tiberius' successor. Only a year later, he suddenly died, saying he'd been poisoned. Tiberius descended into depression again, giving his biological son Drusus his responsibilities, including sharing the tribunician power, while he retreated to southern Italy for two years. Then Drusus also suddenly died of mysterious circumstances (likely poisoned by Sejanus, a political rival) in AD 23.

With both Germanicus and Drusus dead, Tiberius had to quickly decide on a new heir. He adopted Germanicus' two sons - Nero (not the same Nero as the nefarious emperor) and Drusus. He then retired from Rome again, leaving the city under the charge of Sejanus - his Praetorian Prefect - unaware Sejanus had probably poisoned his son. While Tiberius fought the demons of depression and descended into debauchery in Capri, Sejanus, now consul, accused Nero of homosexuality and exiled him - where he died soon after. Sejanus imprisoned Drusus in the palace dungeon, starving him to death. The third son of Germanicus - Caligula - was saved when Tiberius summoned him to Capri, where he lived for six years.

After years of absence from Rome, Tiberius awakened to the growing threat of Sejanus and his crafty intrigues. Suddenly, in AD 31, Sejanus was arrested, executed by strangulation, then thrown down the Gemonian stairs, where the crowd tore his body to pieces. His wife committed suicide but first sent a letter to Tiberius, telling him Sejanus had poisoned Tiberius' son Drusus. Tiberius purged anyone in Rome suspected to have colluded with Sejanus.

Tiberius then retired back into seclusion, leaving the government to be run by the Senate, descending into paranoia. He did nothing about appointing a successor and died in AD 37, at age 77 - some whispered Caligula had smothered him.

Tiberius left his estate and titles to Caligula and Gemellus (his grandson by Drusus) - intending them to co-reign. Caligula immediately had the will nullified regarding Gemellus yet adopted the teenage boy. Although known by his nickname

Caligula – meaning 'little boots" for the miniature military boots his father had made for him when he was a small child – his real name was Gaius Caesar Augustus Germanicus.

This cameo shows Caligula and Roma – a personification of Rome.
https://commons.wikimedia.org/w/index.php?curid=12437143

The Senate proclaimed Caligula emperor, hailed by Rome's people as their shining star. The first seven months of Caligula's reign seemed idyllic as he initiated reforms, reinstated elections, awarded the military with bonuses, granted tax relief, initiated construction projects, and entertained the citizens with extravagant games (which quickly emptied the treasury).

Then Caligula developed a serious illness. Cassio Dio said it was a brain fever – suggesting meningitis or encephalitis. By all accounts, he had a sudden personality change – turning diabolical. He was erratic, easily excitable, and narcissistic. Dio said he would impersonate the Roman gods and goddesses, believing himself to have a divine nature.

He probably had lifelong epilepsy – the Roman historian Suetonius said he had the "falling sickness" as a child; the symptoms improved in adolescence, but he would still have episodes of sudden weakness where he could not stand or sit up and would be mentally confused – suggesting atonic seizures. Suetonius also recorded sleep disruption – he could only sleep about three hours a night, tormented by nightmares.

After his near-fatal illness, Caligula became unhinged, paranoid of those around him, and given to sadistic cruelty. Suspecting his adopted son Gemellus of wishing his death, Caligula ordered him to commit suicide – helped by the palace guards. He exiled or killed his relatives, passing murders off as suicide. Treason trials and execution of statesmen became commonplace.

Did he really make his horse a priest? He doted on Incitatus, who lived in a marble stable with an ivory manger. Dio said he made the horse a priest, while Suetonius said he planned to make the horse a consul. Most like, he just made joking comments comparing the senators (with whom he had a running feud) unfavorably to his horse. But then again, this was Caligula, unbound by society's norms.

Caligula expanded the empire by taking over Mauretania, previously a client kingdom of Rome, by inviting King Ptolemy of Mauretania to Rome, executing him, and annexing Mauretania. He set Britain's conquest in motion before his early death at age 28.

After enduring his reign for less than four years, the Romans were ready for a change. The Praetorian Guard (and probably the Senate) conspired to kill him – stabbing him and his wife to death in January AD 41 and smashing the head of his infant daughter against the wall.

This statue of Claudius is found in the Vatican Museum.

Tiberius Claudius Caesar Augustus Germanicus became the next emperor in AD 41 by default – he was the only adult male left in the family! Claudius survived the purges because of a disability – possibly Tourette's Syndrome. His knees were weak, he stumbled when he walked, he would laugh spontaneously at odd times, his head would shake from side to side when stressed, he drooled, he had a speech impediment, and he would make random, bizarre statements completely irrelevant to the matter at hand.

Caligula kept his uncle around for entertainment, encouraging his dinner guests to throw their olive pits at him. Even his mother called him a monstrosity. His symptoms decreased as he grew older, and he was recognized as a scholarly historian, eventually serving with Caligula as consul. While the Praetorian Guard was hunting down Caligula's wife and baby to murder, Claudius was hiding behind a curtain in the palace. Suddenly, a Praetorian Guard swept back the curtain, stared at Claudius, then knelt, telling the other guards, "This is Germanicus - our emperor!"

Claudius proved to be a conscientious and capable administrator, engaging in massive infrastructure projects throughout the empire: aqueducts, roads, ports, and canals. Despite the expenses of these projects, he recouped Caligula's debt disaster through well-balanced control of the treasury and centralizing the government. He expanded Rome's borders by launching 40,000 troops and several war elephants across the English Channel in AD 43, beginning the conquest of Britain, and bringing Thrace, Lycia, Judea, Austria, and Pamphylia under Rome's direct control. He extended Roman citizenship in the provinces. He was active in Rome's judicial system, even serving as a judge.

An avid womanizer, Claudius' love life was lethal. His first wife died on their wedding day. His third wife was a nymphomaniac who gave birth to a son and daughter - Britannicus and Octavia - during their short marriage. His fourth and final wife was his niece Agrippina, Caligula's sister.

Agrippina successfully manipulated Claudius to adopt Nero, her son from her first marriage, making him Claudius' successor over Britannicus. She arranged for Nero to marry his stepsister Octavia in AD 53. By that point, Claudius was having second thoughts about Agrippina and Nero, and was planning to elevate his biological son Britannicus; Agrippina stopped all that by poisoning Claudius with mushrooms at a banquet, killing him in AD 54 at age 63.

Nero Claudius Caesar Augustus Germanicus became emperor of Rome at age 16 when Claudius died; his 13-year-old stepbrother Britannicus conveniently died - suddenly - three months later. Agrippina's plan to rule through her son failed - he banished her from the palace when she criticized his love affairs, then arranged for her to die in a shipwreck, which she survived, only to be stabbed to death in her villa. In the tradition of Caligula, her death was reported as a suicide.

In his first several years, guided by his tutor Seneca and his advisor Burrus, Nero gave the Senate more power, reduced taxes (he wanted to get rid of them altogether, but Seneca and Burrus explained why that wouldn't work), enhanced slave rights, and provided disaster assistance to cities in need. Through his competent generals, he oversaw victories in Armenia, Germany, and Britain, and promoted a successful expedition to discover the source of the Nile.

Of course, he wasn't personally involved in the military campaigns nor most politics. He gave his attention to the arts – singing, playing the lyre, dancing, acting, writing poetry, painting, and chariot racing. When the Olympic games were held in Rome, he added artistic competitions to the athletic contests and joined both competitions, winning all the ones he competed in, even a chariot race where he never finished (his chariot tipped over!)

After his tutor Brutus died in AD 62, his dark side took over. He forced Seneca to commit suicide, then panicked when he had to make decisions on his own. When his lover Poppaea became pregnant with his child, he divorced Octavia, sending her into exile and marrying Poppaea 12 days later. Nero and Poppaea then had Octavia killed in an overly hot bath.

Nero and Poppaea's daughter died at four months old, but two years later, Poppaea was pregnant again. In an intense argument, Nero kicked her in the belly – killing her and the unborn child. Nero was devastated, going into mourning, and giving her a state funeral. About a year later, he came upon a boy named Sporos, who may have been among the *puer deliciae* – male children with delicate features (usually slaves) abused by Roman men for their sexual pleasure. Sporos bore a remarkable resemblance to Poppaea. Nero had Sporos castrated and married him; Sporos accompanied his husband in public, wearing an empress' clothing.

Rome's fire of AD 64 destroyed two-thirds of the city.

A great fire erupted in Rome in AD 64, burning for over a week, destroying countless homes and temples. Most Roman historians of the day laid the blame on Nero, who needed to clear space for his Golden House project requiring at least 100 acres. To deflect suspicion, Nero blamed the Christians. Both Jews and pagans in Rome were drawn to Christianity through a revolutionary concept— an ideology of brotherly love instead of power. Nero rounded up the followers of *The Way*: crucifying them, throwing them to the wild beasts, or lighting his garden with their burning bodies. The apostle Peter was crucified, and Paul was decapitated.

After the fire, Nero's new building plan called for houses to be spaced apart from each other – not connected like townhouses as they had been, built from brick, not wood, and with a portico on the front. To cover the immense cost of rebuilding Rome, Nero devalued Roman currency, demanded tribute payments from the empire's provinces, and raised taxes.

Rome was growing weary of their despotic emperor. In AD 68, three provincial governors – Vindex, Galba, and Otho – rebelled against the heavy taxation, declaring Galba as the new emperor. Otho, Governor of Lusitania, bore a simmering rage against Nero for stealing his wife Poppaea – and then killing her. The Roman forces defeated Vindex's army in Gaul, but then the Roman legions also demanded a new emperor.

When the Praetorian Guard turned against Nero, he left town, intending to sail to the eastern provinces with his boy-wife Sporos, but he didn't get far beyond Rome's walls – his army refused to take him anywhere. Nero realized his only option was suicide. He ordered his servants to dig his grave but then lost his nerve, asking one of his companions to go first. No one volunteered. Still unable to kill himself, he asked his secretary to stab him. Nero died at age 30 on June 9, 68 – the end of the Julio-Claudian Dynasty.

Tacitus described the following year – the Year of the Four Emperors – as "a period rich in disasters ... even in peace, full of horrors." Once again, Rome was embroiled in a bitter civil war. Vindex, the orchestrator of the rebellion, had committed suicide, but on the night of Nero's death, the Senate proclaimed Galba as their new emperor.

Galba faced the immediate threat of Nymphidius Sabinus, the Prefect of the Praetorian Guard, who had his own ambitions for being emperor. Nymphidius had convinced his men to abandon Nero, but when Nymphidius married Nero's boy-wife Sporos and tried to make himself emperor, his own men killed him.

Galba had a reputation for greed and cruelty – as he marched toward Rome through Spain and Gaul, he decimated or heavily fined any cities in his path that questioned his right to rule them. After entering Rome, he canceled Nero's reforms and executed distinguished citizens without trial, based on trivial suspicions. His rule lasted seven months.

The Roman legions in Germany refused to swear loyalty to Galba – proclaiming their own governor – Vitellius – as emperor. Meanwhile, the Praetorian Guard staged a coup d'état, killing Galba in the Forum and putting forward their candidate – Otho – for emperor (who had bribed them well). With great relief, the Senate approved Otho, who wasn't expected to be a brutish despot.

Otho took the boy Sporos (who resembled his late wife Poppaea) for himself and set to work stabilizing Rome – finding that leading a coup was far easier than putting the pieces together afterward. Within weeks, he learned Vitellius was marching from Germany toward Rome. Vitellius dismissed Otho's offer to share the empire. Although the omens were against him, Otho marched north with his legions to defend Italy's borders, but he was too late. Vitellius' forces had crossed the Alps and were already in northern Italy. Vitellius won the ensuing battle, the Roman soldiers quickly switched to his side, and Otho committed suicide – ending his three-month reign.

As soon as the Senate heard of Otho's suicide, they recognized Vitellius as emperor while he marched toward Rome. He enlarged the Praetorian Guard by installing his loyal soldiers from Germany, then began a succession of celebratory banquets and triumphal parades. He also disposed of his rivals by forcing them to participate in cruel games and gladiator shows. He planned to torture and kill the hapless Sporos in a reenactment of the Rape of Proserpina, but the boy killed himself first.

His lavish feasting and parades emptied the treasury, so he resorted to convincing citizens to name him as their heir, then killed them and collected their estates. After three months of gluttony and games, reality struck – in the form of a new contender. Egypt, Judea, and Syria announced their own emperor: Titus Flavius Vespasianus – the hero legate who led the British Conquest in AD 43.

Leaving his son Titus to deal with the Jewish Rebellion in Judea, Vespasian was on his way to Italy when the legions in Switzerland, Germany, Austria, and the Balkans also acclaimed him as their emperor. Before Vespasian arrived in Italy, the northern legions crossed the Alps into northern Italy, scoring an overwhelming victory over Vitellius, who was decapitated and his body thrown into the Tiber, thus ending the Year of Four Emperors with Vespasian on the throne – the founder of the Flavian Dynasty.

Despite the chaos of the Julio-Claudian Dynasty and the Year of the Four Kings, the rest of the empire was experiencing peace – at least, more law and order than the provinces around the Mediterranean had enjoyed for millennia. The *Pax Romana* or Roman Peace extended from around 27 BC (when Augustus Caesar's reign began) to AD 180 (when Marcus Aurelius died). With a central government, common languages (Latin and Greek), and an excellent and extensive road system, the empire could surge ahead with unprecedented trade, economic growth, engineering feats, and cultural growth. Travel was relatively safe due to Roman legions stationed around the empire discouraging bandits on land and pirates at sea.

The *Pax Romana* immensely affected the spread of Christianity. The New Testament records that Jesus was born during the reign of Augustus, and his teaching ministry took place under Tiberius' reign. The Apostle Paul's missionary journeys throughout much of the Roman Empire took place under Claudius and Nero, enabled by the Pax Romana. Rome was generally tolerant of other religions, and Christians had been only sporadically targeted for persecution until the last few years of Nero's reign. As a Roman citizen, Paul appealed to Caesar – Nero – when the Jews arrested him. His appeal was granted, and he was taken to Rome, where he stayed in his own rented house for two years in the custody of the Praetorian Guard, developing friendships that extended into Nero's household.

Chapter 11: The Flavians and the Antonines

Although cursed by a horrific volcanic eruption, another fire in Rome, and a plague, the Flavian Dynasty restored stability and dignity to Rome after the Year of the Four Emperors' violent power struggle. It was followed by the Antonine Dynasty, known for stability in the frontiers, good emperors, prosperity, uncontested successions, and flourishing arts.

Titus Flavius Vespasianus - founder of the Flavian Dynasty - rose from modest origins to bring Rome back to a place of honor, strength, and cohesion during his ten-year reign. His road to power came through distinguished service in the military, capturing the admiration of his forces who proclaimed him emperor in the chaos following Nero's fall. Before becoming emperor, he was a driving force in Britain's invasion, then served as proconsul in Africa - that didn't go so swimmingly - the people bombarded him with turnips, frustrated at his tight budget.

Nero appointed him in AD 67 to crush the Great Jewish Revolt - a rebellion of the commoners against both the Jewish and Roman ruling class. In AD 66, Jewish Zealots attacked Roman citizens; the Roman governor Gessius Florus retaliated by plundering the Temple in Jerusalem. The outraged Jews massacred 6000 Roman soldiers, and that's when Nero sent

Vespasian to destroy the Jewish forces and punish the citizens. Vespasian and his son Titus slaughtered or sold into slavery about 10,000 Jews in Caesarea and Galilee, and the rebel Jewish forces fled north to Jerusalem.

Vespasian returned to Rome to become the new emperor, but Titus besieged Jerusalem for seven months, starving the people. Three decades earlier, Jesus had wept over Jerusalem, prophesying the siege. Titus breached the walls, burned the city – including the temple, and leveled it to the ground. One million Jews died in Judea, and 60,000 were taken as slaves to Rome to build the Colosseum. The temple in Jerusalem was never rebuilt.

One of Vespasian's first tasks as emperor was to raise money to recoup what had been lost from Nero's extravagance, to repair damage to buildings and infrastructure from a year of civil war, and to begin new construction projects on temples, a theater, and the Colosseum. He reclaimed public land and raised taxes, even placing a tax on public toilets, inducing the citizens to mockingly name urinals *vespasiano* after him.

The Colosseum was built in the Flavian Dynasty to host games, gladiator competitions, and wild animal fights.

In AD 70, Vespasian initiated construction on the Colosseum – the largest ancient amphitheater still standing in the world – in the center of Rome, just east of the Forum. It was finished in AD 80 by his son Titus; his second son Domitian made further modifications during his reign. It was known as the Flavian Amphitheater and used for games, gladiator battles, and wild animal fights. During Vespasian's reign, General Agricola expanded and consolidated Rome's province in Britain, thrusting north into Scotland.

Vespasian was known for his common sense and earthy humor. When he was dying from persistent diarrhea, he quipped, "Dear me, I think I'm becoming a god," poking fun at the Romans' custom of elevating their emperors to god status upon their death. He died in AD 79 at 69, and his son Titus assumed the throne – the first time a Roman emperor was succeeded by his biological son.

Titus Caesar Vespasianus was popular and admired for his military and administrative competence along with his reforms, such as outlawing treason trials, which were being used as witch hunts to eliminate rivals. But most of Titus' brief two-year reign was spent in disaster management: three horrific catastrophes struck Italy in quick succession just two months after he ascended the throne.

On August 24, AD 79, Mount Vesuvius exploded – shooting ash and pumice ten miles into the stratosphere, which then rained down on Pompeii. Most citizens fled, but about 2000 sheltered in their homes – but worse peril awaited them the following morning. The volcano engulfed the town of Herculaneum in a lethal cloud of asphyxiating gas and hot ash, then buried it under 60 feet of mud. The same toxic gas killed those still in Pompeii, then 14 feet of ash and pumice covered the city.

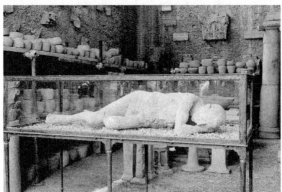

The bodies of Vesuvius' victims in Pompeii were covered in ash, which hardened into a shell, preserving them for almost two millennia. Beginning in 1863, plaster was poured into the hardened shells, forming casts of the victims.
Sparrow (麻雀), CC BY-SA 4.0 <https://creativecommons.org/licenses/by-sa/4.0>, via Wikimedia Commons https://commons.wikimedia.org/wiki/File:Pompeii_casts_18.jpg

Vespasian's friend, Pliny the Elder - author, naturalist, philosopher, and naval commander - was an eyewitness to the eruption, along with his 18-year-old nephew Pliny the Younger. Pliny was stationed with the Roman fleet at Misenum, across the Bay of Naples from Mount Vesuvius, and his nephew wrote of the volcanic cloud rising high and extending out in several branches - like a pine tree. Pliny the Elder organized a rescue mission for Stabiae. As they sailed across the bay, pumice and cinders fell on the ship. They rescued some survivors, but just as they were leaving, they were enveloped by hot toxic gasses which asphyxiated Pliny.

Titus appointed two former consuls to assess and coordinate relief work, donating a generous sum from the state treasury for the victims. He visited the area twice, and while on his second visit in the spring of AD 80, Rome caught fire again, burning for three days and nights, destroying Agrippa's Pantheon, the Theater of Pompey, the Temple of Jupiter, and much more. Titus compensated those who lost their homes or businesses. While the fire was burning in Rome, a lethal epidemic broke out in the countryside, killing 10,000 a day.

Titus celebrated the grand opening of the Flavian Amphitheater (Colosseum) in AD 80, with 100 days of entertainment and games. He also unveiled the new public Baths of Titus just next to the Colosseum. After dedicating these two edifices, he headed for the Sabine territory, but suddenly fell ill, developed a high fever, and died - cut short in the prime of life after only two years as emperor.

When Titus's younger brother Domitian ascended the throne as the last Flavian emperor, he squelched hopes he would follow in his father and brother's footsteps. Rude and tyrannical toward the senators, he stripped their power. He exhibited odd behaviors, disappearing into a room to catch flies and pierce them with a needle, leading the people to joke, "Who was the emperor with today?" "No one! No even a fly."

But Domitian ran the empire with efficiency - tending to micromanage. He enforced rigorous taxes to cover the cost of the two lavish palaces he built for himself - one in Rome and the other in the Alban Hills, and construction of the Stadium of

Domitian for athletic competitions. Toward the end of his fifteen-year reign, he steadily grew paranoid, executing a least twenty senators for treason or corruption. His paranoia was not misplaced – he was assassinated in AD 96 – stabbed in the groin – by Stephanus, a freed slave, in a plot devised by his chamberlain Parthenius, ending the Flavian Dynasty.

On the day Domitian was assassinated, the Senate announced Marcus Cocceius Nerva as Rome's next emperor – ushering in the Antonine Dynasty and the first of the "five good emperors" who brought order, balance, and wealth to Rome.

Why did the Senate choose the elderly Nerva? Perhaps simply because he was older and in ill health – he would be a "place-holder" while the Senate figured out who they really wanted. To his credit, in his 15 months as emperor, Nerva relieved the tax burden, passed economic reforms, granted land allotments to the poor, curtailed the extravagant sacrifices and entertainment draining the treasury, and completed the public works projects initiated by the Flavians.

Nerva did nothing to investigate and punish Domitian's assassins – in the struggle, Domitian had stabbed his killer Stephanus, who died with him. Maybe Nerva feared the conspirators would come after him. Finally, the frustrated Praetorian Guard held him hostage until he agreed to arrest and prosecute the chamberlain and others involved in the plot.

In AD 97, he adopted Marcus Ulpius Traianus as his heir and successor; six months later, he suffered a stroke and died soon after.

Trajan served as the second of the "five good emperors" of the Antonine Dynasty.
https://commons.wikimedia.org/w/index.php?curid=1954744

The new emperor Trajan was born in Spain to Roman parents. Although unrelated, Nerva adopted him, making him his heir due to Trajan's illustrious military career – Nerva desperately needed the support of the military. Trajan had also served as a governor in northern Europe and consul of Rome. Before becoming emperor, Trajan became guardian to his cousins Hadrian and Paulina, whose parents had died.

As emperor, Trajan removed much of the Senate's power but made governmental decisions that the Senate would likely have made anyway, earning the reputation of a virtuous autocrat and a role model of moderation. He was notable for appointing at least fourteen Greek senators to Rome's Senate – making it more representative of the empire's provincial population and helping alleviate simmering tensions with the eastern half of the empire.

Trajan was a soldier more than anything else, and his primary concern was expanding the empire's borders. After two wars, he conquered Dacia (in modern Romania), turning it into a Roman province. He annexed the Nabataean kingdom of the northwestern Arabian Desert after its Bedouin client-king died, consolidating it with Jordan, southern Levant, and the Sinai Peninsula to form the Roman province of Arabia Petraea. In his last military campaign, he annexed Armenia and Babylon as provinces

With the plunder gained from his military victories, Trajan renovated the Circus Maximus and expanded the Forum, but also formed a welfare program for the orphans and poor children of Italy, providing food and education. He hosted three months of games at the Colosseum with five million spectators watching chariot racing, gladiator contests, and fighting beasts – 11,000 gladiator slaves and criminals died.

While on his final campaign in Mesopotamia in AD 117, Trajan suffered heatstroke. On his deathbed, he named Hadrian as his adopted son and successor – although rumors swirled that his wife Plotina forged the document.

This bronze figure of Hadrian is in the Israel Museum.
*Carole Raddato from FRANKFURT, Germany, CC BY-SA 2.0
<https://creativecommons.org/licenses/by-sa/2.0>, via Wikimedia Commons
https://commons.wikimedia.org/wiki/File:Hadrian-
An Emperor Cast in Bronze, Israel Museum (27801269805).jpg*

Caesar Traianus Hadrianus' twenty-year reign raised the Roman Empire to its greatest height. Hadrian spent half his reign traveling outside Rome, ensuring proficient provincial administration and army discipline. In 122, he built the 73-mile Hadrian's Wall in Britain, extending completely across the island from the Irish Sea to the North Sea, protecting Britain from the fierce tattooed Picts of Scotland. Throughout Asia, Africa, and Europe, he built monuments and cities while improving infrastructure and roads. In Rome, he rebuilt the Pantheon, repaired Trajan's Forum, and constructed Roman baths.

In 132, Hadrian rebuilt Jerusalem, provoking the Jews by building a temple to Jupiter just where the sacred Jewish temple once stood, which spurred the Bar-Kochba Revolt. During the fierce war, 580,000 Jews were killed, and 1000 towns were razed. He renamed the province Palaestina, evicted the Jews, burned the Torah, and outlawed the Jewish faith.

After putting down the revolt, Hadrian's health failed, and he retired permanently to Rome. Months before his death in 138, Hadrian adopted Antoninus Pius as his son and successor, who then adopted Lucius Verus and Marcus Aurelius.

With the most peaceful reign of any Roman Emperor, Antoninus Pius had no stunning military conquest, no extravagances, no oddities – other than not being odd. He didn't travel around like Hadrian – he just stayed in Italy and managed the empire as a sensible model of respectability. His long and happy marriage to Faustina produced four children, but only their youngest daughter, Faustina the Younger, lived to see him crowned as emperor. She married her cousin Marcus Aurelius – who had been adopted by Antoninus – and together, they had 13 children with two sets of twins.

Before becoming emperor, Antoninus had excelled as a proficient governor of Asia. As emperor, he was a shrewd political operator with a keen financial sense, leaving the treasury with a surplus. He built the Temple of Antoninus and Faustina in honor of his wife, which was later converted to a Catholic church in the fifth century. He rebuilt the ancient Pons Sublicius bridge over the Tiber, and other bridges, roads, and aqueducts.

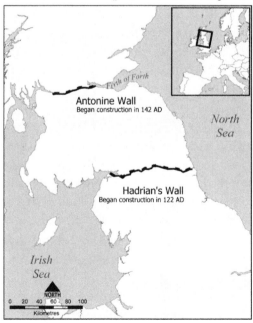

Hadrian's Wall was built during Hadrian's reign and the Antonine Wall during Antoninus' rule.

Although Antoninus remained in Italy, his Numidian general Quintus Lollius Urbicus scored a modest victory when he invaded Scotland, taking additional territory and building the Antonine Wall 100 miles north of Hadrian's Wall. Antoninus was the first Roman ruler to send a diplomatic mission to China (during its Han Dynasty), which went down in Chinese records. Antoninus died in 161, leaving the empire to his two adopted sons – Marcus Aurelius and Lucius Verus – to co-rule.

Marcus Aurelius – a Stoic philosopher – wrote *Meditations*: insights on meaningful life and human behavior. He ascended to the throne with his adoptive brother Lucius Verus – the first time Rome had dual emperors. Verus wasn't scholarly like Marcus – he preferred sports and hunting. In this awkward arrangement, Marcus Aurelius held more authority, but together they continued leading the empire through its peak of power and prosperity.

The pair were almost immediately tested when King Vologases IV of Parthia invaded Armenia. With no military experience, Marcus and Lucius sent Marcus Statius Priscus, governor of Britain, to retake Armenia, but that ended in disaster. Then the Syrians rebelled. One of them needed to head east to deal with things, but who?

Lucius was sent – he had been partying too much and would benefit from military discipline, plus being more cut out for warfare than the erudite Marcus. Lucius leisurely traveled east, feasting, hunting, and visiting the pleasure resorts of Cilicia and Pamphylia before finally reaching Antioch, where he had to assume a modicum of military discipline. The Roman forces were just as dissolute – drinking, gambling, and going soft.

The temporarily reformed Lucius led them through training exercises, marching or running with them on foot. He ordered his men to build a shipping canal on the Orontes River to bypass a waterfall – the construction exposed a massive 18-foot-long earthenware coffin holding the remains of a giant. In the middle of the war, he traveled to Ephesus to marry 13-year-old Anna Lucilla – daughter of Marcus Aurelius.

The Roman generals captured Armenia, and while Lucius was appointing a new king, the troublesome Parthians invaded

Osroene, east of Syria. In 165, Roman forces marched on Mesopotamia, chasing the Parthians to the Tigris, where their general desperately jumped in the river, swimming downstream to a cave where he took refuge. Rome triumphantly took control of all western Mesopotamia, and Lucius returned to Rome and back to partying, hailed as a war hero, although his astute generals had done the real work.

The Antonine Plague – a pandemic of either smallpox or measles – swept the Roman Empire beginning in 165, brought back from the east by the military. Rome lost 2000 souls a day, at least five million died throughout the empire, and the Roman army was decimated. Lucius fell ill, dying in early 169, leaving Marcus as sole emperor.

While Lucius had been fighting in the east, Marcus was resisting invasions of the Germanic tribes, the Iranian Iazyges tribe, and the Costoboci of the Carpathian Mountains. Marcus pushed backed some invasions, but other times the tribes settled in Roman provinces.

Marcus was experienced and adept in legal affairs and conscientious about freeing slaves and providing guardianship for orphans. He diplomatically asked the Senate permission for funding and spoke of his palace as belonging to the people. His death in 180 brought an end to the Pax Romana, as his son Commodus ascended the throne. In the words of Cassius Dio, Rome descended "from a kingdom of gold to one of iron and rust."

Commodus – Rome's new 18-year-old emperor – was a sociopathic megalomaniac. Cassius Dio, an acquaintance, was kinder, saying he didn't have an evil nature but was easily manipulated by his companions, who introduced him to a cruel and indecent lifestyle. Having co-ruled with Marcus Aurelius for two years before his father's death, he had acquired valuable military and administrative experience. But when Marcus Aurelius died, Commodus returned to his reckless and fawning friends, rejecting his father's Stoic asceticism.

His first three years were unremarkable – the empire was relatively peaceful, and his father's advisers kept things running smoothly. But then, it happened. His older sister Lucilla conspired to assassinate him, perhaps concerned his erratic behavior would destroy Rome. The assassins bungled things, and Commodus survived, executing his would-be killers and exiling and later executing Lucilla.

Commodus became paranoid, imaging treachery and plots all around him. He wasn't off-base – conspiracies to kill him continued throughout his reign. Two men – Perennis and Cleander – murdered his chamberlain. Unaware of their involvement, Commodus appointed Perennis as his Praetorian Prefect and Cleander as his new chamberlain. Disinterested in administration, Commodus gave Perennis charge over most of his duties – which Perennis conducted competently, that is, until he was named in a plot to overthrow Commodus and executed.

Perennis' successor Aebutianus was also accused – by Cleander – of plotting to kill Commodus, and after Aebutianus' execution, Cleander took over as Prefect, enriching himself by selling coveted political positions to the highest bidder. Unfortunately for Cleander, a food shortage hit Rome, and the man responsible for grain – Dionysius – blamed Cleander, who hid in Commodus' palace from an angry mob. On the urging of his mistress Marcia, Commodus beheaded Cleander, handing his head on a pike to the mob, then had the mutilated bodies of Cleander's wife and children dragged through the streets.

Commodus was obsessed with playing gladiator, striding into the arena to fight men and animals. He especially enjoyed fighting disabled people. Gladiator contests didn't always involve killing; often, it was a competition to demonstrate which fighter had the superior skill. But the bloodthirsty Commodus always demanded gory death – whether he was watching a contest or fighting himself. Whenever Commodus showed up in the arena, the state had to pay a fee of a million sesterces, driving the struggling economy toward collapse.

Commodus wore a lion skin, impersonating the god Hercules.
© José Luiz Bernardes Ribeiro
https://commons.wikimedia.org/wiki/File:Commodus_as_Hercules_(detail)_-
Palazzo_dei_Conservatori_-_Musei_Capitolini_-_Rome_2016_(2).jpg

Commodus believed he was a god – he pressured the Senate to declare him the incarnate Hercules, son of Zeus, and walked around impersonating Hercules in a lion-hide cloak. After receiving a cold response, he massacred most of the Senators and other administrators on New Year's Eve, intending to be the sole dictator. In the words of Dio, the Romans felt "Commodus was a greater curse to the Romans than any pestilence or crime." His mistress Maria colluded with others to kill him, putting poison in his food, which he vomited up. As he was cleaning off the vomit in the bath, his wrestling partner Narcissus choked him to death, ending the reign of madness in March 193.

Just as the Julio-Claudian Dynasty ended with the Year of Four Emperors, the Antonine Dynasty ended with the Year of Five Emperors. Pertinax, a senator who had served as Proconsul of Africa, was chosen as emperor by Commodus' assassins – basically because he was one of the few nobles still alive after Commodus' purge. Pertinax was a disciplined administrator, but he offended the Praetorian Guard by failing to give the usual monetary gifts at his accession and then imposed stricter discipline over them; the disgruntled Praetorian Guard killed him, then enriched themselves by auctioning the position of emperor.

The highest bidder was the affluent senator Didius Julianus, who had served as Proconsul of Africa after Pertinax. Hated by the people for buying his position, his reign as emperor lasted two months. He was overcome and killed by Septimius Severus, a governor in central Europe, who expected to become emperor. Before that could happen, Septimius had to get rid of his rivals.

Pescennius Niger, governor of Syria, declared himself emperor with the backing of the eastern legions. Severus appointed Clodius Albinus (another contender for emperor) as temporary Caesar while Severus was in the east fighting Niger. Severus defeated Niger, decapitating him, then turned on Albinus, defeating and killing him. After purging his rivals' followers, Severus became sole emperor and the founder of the Severan Dynasty. Although the new dynasty had some successful emperors, it would never again experience the wealth, power, and stability of the Antonine Dynasty.

Chapter 12: The Severan Dynasty

An African family of Semitic-Phoenician descent headed up the new dynasty in Rome. The cruel tyrant Commodus was dead, and Severus had risen to take his place, founder of the Severan Dynasty. Five Severan emperors ruled the Roman Empire for 47 years, from AD 193-235, with an interlude of one non-Severan emperor. The empire fell into decline on their watch, due to incessant barbarian invasions, conflict with the Praetorian Guard prohibiting strong sovereignty, unstable Severan family dynamics, and constant political turmoil rocking Rome.

Septimius Severus was born into a Phoenician family in northern Africa. With exemplary military service, he rose through the ranks until he became governor of Upper Pannonia in central Europe. His Syrian wife Julia Domna was actively involved in politics while he was emperor - unusual for Roman women who ruled through their husbands or sons.

In 195, attempting to gain credibility with the Roman people, Severus had himself posthumously adopted by Marcus Aurelius, so he could claim lineage from the respected emperor of the Antonine Dynasty. He then gave his older son, Caracalla, the imperial rank of Caesar and pronounced him Latin (ethnically, he was north African and Semitic).

The Severan Tondo, circa AD 200, depicts the African-Phoenician Severus with his Syrian wife Julia Domna, and two sons, Geta and Caracalla. Geta's face was blotted out as part of the damnatio memoriae (damnation of memory).
© José Luiz Bernardes Ribeiro
https://commons.wikimedia.org/wiki/File:Portrait_of_family_of_Septimius_Severus_-_Altes_Museum_-_Berlin_-_Germany_2017.jpg

Severus triumphed against the Parthians, sacking their capital city and extending Rome's borders to the Tigris River. He expanded and fortified Rome's Arabian Provence and rebuilt Hadrian's Wall in northern Britain. In Africa, he fought the Garamantes (Berber tribes from the Sahara desert), conquering their capital Garama in Libya and expanding the Roman desert frontier between Libya and Tunisia.

His relationship with the Senate was frosty, having seized power without their blessing and making himself a military dictator, but the military and the common people admired him for bringing stability after the horrors of Commodus' reign. Severus executed many senators on charges of corruption or conspiracy, installing his supporters in their place.

Throughout the Severan Dynasty, sporadic persecution of Jews and Christians took place – mainly because they persisted in monotheistic worship – refusing to embrace the Roman pantheon of gods. Most of Rome's conquered people were already polytheistic, so they would include the Roman deities while still worshiping their own gods. In return, the Romans would even build temples for foreign deities in the provinces and occasionally incorporated the gods of other people into their pantheon.

But the Jews and Christians were a different story. They only worshiped the god of Abraham, Isaac, and Jacob. They refused to offer sacrifices to Roman gods or participate in Roman religious festivals – which seem disloyal to the Romans, testing their religious tolerance. Since the Jews had a monotheistic history going back for millennia, the Romans usually gave them a pass. But Christianity was a new cult in Rome's eyes – an illegal superstition. They thought that holy communion was literal cannibalism and drinking blood.

As for Severus, his Christian doctor had successfully treated him through a severe illness, so he was personally not against Christianity and even protected some of his Christian acquaintances. The persecutions mostly took place at the local level – not by imperial edict – in the provinces. Christians were thrown to the wild beasts, beheaded, and thrown into scalding baths. At least two bishops of Rome were executed in the later Severan Dynasty.

When his oldest son Caracalla was ten years old, Severus proclaimed him as co-emperor and *Pontifex Maximus* (high priest) on the day Severus celebrated his triumph over the Parthian Empire. This was mostly honorary until the boy was old enough to assist his father in ruling, but it paved the way for an easier succession. In 209, Severus made his younger son Geta co-emperor; thus, Rome had three emperors reigning together for two years until Severus died. After he died in 211, the brothers ruled together – unsuccessfully.

Caracalla's real name was Lucius Septimius Bassianus, but he liked wearing hoodies, even when he slept, so he was nicknamed Caracalla after the Gallic hooded tunic. His father had intended him to rule jointly with his younger brother Publius Septimius Geta – but sharing power ended in failure and tragedy. When their father was alive, Caracalla was Severus' military second-in-command, while Geta oversaw the administrative and bureaucratic end of things. But even then, rivalry and antagonism simmered between the brothers.

The brothers had been with their father in Britain when he died, but on their return journey to Rome with their father's ashes, they were either arguing or avoiding each other – staying in different lodging and never sharing a meal. Their mother, Julia Domna, who had been their father's confidante and key advisor, desperately tried to mediate – to no avail.

When they got back to Rome, they lived and worked in separate sections of the palace – even their servants could not cross to the other's side of the building. They were petrified of assassination by the other – always keeping bodyguards around them and only meeting when their mother was present. Julia Domna was the stabilizing force in their tense standoff, acting as a go-between and collaborating cooperatively with the generals and courtiers.

Julia Domna was torn between her two sons, Caracalla and Geta.
https://commons.wikimedia.org/wiki/File:Julia_Domna_Glyptothek_Munich_354.jpg

The brothers even proposed splitting the empire in half – each ruling their own section – but their mother talked them out of it, crying, "as you say, the Propontic Gulf separates the continents. But your mother, how would you parcel her? How am I to be torn and ripped asunder for the pair of you?"

Herodian wrote that she clasped both in her arms, with tears streaming down her face. The meeting adjourned, and the brothers walked out – each to their side of the palace. Their antipathy grew, and in every joint decision they had to make, the brothers were diametrically opposed. They each tried to devise ways to poison the other, but both took precautions. Finally, Caracalla produced a plan.

He told his mother he was ready to reconcile with Geta, asking her to summon him to her apartment, so they could meet with her. Domna persuaded Geta to come, but once he was inside her room, the centurions suddenly rushed toward Geta and stabbed him. Geta staggered toward his mother, falling into her embrace, as the soldiers continued to run him through, even cutting Domna, soaked in her son's blood.

Caracalla fled to the Praetorian camp, telling the troops that Geta had just attempted to kill him and had been killed in the struggle. After he heavily bribed the praetorians (and emptying the treasury), the Praetorian Guard proclaimed Geta an enemy and Caracalla sole emperor. Cassius Dio said everyone that lived on Geta's side of the palace was immediately butchered, even women and babies, and altogether 20,000 of Geta's soldiers, servants, and supporters were slain. Domna – wife and mother of emperors – was forbidden to weep for Geta; not even in private could she express her sorrow for her dead son.

Not satisfied with killing his brother, Caracalla set out to erase Geta's existence in the *damnatio memoriae* (damnation of memory). His name was blotted from documents, his image on paintings, coins, and statues was destroyed. With his brother erased, Caracalla survived through the loyalty of his troops, but that would not last long. Before he was 30, his sins would catch up with him, and he would be betrayed.

Caracalla ruled jointly with Geta, until he assassinated his brother, taking the throne completely for himself.

Caracalla found administrative affairs tedious – his brother had managed those things before, and now his mother Domna assumed much of the everyday running of the empire. Caracalla gave his attention to military affairs – as he always had done.

When he was 14, Caracalla's parents had forced him into an arranged marriage to Fulvia Plautilla, whom he hated. They had one daughter, but then her father was executed for treachery, and Plautilla was sent into exile. Caracalla ordered her strangled after his father died. Neither Geta nor Caracalla had a son to continue the dynasty.

Caracalla passed the Antonine Constitution, extending Roman citizenship to all free men in the Roman Empire; previously, citizenship had mostly been limited to those living in or born in Italy. Cassius Dio felt Caracalla did this for tax revenue – only citizens had to pay inheritance taxes. Caracalla needed to refill the treasury to pay the military well and keep their support. Caracalla also constructed the Baths of Caracalla and introduced a new currency – the antoninianus – a coin worth two denarii.

Caracalla left Rome within a year after his brother's assassination – never to return. He saw himself as a modern-day Alexander the Great, affecting his style and implementing his battle strategies. Caracalla headed north to push back the Alemanni (Germanic tribes). Through strengthening frontier fortifications, he effectively blocked any further invasions for two decades.

The following year, he toured the eastern provinces, reaching Egypt in December 2015, where he had a score to settle with the Alexandrians, who had produced a mocking satire of his claims that Geta was killed in self-dense. Arriving in Alexandria, he reaped his revenge by slaughtering the dignitaries welcoming him at the gate and plundering the city.

In April of 2017, he was traveling through what is now southern Turkey and stopped to urinate, when, suddenly, one of his soldiers, Justin Martialis, stabbed him to death. Martialis was instantly killed by the other soldiers, but the Praetorian Prefect Macrinus, with the military behind him, declared himself emperor three days later. The Senate, far away in Rome, was helpless to do anything, although they were thanking the gods that Macrinus had gotten rid of the homicidal Caracalla.

At the time of Caracalla's death at age 29, Julia Domna was in Antioch, managing his correspondence. Suffering from breast cancer, she committed suicide on hearing the news. Her feelings for Caracalla were complicated – she hated him for killing Geta, yet he was still her son, and part of her loved him anyway. Through him, she had power over the empire. Now she had lost her reason for living. Macrinus would be the emperor of the interlude, but within months, Domna's sister Julia Maesa would restore the Severan Dynasty in 218.

Marcus Opellius Macrinus never visited Rome during his 14-month reign, choosing to rule from Antioch. Born in Caesarea, he was African, like the Severan family, but of Berber descent, with a pierced ear, which the historian and senator Cassius Dio found unseemly.

Macrinus had two military issues to address immediately: finishing the war that Caracalla had started in Parthia and dealing with an Armenian rebellion. He took care of both situations with diplomatic negotiations, then turned his attention to Rome's internal affairs, which were in disarray – especially the dire financial straits.

He reversed Caracalla's fiscal policies – something had to be done about the exorbitant pay for soldiers that had drained the treasury. Unwilling to rock the boat with his current soldiers, he permitted them to retain the same inflated pay, but newly-enlisted men received the salary paid in Severus' time. Macrinus' goal was economic stability, but it angered the military. Even though only new recruits were affected by reduced pay, the veterans guessed that it wouldn't be long before their own pay was reduced.

Julia Domna's sister, Julia Maesa, was still living in the imperial court in Rome, where both her husband and daughter had reached senatorial rank. Macrinus sent her back to Syria. Her hometown in Emesa, Syria was next to a Roman military base, and her family socialized with some of their former friends from Rome, along with some new friends, forming a tight bond with the Roman legion.

Her grandson Elagabalus bore a strong resemblance to his second cousin, Caracalla, and Maesa capitalized on this by spreading rumors he was the lovechild of Caracalla and her daughter Soaemias. She also generously spread her immense wealth among key military leaders and played on their dissatisfaction with Macrinus, instigating a coup. The Roman legion took the boy into their camp one night, wrapped him in purple, and declared him their legitimate emperor of Severan lineage: son of Caracalla and grandson of Severus. Other legions began abandoning Macrinus and defecting to Elagabalus.

Macrinus marched on Syria, but his army defected to Elagabalus, and Macrinus had to escape to Antioch. Elagabalus' army (formerly Macrinus') marched on Antioch, fighting the Praetorian Guard protecting Macrinus. The Praetorian Guard was prevailing, but suddenly Maesa and her daughter Soaemias charged toward the fray in their chariot, leaping out to rally the men and turn the tide of the battle. Elagabalus' army roared at the sight of the women and routed the Praetorian Guard. Macrinus fled, hiding out in Antioch, shaving his beard and hair to disguise himself. He slipped out of Antioch, trying to escape Elagabalus, but he was caught and executed in Cappadocia.

Elagabalus became emperor at age 14, shocking Rome with controversial behaviors.
© José Luiz Bernardes Ribeiro https://commons.wikimedia.org/wiki/File:Bust_of_Elagabalus_-_Palazzo_Nuovo_-_Musei_Capitolini_-_Rome_2016_(2).jpg

Rome now had a 14-year-old emperor, the child of Arab parents from Syria. His grandmother had been promoting him as Caracalla's bastard son; upon ascending the throne, he took

Caracalla's official name: Marcus Aurelius Antoninus. His name Elagabalus came from his position as high priest of Elagabal – the sun god in Syria. He reigned for less than four years, scandalizing Rome with weird behaviors, sexual promiscuity, and strange religious customs. The woman who put him on the throne eventually ripped his life away when he was only 18.

The Senate acknowledged Elagabalus as emperor, along with his claims to be Caracalla's son. Macrinus was expunged from the record – Elagabalus was recorded as the direct successor to Caracalla. Elagabalus' mother and grandmother became senators and influenced the teenage Elagabalus throughout his reign.

He almost immediately married his first wife Julia Paula, divorced her a year later, then married a Vestal Virgin – Aquilia Severa. This created an uproar; traditionally, if a Vestal broke her vow, she was buried alive. His grandmother engineered the annulment of this marriage and married him to Annia Faustina (whose husband he'd just executed), but he went back to Severa, living with her unfaithfully until he died.

Referring to Elagabalus as a woman, Cassio Dio wrote about "her" falling in love with several men "she" married (or wanted to marry): his tutor Gannys – who helped overthrow Macrinus, a chariot driver named Hierocles (he was the husband and Elagabalus the wife), and an athlete named Zoticus.

Rome was also shocked when Elagabalus forced the worship of his Syrian god, Elagabal, as the chief deity of the Romans, over that of Jupiter. To increase his purity as a priest, he had himself circumcised and swore off pork – which utterly mystified the Romans, unfamiliar with Semitic customs. These behaviors alienated him from the Praetorian Guard – his protectors. His grandmother Maesa realized Elagabalus was too controversial to be taken seriously as emperor. No doubt someone would assassinate him eventually.

But it didn't have to mean the end of the Severan Dynasty. She had another grandson who might work out better – Severus Alexander, the 15-year-old son of her other daughter Julia Mamaea. She influenced Elagabalus to appoint his cousin Alexander as his heir, which he did – but then he suspected a coup d'état was in the works – which worried him because the

Praetorian Guard liked Alexander better.

Elagabalus was right. On March 11, the Praetorian Guard attacked him and his mother, who was clinging tightly to him, killing them both and throwing their bodies into the Tiber. The Praetorian Guard then hailed Alexander as their new emperor on March 13, 222.

Alexander became emperor when his grandmother plotted the murder of her other grandson Elagabalus.
https://commons.wikimedia.org/wiki/File:Alexander_Severus_Musei_Capitolini_MC47 1_(cropped).jpg

Alexander ascended the throne at age 15 and reigned for 13 years as the last Severan emperor. He brought some stability to the empire but also confronted numerous, almost insurmountable challenges. He was admired by the Romans for his moderate, thoughtful, and dignified behavior – so different from his cousin Elagabalus.

He was a pious young man who prayed every morning in his private chapel – to the usual Roman deities, but also to Jesus, Abraham, and his ancestors – in a syncretistic mix reflecting his identity as a Roman along with his Middle Eastern heritage. Eusebius, Bishop of Caesarea in Palestine, wrote that he and his mother sat under the teaching of Origen – a well-known Christian scholar.

The peace and prosperity Rome had enjoyed in Alexander's first two years as emperor was threatened by the emergence of menacing challengers on the empire's eastern and northern borders. The ruthless and antagonistic Ardashir, the Persian founder of the Sassanid Dynasty, overthrew Parthia in 224 and invaded Roman provinces in Mesopotamia. Severus, accompanied by his mother, Julia Mamaea, led the Roman legions in a campaign against the Sassanians.

From Antioch, Alexander organized a three-pronged attack on the Sassanid Empire: his forces confronted Mesopotamia, while a second army marched through Armenia's mountains to invade Media, and a third army advanced on Babylon. The war ended inconclusively, with some embarrassing beatings by Ardashir's forces. Yet Alexander declared it a victory because Mesopotamia was retaken, and the Sassanid invasions stymied for a time.

Severus and Julia Mamaea then had to move their forces to the northern frontier – to the onslaught of Germanic tribes besieging Gaul and Raetia. Alarming hordes of Alemanni were crossing the Rhine and Danube. While traveling to confront the invaders, Severus and his mother were concerned about the breakdown in their army's discipline. When they were fighting the Sassanids, the Syrian legion had mutinied and declared a man named Taurinius their emperor. Alexander had crushed the revolt, and Taurinius drowned in the Euphrates. But could they trust their men now? Would they give up in the face of the Germans?

Unsure if they could defeat the invaders, Alexander and Julia paid a large bribe to induce the Germanic Alemanni to back down. This did not go over well with the military – they'd already received pay cuts and lapses in benefits. They thought Alexander was too docile and uninspiring as a leader. They sneered at him for following his mother's advice rather than listening to experienced generals and paying off the enemy rather than fighting them.

In 235, the northern legions rebelled, killing Alexander and his mother, and proclaiming Maximinus Thrax, a giant almost seven feet tall, as their new emperor. The assassination of

Alexander, the last Syrian emperor, marked the close of the Severan Dynasty. The Crisis of the Third Century had begun. Without a clear candidate for emperor, the Roman Empire descended into a half-century of chaos, to the brink of collapse, faced with multiple contenders for the throne, increased invasions on the frontiers, civil wars, peasant revolts, plague, and economic disaster.

SECTION FOUR: FINAL YEARS, SEPARATION, AND FALL (AD 235-476)

Chapter 13: An Empire in Crisis

Chaos reigned for the next fifty years, from AD 235 to 284, as wars and internal chaos almost destroyed the empire in the Crisis of the Third Century. Peril loomed from without as barbarians continued to invade Roman territory. Multiple usurpers – 52 in all – competed for power; 26 claimants were approved as emperors by the Senate. A ghastly plague, the debasement of the currency, and economic depression were nearly Rome's undoing. Ultimately, Aurelian reunified the empire, and the ascension of Diocletian in 284 brought an end to the crisis.

Rome never had clear guidelines for who could be emperor, and this precipitated the Crisis of the Third Century. Traditionally, four factors came into play regarding the legitimacy of a new emperor: Senate confirmation, citizen's approval, military backing, and relationship to the previous emperor. The Severan Dynasty relied more on confirmation by the military than Senate approval, and several times after Nero's assassination, the military proclaimed a new emperor with no connection to the ruling dynasty and without asking the Senate first. However, if all four aspects backed a new emperor's ascension, he stood a better chance of staying on the throne.

Whenever an emperor died without a clear-cut heir, the empire usually descended into a chaotic situation, with various popular and powerful generals attempting to seize power, igniting civil wars. After Alexander's assassination, in powerplays that ravaged Rome, one general after another snatched power and proclaimed himself emperor.

In the pandemonium of the next five decades, Rome was led by a series of *barracks emperors*: men lacking political experience, aristocratic family lines, or any family connection to previous emperors. Barracks emperors got their power and backing from the barracks – the troops they led. They were warlords, relying on their successful experience as generals and the support of their legions.

This denarius, struck in 236, depicts Maximus Thrax, who was almost seven feet tall. *Johny SYSEL, CC BY-SA 3.0 <https://creativecommons.org/licenses/by-sa/3.0>, via Wikimedia Commons https://commons.wikimedia.org/wiki/File:Maximinus_Thrax.jpg*

The exceptionally tall Maximus Thrax, declared the new emperor by the northern legions, was a prime example of a barracks emperor. His father was an accountant, probably from the Thracian tribe of eastern Europe. The Senate sniffed at his pedigree, but military men loved him for his legendary strength and skill as a soldier – and he certainly stood head and shoulders above anyone else.

Maximus never set foot in Rome during his three years as emperor. He immediately focused on defeating the Alemanni-Germanic tribes crossing the Rhine and infringing on Roman territory, establishing a temporary peace. The costs involved in his war campaigns and excessive soldiers' pay demanded high taxes, which irritated Rome's Senate and citizens.

When a revolt flared up in Africa in 238, the Senate threw their support behind the new usurpers: Gordian I and his son

Gordian II. Maximus' problem was solved when Capelianus, governor of Numidia and archenemy of Gordian I, raided Carthage and killed Gordian II, after which Gordian I committed suicide. The senators feared Maximus' wrath because they'd supported his contenders; even so, they declared the grandson Gordian III as Caesar and two elderly patrician senators – Pupienus and Balbinus – as co-emperors.

Maximus marched on Rome to settle things, but his once-loyal troops, out of provisions and starving, were enraged at Maximus for executing his generals for what he considered cowardice in the unsuccessful siege of Aquileia. They mutinied, decapitating Maximus and his son, carrying their heads to Rome mounted on poles. Then the Praetorian Guard murdered Pupienus and Balbinus.

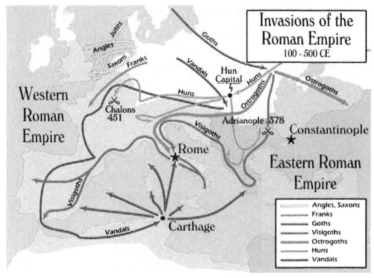

The incessant barbarian invasions contributed to the Roman Empire's ruin.

Once again, a power vacuum ensued, leading to multiple and successive uprisings of dozens of Roman generals – so fixated on power grabs they neglected defending the empire. The tribes surrounding the empire's frontiers exploited the exposed borders: the Carpians, Vandals, Goths, and Alamanni poured over the Danube and Rhine to raid Rome's northern provinces.

Philip the Arab, the former Praetorian Prefect, rose to the throne in 244 with Senate backing, bringing a measure of stability to the empire. During his five-year reign, Rome celebrated its millennium in 248 with three days of games in the Colosseum. According to Eusebius and Jerome, Philip – who grew up near Galilee – was the first Christian emperor, although coinage during his reign implied that he adhered to the polytheistic imperial religion. Even if not a Christian, he was sympathetic toward Christianity.

Because the new emperors were now mostly military men out on campaign somewhere, the center of government shifted away from Rome and to wherever the emperor was stationed with his troops – usually somewhere in the eastern provinces. The Senate no longer held sway as the chief governmental body – it was now the equestrian class (cavalry) of the military rising to prominence.

Rome was not only cursed by invasions and inner turmoil, but from 249 to 262, the Plague of Cyprian swept the empire. From house to house, families would be infected, experiencing acute onset of symptoms including diarrhea, vomiting, fever, throat lesions, bleeding from the eyes, and tissue death in the arms and legs. Some experienced hearing loss, blindness, or loss of limbs. This was a new, terrifying plague – with symptoms never seen before – no one had acquired immunity. It killed the young adults and children as quickly as the older folks.

Cyprian, an African Berber and Bishop of Carthage, chronicled his first-hand observations of the horrific plague that bore his name. Bishop Cyprian preached to his flock to tend to the sick, as Jesus had commanded. The Christians provided care for those ravaged by the pandemic and buried the dead, heedless of their own danger
https://commons.wikimedia.org/wiki/File:Cyprian_von_Karthago2.jpg

The pandemic began in Alexandria, Egypt, and spread to coastal centers throughout the empire, then moved inland. Physicians have analyzed the eyewitness account of Bishop Cyprian and other accounts to make educated guesses on what pathogen caused the deadly plague. Perhaps it was a hemorrhagic form of smallpox - but no one mentions the characteristic rash. More likely, it was a viral hemorrhagic fever - possibly a filovirus often transmitted from animals, such as monkeys or bats. Ebola is one example of a filovirus - it kills at least half of those infected - even with today's sophisticated medicine.

The plague severely weakened the empire - some cities lost over half their population. As the streets filled with the bodies of the dead, there was hardly anyone left to tend the farms - leading to famine. The military was also decimated - leaving the empire even more vulnerable to invasions.

Although the Germanic tribes in the north continued isolated attacks, the greatest threat to the empire was the Persian Sassanid Empire. Alexander had barely fended them off before his assassination, but now they were on the offensive again and had taken Antioch and Syria. After Valerian became emperor in 253, he headed east to confront the Sassanids, successfully recovering Antioch and Syria.

While fighting the Sassanid Empire, Valerian sent orders to the Senate ordering the empire-wide execution of Christian ministers and Christians who were Roman senators or equites (a wealthy political class) unless they worshipped the Roman gods. Lower-class citizens who refused to worship the Roman gods would be reduced to slavery. This indicated a shift toward the persecution of Christians by imperial decree but also revealed Christians had penetrated all classes of Roman society, including the Senate.

Among those executed were Pope Sixtus, Bishop Denis of Paris, Bishop Cyprian of Carthage, and Bishop Fructuosus of Tarragona, among countless others throughout the empire who were beheaded or burned at the stake. Two years after issuing this edict, the Sassanids captured Valerian, and he died in captivity. His son rescinded the anti-Christian orders.

And then it happened – the empire broke into pieces. Lacking a powerful central authority, the empire was divided into three competing empires. Gaul, Hispania, and Britain became the Gallic Empire in 260. Syria, Palestine, and Egypt broke off to become the Palmyrene Empire in 267. The central provinces remained under Rome's rule.

The three-way split rocked the Roman Empire to the core, already reeling from the incessant incursions of barbarian tribes and by ongoing internal unrest. Instead of building wealth by plundering other countries, they were now bleeding money to fund wars and losing soldiers faster than they could replace them. Rome increasingly relied on barbarian mercenaries known as foederati – tribes bound by treaty to support Rome.

Looting raids devastated the unprotected provinces. Barbarians continued streaming through the borders to settle in the empire; most were peacefully assimilated, but others came armed and ready to displace the existing populations. Eventually, the Illyrian emperors came to the rescue to stabilize the frontiers, beginning in 268. The Illyrians, from what is now the Balkans, had risen through Rome's military ranks to become commanders and eventually barracks emperors. They played an intrinsic part in recovering the provinces lost during the crisis and restoring a unified empire.

Claudius II Gothicus' stunning military defeat of the Goths helped end the Crisis of the Third Century.
Museum of Fine Arts, Boston, CC0, via Wikimedia Commons
https://commons.wikimedia.org/wiki/File:ClaudiusGothicusSC265569.jpg

One Illyrian emperor, Claudius II Gothicus, defeated a Gothic invasion into Macedonia and Greece in 268 – the turning point in the Crisis of the Third Century. He pushed the Alamanni back and recouped Hispania from the Gauls. Other resolute and zealous barracks emperors rehabilitated Rome's central authority. The pendulum was now swinging in the other direction.

But the damage had been done. Numerous once-flourishing cities of the western empire lay in ruins, their citizens dead or scattered. The economy was crushed. The Pax Romana was no more – now cities built thick, high walls for protection.

The Crisis of the Third Century included a financial catastrophe caused by multiple issues, including expensive military action, a corrupt and inefficient tax collection system, poor money management, bribing barbarians to stay away, and loss of manpower from the plague and warfare to work the farms, produce goods, and tend shops to sell them. For years, coinage devaluation persisted, leading to hyperinflation.

The Romans had a tradition that when a new emperor took the crown, he gave the soldiers a bonus. That money had to come from somewhere – especially when the country went through 26 emperors in 50 years. The emperors resorted to deflating the value of silver coins by adding in copper and bronze – rendering the silver denarius of no value – useless in trade and spawning rising prices.

The devalued coinage, unsafe travel, and sporadic pillaging by invading tribes profoundly disrupted the empire's vast trade network. The Pax Romana had collapsed, and merchants could no longer safely travel with agricultural and manufactured goods. The large plantations had no way to trade cash crops for manufactured goods, metals, wine, and grain. Commodities could no longer move freely from one end of the empire to the other. This led to economic decentralization. The Roman trade network never fully recovered.

Landowners changed their crops to ones that would sustain them and could be sold in local markets. Because they could no longer reliably import manufactured goods, they began local small-scale manufacturing, gradually becoming self-sufficient. The urban commoners transitioned to the safer rural areas with more food, giving up basic civil rights in exchange for protection. Urban regions throughout the empire slowly transitioned from sprawling metropolises to smaller walled cities defendable against raiding barbarians or opposing forces.

The transition of workers to rural areas produced the *coloni* – the beginnings of the medieval peasantry – half-free citizens that evolved into serfs in what would become a feudal society. In the western empire, the large landowners were becoming a law unto themselves, disregarding tax collectors and Rome's authority. Massive agricultural estates produced the only commodity of recognized value – food. The landholders rose in nobility status, while the merchant class shrank.

Some regions prospered through the chaotic Crisis of the Third Century – notably Egypt and Hispania – regions not especially affected by invading tribes and internal conflict. Trade flourished in these areas, and the people enjoyed a healthy economy. Because the eastern empire was more stable, Emperor Diocletian – who finally ended the Crisis of the Third Century – chose Nicomedia in Asia Minor as his seat of government, with Milan as the secondary governmental center. In the last days of the empire, the eastern section was far wealthier and more durable – able to survive when the western empire collapsed.

A crippling manpower shortage sprang from the plague and incessant warfare. Diocletian attempted to end the exodus from the cities by compelling workers to remain within their trades and forbidding workers and civil service workers to leave their jobs. Caught between economic collapse and authoritarian demands, the maltreated peasants banded together with escaped slaves, disillusioned civil officials, and military deserters in groups called *Bacaudae* or *Bagaudae* (from *fighters* in the Gallic language) – especially in Gaul and Hispania.

The mostly-peasant insurgents arose to defy imperial authority in the Crisis of the Third Century, persisting until the western empire collapsed. The Bacaudae attempted to counter the merciless exploitation of the coloni workers on the large manors and unjust laws against commoners and middle-class artisans and civil servants. Even some landowners rebelled against the crushing taxes, conscription of their workers for the military, and land garnishment by the state.

The Bacaudae revolts increased Rome's reliance on the barbarian foederati mercenaries – employing them to respond to the local unrest. Rome even settled the Iranian Alans tribe around Aurelianum (Orléans) in Gaul to subdue the Bacaudae. Although Emperor Diocletian reinstituted order to the Roman Empire in the late third century, he appointed Maximian as his second-in-command to quash the Bacaudae. Maximian subdued them but never fully defeated them – in part because his army revolted, unwilling to fight the peasant rebels.

The Illyrian emperor Claudius II Gothicus, who had turned the tide of the crisis, died in the Plague of Cyprian in 270. The cavalry commander Aurelian rose to take his place as another Illyrian barracks emperor. Thought to be the son of a peasant farmer, he had proven himself in the military and, as emperor, achieved stunning victories in his five-year reign, restoring the broken Roman Empire.

The Aurelian Walls enclosed all the seven hills of Rome.
MrPanyGoff, CC BY-SA 4.0 <https://creativecommons.org/licenses/by-sa/4.0>, via Wikimedia Commons https://commons.wikimedia.org/wiki/File:Aurelian_Walls_-_Porta_Asinaria.jpg

Aurelian expelled the Vandals, Sarmatians, and Juthungi from northern Italia, defeated the Goths at the Danube, recovered the Palmyrene Empire from Queen Zenobia, restored the Gallic Empire to Rome, built massive ramparts encircling Rome that still stand today, and brought the three sections of the empire back into a unified whole by 274. Aurelian also reformed the coinage, which resulted in a rebellion of the mint workers, accustomed to stealing the silver. He enhanced the free-food distribution to the poor, giving bread, salt, olive oil, and pork.

Seizing the opportunity to vanquish the Sassanid Empire, which was experiencing a leadership crisis, Aurelian embarked on a new campaign in 275. However, he was murdered on his way east by Praetorian Guard officers who erroneously thought they had been marked for execution. His wife, Ulpia Severina, continued his reign in the eight-month interval while the military and Senate were trying to decide what to do next.

Remorseful over their popular emperor's murder, the army handed the right to choose his successor back to the Senate. The Senate was hesitant –, they hadn't elected an emperor in decades – after this election, they never would again. Finally, they proclaimed the elderly Marcus Claudius Tacitus as the new emperor, with the army's polite sanction.

Tacitus restored the Senate to the powers they held in the old days, then turned his attention to the Foederati mercenaries supplementing Aurelian's forces. Once Aurelian was dead - and the Sassanid campaign canceled - they were stranded in the eastern provinces and started plundering towns. Tacitus subdued the tribal mercenaries, gaining the title Gothicus Maximus, then died of a fever on his way back west. His half-brother Florian, the Praetorian Prefect, became the next emperor for three months until he was assassinated by his army.

Florian was succeeded by Probus, another Illyrian barracks emperor who had distinguished himself in the military and had been appointed Supreme Chief of the eastern provinces by Tacitus. In his six-year reign, he continued his successful military campaigns, said to have fought in every front in the empire during his lifetime. By protecting the frontiers, the empire once again experienced stability and prosperity. Whenever there was a lull in fighting, Probus put his soldiers to useful tasks, such as draining marshes or replanting vineyards – further enhancing the economy. Some of the military men were disgruntled with these orders and assassinated Probus, proclaiming Marcus Aurelius Carus, commander of the Praetorian Guard, as their new emperor.

Before he was struck by lightning – ending his nine-month reign – Carus suppressed the Senate's authority for good. His sons Carinus and Numerian succeeded him as co-emperors until Numerian's soldiers smelled a putrid odor coming from his covered litter while marching home from Persia and discovered he was dead. The commander of his bodyguard, Diocletian, declared Numerian's father-in-law Aper had murdered Numerian and ran his sword through Aper. The military hailed Diocletian as their new emperor, but Carinus (rumored to have married nine wives) was still co-emperor. Heading east from Rome and confronting Diocletian, Carinus died in the struggle.

Diocletian ended the Crisis of the Third Century as the new emperor of Rome, but systemic difficulties remained. The issue of succession had still not been settled, leaving the door open for more civil wars. The empire's stupendous size – stretching across three continents – made it impossible for one man to tackle multiple invasions or other challenges simultaneously. Although Diocletian rescued the empire from total collapse, its foundations were weakened, and the beginning of the end loomed ahead.

Chapter 14: Diocletian and Constantine the Great

Two eminent emperors – Diocletian and Constantine the Great – dominated the next five decades, from 284 to 337, bringing momentous changes to the Roman Empire. Diocletian was distinctive for dividing the empire into four parts, persecuting Christians on the greatest scale ever, and being the first emperor to abdicate his throne. Constantine was renowned for transitioning the empire's capital from Rome to Byzantium, protecting Christians and all religions with the Edict of Milan, convening the Nicaean Council to sort out Christian theology, and receiving Christian baptism on his deathbed.

Diocletian instituted reforms to further stabilize the empire and address systemic issues, transforming ideological, administrative, legal, military, and economic affairs. His ideological reforms involved a strong central authority imposing imperial values on the provinces, using revisionist history. Imperial propaganda characterized the empire's history from Augustus until the tetrarchy as incessant internal conflict, tyrannical totalitarianism, and disintegrated government – all now repaired by Diocletian, "founder of eternal peace."

Administrative reforms supported an autocracy, dismissing a cooperative government between the emperor, Senate, and military. Everything was now run from the top down, with everyone answering ultimately to Diocletian. He reduced the Praetorian Guard to a defensive garrison for Rome – it would no longer choose emperors and assassinate them.

Diocletian ended the Crisis of the Third Century and masterminded the Tetrarchy.

In legal affairs, Diocletian's government published law books on precedent and law codes. Governors were now called judges (*iudex*), and the entire empire had a right of appeal. Diocletian was the last emperor to follow classic Roman law; his successors followed eastern and Greek legal philosophy.

Diocletian beefed up the size of his troops – boasting that the four tetrarchs each had more soldiers than previous emperors had for the whole empire. He stationed his men on the frontiers, keeping the borders secure. More soldiers meant more people to pay, meaning higher taxes.

Diocletian's new tax system was tied to an annual census of the entire population and how much land was owned. Tax day was September 1. He instituted a new system of coinage, with five coins: gold, silver, copper-silver, and two copper-only coins of two sizes. Their value didn't reflect the intrinsic worth of the metal, so inflation reared its head, causing Diocletian to order a price freeze.

Realizing the impossibility of one person maintaining the stability of the gigantic empire, Diocletian appointed Maximian, a stellar general, as Caesar and his co-ruler. Diocletian gave primary attention to the eastern part of the empire, and Maximian dealt with subduing the irksome Bagaudae in the west. In 293, Diocletian further organized the empire into a *tetrarchy (rule of four)* with two lead emperors called *Augusti* – Diocletian and Maximian – and two junior emperors – the *Caesares*, who answered to the Augusti and would succeed them. The two Caesares were Galerius and Constantius, who were adopted by Diocletian and Maximian.

Maximian's son (Maxentius) and Constantius' son (Constantine) were groomed in Diocletian's court to step into the Caesares (junior emperor) positions whenever Diocletian or Maximian died, and Galerius or Constantius moved to the top emperor positions. With this system, Diocletian hoped to install a fixed system of succession and avoid all the usurpers and civil wars. Strategically, four co-rulers could be positioned in four points of the empire to resist invaders and sustain smooth internal affairs.

The Tetrarchy divided the Roman Empire into four sections ruled by Diocletian, Maximian, Galerius, and Constantius.

Rome was no longer the capital of the empire – now, the four co-rulers were stationed in four capitals. Diocletian's capital was Nicomedia (in modern-day Turkey), defending against the Persian Sassanids and the Balkans. Galerius' capital was Sirmium (modern Serbia), close to the Danube river – the homeland of the Illyrian emperors. Maximum was stationed in Milan in northern Italy – guarding against invasions from over the Alps. He was the administrator for Italy and the African provinces. Constantius was stationed in Augusta Treverorum (Germany), near the Rhine, and he kept affairs in western Europe running smoothly.

Following a successful war against the Sassanids, in which Galerius captured King Narseh's harem, children, and treasury, the king was eager to sign the Peace of Nisibis to get his wives and children back. Flushed with victory, Diocletian and Galerius returned to Antioch, where they offered sacrifices of thanksgiving to the gods. But there was a problem – the divinators couldn't read the entrails of the sacrificed animals – and thus couldn't predict the future.

Why were the gods silent? What was blocking the divinations? It must be those Christians in the imperial household. Galerius, a passionate pagan who viewed a purge of Christians as a convenient way to get rid of political rivals, pushed Diocletian to violent extermination of Christians, although Diocletian hoped to do so without bloodshed.

At Galerius' urging, Diocletian ordered a purification of the palace and the entire army – all members of the court and every soldier in the army must sacrifice to the Roman gods or be discharged – or worse. When one Christian centurion, Marcellus, heard that he had no choice, he immediately resigned his position, throwing his belt, sword, and insignia to the ground, loudly proclaiming he would only obey Jesus Christ the eternal King. He was arrested on the spot and beheaded. Diocletian's Christian butler Peter was boiled alive.

Thus began the Great Persecution of Christians, who made up about ten percent of the population. Galerius and Diocletian issued edicts purging Christians in the government and military, razing churches, burning Bibles, forbidding Christians to assemble, imprisoning all bishops and priests, and punishing everyone refusing to sacrifice to the Roman deities. The deacon Romanus of Palestine had his tongue cut off and was later executed. An entire congregation in Phrygia was burned alive. Young men were castrated, and virgin girls were sent to brothels. In Africa and the Middle East, Maximinus had Christians blinded in one eye and sent to work in the mines.

Constantius only halfheartedly enforced the edicts at his end of the empire: he mostly only worshiped one god – Sol Invictus, the sun god – and was sympathetic to Christian monotheists. Christians in Gaul and Britain largely escaped the atrocities of Galerius, Maximinus, and Diocletian. Even most pagans throughout the empire were unwilling to support the persecution.

In Armenia, a client-state of Rome, King Tiridates of Armenia had thrown his Christian secretary Gregory into a pit for refusing to worship a goddess with him. Thirteen years later (now in Diocletian's day), King Tiridates fell prey to mental illness, wandering through the forests like a wild boar. His sister had a dream that Gregory could cure him. They hauled the emaciated Gregory up from underground, and he prayed for King Tiridates. The king was healed and converted to Christianity, declaring it the official religion of Armenia in 301. Armenia became the first Christian state, right in the middle of the Great Persecution.

Eventually, Galerius rescinded the edicts against Christianity in 311, passing the Edict of Toleration – stating persecution had done nothing to convert Christians to the Roman gods. Quite the reverse – the Christians' resolve to remain true to their faith had precipitated great admiration, impelling more converts to Christianity. In the words of Tertullian, "The blood of the martyrs was the seed of the church."

Diocletian fell ill in 304, collapsing soon after the grand opening of a circus just next to his palace. Throughout the winter, he remained confined inside, sparking rumors he had died. Finally, on March 1, 305, he appeared in public again, ghastly thin. Galerius quickly snatched the opportunity of Diocletian's illness to rearrange the tetrarch to his advantage. In Diocletian's original plan, Galerius would succeed Diocletian, and

Constantius would replace Maximian, then Constantine and Maxentius would become the Caesars. Galerius bullied the weakened Diocletian into putting Constantine and Maxentius to the side and choosing Severus (Galerius' drinking buddy and a senior army official) and Maximinus (Galerius' nephew) as the new Caesars.

Gravely ill, Diocletian abdicated in 305 - a first for Roman emperors - and his co-emperor Maximian retired with him. As planned, Galerius and Constantius moved up to become the top emperors, and as unplanned by Diocletian, Severus and Maximinus became the two junior emperors. Diocletian lived four more years, watching his carefully planned tetrarchy fall to pieces.

Constantine had been living in Diocletian's palace for the past 12 years, receiving a formal education to prepare him to become the next Caesar. Now, his destiny had abruptly changed. Diocletian had retired to Dalmatia, Galerius was the new emperor living in the palace, and it was not a safe place for Constantine - who represented a threat to Galerius's ambitions.

Constantine's father - Constantius, Galerius' co-emperor now - came to the rescue, recalling his son from Nicomedia to help his campaign in Britain. Constantine got Galerius drunk, and he granted Constantine leave to go to Britain; Constantine fled during the night, charging down the road on his horse before Galerius sobered up and changed his mind. For the next year, Constantius and Constantine campaigned in Britain, fighting the blue-tattooed Picts beyond Hadrian's Wall.

Constantius succumbed to a prolonged illness - probably leukemia - in July 306; before he died, he declared his wish for Constantine to become Augustus in his place (as was Diocletian's intent but overturned by Galerius). King Chrocus, a Foederati from the Germanic Alamanni, proclaimed Constantine as Augustus - the new co-emperor. Constantius' troops backed Constantine; Gaul and Britain welcomed his rule, but Hispania spurned it.

Constantine the Great enacted the Edit of Milan, granting safety and freedom of religion for Christians and all religions.

Constantine sent a dispatch to Galerius, informing him of his father's death, explaining that his army had forced upon him the rank of Augustus in his father's place. He apologized for the irregularity but asked Galerius to recognize his natural claim as his father's successor.

Galerius was enraged – threatening to set both the letter and Constantine on fire. His counselors advised him to take a middle path to avoid outright war – neither rejecting Constantine's claims nor accepting them. Rather, he should grant Constantine the rank of Caesar, replacing Severus, who would move up to Augustus. Both Galerius and Constantine agreed to this compromise, making Constantine ruler of Gaul, Britain, and Hispania.

Although not yet a Christian, Constantine decreed an end to the persecution of Christians in his section of the empire. His ascension to Caesar made Maxentius – Maximian's son – jealous. Like Constantine, Maxentius had been trained under Diocletian to become Caesar. Now Maximinus had usurped Maxentius' spot, due to Galerius' manipulation of Diocletian. So, Maxentius declared himself emperor in Italy.

Just to review – we now have three men named Max to keep straight: Maximian – the retired Augustus, Maxentius – his son, and Maximinus – Galerius' nephew and the current Caesar.

Galerius sent Severus to deal with Maxentius – but Severus' army had previously been Maximian's – and they defected to their former commander's son. Severus was imprisoned and later executed. Maximian came out of retirement to become Maxentius' co-emperor, offering his daughter Fausta in marriage to Constantine and promising to help him ascend to emperor if he would help them against Galerius. Constantine gave verbal support to father and son but never sent troops to help. Then Maximian and Maxentius fell out.

Now, Diocletian also came out of retirement briefly in 308 for a conference with Galerius and Maximian. Their joint decision made Galerius' old friend Licinius the Augustus (emperor) in the west, with Constantine as his Caesar. Galerius would still be Augustus in the east, with Maximinus continuing as his Caesar. Maximian and Diocletian would go back into retirement. This made Maxentius a nobody – a usurper. No sooner had that been decided than Maximinus declared himself Augustus, and Constantine refused to be demoted back to Caesar. Maximian committed suicide in 310, and Galerius died in 311.

Now we're down to two men named Max: Maximinus – Galerius' nephew and Maxentius – Maximian's son, both self-proclaimed – but mostly unrecognized – emperors.

The tetrarchy was in tatters – the contenders at this point were Licinius, Constantine, Maxentius, and Maximinus. Constantine allied with Licinius, and Maxentius allied with Maximinus. In 312, Constantine crossed the Alps into Italy. After defeating two cities, the rest of Italy welcomed him with open arms. Surrounded by the Aurelian Walls, defended by the Praetorian Guard, and with an army twice the size of Constantine's, Maxentius felt safe in Rome.

After his vision, Constantine went to battle with the labarum – the first two letters of the Greek word for Christ – on his helmet, his soldiers' shields, and his banners.

Then, Constantine had a vision while marching in the heat of the day. Above the sun, he saw a cross of light with the inscription, *"In Hoc Signo Vinces"* ("In this sign, you shall conquer"). He had a dream that night where Jesus repeated the same message. Still a pagan at this point (but growing less so by the minute), Constantine had insignia made with the *labarum* – an X (Chi) over a P (Rho) – the first two letters in the Greek word ΧΡΙΣΤΟΣ (Christos). He wore a helmet adorned with the Chi Rho, and his soldiers marched into battle with the labarum of Christ on their standards and shields.

Constantine and Maxentius faced off at the Tiber. After a brief battle, Constantine forced Maxentius' cavalry and infantry back, some falling into the river and drowning, Maxentius among them. Constantine marched into Rome, received with rejoicing. He chose not to offer the usual sacrifices to Jupiter but did meet with the Senate, promising them a return to their former status in his new government. The Senate declared him "greatest Augustus."

In 313, Constantine headed to Milan for the wedding of his half-sister Constantia to his ally Licinius. While there, the two emperors agreed on the Edict of Milan, which granted legal status to Christians and protection from persecution. It mandated freedom of worship to Christians and other religions: "that each one may have the free opportunity to worship as he pleases." The Edict directed that buildings used for Christian meeting places be restored to the Christians. Christians were to be released from prisons and forced labor in the mines.

Was Constantine still a pagan? Licinius was, but Constantine likely was not – for one thing, he didn't worship the gods in Rome in the previous year, although his coinage showed Sol Invictus – the sun god – for several more years. Eusebius said that after his vision, Constantine sought some Christian teachers to help him understand what was going on. They told him that Jesus was the only son of the one and only God and that the sign of the cross he saw in the sky was a symbol of immortality – Jesus' victory over death. Constantine devoted himself to reading the Bible, making Christian priests his advisors, and honoring Jesus with his devotion. He did not get baptized (yet), but he invited Christian ministers to spend time with him, eat with him, and travel with him. He donated copious amounts to church building projects.

When Diocletian was emperor, he chose Nicomedia as his capital, strategically located in western Turkey between the Aegean and the Black Sea – where Europe and Asia meet, easily accessible by sea to Africa and the Middle East. Constantine wanted to build a new capital in the same region that would represent the unification of the east with the west, serving as a center of culture, learning, and trade. He chose Byzantium, a Greek city close to Nicomedia but right on the Strait of Istanbul. In 324, he enlarged and rebuilt Byzantium – now known as "New Rome" or Constantinople. It became the most affluent city in Europe; within two centuries, its population would grow to an estimated one million – the largest city in the world at that time.

Constantine convened the Council of Nicaea to unite Christians on basic theology.
https://commons.wikimedia.org/wiki/File:Nicea.jpg

In 325, several hundred Christian deacons and bishops gathered in Nicaea – near to where Constantinople was being built. An open copy of the Gospels lay on the conference table. Constantine entered the hall in his royal robes, briefly greeting the Christian leaders and advising them of the purpose of the meeting: to agree on some divisive issues. "Division in the church is worse than war," he said.

The bishops and deacons had met to debate the doctrine of the Holy Trinity. Arius, a priest in Alexandria, thought Jesus wasn't equal with God because he was born as a human – thus having a beginning, while God was infinite, with no beginning or end. The churchmen compared Arius' teaching to the Gospel of John, which begins by stating that the *Logos* – Jesus – was in the beginning with God, and through him, all things were made. Thus, even though Jesus's physical body had a beginning, he existed as part of the Godhead from infinity. From their discussion, the council determined that the Father, Son, and Holy Spirit were equal members of the Trinity. They banished the Arian leaders for heresy and established the *Nicene Creed* – a statement of the basic doctrines of Christianity.

Just after the Feast of Easter in 337, Constantine became critically ill. Realizing death was near, he called the bishops, telling them he'd hoped to be baptized in the Jordan River, where Jesus was baptized, but he now understood he needed to be baptized immediately. The historian Eusebius of Caesarea wrote that Bishop Eusebius of Nicomedia baptized Constantine into the Christian faith. The emperor died shortly after on May 22, 337.

The reigns of Diocletian and Constantinople guided Rome through its greatest persecution of Christianity, followed by freedom of religion for all faiths, with an emperor who actively promoted Christianity. The long reigns of both men brought stability to the empire. Although Diocletian's tetrarchy failed, it was an ingenious plan to provide administrative centers in four points of the far-flung empire and an organized means of succession. Constantine replaced the tetrarchy with dynastic succession; however, he followed Diocletian's concept of multiple rulers by designating his three sons as co-rulers after his death.

Chapter 15: The Constantinian Dynasty and the Fall of the West

Constantine had intended the running of the empire to be a family affair after his death, with his three sons – Constantine II, Constantius II, and Constans – as the emperors, and their cousins – Dalmatius and Hannibalianus – as the Caesars. The empire was meant to be divided five ways, with each emperor or Caesar ruling a section. Constantine's arrangement only lasted weeks, as his three sons slaughtered Dalmatius and Hannibalianus, along with two uncles and three other cousins.

The three brothers then divided the empire three ways. The oldest – Constantine – took Britain, Gaul, and Hispania, but as guardian of his youngest brother Constans – not yet of age – Constantine also oversaw Italy, Africa, and Illyricum. Constantius received the Asian provinces, Egypt, Greece, and Thrace.

Constantine II resented sharing power with his younger brothers. When Constans came of age, Constantine refused to relinquish Italy, Africa, and Illyricum. In the ensuing battle, Constantine II was killed in AD 340, leaving Constans with the entire western empire and most of northern Africa to rule – in uneasy peace with Constantius II, ruler of the eastern empire. Ten years later, Constans' inept leadership cost him the support of his troops, who defected to the usurper Magnentius and killed Constans in 350. Three years later, Magnentius faced off against Constantius II. After spending the day praying in a nearby church, Constantius defeated Magnentius, becoming sole emperor of the entire Roman Empire.

Constantius II, son of Constantine the Great, ruled with his brothers and then on his own for 24 years.
https://commons.wikimedia.org/wiki/File:07_constantius2Chrono354.png

The three sons of Constantine the Great were, nominally at least, Christians – although they overlooked the "love your brother as yourself" part. Constans supported the stance of the First Nicaean Council regarding the Trinity. Constantius did not agree with the Nicene Creed, but he didn't agree with Arius either – he followed Semi-Arianism. Most Christians in the empire had no clue what the controversy was all about.

At the urgent request of Pope Julius, Constans and Constantius convened the Council of Serdica in 343 to resolve the theological conflict. Instead, it accentuated the tensions between the theological camps, causing a greater divide, with the eastern churches leaning toward Arianism, and the western European churches supporting the Nicene Creed. The two emperors agreed that each would support their preferred clergy and theology in their ends of the empire.

Throughout his reign, Constantius clashed with the Sassanid Empire in the Perso-Roman wars, in which King Shapur II usually prevailed but never achieved a conclusive triumph. Shapur attacked Nisibis (on the border of what is now Turkey and Syria) in 350, with an incredible strategy. He broke the dams on the Mygdonius River, flooding the valley, then sailed his fleet right up to the city's ramparts, collapsing a section of the wall. His plan went awry when his war elephants got bogged down in the mud, and he had to retreat. Overnight, the industrious Nisibis forces repaired the breach; then, Shapur got word that the Huns were invading Persia, so he had to abandon Nisibis to defend his lands.

Supported by the local tribes, Shapur invaded Roman Mesopotamia in 359. With 100,000 men, he encircled Amida (in Asian Turkey) where six Roman legions waited. Although the legions fought fiercely, and the Roman Scorpion siege engines decimated the Sassanids, Shapur eventually breached the walls. He sacked the city, killing most of the Roman officers and deporting the population to Persia. It was a Pyrrhic victory – Shapur lost one-third of his army, and his tribal allies deserted him.

After Constans died, Constantius discovered that single-handedly running an empire stretching across three continents was overwhelming. His brothers were dead – who would help him? His cousin Julian was only six when Constantius and his brothers were killing off most of their male relatives, and now Julian was a young man. In 354, Constantius appointed Julian to rule Gaul, which he did so superbly that his soldiers declared him emperor in 360. Constantius was too busy fighting the Persians to do anything about Julian.

Finally, during a lull in the hostilities with the Sassanids, Constantius marched west with his armies to confront Julian but fell deathly ill with a fever on the way. He asked Bishop Euzoius to baptize him, then died in November 361, declaring Julius as his successor.

Julian was raised Christian but converted to paganism around age 20, initiated into the secret Eleusinian Mysteries for the cult of Demeter and Persephone. He was eager to revive the ancient Greco-Roman polytheistic religion while subduing Christianity. Julian's religious reforms targeted affluent, upper-class Christians; he didn't mind if the commoners were Christians, but he wanted the ruling classes to follow the traditional pagan ways. He did not promote the violent persecution of Diocletian's day, knowing it had backfired and strengthened the church. He preferred softer measures, such as removing state stipends for bishops and reversing privileges and favors Christians had enjoyed.

His biggest obstacle – one he complained about bitterly – was Christian charity. Julian wrote to the pagan priest Arsacius, "It is disgraceful that, when no Jew ever has to beg, and the impious Galileans [Christians] support not only their own poor but ours as well, all men see that our people lack aid from us."

Although Rome had a state-funded food dole for the poor, the concept of personal charity – individuals helping those who couldn't return the favor – was foreign to Greco-Roman polytheists. In stark contrast, Jesus taught his followers to throw banquets and invite the poor, the crippled, the lame, and the blind (Luke 14:12-14). And that's what the pagan world observed: Christians caring for the poor, the orphans, the widows, and the sick – even burying the dead during the plagues.

At any rate, Julian did not have long to overturn Christianity and reinvigorate paganism. His reign lasted less than two years. Despite peace offers from the Sassanids, he wanted to gain fame and glory by trouncing the Persians once and for all, which didn't go well. In the Battle of Samarra, a spear pierced his gut, and he died three days later in 363.

The day after Julian died, the Roman military elected their commander Jovian as emperor. Although he lived only eight months, he restored Christianity to favored status in the empire.

He died in mysterious circumstances, found dead in his tent while traveling to Constantinople – perhaps from poisonous fumes.

Valentinian ruled the western Roman Empire beginning in 364

The military and civil officials met in Nicaea, finally choosing Valentinian, a tribune who had served under Constantius and Julian. Valentinian was crowned emperor in February 364, then appointed his brother Valens to be his co-ruler. Valens made Constantinople his capital, while Valentinian ruled from Milan in northern Italy.

Two simultaneous challenges confronted Valentinian on November 1, 365: the Germanic Alamanni were invading Gaul, and Procopius – the last descendent of the Constantinian Dynasty – had revolted. His first instinct was to head east to help Valens, but the cities in Gaul urgently begged him to come. After a year of battles and initial defeats, he forced the Alamanni out of Gaul. Meanwhile, Valens captured Procopius and executed him by having him torn apart.

When a crisis in Britain distracted Valentinian, the Alamanni crept back across the Rhine, raiding and plundering. This time, Valentinian conspired to have Vithicabius – a key Alamanni chieftain – assassinated by his bodyguard. Valentinian then mustered a gigantic force to cross the Rhine and invade the Alamanni lands in southwestern Germany, determined to permanently overcome them. While on a reconnaissance mission, Valentinian was almost captured by an enemy ambush. The Romans defeated the Alamanni mountaintop encampment in the fierce Battle of Solicinium, but with heavy casualties. Valentinian then ordered a series of fortresses built along the Rhine to keep the Alamanni on their side of the river.

The crisis in Britain that had distracted Valentinian was the Great Conspiracy. The Roman garrison guarding Hadrian's Wall had defected, letting the fierce Picts into Britain. Meanwhile, a joint force of Scots, Saxons, and Attacotti (possibly from Ireland) invaded by sea. Simultaneously, Franks and Saxons attacked northern Gaul. Nearly all the Roman settlements of northern and western Britain were overcome: the tribes sacked their cities, murdering, raping, and enslaving the population.

The Roman response was initially unsuccessful, but finally, the commander Flavius Theodosius with his son Theodosius I (who later became emperor) crossed the channel and marched to Londinium (London). Using stealth and ambush, his forces attacked the raiding tribes, recouping the captured people and livestock. His forces chased the barbarians back to their homelands, retook Hadrian's Wall, and regarrisoned the abandoned forts.

In 373, war broke out on the Danube with the Germanic Quadi and their Iranian-Sarmatian allies, who had been steadily migrating west. Tension flared over Valentinian building forts in Quadi territory. Marcellinus, in charge of the building project, held a banquet for the Quadi and Sarmatians, under the pretense of initiating peace negotiations, but then he killed the Quadi king Gabinius. The enraged Quadi and Sarmatians charged across the Danube, ravaging the region of Valeria.

Valentinian marched to Carnuntum (in what is now southern Austria), where the apprehensive Sarmatians sent ambassadors seeking forgiveness for participating in the fray. Overlooking Marcellianus' treachery and determined to make an example of the Quadi, Valentinian crossed the Danube, pillaging their lands.

In November 374, a Quadi deputation arrived at Valentinian's camp. They complained about Roman fortresses being built on their land and explained that not all the Quadi chiefs had entered peace treaties with Rome – it was the hold-outs who were attacking. Valentinian exploded in a rage, screaming at the envoys, when he suddenly had a stroke and dropped dead. As founder of the Valentinian Dynasty, his sons Gratian and Valentinian II succeeded him as rulers of the western empire, while his brother Valens continued to rule the eastern empire from Constantinople.

The Aqueduct of Valens in Constantinople (now Istanbul) was completed in 373. *Lowcarb23, CC BY-SA 4.0 <https://creativecommons.org/licenses/by-sa/4.0>, via Wikimedia Commons https://commons.wikimedia.org/wiki/File:Valens_2012_DK.jpg*

While Valentinian had been contending with the Alamanni, Quadi, and Sarmatians, Valens was campaigning against the Goths, the Persians, and the Saracens. A bungled attempt to resettle the Goths (displaced by the Huns) in the Balkans led to the Gothic War of 376-377. Valens' forces unsuccessfully collided with the Goths for two years. Jealous of the western emperor Gratian's recent victory over the Alamanni, Valens took over the campaign against the Goths himself – not a great plan, given his mediocracy in military affairs. As 10,000 Goths were marching on Adrianople (in Thrace), Gratian sent a message that his troops were on the way to assist Valens, urging Valens to wait for them before engaging the Goths. The headstrong Valens, not wanting to share the glory, proceeded anyway.

The battle was one of the worst defeats in Roman history. Some overeager Roman forces attacked without orders, leaving the lines in disarray. The Gothic cavalry returned from a raiding mission just in time, surrounding the Roman troops and decimating their numbers. Abandoned on the field, Valens was presumably killed, although his body was never found. At least two-thirds of Rome's eastern forces were destroyed, including most of the experienced generals.

After Valens' death, Gratian appointed Theodosius I as the next co-emperor. He was the son of the hero Flavius Theodosius, who vanquished Britain's Great Conspiracy. Theodosius negotiated peace with the Goths by permitting them to settle in Roman territory but maintaining their military and political autonomy – and serving as mercenaries in Rome's imperial forces.

In 383, the usurper Magnus Maximus proclaimed himself emperor, invaded Gaul, killed Emperor Gratian, and assumed rule over Gaul, Britain, and Hispania. Theodosius counterattacked in 388, defeating Maximus, executing him, and restoring his younger half-brother Valentinian II as emperor of the west.

When Theodosius I died in 396, his throne went to his two sons: Honorius was to rule in the West and Arcadius in the East – but both boys were still under ten years old. Honorius was dominated by his uncle, Stilicho the Vandal, and Arcadius' Praetor Prefect Rufinus controlled the eastern empire. Instead of cooperating, Stilicho and Rufinus undermined each other's military efforts, weakening the already stressed empire. Even when Honorius and Arcadius came of age, they remained puppet emperors.

The Visigoths spoke a Germanic language and probably originated in Scandinavia, then migrated north of the Black Sea. This map shows their migration south and west in the last days of the Roman Empire.

https://commons.wikimedia.org/wiki/File:Visigoth_migrations.jpg

Stilicho had several run-ins with Alaric – a Visigoth who'd once served as a mercenary under Theodosius I but had gone rogue, becoming King of the Visigoths (western Goths). Sometimes Alaric was fighting Stilicho, and other times Stilicho was plotting to take over the eastern empire with Alaric's help. Alaric invaded Italy during a famine in 410, raiding the countryside to feed his army of Goths and runaway slaves. He contacted Honorius, offering to leave Italy in exchange for food, but Honorius refused.

The famine was so dreadful that Jerome reported cannibalism going on in the city of Rome. Alaric easily took Rome and sacked it – the starving people were helpless. His men stole anything of value they could carry away and ransacked and burned the important buildings around the Senate House and Forum, but mostly spared the basilicas of Peter and Paul. The Goths captured many Romans, ransoming some, selling some as slaves, and raping and killing others. Rome had not been sacked in nearly eight centuries – the eternal city was increasingly vulnerable and frail.

Alaric and the Visigoths ravaged southern Italy, but their plan to cross to Africa failed when a storm destroyed their ships. A few months after sacking Rome, Alaric fell ill and died in Italy. His band headed to southwestern Gaul, establishing the Visigoth Kingdom, which helped the western empire fight Attila the Hun four decades later.

While Rome was being sacked in 410, Britain was falling apart, as the remaining Roman troops proclaimed a series of usurpers. The last – Constantine III – raided Gaul and defeated Honorius' army. When the Roman citizens in Britain asked Honorius to help them evict Constantine, he told them they were on their own. Rome had essentially abandoned Britain.

Arcadius' only son Theodosius II became co-Augustus with his father while still an infant – the youngest Roman emperor. When Arcadius died in 408, Theodosius became emperor of the eastern empire at age seven. His Praetorian Prefect, Anthemius, managed governmental affairs at first, then in 414, Theodosius' older sister Pulcheria was pronounced Augustus, ruling until Theodosius came of age.

The Huns threatened Constantinople while Theodosius was campaigning in Persia. Theodosius returned to Constantinople in 424 and paid the Huns 350 pounds of gold to live peacefully in the empire. Nine years later, when Attila the Hun rose to dominance, he doubled the annual payment to 700 pounds. In 423, the western emperor Honorius died, and Theodosius killed the usurper Joannes and installed his six-year-old cousin Valentinian III as emperor of the western empire, with the boy's mother, Galla Placidia, as regent.

The western Roman Empire was crumbling around the edges. Britain was gone, part of Africa was gone, Hispania was slipping away, and Gaul was held by the Visigoths in the southwest and the Franks in the northeast. In 428, 80,000 Alans and Vandals, united under King Genseric, crossed the Straits of Gibraltar to Mauritania in Africa, then spread to Numidia, kicking out the Roman ruler Boniface.

In 439, the Vandals captured Carthage. Their powerful navy controlled the area, crushing the western empire's economy, dependent on Africa for tax revenues and grain. Both emperors sent troops to launch an attack from Sicily. But Attila the Hun and the Persians took this opportunity to attack on two fronts, so the forces in Sicily were recalled. After a catastrophic loss to the Huns, the Romans' annual tribute tripled to 2100 pounds of god.

Theodosius II fell from a horse and died in 450, with no sons and no chosen successor. After a month of discussions (but *not* consulting the western emperor Valentinian III), Theodosius' personal assistant Marcian was chosen as the next emperor of the eastern empire. The lack of input from Valentinian III indicates how politically separate the eastern and western sections of the empire had become by AD 450. The relationship between east and west at this point was more like two large countries in friendly alliance rather than two sections of the same empire.

Atilla the Hun was one of the most feared barbarians who menaced the Roman Empire.

Marcian immediately revoked the treaties with Atilla the Hun and stopped annual payments. In Italy, Valentinian III's sister Honoria sent a desperate message to Attila, begging him to rescue her from a forced marriage her brother was negotiating. Attila interpreted this as an offer of marriage and a potential way to grab the western empire. In 452, he invaded Italy to claim his bride but only ended up plundering the land. While Attila was in Italy, Marcian slipped into the Hungarian heartland, defeating the Huns in their territory. Meanwhile, the western empire, beleaguered by famine and the plague, bribed Atilla to leave Italy.

In 455, a Vandal fleet sailed to Italy and sacked Rome, first knocking down the city's aqueducts. When they reached the gates, Pope Leo I made them promise not to destroy Rome or murder its people. The Vandals agreed, and the gates opened. The Vandals kept their promise – they burned nothing, and they didn't kill masses of people, but they plundered the city's treasures for two weeks and took captives as slaves – including Princess Eudocia, whom the Vandal king married. The Vandals conquered Sicily and menaced sea traffic in the western Mediterranean.

Western Europe was now ruled by a series of puppet emperors controlled by the barbarian warlords who swarmed the western empire. In 475, the Roman general Orestes, who had served as Attila the Hun's secretary and envoy, proclaimed his son Romulus Augustus as emperor – the last emperor of the west. Several months later, the barbarian Odoacer of the Ostrogoths (eastern Goths) invaded Italy, killed Orestes, and forced the 16-year-old Romulus to abdicate.

With Romulus' abdication on September 4, 476, the collapse of the western Roman Empire was almost complete. The remnant of a few western European states continued under some form of Roman rule for a few more years. Odoacer proclaimed himself King of Italy – the client of the eastern Emperor Zeno in Constantinople. In 488, Theoderic the Goth invaded Italy; after fighting for five years, Odoacer agreed to rule jointly with Theoderic. At the banquet celebrating the union, the Goths murdered Odoacer's men, and Theoderic hewed Odoacer in half. Technically, Italy remained under the authority of the eastern empire, but Theoderic was a law unto himself, King of the Visigoth Kingdom – a superstate stretching from the Danube to the Atlantic.

No single cataclysmic event ended the western Roman Empire. It disintegrated slowly, unable to cope with internal conflict, imperial incompetence, and the incessant hordes of barbarians. The eastern empire would continue into the Middle Ages as the Byzantine Empire, with Constantinople still the capital city. The city of Rome, although no longer the capital of a political empire, continued as the center of Catholic Christianity.

Conclusion

Ancient Rome left an indelible imprint on today's world. Traces of this remarkable ancient civilization still impact our legal and political systems, language, literature, religion, infrastructure, architecture, art, and technology. The Roman legacy survived the empire's collapse and continued to shape civilizations throughout the centuries. Rome's enduring legacy laid the groundwork for many aspects of today's society.

Classical civilization – the Greco-Roman world – emerged from the geographical regions that the Greeks and Romans influenced through literature, culture, politics, and religion. Greek philosophy, religion, art, medicine, astronomy, higher mathematics, engineering, and architecture strongly influenced early Roman civilization. Evander – Aeneas's ally, had settled the region that would later become Rome – bringing Greek political, cultural, and religious traditions with him. Alexander the Great believed Hellenistic (Greek) culture was the god's gift to mankind; thus, he felt called to export it to the regions he conquered – much of which later became part of the Roman Empire. Rome assimilated the Greek knowledge and worldview, then disseminated it through the empire and through the pages of history.

Galen – the Greco-Roman philosopher, physician, and surgeon – guided Western medical theory and practice for over a millennium. Ptolemy – astronomist, geographer, and mathematician – produced the *Almagest:* the most in-depth and enlightening astronomical-mathematical treatise of the ancient world, recording 48 of the 88 constellations recognized by today's International Astronomical Union. Hero of Alexandria – a first-century Greek mathematician and engineer – formed the Heron geometric formula and established the study of pneumatics and mechanics. Also in Alexandria, Diophantus – the Father of Algebra – wrote the *Arithmetica:* a series of books covering algebraic equations, geometry, and approximations. He was the first Hellenist mathematician who identified fractions as numbers.

Besides science and mathematics, the Greco-Roman world profoundly shaped literature, philosophy, and theology, which were preserved and passed on by the Christian church after the Roman Empire crumbled. The medieval Christian universities focused on Greco-Roman classics, including Boethius' *Consolation of Philosophy* and his translations of Plato and Aristotle.

Marcus Aurelius was the last of the "Five Good Emperors" but also a Stoic philosopher and writer.

Saint Augustine drew from Cicero, Homer, Varro, Virgil, and especially Plato in the *City of God* – his philosophical treatise about moral decay causing Rome's fall and comparing the "City of God" with the "City of Man," symbolic of the perpetual struggle between faith and unbelief. The Renaissance's syncretism of Hellenism with Christianity revived interest in the Greek and Roman philosophical classics, such as the writings of Marcus Aurelius, Epictetus, and Seneca the Younger.

"Innocent until proven guilty!" This well-known concept, which sprang from ancient Roman law, underlines the Roman influence on the western criminal justice system. The Romans set the precedent for today's court proceedings in modern judiciary systems. Like today's court system, the accused would have a preliminary hearing to determine just cause for a case. If sufficient grounds merited going forward, a formal indictment or charge would inform what the charges were, and a trial by jury would hear from the witnesses and examine the evidence.

The Law of the Twelve Tables, dating to 450 BC, contained the written laws of Rome engraved on 12 bronze tablets – the beginning of a codified system – permitting all citizens to know what the laws were and be treated equally. Before that, citizens often only found out about laws when they broke them and were arrested. The *Twelve Tables* focused on civil law – usually disputes between individuals, such as contracts or property damage, but the state also had public law dealing with things like taxes or treason. The Roman codified law system is the common foundation of today's systematic and comprehensive written laws.

Who made the laws in ancient Rome? During the Republic era, lawmaking involved two bodies of legislation (like America's House of Representatives and Senate). The *comitia* or assembly of citizens first passed legislation, which then went to the Senate for approval. This model of lawmaking continues today in most democratic governments.

Rome overtly influenced the United States in the realm of politics and government. America's founding fathers intentionally imitated the model of government used in the Roman Republic, including features such as a senate, checks and balances, vetoes, separation of powers in three branches of government, term limits, impeachments, quorum requirements, filibusters, and regularly scheduled elections.

The Romans left their mark on the Western world through the Latin language, used as the *lingua franca* (common language) throughout the empire. The Latin language gave birth to the Romance languages, including French, Italian, Portuguese, Romanian, and Spanish. Roughly one-third of English words derive from Latin root words, and another one-third comes from the Romance languages descended from Latin, especially Anglo-Norman and French. Latin words or Latin-derived words comprise 90% of legal, medical, and scientific terminology in the western world.

Some examples of English words derived from Latin are *scholar* for scholar, *cattus* for cat, *familia* for family, *Senatus* for Senate, *sermones* for sermon, *lingua* for language, *musicorum* for music, *cultura* for culture, *consensu* for consent, and *orbis* for orbit.

If you look at old Roman engravings on monuments, you will recognize most letters – the Roman alphabet is the prototype for the English alphabet and most European languages (although the Romans wrote everything with capital letters). The Latin alphabet evolved from the Etruscan alphabet, which derived from the Cumaean Greek alphabet, which came from the Phoenician alphabet, which descended from Egyptian hieroglyphics.

English literature is indebted to Roman influence. Examples of English classics inspired by Roman history or Roman literary style include Chaucer's *The House of Fame,* Dante's *Inferno,* James Joyce's *Ulysses,* Milton's *Paradise Lost,* Robert Graves' *I Claudius,* and, of course, Shakespeare's *Julius Caesar* and *Antony and Cleopatra.* Chaucer, Dante, Milton, and Shakespeare were all influenced by Ovid's *Metamorphoses.*

Throughout the modernist T. S. Eliot's satirical and complicated poetry are allusions to Greco-Roman myths, including Sybil, Hercules, Cupid, and Chronis. C.S. Lewis' works reveal a mind intimately familiar with Roman mythology and literature: *Till We Have Faces* is a retelling of the Cupid and Psyche story from Lucius Apuleius Madaurensis' second-century *Metamorphosis.* Lewis's friend J.R.R. Tolkien believed the pagan myths of Rome retained a semblance of eternal truth. In Tolkien's *Lord of the Rings*, Gondor reflects the eastern Roman empire with a Numenorean history that parallels Aeneas.

The Old Testament was translated into the Greek Septuagint version in Alexandra, Egypt, in the second century BC, and this is the version Jesus read from in the synagogue in Nazareth (Luke 4:16-20). Greek and Latin were the official languages of the Roman Empire; the New Testament was written in Koine Greek – the Lingua Franca of the eastern Roman Empire. Most people in the eastern part of the empire – and some in the west – could have read (or have read to them) both the Old and New Testaments in Greek.

Latin was Rome's original language and continued to be used for administration, legal affairs, and in the military, gradually replacing Greek as the major common language in western Europe. Many people in the western empire could not read Greek or understand it; therefore, parts of the Old and New Testaments were translated into Latin – as early as the first century after Christ.

Jerome was an ascetic who spent the last years of his life in a cave outside of Bethlehem translating the Bible into Latin. He is often pictured with a skull – symbolizing the struggle of the spiritual nature over the earthly nature.
https://commons.wikimedia.org/w/index.php?curid=10285609

Jerome was a priest who knew Greek, Latin, and Hebrew; sensing the need for a good Latin translation of the entire Bible – especially for the western church, he moved to a monastery in Bethlehem in 382 to start translating. Using the earlier Latin translations, he first translated the New Testament Gospels – Matthew, Mark, Luke, and John – into Latin. He then translated the entire Old Testament into Latin by cross-referencing the original Hebrew texts with the Greek Septuagint translation and – since he was in Bethlehem – consulting with the Jewish scholars there on difficult texts. He finished translating the entire Old Testament and the Gospels into Latin – in what's known as the Vulgate – by 405. It was called the Vulgate (meaning *commonly used*) because he used everyday, easier-to-understand Latin rather than scholarly, classical Latin (which he knew well but wanted a version the ordinary people could understand).

Jerome's new Latin translation of the Bible had its critics – but now the western empire had a Bible in a language they could read and understand. This aided the spreading of Christianity throughout western Europe. The Vulgate was the Latin translation used by the Roman Catholic church for centuries – right up until 1979. The Latin Bible helped grow the church; in return, the church preserved the Latin language through the centuries with Jerome's translation.

"All roads lead to Rome" reflected the days of the Roman Republic and Empire when the *Viae Romanae* or Roman roads traveled like rays of the sun from Rome to points throughout the empire – providing efficient travel for the military, government officials, merchants, and ordinary people. Roman roads still exist today, two millennia later; some even have their original cobblestones. Others have formed the routes for modern-day roads and highways.

Roman roads were constructed with a three-level substructure of dirt, gravel, and bricks with the paving stones on top made from rock slabs. They were amazingly strong and resilient, resistant to harsh weather, and built with a slight lift in the center to allow efficient rain drainage.

Rome's sweeping network of over 250,000 miles of roads was an extraordinary achievement for its day. They connected the colonies to each other and to Rome, enabling travel with wheeled carts. The roads had signposts marking the miles and the distance to the next town. One great advantage of the road system was permitting the Roman legions to travel by foot about 20 miles a day to quickly respond to uprisings in the cities or invasions on their borders.

Roman roads engendered another great invention used today – the postal service! The roads permitted relatively fast travel of messages from city to city, and they even had express delivery using horses.

Echoes of ancient Rome still resound in different spheres of life, more than we realize. Our calendar, holidays, philosophy, and sense of justice are part of the treasure trove left by the Romans. The rise and fall of Rome inspire us but also provide cautionary lessons we must learn for our survival. Ancient Rome still matters. Studying its history is still important: it continues to define our worldview, our self-concept, our spirituality, and our political ideals.

Part 3: Ancient Mesopotamia

An Enthralling Overview of Mesopotamian History, Starting from Eridu through the Sumerians, Akkadians, Assyrians, Hittites, and Persians to Alexander the Great

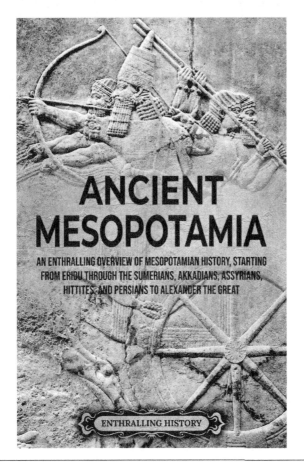

Introduction

"All the evil winds, all stormy winds gathered into one and with them, the Flood was sweeping over the land, for seven days and seven nights. After the Flood had swept over the country, after the evil wind had tossed the big boat about on the great waters, the sun came out spreading light over heaven and earth."

The Eridu Genesis from a Sumerian cuneiform tablet, circa 1600 BCE

Sound familiar? The *Eridu Genesis* flood story echoes other ancient Mesopotamian flood stories, such as those found in the Hebrew Torah, the Sumerian *Epic of Gilgamesh*, and the Akkadian *Epic of Atrahasis*. Mesopotamia, "the cradle of civilization," gave birth to the world's first pieces of literature and many other innovations, including the first agricultural systems, the first cities, the first writing system, the first wheel, the first maps, the first sailboats, the first written mathematics, the first kings, and the first great empires. Mesopotamia was indeed a land of many beginnings!

This overview gives an in-depth insight into the intriguing people of ancient Mesopotamia and their astonishing achievements. Traveling back 7,400 years, we will begin with ancient Eridu, the first city of southern Mesopotamia. We will then explore the Sumerian civilization, the Akkadian Empire, the Assyrians, the Hittites, the Persian-Achaemenid Empire, and end with Alexander the Great of Macedonia, who conquered most of

Mesopotamia. We will unlock the mysteries of these ancient people, explain the distinctive features of the various civilizations, and discover what made them exceptional.

The great Euphrates and Tigris Rivers flow through Mesopotamia.
No machine-readable author provided. Kmusser assumed (based on copyright claims).,
CC BY-SA 2.5 https://creativecommons.org/licenses/by-sa/2.5 via Wikimedia
Commons;https://commons.wikimedia.org/wiki/File:Tigr-euph.png

Where is Mesopotamia? It encompasses part of the Middle East. Mesopotamia literally means "between the rivers," referring to the Euphrates and Tigris, which the Torah said flowed out of the Garden of Eden. Both rivers flow from Turkey's Taurus Mountains through Syria, meeting in Iraq, then flowing together through Iran and into the Persian Gulf. Ancient Mesopotamia included modern-day Iraq and Kuwait, as well as portions of Iran, Turkey, Syria, and Saudi Arabia.

Many books written about ancient Mesopotamia were written by scholars for other scholars, which means they use academic language. Some were written decades before the most recent archaeological finds and the latest information. Other books are meant for children or cover specific aspects of Mesopotamian civilization. This comprehensive overview draws from scholarly research yet endeavors to unlock Mesopotamia's majestic history in clear, compelling, easy-to-understand prose. It is great for beginners and history buffs alike.

Knowledge of past civilizations helps us discern our world today. We will discover how Mesopotamia's ancient civilizations contributed to today's cultures. How did they inform our worldview and lay the foundation for our belief systems? How do the catalysts for change in ancient Mesopotamia, the rise and fall of great empires, impact us today? How have the struggles of ancient Mesopotamia influenced contemporary Middle Eastern conflicts?

This overview is divided into four sections, beginning with "An Age of Firsts," when people began forming agricultural communities, domesticating animals, and devising irrigation techniques that took advantage of the Tigris and Euphrates Rivers. We will explore Eridu, the first of five cities established before the Great Flood, according to the *Sumerian King List.*

We will then examine the Sumerians, who developed the earliest written language and built Ur, the patriarch Abraham's birthplace. This city was seven miles northeast of Eridu and fifty miles southeast of Uruk, the hero Gilgamesh's city. What spurred their sophisticated architecture, notably the terraced pyramid-shaped ziggurat towers? How did trade expand their territory? We will analyze the Code of Ur-Nammu, the world's oldest law code. What did it say about witchcraft, runaway slaves, and bodily injury? We will also look at Sargon the Great, who conquered all of Macedonia and part of Syria, Lebanon, Turkey, and Iran, establishing the Akkadian, the first empire in recorded history.

Part Two, "Age of Empires," delves into Assyria and Babylonia, the mighty empires that ruled Mesopotamia. How did they take control, what made them famous, and who were some of their renowned leaders? What intriguing aspects of ordinary people's lives can we learn from archaeology and ancient documents? How did the Amorites seize control and establish Babylon as their capital? What was the Babylonians' religion, and what was their creation myth? And what led to the collapse of the

Assyrian and Babylonian Empires?

Part Three, "Age of Innovation," dives into the adventures of King Gilgamesh and his half-wild companion Enkidu in the *Epic of Gilgamesh*. We will discover the incredible innovations and inventions that took place from 1800 to 1400 BCE. How did the famous King Hammurabi expand his empire, and what laws did he include in his law code? What happened when the Elamites conquered Ur?

When Nebuchadnezzar conquered Mesopotamia, including Jerusalem in 586 BCE, why did he take the Jews into captivity? What happened to them in Babylon? Did Babylon really have hanging gardens? What inspired the ornate Ishtar Gate and the walls of Babylon? How did the Zoroastrian religion influence Mesopotamian culture and other beliefs?

Part Four, "Here Come the Persians," uncovers how Cyrus the Great seized power and founded the Achaemenid Empire. We will explore everyday life in Persia and review the exquisite Persian art, stunning architecture, and extraordinary technology that changed the known world. How did the clash play out between King Darius III and Persia's great enemy, Alexander the Great?

Now, let's step back seventy-four centuries to begin our exploration of Mesopotamia. Why was Mesopotamia's legacy so revolutionary? And how has it molded society as we know it today?

SECTION ONE: AN AGE OF FIRSTS (5500–2000 BCE)

Chapter 1: Eridu: The First City

If you visited the site of the world's oldest city today, you would see an unprepossessing mound rising over a vast expanse of desolate desert. If you looked closer, you'd realize what looks like a natural mesa is actually the crumbling ruins of ancient buildings. The mound is a tell, the accumulated stratified debris of a city occupied from around 5400 BCE until the 5th century BCE. Houses, temples, and cemeteries were built on top of old ones for millennia, creating an artificial hill.

Eridu wasn't always located in a barren wasteland. If you traveled back in time thousands of years, you'd find a prosperous, bustling metropolis covering one hundred acres on the northern shores of the Persian Gulf, close to the mouth of the Euphrates River. Outside the city walls, the fertile wetlands of Lake Hammar, which was fed by the Euphrates, came right up to the city's eastern wall. The lake is saline today, but it was freshwater in ancient times, according to an archaeological and geological survey from 2010. A canal came in from the lake and around the northern and western walls of the city, with channels irrigating the agricultural fields and fruit groves. Farther away were the vast pasturelands, where sheep and goats grazed. In the wetlands, workers would press clay and mud into forms that would dry in the sun, forming bricks.

Thousands of years ago, the Persian Gulf extended far north to Eridu and Ur.

NordNordWest, usingUbaid culture sites map.jpg by John D. CroftGroßer Atlas zur Weltgeschichte, Westermann SchulbuchverlagPutzger Historischer Weltaltas, Cornelsen Verlagdtv-Atlas Weltgeschichte, Deutscher Taschenbuch VerlagGTOPO-30 Elevation Data by USGS, CC BY-SA 3.0 https://creativecommons.org/licenses/by-sa/3.0 via Wikimedia Commons; https://commons.wikimedia.org/wiki/File:Map_Ubaid_culture-en.svg

Moving south, you would find fishermen in picturesque sailboats on the Persian Gulf, casting their nets. Along its shore, people would be harvesting shellfish and drying fish on platforms. Other boats would trade up the Euphrates or with other settlements around the Gulf. You would hear the grunts and grumbles of camels as they set out in caravans, following the Fertile Crescent north into what is now Turkey, east to the Mediterranean, and down its shores past Sidon and Tyre to Egypt.

Enki's temple, the House of the Aquifer, stood in the city center inside the city walls. The original temple dates to 5300 BCE, when Ur was a settlement of the Ubaid civilization. The first temple was a modest one-room structure with an altar for sacrifices at one end and a cult niche for an idol at the other. Grander temples were built over the first site as time passed; there were eighteen of them over several thousand years. In the

3rd millennium BCE, a multi-storied, tiered pyramid-shaped temple called a ziggurat towered over the city rooflines. Adobe brick residential buildings that housed four thousand people surrounded the thirty-acre city center.

The Ziggurat of Enki may have looked like this model.
https://commons.wikimedia.org/wiki/File:SumerianZiggurat.jpg

Do we know for sure if Eridu was the world's oldest city? The *Sumerian King List* identified Eridu as the first city (of five), as does Babylonian literature. Archaeological excavations at Eridu revealed constructions from the prehistoric Ubaid period (6500–3800 BCE), with the first structures dating to about 5400 BCE. Urbanization first began in Mesopotamia before China, India, or Egypt. So, which Mesopotamian city, if not Eridu, came first?

Scholars sometimes propose Uruk was the oldest city, but archaeological evidence suggests it was first settled around 5000 BCE, about four centuries after Eridu. The ancient city of Jericho is another contender, and it does have evidence of human occupation going back to the Neolithic Age. However, it did not reach city status (in terms of population size) until the Bronze Age, which was after Eridu. A third contender is Çatalhöyük in Turkey, which did have a settlement of several thousand people prior to Eridu. However, it lacked a city's infrastructure; it didn't even have streets! People had to get around on the rooftops.

Depending on one's definition of what a city actually *is* (and archaeologists and other scholars hotly debate this), Eridu takes the prize as the oldest settlement that: 1) was the center of religion for the surrounding area, 2) was densely populated, 3) had a central government, and 4) had infrastructure. As Enki's main sanctuary, Eridu was a religious center of Mesopotamia until the 6th century BCE. According to Sumerian mythology, Enki, the god of deep waters, magic, and wisdom, was Eridu's founder.

Eridu started as a cluster of people living in reed-thatched huts. They had herds of goats and sheep, fished from the Persian Gulf and the nearby Lake Hammar, and hunted waterfowl, gazelle, deer, and other wild animals. They engaged in simple agriculture and began growing grain. Einkorn wheat grew wild throughout the region, and they learned to cultivate it. The early settlers had an adequate and healthy diet with plenty of protein, mainly fish, and their population quickly grew. Over time, sun-dried clay-brick houses replaced the reed structures. Eventually, they began building multi-storied buildings, and their humble beginnings grew into a stunning city!

This pottery jar dates to the Ubaid III period (5300–4700 BCE).

They began producing a type of pottery called Hadji Muhammed ceramics with striking geometric patterns. They built canal networks to irrigate their fields. They also started trading with what is now Turkey for obsidian, black volcanic glass or igneous rock from which they formed knife blades and weapons.

At the end of the Ubaid period (around 3800 BCE), Eridu lost most of its population. Nearby Ur, which was just several miles away along the coast, was also simultaneously uninhabited for a time. A layer of sediment in Ur indicates a flood swept over it, covering the city in silt. A flood of this magnitude may have impacted its neighbor Eridu, although Ur was much closer to the cojoined Euphrates-Tigris River system.

Lake Hammar's levels fell due to over-irrigation and climate change, making its water more saline and harmful to the crops. The land became arider since there was less rainfall, turning it from semi-desert to desert. As the lake levels dropped, sand dunes formed around the lake's perimeter that may have cut off the irrigation canals. For centuries, Eridu and its neighbors lay abandoned under the desert sun.

Around 2900 BCE, Eridu was again inhabited, and it grew into a major city. By this time, Semitic-speaking herdsmen were entering the area. An unknown king, or more likely a series of kings over time, built a grand palace with dozens of rooms, buttresses, and drains for water. Eridu went into decline again by 2050 BCE, and it was uninhabited or sparsely inhabited after this point. In the 7th century BCE, the Neo-Babylonians rebuilt its temple site, honoring Enki's city. However, it never rose as a city again. The receding Persian Gulf eventually left almost two hundred miles of desert between the city and the sea, which had once been its source of food and trade. The rising salinity of the available water supply could not provide enough fresh water to sustain life and support agriculture.

Although Eridu was located almost within sight of Ur and other cities that shared a common language, religion, and culture, each was an independent political entity with its own king: a city-state. Eridu and its neighboring city-states consisted of a densely-populated urban residential area with narrow streets that wandered through the maze of buildings. In the city's center stood a temple, palace, markets, and public buildings

Tall, thick walls encircled Eridu to protect it from neighboring city-states. Outside the walls stretched lush, irrigated farms; sheep, goats, and camels grazed along the wetlands. Like other city-states of southern Mesopotamia, Eridu was a politically self-contained bubble, with enough agriculture, domesticated animals, and fish to sustain its population. However, trade was an essential element of Mesopotamian culture, especially long-distance transactions in lands with resources like metal ore, which the people used to make weapons and farming utensils. Camel caravans traveled overland, and boats on the Euphrates and the Persian Gulf were trade conduits.

Eridu had three different ecosystems. The first was agricultural, with an extensive canal and irrigation system necessary in a semi-desert climate with limited rainfall. Like most early Mesopotamian regions, the people grew barley and einkorn wheat. Under the shade of date palms, farmers grew beans, cucumbers, garlic, leeks, lettuce, and peas. They also grew fruit, including pomegranates, grapes, figs, and melons.

The second ecosystem was mainly sea-based. Eridu was a coastal city in ancient times, and fish was the primary protein source. Archaeological excavations have discovered whole rooms full of dried fish! Extensive middens (refuse heaps) along the Persian Gulf reveal that shellfish harvesting was vital for food and exquisite pearls. Shells would be pressed into the walls of palaces, temples, and homes, acting as decorations.

In the area around Eridu, nomadic herders of camels, goats, and sheep lived in tents, tending about 1,400 sheep in flocks of about 70 animals (the ancient cuneiform tablets recorded information on the herds). The nomads milked the ewes to make butter, yogurt, and cheese. They used their wool for clothing and slaughtered the animals for sacrifices and meat. In addition to domestic animals, gazelle and wild ass herds roamed the grasslands of the river and lake system, which were hunted for meat and skins.

In Eridu and other early Mesopotamian cities, the kings were first known as *Ensi* or priest-kings. Later, as cities grew and needed more complex leadership, the king became primarily a secular ruler called *Lugal* or strongman. The strongman-king of Eridu administered the work of farmers, fishermen, and herdsmen, and he oversaw the merchants, craftsmen, and construction workers within the city.

Although the king continued having a dual role of city-administrator and religious leader, a priestly caste evolved to perform sacrifices and other religious rites and to gaze at the stars to discover omens. The people believed the heavens chose the king; to obey their king was to obey the gods. The king was considered the intermediary between the people and the gods. In addition to administrative and religious functions, the strongman-king protected Eridu from invasion, led his men in wars against other city-states, supported law and order in the city, and provided for widows and orphans.

The farmers, herders, fishermen, and workers, who built and maintained the dams and irrigation canals, mostly lived in villages or nomadic tent dwellings around the city. The craftspeople—carpenters, weavers, and blacksmiths—lived within the city, along with the priests and administrators.

In the earliest days of Eridu, people discovered that intense heat could shape metal. They also found that heating rocks like azurite and malachite released copper. As their knowledge of metallurgy evolved, they learned they could mix copper with tin to produce stronger bronze. By 4000 BCE, the people of Eridu and other Mesopotamian cities were using bronze, copper, gold, iron, lead, mercury, silver, and tin.

A city the size of Eridu required a bureaucracy of city officials, tax collectors, and scribes to keep records. The farmers, herders, craftsmen, and other workers paid a tithe or part of their product to the city to pay for the cost of the defensive wall around the city, the irrigation canals and aqueducts, and other infrastructure. By 3500 BCE, a pictograph writing system had developed in Mesopotamia, and clerks used cuneiform writing to track taxes, merchants' and traders' sales, and other vital information.

Writing in Eridu began with pictographs like these.
https://en.wikipedia.org/wiki/Cuneiform#/media/File:Tableta_con_trillo.png

By 3200 BCE, Eridu's scribes were using cuneiform writing, making wedge-shaped indentations with a reed stylus onto clay tablets. They also began chiseling cuneiform into stone. The cuneiform marks represented syllables, and putting them together formed words. As writing developed, the first schools opened to teach some young people how to read and write. Early writing was mainly used for administrative purposes, but scholars also put oral traditions and histories into written form.

The *Eridu Genesis* (the *Sumerian Flood Story*), an ancient Sumerian text written approximately 2300 BCE, might be the oldest Mesopotamian account of the Great Flood. A similar story later appeared in the *Epic of Gilgamesh* (circa 2150 BCE), the *Epic of Atrahasis* (circa 1640 BCE), and a detailed description in the Hebrew Bereshit (Genesis, circa 1446 BCE). These accounts likely retold stories from older documents or oral tradition.

Fragments of the *Eridu Genesis* are found on several clay tablets; the first one was discovered in ancient Nippur, Iraq. The tablets have been broken or damaged and have missing lines; however, what is there is clearly an account of a Great Flood story. Scholars relied on the later *Epic of Atrahasis* to fill in the missing sentences. In the *Eridu Genesis*, the righteous man chosen to survive the deluge and continue human life is Ziusudra, the priest-king of Suruppak. In the *Epic of Gilgamesh*, he is called Utnapishtim. In the *Epic of Atrahasis*, he is Atrahasis, and in Genesis, he is Noah.

The *Eridu Genesis* begins with the mother-goddess Nintur leading humans back from their trails and having them build brick cities with temples. There, she can relax in the cool shade, and the people could live in peace, practicing divination. Then she instituted the kingship, saying the king was to advise the people, oversee their labor, and teach them to follow like cattle. A royal scepter, a crown, and a regal throne descended from heaven.

The people built the first city, Eridu, and the goddess appointed Nudimmud as its king. Four other cities were built with four other kings. The people dredged irrigation canals, which enabled abundant crops. But they made so much noise while they worked that they annoyed Enlil, the god of the wind, earth, and storms. Enlil colluded with the other gods to kill mankind.

Distraught, the mother-goddess Nintur wept over her creatures, and the god Enki, who had founded the city of Eridu, determined to save humankind. He warned the priest-king Ziusudra. "Listen! Heed my advice! A flood will sweep over the cities and the country. The gods decided to destroy mankind! Their command is irrevocable!"

Enki counseled Ziusudra to build a great ark and load it with pairs of animals. Then the winds blew, and the flood swept over the cities for seven days and nights as the ark tossed about on the raging sea. Finally, the sun came out, spreading light through the sky and down onto the earth. Ziusudra cut an opening in the boat, and the sun shone inside. Ziusudra stepped out in front of the sun, kissing the ground.

Ziusudra then butchered oxen and many sheep to sacrifice, along with barley cakes. At this point, the enraged Enlil discovered Ziusudra had survived the flood. Enki explained his actions, saying the man was an ally with the gods. Ziusudra then kissed the ground and honored Enlil and his father, the supreme god An (or Anu), and the gods rewarded Ziusudra with immortality. Ziusudra guided the animals off the ark and went to live in the east, over the mountains of Dilmun.

Another Mesopotamian myth tells of Inanna, the patron goddess of Uruk and the daughter of Enki, the patron god of Eridu. According to the myth, Inanna traveled fifty miles south from Uruk to Eridu to persuade her father to give her the *mes* (gifts of civilization) for her fledgling city. At first, Enki refused.

So, Inanna challenged him to a drinking contest. When he was drunk, he gave the *mes* to Inanna. The following day, he awoke with a dreadful hangover. He realized what he'd done and tried to retrieve the *mes* from Inanna. But she had already fled the scene and was back in Uruk, developing it into a great city.

This myth seems to represent the transition in power from Eridu to Uruk. The southern cities became less important (or faded away altogether) while Uruk became the new power center. The Torah records that the patriarch Terah (Abraham's father) packed up his extended family and left Ur (seven miles from Eridu), following the Euphrates north with his sheep, goats, and camels to Haran. According to genealogies, this emigration was around 2100 BCE. Perhaps it was part of an extensive migration north from the Eridu-Ur region.

Chapter 2: Sumerians: The First Civilization

For over two thousand years, the scorching sands of Iraq and Kuwait hid the relics of the Sumerians: the world's first civilized group of people. Sumer, the "cradle of civilization," lay in southern Mesopotamia, stretching along the Euphrates and Tigris Rivers to the Persian Gulf. *Sumer*, an Akkadian word, means "land of the civilized kings." The Hebrews called the land *Shinar*, "land of two rivers." But the Sumerians' name for their land was *kiengir*, simply meaning "the land," and they called themselves *sagiga*, the "black-headed people."

Three of their earliest cities were Eridu, Uruk, and Ur, which were all settled during the prehistoric Ubaid period (c. 6500–3800 BC). However, Eridu and Ur were abandoned and then reinhabited by the Sumerians at the cusp of the Bronze Age (3500 BCE). By that time, the Sumerian language, which is unrelated to any known language group, was the dominant language of southern Mesopotamia.

The Sumerians built most of their cities on the Tigris and Euphrates Rivers or their tributaries. City-states were usually independent entities, but occasionally, a strong leader of one city-state would conquer and absorb other city-states into his kingdom. King Eannatum of Lagash is a prime example. He drove out Elamite invaders and then conquered Ur, Uruk, Kish, and other Sumerian cities, forming a small empire.

The *Sumerian King List* provides invaluable information on the kings of each era and the eras' most important cities. The earliest kings, before the Great Flood, lived fantastically long lives: eight kings ruled for a total of 385,200 years. After the flood, the kings enumerated in the *Sumerian King List* gradually had shorter lives, similar to the genealogies in the Torah, where lifespans grew much shorter after the Great Flood.

After Gilgamesh's rule, most kings reigned for less than a century and often less than a decade. The latter part of the *Sumerian King List* following Gilgamesh is probably actual history and not mythical. Excavations from Sumer back up part of the *Sumerian King List*, such as grave markers and other artifacts that recorded the names of the kings.

Archaeology also confirms that before 5000 BCE, the Sumerians had already established an agrarian society. The people worked with stone tools, including adzes (a digging tool similar to an ax), hoes, knives, and sickles. By this time, they were also making bricks for construction, creating striking painted pottery, and sculpting intriguing figurines, some with sci-fi appearances, such as reptilian people or individuals with elongated necks or enormous round eyes.

The Sumerians' well-rounded diet featured fish, cheese, and yogurt for their main protein, and it was occasionally supplemented with mutton or wild game. They ate bread and porridge made from einkorn wheat, millet, or barley and consumed various fruit and vegetables, including pomegranates, dates, lentils, chickpeas, melons, and cucumbers.

A husband-and-wife toast each other while drinking beer (this time without a straw).
Osama Shukir Muhammed Amin FRCP(Glasg), CC BY-SA 4.0
https://creativecommons.org/licenses/by-sa/4.0/ via Wikimedia Commons;
https://commons.wikimedia.org/wiki/File:Detail,_Part_of_the_so-
called Banquet Plaques. Beer was a common daily dietary staple in ancient Mes
opotamia. From Ur, Iraq. Early Dynastic Period, 2900-
2350 BCE. Sulaymaniyah Museum, Iraqi Kurdistan.jpg

They needed to drink lots of water in the hot, dry climate, which they kept in earthenware pots. Water would condense on the surface of these large jars, keeping the water cool. The people also drank beer! They even had a goddess of beer: Ninkasi. The world's first recipe for brewing beer comes from the Sumerians in the *Hymn to Ninkasi*. Beer was a bit different then. It had about the same alcohol content as today, but it had a thick,milkshake consistency. Like we drink milkshakes with straws, the Sumerians often drank their beer through long straws from large jugs; several people would drink from the same jar. A recurring theme in Sumerian pottery art was a husband making love to his wife while she drank beer from a straw!

Homes were initially made from bundled marsh reeds and later replaced by mud-brick houses with arched doorways and flat roofs. Families enjoyed gathering on the rooftops in the cool evenings and usually slept there. They would also spread grain or grapes out to dry on their roofs. Temples, palaces, and other grander-scale buildings featured elaborate constructions with terracotta decorations, bronze accents, mosaics, columns, and mural paintings. Relief carvings in stone, which had remarkably realistic figures, adorned many Sumerian temples. Sumerians surged ahead in metal-casting technology, which they used for some sculptures.

Sumerian men and women wore wraparound wool or sheepskin skirts that fell to their knees or ankles—longer skirts showed higher status. Men usually wore no clothing above the waist in the heat of the day. The women's skirts often had a section wrapped over one shoulder, sometimes leaving one breast exposed. Both men and women wore earrings, necklaces, and bracelets of gold, turquoise, and lapis lazuli.

The highly innovative Sumerian people engaged in complex and cooperative efforts, such as building thick, high city walls, complex irrigation systems, magnificent ziggurats, and splendid palaces. After inventing the world's first writing system—pictographs that evolved into cuneiform—they wrote down the world's first literature: epic poetry, hymns, and prayers. They also used their writing system for law codes and administrative record-keeping.

Sumerians used herbalism and magic in their medical practices but learned to extract chemicals from plants and other substances to produce medications. They had an advanced understanding of anatomy, and doctors performed surgeries (archaeologists have unearthed surgical instruments). They understood that bodily organs could malfunction, causing illness. Cuneiform tablets dating to 1770 BCE demonstrate knowledge of lethal pathogens.

The Sumerians made astounding advances in hydraulic engineering. Not only did they invent crop irrigation, harnessing the Euphrates and Tigris for their agricultural fields, but they also learned to build ditches and dikes to control the frequent flooding of these great rivers. Their skill in these engineering feats, not to mention their stunning architecture, demonstrates their sophisticated knowledge of measurements, geometry, calculus, and trigonometry.

Sumerians believed in an assortment of gods with human-like forms: anthropomorphic polytheism. Each city-state had a patron deity and was the terrestrial home of that god. In their core pantheon, An (Anu) ruled as the supreme god of heaven. Enki (Ea) was the god of the earth, healing, and groundwater. He was Eridu's patron god and protected humans when the other gods wanted to kill them. Enlil (Nunamnir) was the god of the atmosphere and wind. An, Enlil, and Enki formed a triad that ruled heaven, earth, and the underworld.

Inanna, the patron deity of Uruk, was the planet Venus's divine personification; she represented love, sex, beauty, justice, political power, and war. The Akkadians, Assyrians, and Babylonians worshiped her as Ishtar. Inanna's twin brother, Utu, was the sun god and represented truth and morality. Sin (or Nanna) was Enlil's son; he was the moon god and represented wisdom.

The Sumerians thought that mankind's reason for existing was to serve the gods. If they failed to please the gods, humans would suffer. If a flood destroyed a village, it was because the people had offended the gods. Thus, they needed priests to engage in rituals to discern the gods' will and what people needed to do to stay on their good side. The Sumerian priests were astrologists. They read omens and predicted the future from the stars, planets, and sun. All Sumerians were expected to pray daily to the gods, honoring them with hymns and incense, and atone for their sins. They prayed while raising both hands in the air or with one hand in front of their mouths. They often kneeled or prostrated themselves face-down on the ground.

This silver lion's head guarded the entrance of Puabi's burial chamber.
Mary Harrsch, CC BY 2.0 https://creativecommons.org/licenses/by/2.0 via Wikimedia Commons; https://commons.wikimedia.org/wiki/File:Silver_Lion%27s_Head_Finial_for_the_arm_of_a_chair_with_shell_and_lapis_lazuli_inset_eyes_recovered_from_the_royal_cemetery_of_Ur_2550-2450_BCE.jpg

One astonishing ritual was how the Sumerians buried their dead, particularly their royalty. British archaeologist Leonard Woolley discovered Ur's "death pit" in 1926, where the priestess-queen Puabi was buried around 2600 BCE. More than one hundred attendants and soldiers, draped with gold and silver, were sacrificed to accompany her to the afterlife. Woolley unearthed a staggering amount of treasure in her tomb: a spectacular golden headdress with gold leaves, a lyre with a gold and lapis-lazuli bull's head, gold tableware, gold and lapis lazuli necklaces and belts, and a chariot covered with silver.

Ur's location on the Persian Gulf at the mouth of the Euphrates-Tigris made it an important trade city with astounding wealth. Surrounded by marshy land, farming was relatively easy. In fact, sophisticated farming techniques may not have been necessary to support a relatively large population since abundant fish, waterfowl, tubers, and other food sources were readily available. Ur was, however, susceptible to frequent flooding.

A small settlement existed there from about 5000 BCE until 3800 BCE. At that time, Ur experienced a devastating flood, leaving an eleven-foot layer of silt that was discovered by archaeologists. By 3500 BCE, it was inhabited again, and it eventually grew into a city of thirty-four thousand people. The extravagance and wealth with which the priestess-queen Puabi was buried imply an advanced and wealthy civilization.

King Mesannepadda initiated the First Dynasty of Ur (2500–2445 BCE), gaining ascendency over the city of Uruk, which had been dominating Sumer. Four kings followed him before the Elamites invaded, ending the First Dynasty. The Elamites ruled Ur until they were overthrown by Sumerian King Eannatum of Lagash, who controlled much of Sumer as head of one of the world's first empires. Ur reestablished self-rule briefly in an obscure Second Dynasty until the Akkadians took over. They were followed by the "barbarian" Gutian nomads of Iran.

After a coalition army of Uruk and Ur expelled the Gutians, Ur-Nammu ushered in Ur's Third Dynasty (2112–2004 BCE). At this time, according to the Torah, the Semitic patriarch Abraham was living in Ur with his father Terah, his half-sister and wife Sarah, and other family members. They migrated north around the time of Ur-Nammu's death in 2096 BCE.

Ur-Nammu unified the southern floodplain cities and gained supremacy over most of Mesopotamia. He reestablished Sumerian as Mesopotamia's official language and initiated astounding building projects around Mesopotamia; his figurines often show him carrying building materials. He built walls around his capital, constructed numerous ziggurats (including the Great Ziggurat of Ur), and more irrigation canals. He also instituted schools to train government officials in cuneiform writing and other skills.

This cylinder-seal impression, circa 2100 BCE, depicts King Ur-Nammu.
Steve Harris, CC BY-SA 2.0 https://creativecommons.org/licenses/by-sa/2.0 via Wikimedia Commons; https://commons.wikimedia.org/wiki/File:Sumerian_Cylinder_Seal_of_King_Ur-Nammu.jpg

Ur-Nammu is most famous for writing the first law code that has survived. It covered murder, kidnapping, slave rights, premarital sex, sorcery, and more. If someone accused a person of witchcraft or a husband accused his wife of adultery, they had to endure an ordeal by water.

What was ordeal by water? The tablets didn't say, but the Torah and the Code of Hammurabi give some clues. The Torah stipulated that if a man suspected his wife of adultery but had no proof, the priest would give her holy water mixed with a sprinkling of dust from the tabernacle floor. If nothing happened when she drank it, she was innocent. But if she were impure, her belly would swell, her thigh would shrivel, and she would be unable to conceive children (Numbers 5:11-31). Hammurabi said that if someone were accused of a crime with no hard evidence, they could jump into the river. If they drowned, they were guilty, and if they survived, they were innocent. Perhaps one of these "water tests" was similar to Ur-Nammu's ordeal by water.

At the end of Ur-Nammu's reign, Ur was the largest city globally, with approximately sixty-five thousand people. Ur-Nammu's son Shulgi succeeded him; a hymn recounts his incredulous achievement of running one hundred miles from Nippur to Ur in one day. And yes, that can be done! Today, ultra-distance runners can run one hundred miles (on level ground) in about twenty hours, but an elite runner can complete that distance in eleven hours. Whether Shulgi actually ran that distance or hopped in a chariot once he was out of sight of the cities is another question.

Shulgi built a remarkable 155-mile-long wall to keep the Amorites out of Sumer, which his descendants maintained and reinforced. However, it failed to protect Sumer from a 1940 BCE invasion from the southeast. The Elamites simply went around the end of the wall, got into Sumer, sacked Ur, and captured the king. Ur never regained political power, but its access to the Persian Gulf and the Euphrates enabled the city to continue as a vital trade conduit for the next thousand years.

The Amorites of Babylonia, the Akkadian Sealand dynasty, the Kassites, the Elamites, and the Assyrians ruled Ur successively during the next millennia. Ur declined after Babylon fell to the Persians in 530 BCE. The city lost its entire population when the Euphrates shifted west, which caused its outlet to the Persian Gulf to silt over.

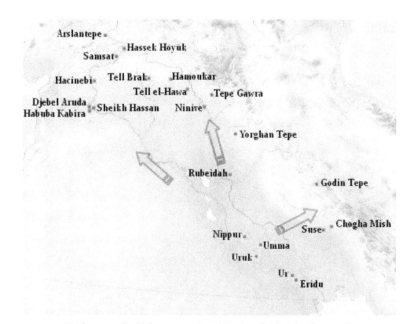

Uruk controlled Mesopotamian cities hundreds of miles north.
Middle_East_topographic_map-blank.svg: Sémhur (talk)derivative work: Zunkir - This file was derived from: Middle East topographic map-blank.svg:, CC BY-SA 3.0 https://creativecommons.org/licenses/by-sa/3.0 via Wikimedia Commons; https://commons.wikimedia.org/w/index.php?curid=25540654

Uruk was a key city, the dominant city for a time, in ancient Mesopotamia. It was located about forty miles north of Ur on the east bank of the Euphrates. The *Sumerian King List* names King Enmerkar as its founder around 4500 BCE, although archaeological evidence shows an Ubaid settlement dating to about 5000 BCE. The Torah (Genesis 10:10) identifies Uruk as ruled by the mighty warrior and hunter Nimrod. The *Epic of Gilgamesh* says Gilgamesh built Uruk's walls and ruled the city in the 27th century BCE.

Although Eridu was established hundreds of years earlier, Uruk was Mesopotamia's powerhouse for 1,600 years until Ur rose to preeminence. At its peak, Uruk had an astonishing population of forty thousand inside the city walls and eighty thousand people in its immediate area. It was probably the largest city in the world around 3100 BCE. Uruk had an organized military, full-time civil servants, and a stratified society.

Archaeologists believe Uruk was the first city to build immense stone or brick structures, including the first ziggurat. It was the first to mass-produce beveled-rim pottery bowls, and its people invented the cylinder seal, which was rolled in soft clay to produce pictures and written characters. It may have been where the first writing was devised (if not Eridu). The entrancing Lady of Warka mask (Warka is another name for Uruk) is the first preserved depiction of a human face. It perhaps is a sculpture of Uruk's patron goddess Inanna.

The Lady of Warka mask dates to about 3100 BCE in Uruk.
Osama Shukir Muhammed Amin FRCP(Glasg), CC BY-SA 4.0
https://creativecommons.org/licenses/by-sa/4.0 via Wikimedia
Commons;https://commons.wikimedia.org/wiki/File:Warka_mask_(cropped).jpg

The extraordinary Uruk period, spanning from 4100 to 2900 BCE, saw a rapid expansion of cities in southern Mesopotamia, of which Uruk was the trade and administrative hub. Uruk had a wall around its perimeter, supposedly built by the great Gilgamesh, but it also had an interior wall dividing the newer Eanna district from the older Anu district. Like Eridu, Uruk had an elaborate irrigation system, producing an agricultural surplus of domestic grain.

After 2900 BCE, Uruk faded somewhat in power and population; however, it continued as a city long after Eridu and Ur dissolved into oblivion. Although it declined in prestige and people after Eridu and Ur were abandoned in the 6th century BCE, Uruk's fascinating 5,200-year history of inhabitation continued until 700 CE. By that time, the Euphrates had changed course, leaving Uruk in the middle of a bleak desert. The shifting sands quickly covered the abandoned city, hiding its mysteries until the mid-1850s when British archaeologist William Loftus rediscovered it.

The Neo-Sumerian civilization declined and finally collapsed in 2004 BCE, and within two centuries, Sumerian was a dead spoken language. However, the Sumerian language continued in written literary works and religious liturgy, and the brilliant Sumerian culture exercised considerable influence over the Assyrian and Babylonian civilizations. The Akkadians and fierce Amorites swept into the land between the rivers, synthesizing their language and culture with the Sumerians' ways.

What, specifically, was the Sumerian legacy? Where do we start? The enthralling Sumerians instituted the first schools to teach the first written language, with which they wrote the first law code and epic poetry. They also used it to keep track of administrative affairs. They ingeniously developed the concept of time, creating the sixty-second minute and the sixty-minute hour. They divided day and night into twelve-hour periods and instituted a workday time limit and days off for holidays.

The Sumerians astutely developed measurements around 4000 BCE, which led to the rise of arithmetic, algebra, and geometry. They were the first to build large buildings, like ziggurats, from stone or brick and the first to build empires. They invented the sailboat, initiated large-scale pottery production, and developed metallurgy. They invented the wheel, created the arch, and were the first to have irrigated fields and cultivate grain on a large scale to make bread. And that led to beer! Let's not forget beer!

Chapter 3: Sargon of Akkad: The First Ruler

From mysterious origins, Sargon the Great rose to establish the world's first multi-ethnic empire with a central government. Through subterfuge and switching alliances, he conquered Kish and Uruk, then continued brazenly expanding his massive empire to include all of Mesopotamia and parts of Anatolia (Turkey), Elam (western Iran), and Syria. Reigning from 2334 to 2279 BCE, Sargon founded the first Semitic dynasty, known as the Sargonic or Old Akkadian dynasty.

Some scholars equate Sargon with the exceptional warrior Nimrod, a distant descendent of Noah who built a massive empire in Shinar (Sumer), then expanded north. According to the Torah, "The first centers of his kingdom were Babylonia, Uruk, Akkad and Kalneh in Shinar. From that land he went to Assyria, where he built Nineveh, Rehoboth Ir, Calah, and Resen" (Genesis 10). Where was Akkad, and who were the Akkadians?

Akkad (Agade) most likely existed before Sargon; perhaps he enlarged a village into a city or restored an older city. In the early 3rd millennium, the Semitic Akkadian tribes began settling in central and southern Mesopotamia after migrating from the Arabian Peninsula. Akkad's location is a mystery; its ruins lay undiscovered under the desert's shifting sands, presumably along the Tigris or Euphrates somewhere north of Uruk.

The Akkadian language, the earliest documented Semitic language, preceded Sargon. The language first appeared in its written form in the mid-3rd millennium, borrowing from the Sumerian cuneiform script. A bowl discovered in Ur has an inscription in Akkadian from Queen Gan-saman (probably from Akkad) to her husband King Meskiagnunna (circa 2485–2450), about a century before Sargon's rise to power.

Most of us are familiar with the baby Moses drifting in a basket down the Nile to be found by the pharaoh's daughter or the twin newborns Romulus and Remus floating down the Tiber in a basket to be found by a she-wolf. In a 7th-century BCE Neo-Assyrian text, Sargon described his origins:

"Sargon, the mighty king, king of Agade, am I. My mother was a changeling; I didn't know my father. The brother(s) of my father loved the hills. My home was in the highlands, where the herbs grow on the banks of the Euphrates.

My mother conceived me in secret; she gave birth to me in concealment. She set me in a basket of rushes; she sealed my lid with bitumen. She cast me into the river, but it did not rise over me.

The water carried me to Akki, the drawer of water. He lifted me out as he dipped his jar into the river. Akki took me as his son; he raised me and made me his gardener. While I was a gardener, Ishtar granted me her love."

When Sargon referred to his mother as a "changeling," he might have been referring to the androgynous nature of the priests/priestesses of Inanna (Ishtar). In other traditions, Sargon's mother was a high-priestess (or cult prostitute) of Inanna. She had to hide her apparently illegitimate pregnancy and birth, so she sent him down the river. Sargon said the goddess Ishtar visited him as a youth, inspiring him to rise to greatness.

The goddess Inanna (Ishtar) rests her foot on a lion on this cylindrical seal.
https://commons.wikimedia.org/wiki/File:Ancient_Akkadian_Cylindrical_Seal_Depicti
ng_Inanna_and_Ninshubur.jpg

Akki, Sargon's adopted father, made Sargon his gardener; most likely, Akki was a palace gardener and trained Sargon in the art. According to the *Sumerian King List*, Kish was the first city built after the Great Flood, and it was located in northern Sumer. Sargon somehow rose to the position of cupbearer to King Ur-Zababa, a remarkable feat for a foundling child and palace gardener. A cupbearer was a trusted official who protected the king from poison and was his confidante and informal advisor.

One day, Sargon had an appalling vision: the goddess Inanna (Ishtar) told him she was planning to drown King Ur-Zababa in a river of blood. As he dreamed, Sargon groaned and gnashed his teeth in horror. Hearing of this, the king called Sargon to him, demanding that he reveal his dream. What Sargon told him was frightening. The king bit his lip in fear, certain that Sargon aspired to usurp his throne and assassinate him. He had to kill Sargon before Sargon could kill him!

King Ur-Zababa sent Sargon with his bronze mirror to the chief smith, Beliš-Tikal, supposedly to repair it. But Ur-Zababa had secretly ordered Beliš-Tikal to throw Sargon into the statue mold so he would be covered with molten metal! Everyone would think his dead body was a metal figurine. But the goddess Inanna intervened, ordering Sargon not to enter the gates of the smith's house. The king paled in fear when Sargon later showed up at the palace, healthy and whole.

With his murderous plot foiled, the king had to find another way to eliminate his would-be assassin. Then, he heard his great enemy, King Lugal-Zage-Si of Umma, was approaching Kish after systematically conquering the other city-states of Sumer, uniting them into one Sumerian empire. After taking Uruk, he marched toward Kish in the far north of Sumer. King Ur-Zababa was worried when he heard Lugal-Zage-Si was heading his way. But could he somehow work this to his advantage?

He sent Sargon to Lugal-Zage-Si with a clay tablet, ostensibly suing for peace. But the secret message on the tablet asked Lugal-Zage-Si to kill Sargon. After reading the tablet, Lugal-Zage-Si looked at Sargon and chuckled. Why would he kill this man when he could use him? After all, he was the king's cupbearer; he had inside information! Lugal-Zage-Si invited Sargon to join forces with him. Sargon accepted, and together, they successfully attacked Kish. Ur-Zababa fled.

This bronze mask, possibly of Sargon, might be the world's first depiction of a man-bun.

https://commons.wikimedia.org/wiki/File:Sargon_of_Akkad_(1936).jpg

It wasn't long, however, before Sargon and Lugal-Zage-Si had a falling out. Rumors that Sargon was sleeping with the king's wife enraged Lugal-Zage-Si, and the two allies became sworn enemies. Sargon attacked Uruk and tore down its walls. Lugal-Zage-Si rushed to defend the city he'd only recently taken for himself, but Sargon defeated him in battle, dragging him in chains with a yoke on his neck to Nippur, the sacred sanctuary of the god Enlil. This was the god that Lugal-Zage-Si had always called upon. Sargon forced him to walk in humiliation through Nippur's gate before proclaiming himself king of Kish with Ishtar as his patron goddess.

Sargon had this inscription carved into a statue's pedestal in the temple of Enlil:

"Sargon, king of Akkad, overseer of Inanna, king of Kish, anointed of Anu, king of the land, governor of Enlil. He defeated the city of Uruk and tore down its walls; in the battle of Uruk, he won, took Lugal-Zage-Si, king of Uruk, in the course of the battle and led him in a collar to the gate of Enlil."

By defeating Lugal-Zage-Si, Sargon nominally inherited all the city-states of Sumer that Lugal-Zage-Si had conquered and formed into one unified Sumerian state. And it was not just Sumer; the ambitious Lugal-Zage-Si had pressed west as far as the Mediterranean! Of course, assuming control over Lugal-Zage-Si's former mini-empire was not an easy matter. Most Sumerian cities were reluctant to submit to a new overlord, especially one that wasn't even Sumerian. One by one, Sargon had to retake the Sumerian cities.

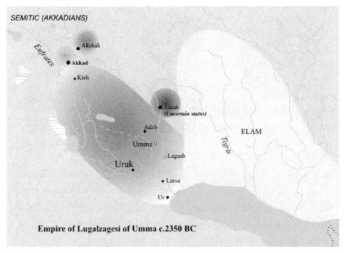

This map depicts the area Lugal-Zage-Si controlled and a possible location of Akkad.
CC BY-SA 3.0, https://commons.wikimedia.org/w/index.php?curid=1084105

Sargon also had to prove his legitimacy. He had no known royal heritage, and his birth was mysterious and likely illegitimate. Abandoned by unknown parents, he labored as a gardener until he was abruptly raised to be the king's cupbearer; he then turned on that king (admittedly in self-defense) and forcibly stole his throne. He renamed himself Sargon or Sharrukin (Akkadian for "legitimate king"); we have no idea what his original name was. He had to vigorously promote his right to rule by reminding everyone of Ishtar's favor and the support of the god Enlil and other deities.

"Sargon, king of Agade, was victorious over Ur in battle, conquered the city and destroyed its wall. He conquered Eninmar, destroyed its walls, and conquered its district and Lagash as far as the sea. He washed his weapons in the sea. He was victorious over Umma in battle. The god Enlil made Sargon the unrivaled lord of the land and gave him the Upper and Lower Sea."

(Inscription of Sargon, Old Babylonian copy from Nippur)

Once Sumer's cities capitulated to Sargon's control, he turned north to open trade routes and control sources of silver and other riches. He conquered his way up the Euphrates to Syria and then northeast to Anatolia and its silver-rich mountains. He took Susa, the Elamite capital in the Zagros Mountains (today's Iran).

An epic tale preserved in the Hittite and Akkadian manuscripts called *King of Battle* tells how some Akkadian merchants in Buru Shanda (Purshahanda) in Anatolia asked him to arbitrate a regional dispute with the oppressive ruler Nur-Dagan. In a lightning-fast attack, Sargon literally brought Nur-Dagan to his knees, and Buru Shanda came under Akkadian control.

Although the goddess Ishtar (Inanna) was Sargon's first patroness, he later began worshiping the Semitic god Dagan, who is often equated with the Mesopotamian god Enlil, whom Sargon considered a patron or supporter-champion. Dagan, the father of the god Baal, was a deity of the Syrians and the middle region of Mesopotamia (including Akkad). Dagan later became the god of the Philistines in Canaan. The Mesopotamians considered Dagan capable of granting kingship, and Sargon desired all the legitimacy he could acquire.

After bowing to Dagan, Sargon overcame northern Mesopotamia and the Levant (modern-day western Turkey, Syria, Lebanon, Jordan, Israel, and Palestine). He also invaded Canaan and Syria four times, up to Lebanon's cedar forest.

According to the *King of Battle*, he set sail across the Mediterranean, arriving in Kuppara, which was probably Crete or Cyprus. Sargon ruled a vast empire from the "Upper Sea" (the Mediterranean) to the "Lower Sea" (the Persian Gulf).

In 1867 CE, archaeologist Sir Henry Rawlinson unearthed the Library of Ashurbanipal while excavating the ancient Assyrian city of Nineveh. He found the *Legend of Sargon* in the library, which is purportedly Sargon's autobiography. Sargon speaks of an uprising during his "old age."

"In my old age of 55, all the lands revolted against me, and they besieged me in Agade [Akkad], but the old lion still had teeth and claws. I went forth to battle and defeated them: I knocked them over and destroyed their vast army. Now, any king who wants to call himself my equal, wherever I went, let him go!"

Sargon's principal wife was Queen Tashlultum, and his daughter Enheduanna was a powerful priestess who composed hymns, including the *Exaltation of Inanna*, which was sung by devotees of Inanna (Ishtar) for centuries. Sargon's son Rimush succeeded him as king, and another son, Manishtushu, assumed the throne after Rimush's courtiers murdered him. Sargon had at least two more sons: Shu-Enlil and Ilaba'is-takal.

This Akkadian cylinder seal depicts a hunting scene. It is dated to about 2250 BCE.
Metropolitan Museum of Art, CC0, via Wikimedia Commons;
https://commons.wikimedia.org/wiki/File:Akkadian_cylinder_seal_and_modern_impre ssion_hunting_scene_ca_2250_2150_BC.jpg

To maintain the lands he had conquered, Sargon organized a well-structured bureaucracy. He astutely placed his finest and most dependable Akkadian administrators, known as the

"Citizens of Akkad," as city leaders and provincial governors throughout his empire. He ingeniously placed his daughter Enheduanna in Ur as the high priestess of Inanna, where she engineered religious and cultural affairs in the southern regions.

Sargon did not dismantle the Sumerian religion; he actually embraced it. But he did make the Akkadian language the official administrative language of his empire, although he used Sumerian cuneiform for its script. Most Sumerians were probably bilingual in both Akkadian and Sumerian. He unified his realm by placing Akkadian as the lingua franca (common language to all).

By controlling such a large region of the known world, Sargon promoted trade throughout today's Middle Eastern countries. The cedars of Lebanon and the silver of Anatolia provided treasures in raw goods. His trade routes extended to the Indus Valley (modern-day Pakistan and northern India) and the regions around the Persian Gulf (modern-day Saudi Arabia, the United Arab Emirates, Oman, and Iran). He traded wool and olive oil for India's pearls and ivory, the lapis lazuli of Badakhshān (northeastern Afghanistan), and Anatolia's copper, silver, and other precious metals. Sargon taxed the merchants to support his military, scribes, and royal artists.

After sensationally conquering what he called the "four corners of the universe," Sargon's military forces and administrators maintained peace and order throughout his empire. This stability enabled road construction, enhanced irrigation projects, extensive trade, and astounding developments in the sciences and arts. Using the Akkadian language in cuneiform script, the clay tablets and cylinder seals of Sargon's era display an innovative spirit of calligraphy with exquisite scenes depicting festivals and mythology.

The first postal system emerged in the Akkadian Empire; these were outer clay envelopes encircling clay tablets with cuneiform messages. The sender inscribed the name and address of the recipient on the outer clay envelope and pressed his or her official seal on it. The only way to open the clay envelope was to break it, thus preserving the message inside for the person meant to read it and no one else.

According to the *Sumerian King List*, Sargon ruled for fifty-five years. But was he a good or a bad emperor? Did he deserve the nomenclature "Sargon the Great?" He was great in the sense that he conquered an incredible section of the known world and organized it into a stable, relatively peaceful empire. He ensured the ease of trade, allowed the arts and sciences to flourish, and oversaw a secure, affluent, orderly, and progressive society for his citizens. Accounts of his life say he protected the weak, the widows, and the orphans. Apparently, everyone had enough to eat in Sumer; no one needed to beg for food.

The Mesopotamians called Sargon's reign their golden age in the centuries following his death. He enriched his empire with widespread trade, bringing precious goods and raw materials from distant lands, and he enlightened the provinces he ruled by spreading vast amounts of knowledge. The Sumerians had previously developed mathematical and scientific understandings; they experienced further breakthroughs since Sargon encouraged scholarly studies and the interchange of ideas with other lands. Sculptures, paintings, mosaics, metallurgy, and architecture rose to new heights once various cultures shared their techniques and styles.

Yet, especially in his later years, incessant rebellions rocked Sargon's empire, which, in his own words, were met by "a lion with teeth and claws." What caused the uprisings? No literature or inscriptions survive that portray him as unjust. Yes, he was harsh if cities resisted being conquered by him, and he was ruthless when suppressing uprisings. But once Sargon established peace and justice, his rule was relatively benign. The rebellions do not appear to be racially motivated; the Sumerians did not seem to take issue with him being a Semite.

His biographers said the problem was spiritual, attributing the revolts to the anger of the god Marduk and "because of the evil which he had committed." The specific evil has not been identified. Perhaps the god was angry about all the violence involved in conquering nations. Maybe he was vexed by the abuses of justice (Marduk was the god of fairness and truth). According to *The Curse of Agade*, written two centuries later, Marduk also brought a famine that destroyed Sargon's people.

At any rate, Sargon marched out to meet his mutinous aggressors, turning the rebel city of Kassala into heaps of ruins and leaving no tree or building for a bird to rest. He attacked Subartu (northern Mesopotamia) and overthrew the insurgents, destroying countless combatants, pillaging their city, and bringing the loot back to Akkad.

What was Sargon's legacy? He continued building the empire started by Lugal-Zage-Si, consolidating all of Sumer and then expanding into the Levant and Anatolia. He founded a military tradition that continued through Mesopotamia's history. His half-century reign formed a strong command that stood firm through the rule of his two sons and his remarkable grandson Naram-Sin. Mesopotamian kings regarded him as an exemplary archetype of leadership.

Chapter 4: Akkad: The First Empire

The astounding Akkadian Empire was history's first true multi-ethnic empire with a strong, centralized state. Although "mini-empires" of several city-states had previously existed in Sumer, such as under King Eannatum of Lagash, they were monocultural. They had the same ethnicity, same language, same religion, and same culture. The Akkadian civilization had already begun to flourish in central Mesopotamia's fertile alluvial plain. As Sumer's Early Dynastic period drew to a close, the Akkadian Empire rose to dominate from 2334 to 2154 BCE, coinciding with the Early Bronze Age civilizations in Canaan (Israel), Syria, and Turkey. At its peak, the Akkadian Empire stretched for thousands of miles from the Mediterranean to the Persian Gulf and encompassed numerous ethnic groups and cultures.

The political landscape in the Early Dynastic period had been fragmented, with no lasting central government. Each city-state was like its own small country, although one city would occasionally rise to dominance and exert power over the others for a while. Sumer had been the dominant culture in southern Mesopotamia, and as time passed, Akkadian immigrants from the Arabian Peninsula rose to become the preeminent civilization of middle and northern Mesopotamia. Like the Sumerians, the Akkadians had independent, self-governing city-states but shared a Semitic language, religion, and culture. When Sargon the Great conquered all of Sumer and then the rest of Mesopotamia (and beyond), he brought the Sumerians and Akkadians together under one government and language. He then expanded into Syria, Lebanon, Canaan, Anatolia (Turkey), and Elam (Iran), forming a multi-cultural empire.

Even before Sargon the Great's stunning empire-building feats, kings with Semitic names ruled Kish, including Ur-Zababa, under whom Sargon had served as cupbearer. But Sargon's fame eclipsed these early Semitic rulers. He raised statues of his image along the Mediterranean to celebrate his victories in Canaan and Syria. He also brought home spoils from his conquests to adorn his palaces and temples. He campaigned to the west, subduing the Elamites and contending with King Sarlak of Gutium.

This scene is a segment of the Victory Stele of Rimush over Lagash.
Louvre Museum, CC BY 3.0 https://creativecommons.org/licenses/by/3.0 *via Wikimedia Commons;*
https://commons.wikimedia.org/wiki/File:P1150890_Louvre_st%C3%A8le_de_victoire_Akkad_AO2678_rwk.jpg

Sargon the Great ruled from 2334 to his death in 2279 BCE, after which his son Rimush ascended the throne as the second ruler of the Akkadian Empire. Rimush reigned for nine turbulent years, struggling to hold the empire together as numerous revolts broke out in Ur, Umma, Adab, Lagash, Der, and Kassala. In response to the Sumerian uprisings, he ruthlessly annihilated enormous numbers of people and uprooted the cities' foundations.

In three merciless battles against rebel princes in Sumer, he killed fifty-six thousand people, enslaved over twenty-nine thousand, and sent over twenty-five thousand into exile. The 6 cities lost a shocking total of about 111,000 people to the mass slaughter; this was most of their population! He parceled out the agricultural lands around the vanquished cities to the Akkadian Empire's new land-holding class. The few survivors of the massacres had no legal right to farm their ancestral lands.

Rimush destroyed Sumerian cities and even his own Akkadian cities, including Kassala on the Euphrates River between Kish and Akkad. Sargon had already flattened Kassala following an earlier revolt. After rebuilding, they challenged Rimush, who retaliated by killing twelve thousand Akkadian rebel soldiers, enslaving five thousand citizens, and leveling the city to the ground a second time.

Rimush's own officials assassinated him in 2270 BCE, bashing him to death with their marble or metal cylinder seals. Perhaps the atrocities against the fellow Akkadian city of Kassala were too much for his people to endure. It's likely some of his officials hailed from Kassala. Even if not, they probably thought that decimating the empire's population was not the way to go. No doubt, his officials worried that the constant instability would disrupt the empire's lucrative trade. It is possible Rimush's brother Manishtushu was plotting against him, desiring a return to stability.

Manishtushu assumed the throne upon his brother's death and ruled for fourteen years. The *Sumerian King List* said he was the older brother of Rimush. Why wasn't he king first before his brother then? Some scholars theorize the two were twins. Others speculate that Sargon may have selected Rimush as his successor, feeling that Rimush had a more resolute character and could manage rebellions better.

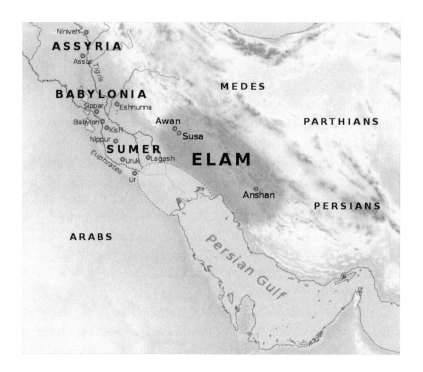

This map depicts the regions around the Persian Gulf that Manishtushu controlled and shows how far the Persian Gulf extended into Mesopotamia in the Bronze Age.

File:Near East topographic map-blank.svg: SémhurFile:Elam-map-PL.svg: Wkotwicaderivative work: Morningstar1814 - File:Elam-map-PL.svg, CC BY-SA 3.0, https://creativecommons.org/licenses/by-sa/3.0 via Wikimedia Commons; https://commons.wikimedia.org/w/index.php?curid=61956849

Because Rimush had ferociously squelched insurgencies within the empire, Manishtushu could focus on regions outside the empire's borders. He launched ambitious military campaigns to expand Akkadian territory and strategically enhanced trade relations with foreign civilizations. He sailed a fleet around the Persian Gulf, gathering a coalition of thirty-two kings through conquest or alliances to commandeer trade in the coastal lands. Manishtushu spectacularly invaded Elam via the Persian Gulf, looted its silver mines in Susa, and installed Akkadian governors. He sent his fleet up the Tigris River and traded with thirty-seven other city-states.

Manishtushu erected statues of himself throughout multiple cities under his reign. The images were the same, but the inscriptions honored a different god in each city, as the city-states all had their own patron deity. All the inscriptions lauded his successful overseas expedition around the Persian Gulf, an accomplishment that must have made him exceptionally proud. He also might have been exercising diplomacy. While Sargon's and Rimush's statues touted their violent repression of local insurgencies, Manishtushu focused on military successes overseas that had enriched Akkad and Sumer.

Like his brother, Manishtushu fell victim to palace intrigue. For unclear reasons, his officials assassinated him, and his son, Naram-Sin, ascended the throne as the fourth king of the Akkadian Empire. Naram-Sin sprang to greatness much as his grandfather Sargon had. He took the empire to exceptional heights in his thirty-sixth regnal year. During his rule, which lasted from 2254 to 2218 BCE, the Akkadian Empire reached its peak of power.

Naram-Sin picked up where his father had left off with victorious military campaigns in northern Syria and western Iran. He besieged Magan (probably modern-day Oman), taking its king captive. He fought multiple wars against the Armenian (Armeni) people of Ararat in today's eastern Turkey (where the Torah said Noah's ark landed). Like his grandfather, he assumed the title "ruler of the four corners of the universe."

Naram-Sin was not only a military man; he was also astute with financial affairs and standardized his kingdom's accounts. He appointed his daughters as high-priestesses of several important cults in Mesopotamia, which increased the people's acceptance of his dynasty and enhanced his control of the regions they were in.

The Victory Stele of Naram-Sin, now on display in the Louvre Museum in Paris, depicts him as larger than life, towering over other people and wearing a horned helmet, both of which imply divine standing. His admiring citizens deified him, raising him to the status of a living god of Agade (Akkad). And yet, accepting his citizens' adulation offended the gods, according to *The Curse of Agade*, and they poured out their wrath on the empire after Naram-Sin's death.

This cylinder seal impression reads "The Divine Shar-Kali-Sharri, Prince of Akkad."
Mbzt 2011, CC BY 3.0 https://creativecommons.org/licenses/by/3.0 via Wikimedia Commons; https://commons.wikimedia.org/w/index.php?curid=77501439

After the popular Naram-Sin died, his son, Shar-Kali-Sharri, ascended the throne and ruled for twenty-four years from 2217 to 2193 BCE. He led stellar military campaigns but did not measure up to his father's spectacular reign due to external threats and crippling climate change. The savage Gutian hill tribes had begun sporadically raiding Akkadian territory during Naram-Sin's reign, and they were growing bolder, attacking more frequently and viciously. To support his military campaigns against the Gutians, Shar-Kali-Sharri levied taxes on his vassal city-states, but this led to insurgencies from disgruntled kings. He fortuitously captured Sharlag, King of Gutium, and stymied the Gutian attacks. He waged three successive years of victorious campaigns against the Amorites and fought successfully against the Elamites for two years.

Then, beginning around 2200 BCE, a horrifying drought struck, forcing the populations of some of the hardest-hit areas to abandon their cities for the encroaching desert, migrating in search of more well-watered regions. Seventy-four percent of Mesopotamian settlements lost their population in this catastrophic period. This was more than just a local drought; Egyptian records documented drought in the same period during Pharaoh Pepi's reign.

When Shar-Kali-Sharri died in 2193 BCE, anarchy raised its perilous head. With no clear-cut successor, four would-be emperors wrestled for control while the empire dwindled. As the *Sumerian King List* put it, "Then who was king? Who was not the king? Igigi, Imi, Nanum, Ilulu: four of them ruled for only three years."

As it turned out, none of the four contenders won. Instead, a fifth man, King Dudu, took the throne in 2189 BCE and held it for twenty-one years. But he was only a king, not an emperor; the empire had shrunk down to the city-state of Akkad and several nearby cities. Taking advantage of the instability, the Gutians had made decisive inroads into Mesopotamia during the anarchy period; some scholars even believe that King Ilulu may have been Gutian.

The *Sumerian King List* records that Dudu's son Shu-turul succeeded him in 2168 BCE, ruling as the last-known king of Akkad, Kish, and Eshnunna. Fifteen years later, the Gutians conquered Akkad and ruled over Mesopotamia for half a century. Eventually, a coalition army of Uruk and Ur chased the Gutians out of Sumer, and the Third Dynasty of Ur rose to prominence in 2112.

Who is he? This king's sculpture dates to the Akkadian era, but his identity is unknown.
Metropolitan Museum of Art, CC0, via Wikimedia Commons;
https://commons.wikimedia.org/wiki/File:Head_of_a_ruler_ca_2300_2000_BC_Iran_or_Mesopotamia_Metropolitan_Museum_of_Art_(dark_background).jpg

What was the social and political structure of the Akkadian Empire? Like the Sumerians, the Akkadians were polytheistic and worshiped most of the same gods the Sumerians worshiped: An, the sky god; Enlil, the god of air; Nanna, the god of the moon; and Utu, the sun god. They worshiped Inanna, often under the name Ishtar. The Akkadians believed their kings were the earthly representation of the gods. They perceived their gods to have human forms and alternate between being wise, reckless, humorous, or irate; the gods were unconcerned with morality.

Because the Akkadian Empire covered a vast region with multiple ethnicities, it was politically unified, but each area continued with its own culture and social system. However, most of Mesopotamia continued with the social system in place in Sumer. The Akkadians adopted the Sumerian cuneiform script to write the Akkadian language and assiduously recorded, in minute detail, aspects of life in the cities.

The Akkadians had a hierarchical system of five classes: the nobility, priests/priestesses, upper class, lower class, and enslaved people. The nobility included the kings, governors, and other ruling class members and was intricately linked to the priestly class. The kings often appointed their sons to be governors of strategic provinces and their daughters as high priestesses in significant cities. They also married their daughters to rulers of distant regions of the empire. Most conquered cities had both a civil and military administration that ruled parallel with each other. Akkadian troops were stationed in the conquered cities to ensure compliance with their overlords. Akkadian governors replaced most city administrators.

The priests and priestesses commanded profound respect because they could interpret omens and signs. They were literate and served as doctors and dentists in the temples' outer courts. The upper class consisted of wealthy merchants, teachers, scribes, military officers, architects, shipbuilders, and accountants. Only boys attended school, but girls from leading families learned at home from tutors. Sargon's daughter Enheduanna must have learned to read and write since she was a famous hymn-writer.

The lower classes kept the cities fed and operating. This included the farmers, construction workers, basket weavers, fishermen, lower-ranking soldiers, and craftspeople. Men and women could and did climb the social ladder to have an upper-class standing. Women appeared to have a relatively high status, especially in the arena of religion, where they often served as high priestesses. They also served as tavern owners, doctors, and dentists.

This carving shows Akkadian soldiers on Nara-Sim's victory stele, circa 2250 BCE.
Rama, CC BY-SA 2.0 FR <https://creativecommons.org/licenses/by-sa/2.0/fr/deed.en>,
via Wikimedia Commons;
https://commons.wikimedia.org/wiki/File:Akkadian_Empire_soldiers_on_the_victory_stele_of_Naram-Sin_circa_2250_BC.jpg

Most enslaved people were war captives, but a person could sell themselves or their children into slavery to pay a debt or receive enslavement as punishment for a crime. Slaves came from all ethnicities, including Akkadian, and had wide-ranging responsibilities depending on their skills and education. They were not only manual laborers; they also worked as estate managers, tutors, accountants, and craftspeople. They could buy or earn their freedom.

Trade capabilities for the Akkadian Empire were rich and varied. The Persian Gulf and the Euphrates and Tigris Rivers served as the empire's water highways. From the Persian Gulf, the Akkadians sailed into the Arabian Sea to India. A network of unpaved roads connected Akkad with its far-flung empire. Camel caravans carried goods and people over desert terrain, and mules and donkeys pulled carts and sleds. They even had a postal service!

Their trade routes extended to the silver, tin, and copper mines of Anatolia, Lebanon's cedar forests, and the lapis lazuli mines of Bactria (Afghanistan). The Akkadians had an abundant and varied food supply, thanks to irrigation techniques learned from the Sumerians. Since they usually had a surplus, they could trade grain, dried fish, and dried fruit for resources they did not have, such as lumber, metal ore, and stone for construction.

The Akkadian Empire only lasted about 180 years. What factors influenced its downfall? Climate change drastically impacted the empire's decline, which the Akkadians and other Mesopotamians believed resulted from divine retribution. They felt the gods were offended that King Naram-Sin had accepted and promoted being called a living god by his adoring citizens. The gods punished his excessive pride by wreaking devastation on his descendants, which led to poor harvests and food shortages.

Soil analysis of Akkadian sites in northern Mesopotamia indicates a severe drought began around 2200 BCE and endured for three centuries. Archaeological excavations reveal the sudden abandonment of multiple Akkadian cities in Mesopotamia's northern plains, as well as a southern migration. Scientists attributed the devastating drought to erratic weather patterns due to changing wind currents and a horrific volcanic eruption in Anatolia to the north. The Mesopotamian drought was part of the 4.2-kiloyear BP aridification event that lasted from 2200 to 2000 BCE. It was one of the most severe climate changes in human history, and it caused the collapse of empires in Egypt, Mesopotamia, and even China.

After King Shar-Kali-Sharri's death, a power struggle rocked the empire. Several southern Mesopotamian city-states reasserted their independence, causing the empire's borders to deteriorate. The rapacious Gutian tribes swarmed from the Zagros Mountains (in today's Iraq, Iran, and southern Turkey) in increasing numbers, leaving behind devastation in the regions of Akkad, Sumer, and Elam.

As the Akkadian Empire diminished, the nomadic Gutians took advantage of its weakness to launch a decades-long campaign of incessant guerilla attacks, crippling the empire's economy. They disrupted trade through disastrous strikes on camel caravans. Farmers were terrified of working in their fields, as they were afraid the raiding bands would target them. Climate change had already created crushing food shortages; now, the people sank into dire famine conditions.

Around 2100 BCE, the Third Dynasty of Ur, the "Sumerian Renaissance," rose to preeminence in Mesopotamia, shifting power from Akkad back to the southern regions of Sumer. This shift created a return to the Sumerian language for general communication; however, a modified form of Akkadian continued for the next millennia as the trade and diplomatic language of Mesopotamia. Eventually, the Babylonian language replaced both languages in 1000 BCE.

The Akkadians were astute assimilators but not the inventors and innovators that the Sumerians were. However, the Akkadian Empire served as a vital bridge between the Sumerian culture and other cultures of the Akkadians' far-reaching empire. They incorporated and shared the Sumerian culture throughout the Middle East while learning from the social organization and commercial practices of the regions they conquered. They were the first "melting pot" of civilization.

SECTION TWO: AGE OF EMPIRES (2000–539 BCE)

Chapter 5: Assyria: An Overview

Creators of the largest empire in the known world at that point, the Assyrians struck fear into other nations for centuries. Their siege engines grounded their enemies' walls into dust, and they displaced entire populations. At its height, the Assyrian Empire stretched from northern Africa (Libya and Egypt), up the eastern Mediterranean coast, including Israel, Lebanon, and Syria, into Anatolia (Turkey), present-day Armenia, and Azerbaijan, down through Mesopotamia, and east into part of modern-day Iran.

Who were the Assyrians, and what were their origins? These fierce empire-builders were originally Semitic pastoral herders living in the city-state of Aššur (Ashur) in today's northern Iraq. The Torah identifies Aššur as being on the western banks of the Tigris River and the man Ashur as the son of Shem and grandson of Noah. The Assyrians worshiped a god named Ashur, who was originally the local deity of the city of Aššur and later their supreme god and national patron. The Assyrians were probably distant relatives of the Akkadians since they spoke the same language. The Torah identifies the Assyrians as being distantly related to the Aramaeans and Hebrews.

Ashur is depicted in this Assyrian "feather-robed archer" figure.
https://commons.wikimedia.org/wiki/File:Ashur_god.jpg

When did the Assyrians rule in Mesopotamia and beyond? Its two-thousand-year history spanned from the Early Bronze Age to the Late Iron Age. Historians usually divide Assyria's history into several segments, beginning with the Early Period (2500–2025 BCE), during which the Akkadian Empire conquered Assyria under Sargon the Great. Nomadic shepherds settled the area of Aššur as early as 2600 BCE, and the nation (and eventually the empire) of Assyria continued until 609 BCE.

After the fall of the Akkadian Empire, the Assyrians rose to power with their own empires, achieving astounding heights in cultural and technological achievements. Their three empires were the Old Assyrian Empire (2025–1522 BCE), the Middle Assyrian Empire (1392–1056 BCE), and Assyria's peak of power in the Neo-Assyrian Empire (911–609 BCE).

Aššur grew into a city-state during the Sumerian period of dominance in Mesopotamia. The early settlers were nomads. The *Assyrian King List* named their oldest known king, Tudiya, as "the first of seventeen kings living in tents." Several other Akkadian-speaking city-states arose in northern Mesopotamia near Aššur: Nineveh, Gasur, and Arbela. This region was Assyria proper; it was called *Subartu* by the Sumerians and *Azuhinum* by the Akkadians.

When Sargon incorporated Assyria into the Akkadian Empire (2334–2154 BCE), he made Aššur the administrative center of Assyria. In the early Akkadian Empire period, the Assyrians established trading posts with the Hittites in Anatolia (Turkey). Assyria was one of the regions that rebelled against Sargon the Great in his later years, but he brutally counterattacked and subdued them.

After the Akkadian Empire fell, Assyria became fully independent between 2154 to 2112 BCE. The Gutians invaded and occupied central and southern Mesopotamia, but Assyria never fell under their power. When the Third Dynasty of Ur (the Neo-Sumerian Empire) rose to power in 2112 BCE, Ur extended its rule up to Aššur but did not go as far north as Nineveh. The Assyrians ruled Aššur and other cities under Neo-Sumerian dominance as *shakkanakka*, or vassal governors, for Ur until 2080 BCE, when King Ushpia became Assyria's independent ruler.

Several independent kings ruled Assyria until King Puzur-Ashur I ascended the throne, ushering in the Old Assyrian Empire (2025–1522 BCE). Under his reign, Assyria began expanding its trade colonies in Hittite and Hurrian lands in Turkey. Puzur-Ashur's descendant, King Ilu-Shuma (1995–1974 BCE), engaged in military actions in Sumer, freeing Akkadian settlements from Elamite and Amorite oppressors. Ilu-Shuma built the first temple of Ishtar in Aššur.

King Erishum I (1973–1934 BCE) followed Ilu-Shuma; this indomitable king ruled for forty years and wrote one of the earliest legal codes (he came after Ur-Nammu but before Hammurabi or Moses). Assyria's eighteen trading centers in Anatolia traded in bronze, copper, gold, iron, silver, tin, lapis lazuli, grain, and textiles during his reign. He built a temple for the god Ashur, with two beer vats in its courtyard, and a temple for Ishtar and Adad, the Amorite god of rain.

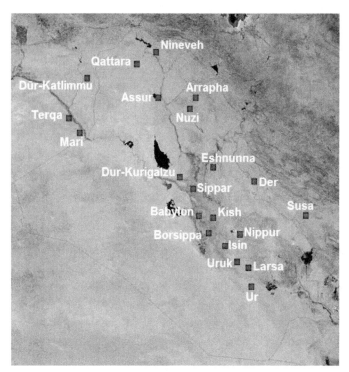

This map shows the major cities of Mesopotamia in the 2ⁿᵈ millennium BCE.
CC BY-SA 2.5; https://commons.wikimedia.org/w/index.php?curid=18438114

In 1808 BCE, Shamshi-Adad, ruler of Terga, usurped the Assyrian throne, overthrowing Puzur-Ashur I's dynasty. He claimed lineage from King Ushpia, but the Assyrians considered him an Amorite. Interestingly, a 2013 DNA analysis of four people's teeth buried in Terga during this era carried haplotypes from the Indian subcontinent. Shamshi-Adad may have been neither Amorite nor Assyrian but rather Mitanni, a people from the north. The Mitanni elite had Indo-Aryan names and worshiped Hindu gods, but the common people spoke the Hurrian language of the Armenian highlands. Apparently, a tribe from the Indian subcontinent had assimilated with the Hurrians but held upper-class status.

Shamshi-Adad was a dynamic leader. He expanded the Assyrian Empire from a small group of city-states to encompass all of northern Mesopotamia and a large swathe of today's Turkey, Syria, Lebanon, and Canaan (Israel). His son, King Ishme-Dagan (1775–1763 BCE), could not hold on to Sumer or the Mediterranean region, although he was a fierce warrior, one "not afraid to risk his own skin." He held a tenuous relationship with King Hammurabi, who was rapidly turning obscure Babylon into a formidable power; Assyria and Babylon were allies at times but also competitors for dominance.

Babylon won the race for power, at least temporarily. The subsequent three Assyrian kings were Babylon's vassals during Hammurabi's long reign. But after Hammurabi's death, Puzur-Sin, an Assyrian vice-regent, threw off the shackles of Babylon, returning Assyria to self-rule by a series of usurpers. The seventh contender for the Assyrian crown, Adasi, "son of nobody," ascended the throne, bringing stability and ending Babylonian and Amorite control.

His successors, the Adaside dynasty, continued to rule Assyria independently. They gradually grew in strength and led Assyria through several peaceful, prosperous centuries. When the Hittites attacked and sacked Babylon, Assyria serenely stood firm. When the Kassites conquered Babylon in 1594 BCE, Assyria was impregnable, calmly upgrading its infrastructure and building temples.

Assyria's strength, stability, and prosperity were interrupted when Egypt enlisted help in a power play against Mitanni. Egypt was concerned about Mitanni's bourgeoning power. They were building their own vast empire that stretched along the Fertile Crescent, from the Mediterranean Levant (Canaan, Lebanon, and Syria) to Anatolia and down into Mesopotamia. Pharaoh Amenhotep II sent King Ashur-nadin-ahhe of Assyria gold in exchange for allying with Egypt against the Mitanni-Hurrians, who had extended their empire down to Egypt's border and were claiming Egypt's tributary cities in the Levant.

Hearing of the alliance, King Shaushtatar of Mitanni allied with the Hittites and launched a preemptive strike on Assyria. They sacked Aššur and made Assyria a vassal state. But similar to their experience with Babylon, the Assyrians survived with their monarchy intact and minimal Mitanni interference for the reign of three Assyrian kings. In less than two decades, Assyria was independent of Mitanni. King Ashur-bel-nisheshu of Assyria (r. 1417–1409 BCE) signed a treaty with the Kassite king of Babylonia. He also rebuilt Aššur and recouped its advanced economic system. By the time King Eriba-Adad I was crowned in 1392 BCE, Assyria was exerting power over Mitanni.

King Eriba-Adad I's reign marked the beginning of the Middle Assyrian Empire (1392–1056 BCE). It was an era of comeback and recovery for Assyria, as it seized most of the Hittite territory and recovered northern Mesopotamia and the Levant. King Ashur-uballit I (1365–1330 BCE) crushed the Kingdom of Mitanni, which spurred the Hittites to join forces with Babylon against Assyria, but to no avail. King Ashur-uballit conquered Babylonia, installing a vassal king loyal to Assyria.

King Arik-den-ili (r. 1318–1307), whose name meant "long-lasting is the judgment of God," marched into northern Iran and pulverized the Gutians, who had wreaked havoc on central and southern Mesopotamia for centuries. He then turned his attention to the Levant, conquering Canaanite and Aramaean tribes. He instituted annual military campaigns and erected the great Ziggurat of Aššur.

Shalmaneser I (r. 1274–1245 BCE) subdued eight Anatolian kingdoms, overpowering a Mitanni and Hittite coalition. He supervised ambitious construction projects in Aššur and Nineveh and established Kalhu (the biblical Calah). His enterprising son, Tukulti-Ninurta (r. 1244–1207 BCE), took thousands of Hittite prisoners at the Battle of Nihriya. He demolished Babylon's walls and plundered the city's temples. He ruled Babylon for seven years as Babylon's first Assyrian king.

Tukulti-Ninurta authored an epic poem championing his victories over the Elamites. He triumphed over the Dilmun kingdom of Saudi Arabia and erected Assyria's new religious center and capital: Kar-Tukulti-Ninurta. Babylon reasserted independence after Tukulti-Ninurta's death, and internal unrest rocked Assyria. Then, Ashur-resh-ishi I (r. 1133–1116 BCE) rose as a forceful, victorious king who annexed the region of Iran's Zagros Mountains. He subdued the Amorites and Arameans and prevailed over Nebuchadnezzar I, subjugating Babylon once again.

The indomitable and renowned Tiglath-Pileser rose to power in 1115 BCE and ruled for forty-one years. He established Assyria as the Near East's leading power, striking terror as the world's premier military force. He overcame the Phrygians and Kaskians of Upper Mesopotamia and drove the Hittites from Assyria's Subartu province. He suppressed Malatia and Urartu (related to the Mitanni people) in eastern Turkey and the Armenian highlands.

Next, Tiglath-Pileser targeted Syria's Aramaeans, then blazed his way down the Mediterranean coast, seizing the Phoenician cities of Aradus (Arwad), Simyra (Sumer), Byblos, Berytus (Beirut), Sidon, and Tyre. An enthusiastic hunter of wild bulls, gazelles, lions, and elephants, he set sail into the Mediterranean, killing a *nahiru* (possibly a narwhal). He embarked on massive building projects and the restoration of ancient temples. His cuneiform tablet collections helped preserve the written history of Mesopotamia.

Within two decades of Tiglath-Pileser's death, a civil war ignited in Assyria between his son, Ashur-bel-Kala, and a usurper named Tukulti-Mer. Although the rebellion failed, it kept Assyria distracted, allowing a massive Hittite and Aramean invasion to take place. This caused the loss of Syria and Phoenicia.

Mesopotamia entered into its "dark ages" during the Bronze Age Collapse (1200–900 BCE) along with the rest of the Near East, North Africa, Greece, and the Balkan and Mediterranean regions. These three centuries saw massive upheavals and even the extinction of once-thriving civilizations because of the marauding Sea People, who devastated sea traffic and annihilated coastal cities from Egypt to Turkey. Since the ancient world was deeply interconnected through trade, its supply-chain breakdown was catastrophic, causing a widespread collapse.

Core samples taken from the Sea of Galilee in 2014 revealed a megadrought that lasted from 1250 to 1100 BCE. It would have killed off populations and encouraged mass migrations, perhaps even the mysterious Sea People. Israel was contending for Canaan's control against the Philistines, who may have been the Sea People who ravaged Greece and other eastern Mediterranean regions. Geophysicists discovered that a series of severe earthquakes rocked the Mediterranean from 1225 to 1175 BCE, which would have toppled cities and triggered tsunamis. This "perfect storm" of disasters plunged many civilizations into an abyss from which they could not recover.

Curiously, Assyria thrived through the first half of this era, as Tiglath-Pileser and other mighty leaders expanded the flourishing empire. However, the Hittite and Aramean invasions during Ashur-bel-Kala's reign began a century-long decline for Assyria. It led to the disastrous loss of territory, reducing the realm to the regions immediately next to Assyria. Nevertheless, Assyria's main domain in northern Mesopotamia persevered as a compact nation with a strong military and stable administration, while other countries were teetering on the brink of destruction. Greece, for instance, lost its written language and all its cities except Athens in these turbulent centuries.

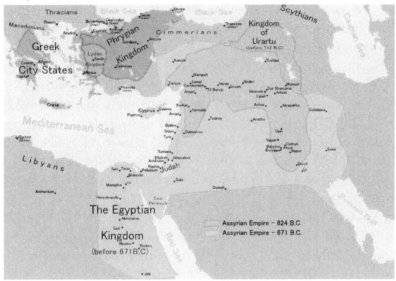

This map shows the extent of the Neo-Assyrian Empire.
Nigyou, CC BY-SA 3.0 https://creativecommons.org/licenses/by-sa/3.0 via Wikimedia Commons; https://commons.wikimedia.org/wiki/File:Neo-Assyrian_map_824-671_BC.png

Assyria recovered from the Bronze Age Collapse to enter its most prominent period: the Neo-Assyrian Empire, which lasted from 911 to 628 BCE. It grew exponentially, subjugating all of Mesopotamia, Egypt, the eastern Mediterranean coast, and part of Turkey. Shortly before the Bronze Age Collapse, the Assyrians began using iron weapons and war chariots. They developed lethal siege engines and engineer corps, making it the most technologically advanced military of the day.

Beginning with King Adad-Nirari II (r. 912–891 BCE), Assyria embarked on a massive expansion campaign. Along with its military technology, the Assyrians exercised brilliant battlefield tactics, using earthen ramps, mobile ladders, and siege towers on wheels to breach city walls. Meanwhile, combat engineers and miners dug tunnels under the walls to cause them to collapse. As the cities fended off the ladders and miners, the Assyrians used multiple battering rams to break down the gates and walls.

The Assyrians were a methodical, indomitable force. City by city and nation by nation, they gained territory in one campaign after another for over a century. Once they besieged a city, all hope was gone. However, after a little over a century, Assyria fell into a slump. Its rulers seemed to lack energy and ambition, their administration was disorganized, and their military was demoralized.

Finally, in 745 BCE, Tiglath-Pileser III ascended the throne, reorganized the bureaucracy, transformed the military into an efficient powerhouse, and retook the provinces that had broken away. He often relocated part or all of their population to prevent further uprisings. The Tanakh provides detailed insights into what it was like to be on the receiving end of the Assyrian war machine and part of its population-relocation program.

"King Pul of Assyria [also known as Tiglath-Pileser] invaded the land and took the people of Reuben, Gad, and the half-tribe of Manasseh as captives. The Assyrians exiled them to Halah, Habor, Hara, and the Gozan River, where they remain to this day."

Ketuvim, 1 Chronicles 5:26

"During Pekah's reign, King Tiglath-pileser of Assyria attacked Israel again, and he captured the towns of Ijon, Abel-beth-maacah, Janoah, Kedesh, and Hazor. He also conquered the regions of Gilead, Galilee, and all of Naphtali, and he took the people to Assyria as captives."

Nevi'im, 2 Kings 15:29

Shalmaneser V reigned next, from 727 to 722 BCE. He resettled part of the population of Babylon and other cities into Israel. A few years later, Sennacherib took the crown (r. 705–681 BCE) and honed Assyria's military the strongest it would ever be.

He moved Assyria's capital to Nineveh, where he built a splendid palace with hanging gardens.

The Judean prophet Isaiah described what happened when Sennacherib sent his second-in-command from Lachish to Jerusalem, where he taunted King Hezekiah:

"Who are you counting on that you have rebelled against me? On Egypt? If you lean on Egypt, it will be like a reed that splinters beneath your weight and pierces your hand. Pharaoh, the king of Egypt, is completely unreliable!

I'll tell you what! Strike a bargain with my master, the king of Assyria. I will give you 2,000 horses if you can find that many men to ride on them! With your tiny army, how can you think of challenging even the weakest contingent of my master's troops?

When we put this city under siege, your people will be so hungry and thirsty that they will eat their own feces and drink their own urine."

Nevi'im, Isaiah

When King Hezekiah heard their report, he tore his clothes, put on sackcloth, and went into the temple. Soon afterward, King Sennacherib received word that King Tirhakah of Ethiopia was leading an army to fight him. Before leaving to meet the attack, he sent messengers back to Hezekiah in Jerusalem with this message: "Don't let your God, in whom you trust, deceive you with promises that Jerusalem will not be captured by the king of Assyria."

"That night the angel of the LORD went out to the Assyrian camp and killed 185,000 Assyrian soldiers. When the surviving Assyrians woke up the next morning, they found corpses everywhere. Then King Sennacherib of Assyria broke camp and returned to his own land. He went home to his capital of Nineveh and stayed there.

One day while he was worshiping in the temple of his god Nisroch, his sons Adrammelech and Sharezer killed him with their swords. They then escaped to the land of Ararat, and another son, Esarhaddon, became the next king of Assyria."

Nevi'im, Isaiah 36-37

The Greek historian Herodotus said millions of field mice had invaded the Assyrian camp, gnawing on bowstrings and destroying Assyrian arms. If so, perhaps the mice carried something like septicemic plague. Sennacherib was assassinated by two of his sons because he passed over the older son, Arda-Mulissu (Adrammelech), and instead made the younger Esarhaddon his crown prince. It did the young men no good to kill their father, as the Assyrians were horrified at the murder and did not support Arda-Mulissu's rule.

This bas-relief of Assyrian soldiers was found in Sennacherib's palace.
Gary Todd, CC0, via Wikimedia Commons;
https://commons.wikimedia.org/wiki/File:Ancient_Assyria_Bas-
Relief_of_Armed_Soldiers,_Palace_of_King_Sennacherib_(704-689_BC)_(c).jpg

Esarhaddon and his son Ashurbanipal were ruthless yet efficient rulers. They continued to enlarge the empire's borders, stabilize the vast provinces, encourage the arts, and develop Assyria's legendary wealth. Yet, soon after Ashurbanipal's death, the Assyrian Empire began to crumble; it had grown too large to manage effectively. Taxes were exorbitant, power-plays and coups destabilized the monarchy, and revolts broke out in the provinces.

In 612 BCE, a coalition army of Persians, Babylonians, and Medes invaded and razed Nineveh, and most of the Assyrian ruling class fled to Harran in Turkey. Three years later, Pharaoh Necho II of Egypt marched toward Harran to lend his support to the remnants of the Assyrian leadership, but King Josiah refused to let him march through Judea. The Egyptians killed Josiah in the Battle of Megiddo, but the delay prevented Necho from reaching Harran in time. The Babylonians and Medes took the city. The fall of Harran spelled the end of the Assyrian state.

Chapter 6: Daily Life in Assyria

What were the lives of Assyrians like 4,500 years ago when they built their first cities? How did their lives change over the next two millennia as their government and military developed? What new language did they begin using due to their vast population-relocation program? And what made the Assyrian religion and architecture distinctive?

We can glean the answers to many of our questions regarding daily life and culture in Assyria from the Library of Ashurbanipal. Around 600 BCE, the last Assyrian king, Ashurbanipal, formed the library with a clay tablet collection containing the literature of ancient Assyria, Sumer, and Babylonia. There were over thirty thousand tablets in his magnificent library, and they provide incredible insight into the Assyrian culture.

Assyria was a monarchy, and the Assyrians believed their god Ashur chose their king to be his earthly representative and high priest. The king served as Assyria's lead administrator, the army's commander-in-chief, and the "king of kings" over vassal nations. In Assyria's hereditary monarchy, the king designated one of his sons as his crown prince, usually the oldest, and appointed other sons as governors of nearby provinces.

The king had a court of chief ministers, including a chancellor to head the administrative staff. As with most Asian courts, many officials were eunuchs. A team of scribes managed the vast correspondence. In Assyria's earliest days, the king's rule encompassed several other city-states that made up the core Assyrian region in northern Mesopotamia. Then, as Assyria's military machine conquered other lands, some kingdoms became vassal states, while governors appointed by the king ruled others.

This painting depicts Ashurbanipal, "King of the world, King of Assyria."
Carole Raddato from FRANKFURT, Germany, CC BY-SA 2.0
https://creativecommons.org/licenses/by-sa/2.0 via Wikimedia Commons;
https://commons.wikimedia.org/wiki/File:Exhibition_I_am_Ashurbanipal_king_of_the_world,_king_of_Assyria,_British_Museum_(45923437402).jpg

In the vassal kingdoms, the Assyrian emperor left the king of a conquered region in place as long as he submitted to Assyrian overlordship. If not, the Assyrian king would kill or imprison the rebel king and appoint a different king, generally from the defeated country's royal family. Most defeated nations continued as they had before, except they had to acknowledge the leadership of Assyria, pay tribute, and send troops to fight with Assyria's army. The tribute was a sort of tax; it was payable in money or goods.

Babylon was a neighbor and powerful rival of Assyria, so rather than make it a vassal kingdom, the Assyrian king himself, beginning with Tukulti-Ninurta (r. 1244–1207 BCE), ruled both Babylon and Assyria. Sometimes, the Assyrian king would appoint his brother or son to rule as a subordinate king.

Until the mid-8th century, the Assyrian Empire consisted of two zones: the conquered nations ruled by vassal kings and Assyria proper. When Tiglath-Pileser III became Assyria's king in 745 BCE, he reorganized Assyria's territorial administration, setting up smaller districts under the central government's control. He also initiated a third zone, which was most of Mesopotamia and Syria that fell under direct Assyrian control. Instead of vassal kings, the Assyrian king appointed provincial governors (usually Assyrian) and stationed a garrison of Assyrian troops in these provinces.

The Assyrians had a detailed law code that was much harsher than other Mesopotamian legal systems, such as Hammurabi's. Their style of imperialism was also despotic. Vassal kingdoms paid crushing tribute payments with nothing in return from Assyria other than "protection" by the Assyrian army, to which the vassal kingdoms had to contribute men. Many vassal kingdoms withered away, their people starving and impoverished, while Assyria reveled in unparalleled luxury.

In the 8th century, the Assyrians began the mass deportation of some especially rebellious conquered nations, as previously noted with Israel. The objective of the deportations was to disrupt the insubordinate strongholds. Sometimes, they deported the ruling class and left the ordinary people to tend the fields. Other times, they exiled the entire population to distant locations and brought the populations of other cities to the now-empty land. The exiles were usually not slaves; the Assyrians gave most of them the same rights as citizens, and some even rose to positions of preeminence in their new lands.

An estimated 4.5 million people were exiled to other parts of the Assyrian Empire, mostly Aramaic speakers. Aramaic became the lingua franca throughout the Assyrian Empire, both spoken and written. Aramaic had an alphabet that was much easier to learn than the cuneiform Sumerian and Akkadian scripts. Even most Assyrians started using Aramaic, although the ruling class continued to speak Akkadian and write in cuneiform. In 752 BCE, Aramaic joined Akkadian as the two official administrative languages.

The sensational Assyrian military developed one stunning innovation after another. They were among the first to fight with iron weapons and wear iron armor. In their Early Bronze Age days, elite warriors in chariots fought battles. With stronger and cheaper iron, Assyria could arm vast armies of foot soldiers who could march out to confront the enemy in terrifying numbers.

Cavalry forces gave the Assyrian military strength and agility in battle.
Osama Shukir Muhammed Amin FRCP(Glasg), CC BY-SA 4.0
https://creativecommons.org/licenses/by-sa/4.0 via Wikimedia Commons;
https://commons.wikimedia.org/wiki/File:Assyrian_horses.jpg

By the 15th century BCE, they had incorporated skilled cavalry riders. The Assyrians' interactions with the equestrian nomads of the Anatolian and Iranian highlands introduced them to cavalry techniques. These incredible horsemen rode without saddles or stirrups while shooting arrows, fighting with swords, or impaling the enemy with spears. They rode in pairs, with one soldier holding the reins of his mate's horse while the other used his weapons.

Until the mid-8th century BCE, the military was composed of young farmers and workers drafted for service. All able-bodied men were required to serve in the military. Usually, the younger men were the first to be called up, and they would train in camps before marching off on campaign. Men could also be summoned for construction projects or to farm the royal estates.

In the Neo-Assyrian Empire, the military continued drafting young Assyrian men each year, but they also had a professional army of highly-trained foreign troops who served for years. In the past, military campaigns took place during the "off" season when farmers weren't planting or harvesting their fields. More prolonged wars could be waged with a full-time military and permanent garrisons, which were set up throughout the empire.

The Assyrian military implemented brilliant, highly organized logistics to assemble the necessary supplies and food for campaigns, transporting them by camels. Soldiers packed inflatable bladders to use as flotation devices when crossing rivers. The innovative Assyrians were the first to use siege towers, battering rams, siege engines, and assault ladders, and the fearful apparatus and engineer corps traveled with the soldiers.

Even after developing a cavalry, the Assyrians continued using chariots. In Sumer, the earliest chariots were four-wheel or even six-wheel carts, but the Sumerians were already using two-wheel chariots before the dawn of the Assyrian civilization. Assyrian chariots had blades extending from the wheel hubs, which could sever the legs of any men or horses that got too close.

The Assyrians used psychological warfare, including terror tactics, to compel cities to surrender, such as capturing enemy soldiers, impaling them on long poles, and torturing them in view of the city walls. When the Assyrian army led by King Tukulti-Ninurta in 1225 BCE finally defeated Babylon, the desolation he wreaked on the city sent shockwaves throughout the region. The Assyrians flattened Babylon's walls, massacred or enslaved the citizens, pillaged the city, stole the sacred idol of Babylon's patron god Marduk (Bel), and stripped the Babylonian king naked, marching him in chains with his harem to Aššur. Tukulti-Ninurta boasted, "I filled the caves and ravines of the mountains with their corpses. Like grain piled beside their gates, I made heaps of their corpses."

Stealing Marduk was horrifically sacrilegious; it not only sparked horror in Assyria's enemies but also left the Assyrians aghast once the initial flush of victory abated. They feared Marduk was incensed at the Assyrians for destroying his city and stealing him from his temple! Crippled by the fear of Marduk's revenge, the Assyrians returned his idol to Babylon and rebuilt the city!

The long wars fought during the Middle Assyrian Empire established Assyria's reputation as a warrior nation. Their social stratification reflected the military's importance and the intrinsic contributions of the priests. The landed nobility farmed large estates and raised horses to supply the army. In its earliest history, Assyria, like other early city-states of Mesopotamia, had a self-supporting economy and grew enough food to sustain the population. There were also nearby resources for building reed or mud-brick houses.

Like other Mesopotamians, the Assyrians believed that each city was the home to its own patron god. Thus, the temple was the center of the city's spiritual and material life. The craftsmen, construction workers, weavers, and even the long-distance trade caravans were considered employees of the city's patron god. The king was simply a vice-regent for the god.

As time passed, the kings grew more powerful as secular rulers rather than simply being vice-regents and priests for the patron god. They began appropriating land and employed scribes and skilled craftsmen for themselves. Later, a private market emerged in the Assyrian cities that was unconnected to the king or the temple. This allowed the weavers, construction workers, and other workers to be self-supporting.

The Sumerians had used metal coinage since Ur's Third Dynasty (2112–2004 BCE); Ur-Nammu's law code mentioned fines of silver shekels. However, Assyria did not use metal currency until the Neo-Assyrian Empire under King Sennacherib (r. 705–681 BCE). Before that, Assyrians used seeds for currency, and law codes stipulated the seeds' value. The Assyrian temples served as banks. They kept written clay-tablet accounts of loans from merchants, landowners, and the temple itself. If the borrower repaid the loan by the due date, he did not have to pay interest, but delinquent payments incurred 20 to 30 percent interest!

Three social groups comprised Assyrian society: free citizens, serfs of the large estates, and enslaved people. Soldiers from conquered countries were incorporated into the Assyrian military. The craftsmen, scribes, and other highly skilled artisans became free Assyrian citizens and employed their trade in their new cities. Most farmers became serfs or tenant farmers on the Assyrian landed estates. Some captives, like Babylon's king and his family, became slaves. Assyrians could also sell themselves or their children into slavery to pay a debt. Even enslaved people had rights under Assyria's laws.

As Assyrian history progressed, women's social status decreased. For instance, older law codes stipulated that the family assets were to be equally divided if a couple divorced. However, a 14th-century Assyrian legal code stated that a man could divorce his wife without owing a financial payment to her. Men could beat their wives and pull out their hair with no penalty. A woman convicted of adultery could receive a sentence of a beating or death. A man could rape a woman (or another man) without punishment if the victim were a cult prostitute or of lower social status. If a man raped a virgin, she became his wife, but if he already had a wife, his wife was given to the virgin's father to rape.

While most ancient Mesopotamian civilizations buried their dead outside the city or cremated them, the Assyrians preferred to keep their departed loved ones at home. Wealthy Assyrians built a tomb for their deceased family members right in the house, while the common citizens dug a hole under their house to bury their dead. They would keep an oil lamp burning at the tomb or grave to signify that their deceased family member was with them.

Art and sculpture advanced swiftly as the Assyrians expanded their empire since they learned new techniques and styles from other civilizations. Assyrian artists reached stunning heights in their production of beguiling artwork. Archaeologists have unearthed captivating treasure troves of intricately worked jewels from the royal tombs of Nimrud and Nineveh. The Assyrian artisans created alluring items of gold, ivory, alabaster, and precious stones.

This bas-relief (circa 640 BCE) depicts King Ashurbanipal impaling a lion.
Osama Shukir Muhammed Amin FRCP(Glasg), CC BY-SA 4.0
https://creativecommons.org/licenses/by-sa/4.0 via Wikimedia Commons;
https://commons.wikimedia.org/wiki/File:Assyrian_king_Ashurbanipal_on_his_horse_t
hrusting_a_spear_onto_a_lion%E2%80%99s_head._Alabaster_bas-
relief_from_Nineveh,_dating_back_to_645-
635_BCE_and_is_currently_housed_in_the_British_Museum,_London.jpg

Assyrian sculptures and friezes followed Mesopotamian styles but on a grander scale; they were much larger than previous carvings. Rather than carving statues, the Assyrians preferred friezes and bas-reliefs: two-dimensional sculptures usually worked into a wall. Assyrian friezes were realistic and depicted fluid motion with exquisite detail. Many Assyrian friezes and bas-reliefs decorated palaces, celebrating the king's power in hunting and warfare.

What did the Assyrians wear? When they were pastoral sheepherders in their earliest days, they wore wool clothing. Early Mesopotamians domesticated flax to weave linen cloth, which would have been cooler for Assyria's hot summers. However, these clothes probably were worn mostly by the wealthy upper classes and priests. Sennacherib introduced cotton from the Indus Valley in the 8th century BCE.

Assyrian bas-reliefs and friezes typically show men wearing a knee-length or ankle-length tunic (the longer tunics denoted a higher rank). However, laborers are depicted wearing wrap-around skirts. Some of the tunics had angular hems: knee-length in the front and ankle-length in the back. In rare cases, men are depicted in the nude. Tunics were elaborately decorated with fringe and embroidery and dyed in bright colors.

Assyrian women wore brightly-colored ankle-length gowns, elaborate necklaces, earrings, headdresses, and fringed shawls. Men wore long capes over one shoulder, similar to Roman togas. Both men and women wore sandals and had braided hair. Small children ran about naked or with a little loincloth.

The Assyrians followed a polytheistic religion similar to the Sumerians and Babylonians. They even had some of the same deities. Their chief god was Ashur. One of Noah's grandsons, through his son Shem, was named Ashur in the Torah. He may have been the Semitic Assyrians' ancestor and acquired god-status over time, which often happened in ancient civilizations. Other important deities were the goddess Ishtar (goddess of love, sex, and fertility), Sin (god of the moon), and Tiamat (goddess of chaos and the sea). Just as each city had a patron god, each home had a household god.

The Assyrians sincerely believed the gods communicated with mankind via signs and omens. They paid close attention to anything unusual about the sun, moon, or stars. They analyzed birds' flights and pigs' actions and investigated bird entrails. The king had an entourage of shamans, astrologists, and priests to advise him on the gods' will concerning crucial decisions.

As Assyria grew from a modest city-state into a vast empire, communication, transportation, and infrastructure became increasingly complex. The Assyrians developed a well-ordered communication system to keep abreast of affairs in faraway provinces, using fire signals and couriers on mule or horseback for longer distances. To ensure swift delivery of messages, they built wooden bridges over rivers, paved roads through mountain terrain, and maintained a network of roads that extended to all points of the empire called the "king's road." Using relay riders, the Assyrians achieved unprecedented speed in message delivery, which was unsurpassed until the introduction of the telegraph over two thousand years later.

The Assyrians used camels to transport goods across desert regions and donkeys and oxen in more accessible terrain. They used barges and boats on the Tigris and Euphrates Rivers, which flowed from the Taurus Mountains of Turkey through Assyria, Sumer, and out into the Persian Gulf. Ships on the Mediterranean, Persian Gulf, and the Arabian Sea transported goods from as far away as India, northern Africa, and Europe.

These two lamassu in King Sargon's palace in Dur-Sharrukin feature the body of a winged ox with the king's head. Notice the creature on the left has five feet!
Vania Teofilo, CC BY-SA 3.0 https://creativecommons.org/licenses/by-sa/3.0 via Wikimedia Commons; https://commons.wikimedia.org/wiki/File:Human-headed_Winged_Bulls_Gate_Khorsabad_-_Louvre_02a.jpg

The Assyrians followed the typical Mesopotamian architectural styles with one notable exception: the scale. They loved constructing colossal buildings, which were protected from evil spirits by a gigantic statue called a *lamassu* that featured the king's head on a mythical creature's body. Assyrian kings enjoyed building projects; if they felt like the noblemen of the capital city were getting too belligerent, they would build a new capital city and move there, leaving the testy nobles behind and building up a new aristocracy.

They built breathtaking palaces and temples and designed captivating gardens and parks, diverting rivers to irrigate them. Assyrian architecture encapsulated Assyrian culture. They freely assimilated new elements from other civilizations and innovated startling new ways of doing things.

Chapter 7: Babylon: An Overview

Driven by a great drought, mysterious nomadic shepherds swept into central and southern Mesopotamia in the 3rd millennium BCE. The Amorites demolished the former power structures like Ur's Third Dynasty. They also usurped the rule of ancient city-states like Kish and Isin and established extraordinary cities, most notably Babylon, which would rule an empire one day. The Sumerians called them Amurru or Martu and considered them uncivilized nomads. An Akkadian cuneiform tablet (circa 2300 BCE) described them as a bitter adversary of Sumer.

In the Sumerian creation myth called *The Marriage of Martu*, an Amorite fell in love with a Sumerian maiden, and she with him. Her girlfriend demanded to know why she wanted to marry this man:

"Now listen! Their hands are destructive, and they have monkey features! They eat what our god Nanna forbids and don't show reverence. They never stop roaming about! Their ideas are confused; they cause only disturbance.

This Amorite! He is dressed in sheepskins: he lives in a tent, exposed to the wind and rain. He doesn't offer sacrifices or bend the knee. He lives in the mountains, ignoring the places of the gods. He digs up truffles and is restless. He eats raw meat. He lives without a house, and when he dies, he will not be buried according to proper rituals. My girlfriend, why would you marry Martu?"

Who were the Amorites? What were their origins? They spoke a northwestern Semitic language that was related to the Canaanite language. The Torah (Genesis 10) identifies the Amorites as descendants of Noah's grandson Canaan, saying they were a Canaanite clan, along with the Hittites and the ancient Phoenicians of Sidon. The Amorite herders migrated into central and southern Mesopotamia from the west, probably Syria, in vast numbers around the time of the devastating drought of the 4.2-kiloyear BP aridification event. The Amorites had become so prolific in Mesopotamia that around 2055 BCE, King Shulgi of Ur built a remarkable 155-mile-long wall to keep the Amorites out of Sumer.

Manuscripts from Babylonian archives stated the city of Babylon was founded on the banks of the Euphrates River in 2286 BCE (during the Akkadian Empire period) by a man named Belus. Belus was later elevated to god-status (Bel or Marduk) and became the patron of Babylon, similar to how the man Ashur became the patron god of Aššur. Babylon existed as a small, unimportant town for about four centuries as the Akkadian Empire drew to a close and the Old Assyrian Empire rose to power. By the 1800s BCE, it was an administrative center and a vassal town to the city-state of Kassala.

The Amorite Sumu-Abum (Su-abu) became the first king of the First Dynasty of Babylon in the mid-1800s BCE. He declared independence from Kassala. Sumu-la-El, who ruled the city-state of Babylon from 1817 to 1781 BCE, extended its territory, defeating Kish and other nearby cities and erecting a series of fortifications around the expanded domain.

Babylon's famous King Hammurabi was a fierce warrior yet keen administrator.

Mbmrock, CC BY-SA 4.0 https://creativecommons.org/licenses/by-sa/4.0 via Wikimedia Commons; https://commons.wikimedia.org/wiki/File:(Mesopotamia)_Hammurabi.jpg

Babylon continued as a modest city-state until its sixth Amorite king ascended the throne in the 1700s BCE: the illustrious Hammurabi, whose extraordinary reign and law code we will explore in Chapter 11. Hammurabi's ambitious construction projects elevated Babylon from an obscure town to a stunning city with an efficient, centralized government. He drove the Elamites out of southern Mesopotamia and annexed Sumer, including Isin, Kish, Ur, Uruk, and Eridu. Within a few years, Babylon metamorphosized into the awe-inspiring Babylonian Empire.

And that was just the beginning! The Babylonian Empire continued to grow. Hammurabi led his army east to invade Iran, subduing the Kassites, Lullubi, Gutians, and Elamites. He then turned west toward his Amorite ancestors of the Levant and conquered the Mari and Yamhad kingdoms in Syria and Jordan.

That last move brought him into conflict with the Old Assyrian Empire, which had been exerting power over the Levant and central Mesopotamia. This led to decades of on-and-off wars until Hammurabi won, making Assyria a vassal kingdom to Babylon.

The Old Babylonian Empire rapidly fragmented following Hammurabi's death. In the southernmost marshlands of Sumer, Sealand declared independence and formed its own dynasty. Assyria's vice-regent Puzur-Sin broke Babylon's shackles, regaining Assyrian independence in 1740 BCE. By the 1600s, Babylonia's territory had shrunk back to what it was before Hammurabi's rule, although it still boasted its large and beautiful city for a few more years.

King Samsu-Ditana reigned as Babylon's last Amorite monarch. In the 1500s, King Muršili I of the Hittites raided and sacked Babylon, carrying off loot and captives. However, he was disinterested in ruling the city. Like the Assyrians did later, he stole the idol of Marduk, but unlike the Assyrians, he kept Marduk, leaving Babylon as a ruined, unoccupied city.

Twenty-five years after the Hittite's savage assault on Babylon, the Kassites took possession of the abandoned city. Who were the Kassites? Their origin is somewhat of a mystery. They spoke a language isolate, which means it was unrelated to other known languages, and they may have come from the Zagros Mountains of Iran. They first appeared in written history when they unsuccessfully attacked Babylon during the reign of Nebuchadnezzar's son, Samsu-iluna (r. 1749–1712 BCE), about 150 years before Babylon fell to the Hittites.

Whatever their origins, the Kassites quickly proved to be a sensational power in Mesopotamia, ruling Babylon for almost four hundred years. Their king, Agum-Kakrîme, trounced the Hittites, retrieved Marduk's idol, and installed it back in Babylon. He built the new capital city of Kar-Duniash and rebuilt the ancient city of Nippur, which had laid neglected and practically abandoned. Within sixty-five years, the Kassites conquered Sumer, including the Sealand dynasty, and expanded northeast into the Diyala River region (present-day Baghdad).

And then, gradually, the Kassite power declined. It was eclipsed by the Assyrians, Elamites, and Aramaeans. The Assyrians staged a comeback during the Middle Assyrian Empire, and King Ashur-uballit brought the Kassites to their knees, installing a vassal king in Babylon. The Assyrian king Tukulti-Ninurta flattened Babylon's walls in 1200 BCE, stole the idol of Marduk, and ruled Babylon himself for seven years.

Then the Elamites attacked and plundered Babylon, and they stole Marduk again! They also stole the renowned stele with King Hammurabi's law code and hauled it back to their capital of Susa. What's worse, they captured the last Kassite king, Enlil-nadin-ahi, and took him back to Susa, ending the Kassite rule in Babylon in the 12th century BCE.

The Sumerian Second Dynasty of Isin rose to replace the Kassites as Babylonia's rulers. Under their King Nebuchadnezzar I (r. 1126-1104 BCE), the Sumerian-Babylonians marched to Elam and stole back Marduk's statue. Following this loss, Elam faded into obscurity for over a century. However, Nebuchadnezzar I was subsequently defeated by the Assyrian king, Ashur-resh-ishi I.

During the Bronze Age Collapse, Assyrian King Tiglath-Pileser I (1115-1076 BCE) pummeled Babylon in war. He annexed a massive swathe of Babylonia's lands and made the Babylonian kings vassals to Assyria until 1050 BCE. A cataclysmic famine weakened Babylonia, permitting the Aramaeans to make inroads in 1026 BCE. The Aramaeans deposed their king and plunged Babylonia into anarchy for twenty years.

The Kassites had been rebuilding power in southern Mesopotamia, and the new Kassite state regained control of Babylon around 1003 BCE. However, the Elamites had also been restoring their strength, and they seized Babylon about two decades later, only to have it fall to the Aramaeans. Meanwhile, another northwestern Semitic nomadic people, the Chaldeans, migrated from the Levant, settling in Babylonia's southeastern region on the banks of the Euphrates.

As Assyria recovered from the Bronze Age Collapse, it expanded once again, integrating Babylonia into its empire in 911

BCE. The Babylonians tried to reclaim independence, but Shalmaneser V cruelly put down the revolt, resettling a sizable portion of Babylon's citizens to Israel. Sennacherib appointed his oldest son, Ashur-nadin-shumi, as Babylon's king in 700 BCE. But when Sennacherib sailed across the Persian Gulf to attack Elam, the Elamites in Mesopotamia invaded Babylon and captured (and presumably killed) Ashur-nadin-shumi in 694.

Sennacherib retaliated by destroying Babylon. He razed it to the ground and diverted the Euphrates to flood the ruins. "I utterly dissolved it with water and made it like inundated land." Sennacherib also stole the god Marduk once again, and he put the god on trial before Assyria's patron god Ashur. The *Marduk Ordeal Text* suggests that Marduk died and was resurrected. After his own sons murdered Sennacherib, his younger son Esarhaddon ruled both Assyria and Babylon. He restored Marduk to Babylon and rebuilt the city his father had decimated, endeavoring to establish harmony between the two nations.

The Neo-Babylonian Empire arose in 626 BCE to become the most powerful Middle Eastern state. It began with Nabopolassar. He was the first of a new dynasty that ruled for over a century. Taking advantage of Assyria's unraveling, which had been caused by internecine conflicts, Nabopolassar led Babylon's rebellion. He and the Chaldeans signed a treaty in 616 BCE with Cyaxares, King of Media, which was located in northwestern Iran (he was also the great-grandfather of Cyrus the Great). A royal wedding between Babylonia's Crown Prince Nebuchadnezzar II and Cyaxares's daughter Princess Amytis sealed the deal.

The Scythians, who came from the far northern steppes and allied with Assyria, held the Medes under their yoke. Cyaxares invited the Scythian overlords to a banquet, where he got them drunk before murdering them, freeing Media from Scythian hegemony. The Scythians switched sides, joining the Medes and the Cimmerians from the Black Sea in a massive coalition against Assyria. On horseback, hordes of Scythians and Cimmerians bombarded Assyria's far-flung provinces: Anatolia, Israel, and Judah. They even ravaged Egypt's coast.

While Nabopolassar fought the Assyrians in central Mesopotamia, the Medes, Scythians, and Cimmerians attacked and sacked Assyria's cities in northern Mesopotamia. In 612 BCE, a stupendous coalition force of Babylonians, Chaldeans, Medes, Scythians, Cimmerians, Persians (from the Eurasian Steppe), and Sagartians (of Iran) all joined together against Assyria. They sacked Nineveh in 612 BCE, ground Assyria into dust, and transferred Mesopotamia's rule back to Babylon.

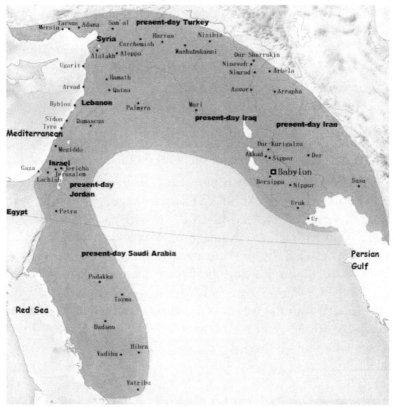

Neo-Babylonia's territory encompassed most of the Assyrian Empire's territory.
Ichthyovenator:Sémhur (base map) - Own work, CC BY-SA 4.0, Photo modified: zoomed-in, names of seas and present-day countries added; https://commons.wikimedia.org/w/index.php?curid=105149705

Nebuchadnezzar II ascended Babylon's throne in 605 BCE; by the end of his illustrious forty-three-year reign, he held sovereignty over all of Mesopotamia, eastern Iran, southern Turkey, Syria, Lebanon, Israel, Jordan, and western Saudi Arabia. In 597 BCE, Nebuchadnezzar marched on the rebellious

Kingdom of Judah in the Levant and stripped the temple and palace of their gold and treasures. He also took King Jehoiachin prisoner, along with ten thousand captives, which included the royal family, military, craftsmen, and artisans.

Among the royal family were four youths: Daniel, Hananiah (Shadrack), Mishael (Meshach), and Azariah (Abednego), who Nebuchadnezzar trained, along with other young people from noble families, to enter his royal service. Daniel, a seer, remained as an advisor and dream interpreter to the Babylonian kings until 539 BCE when King Cyrus of Persia took Babylon. Daniel then briefly served the Persians.

When Judah rebelled again, Nebuchadnezzar laid siege against Jerusalem for two years while its people starved. King Zedekiah tried to escape one night, but the Babylonian troops overtook him, forcing him to watch as they slaughtered his sons. It was the last thing he would see, as the Babylonians gouged out his eyes and hauled him in chains to Babylon. After Nebuchadnezzar died in 562 BCE, his son, Amel-Marduk, released King Jehoiachin from the palace prison, where he'd languished for thirty-seven years. Jehoiachin dined at the king's table for the rest of his life. It is believed Zedekiah perished in Babylon.

Intrigue rocked the palace when Amel-Marduk's brother-in-law, Neriglissar, murdered him two years later, usurping the throne and reigning for six years. Another coup d'état brought Nabonidus to the throne, which he held for seventeen years. On October 12ᵗʰ, 539 BCE, Nabonidus's son and co-regent Belshazzar was at a grand feast with his nobles when he suddenly turned pale, his knees knocking, all strength drained from his body. A disembodied hand was writing on the palace wall! The aged seer Daniel was called in to inform Belshazzar that his days were numbered and that his kingdom would be given to the Medes and Persians. That night, after Cyrus the Great's engineers diverted the Euphrates River, his Persian forces entered Babylon without a struggle.

Babylon's government and political life evolved over time. In the earlier empire of the Amorites and Kassites, the kings micromanaged the government's trivial affairs. Their primary concerns, aside from warfare, centered on building temples, fortifications, and irrigation systems. The Babylonians, especially in the earlier empire, believed their kings were chosen by their patron god Marduk (Bel) and manifested the god's presence on Earth. In addition to their king, the Babylonians had an elected Assembly or Council of Elders. The Assembly was made up of wise men who offered counsel to the people and the king when they needed to make crucial decisions. Their main concern was not angering the gods.

The need for a consistent, established legal system impelled Hammurabi to write his legal code and involve himself in judging minor affairs. He embraced the Mesopotamian concept that the king was the guardian of justice. Hammurabi and other Babylonian kings had a systematic approach to assimilating new provinces they'd conquered; they would send specialists to organize and integrate new territories and coordinate population redistribution.

The Neo-Babylonian Empire exhibited increased interaction with foreign powers, an influential priesthood, and a constantly growing administrative system. Nevertheless, the Babylonians believed their ancient predecessors were nearer to the gods, and thus, they tended to emulate the old political structure. Some change was inevitable, but overall, the Babylonians were politically conservative. Marduk's priesthood grew dramatically in power during this era.

The Neo-Babylonian Empire initiated a cultural renaissance of art, exquisite sculptures, and outstanding architecture. The historian Herodotus spoke of Babylon as the most resplendent city of its time, with luxurious, breathtaking buildings and three rings of impenetrable walls, fifty feet tall and wide enough to host chariot races. The Ishtar Gate glistened with blue glazed tile mosaics depicting lions, dragons, and horses. Nebuchadnezzar's three palaces gleamed with yellow and blue glazed tiles. The god Marduk had finally returned to Babylon after the Hittites, the Assyrians, and the Elamites all stole his cult image, and Nebuchadnezzar ceremoniously enshrined him in the Esagila temple, which was just south of the great ziggurat in Babylon's center.

The reproduction of Babylon's Ishtar Gate is in the Pergamon Museum in Germany.

According to the ancient Greeks, the Hanging Gardens of Babylon were one of the Seven Ancient Wonders of the World. They were supposedly built for Nebuchadnezzar's beloved wife, Amytis. The problem is that archaeologists haven't found evidence of these famous gardens. That doesn't necessarily mean they didn't exist, as new archaeological evidence is constantly unearthed, and much of ancient Babylon hasn't been excavated due to the high-water table. Some scholars think the Greeks meant Nineveh, which *did* have a well-documented garden built by Assyrian King Sennacherib. However, the Babylonian historian Berossus also documented the Babylonian Hanging Gardens, and numerous accounts give explicit details of how the Babylonians constructed the gardens. Despite the lack of archaeological evidence, literary evidence makes the Babylonian Hanging Gardens a near certainty.

From Babylon's inception, its people applied mathematics to observe daylight's length through the solar year. They recorded details of celestial phenomena, such as Venus's risings over twenty-one years, and cataloged constellations and stars in the Enuma Anu Enlil tablets. Medical texts date back to Babylon's First Dynasty, including the *Diagnostic Handbook* by Esagil-kin-apli around 1050 BCE, which described various illnesses, including their symptoms, prognosis, and recommended treatment.

In mathematics, Babylonians demonstrated an understanding of place value, square roots, the Pythagorean theorem (before Pythagoras), and how to measure the diameter and circumference of a circle. Technologically, they used a lever and pulley, a sundial, and a water clock and had a measurement system for long distances. They developed trigonometry and used mathematical models to study the earth's rotation.

Part of Babylonia's population, both men and women, knew how to read and write. Youths from the wealthier families attended school or were tutored at home. Merchants, engineers, and construction supervisors all had to keep records, and scribes recorded annals of government and translated ancient works from Sumer and elsewhere into the Akkadian language. They initially wrote in the cuneiform script, but once Babylonians began using the Aramaean alphabet in the Neo-Babylonian era, they translated masses of ancient literature: epic poems, hymns, and histories. Scholars had to be bilingual or trilingual and adept in both cuneiform and the ancient alphabet.

Babylonia was a civilization infamous for cruel and merciless slaughter on the battlefield, yet it was renowned for extending kindness and mercy to conquered people. The Babylonians could be guilty of impoverishing other cultures to enrich themselves, yet their proverbs taught morality, such as "smile at your enemy" and "treat evil-doers with kindness." They were a paradox, but they were a conglomeration of many cultures: Sumerian, Amorite, Kassite, Assyrian, Median, and more. They were complex, and because they assimilated culture and knowledge from multiple civilizations, the Babylonians reached great heights and left a lasting legacy on the Middle East and the world.

Chapter 8: Babylon: Religion, Myth, and Creation

What were the religious beliefs of the Babylonians? What rituals did they practice, and what meaning did these rituals have? How important was religion to the Babylonians? This chapter will explore these questions and unpack the intriguing details of Babylonian religion. We will compare their creation myth to other Mesopotamian creation myths, investigate their pantheon of gods, and discover several other fascinating Babylonian myths.

Babylon shared many gods with Sumer and other Mesopotamian cultures, but the gods' positions and roles were somewhat different. Babylon's creation myth championed the victory of the younger gods over the older ones, just as the younger Babylonian civilization championed its victory over ancient Sumer.

In its infancy, when Babylon was just an obscure town, Marduk was its patron god, just as most other towns and cities in Mesopotamia had patron gods or goddesses. During Hammurabi's reign (r. 1792–1750 BCE), as Babylon rose from a city-state to an empire, Marduk rose to become Babylonia's national god. He surpassed Inanna (Ishtar) in popularity, and other female deities faded away since the Babylonians focused more on male gods. The Kassites rose Marduk to even greater preeminence, making him the king of the gods.

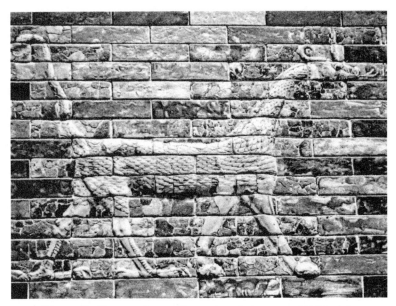

The mušḫuššu was a dragon-like creature that represented Marduk.

It is thought that Babylonians had six hundred gods in their pantheon: three hundred heavenly gods and three hundred gods of the underworld. One of the gods was Anu (An), who was perhaps the most important god to the Sumerians. He was the god of the sky and the father of the gods. However, in the Babylonian creation myth *Enuma Elish,* Anu was one of the younger gods, although he was a leader and the grandfather of Marduk. The myth clarifies that Marduk is more powerful than Anu because Marduk overcame Tiamat when Anu could not resist her sorcery.

Nudimmud was the Babylonian name for the popular Sumerian Enki (Ea), god of fresh water. In Babylonian myths, he was Anu's son; he knew and excelled at everything. He put Apsu, the first of the gods, into a deep sleep and killed him, then lived on (or in) Apsu's body with his wife, Damkina, who gave birth to their son Marduk. In consultation with his son Marduk, Ea (Nudimmud, Enki) created humans to serve the gods.

Adad, another son of Anu, was the Babylonian storm god. His images show him carrying a lightning bolt or hammer with a bull's body or a dragon with a lion's head. Ishtar (Inanna), the sister of Adad and Enki, was the goddess of sexual love and war. In later Babylonia, Ishtar was connected to the planet Venus. She was the most popular goddess throughout Mesopotamia, and in Babylon, she was second only to Marduk in the pantheon.

Religious rituals connected humans to the gods. The humans were responsible for taking care of the gods' need for food and clothing, while the gods were the humans' source of justice, protection, and life itself. Babylon gods had dual characteristics of benevolence and violence. Rituals were intrinsic in keeping the gods happy and appeasing their anger. Religion was not optional; the Babylonians felt that keeping on the gods' good side was imperative for survival.

The Babylonians believed their everyday world overlapped with the spiritual dimension, which created anxiety and speculation. If they didn't keep the gods happy, they could be the victims of floods, famine, or invasion by other nations. Even in their mundane life, if they accidentally spilled or dropped something, they thought it was because of evil spirits. Thus, they often turned to sorcery to cast spells on their enemies or protect themselves from the dark forces. The earlier Babylonian kings and most Mesopotamian kings forbade sorcery, but in the Neo-Babylonian Empire, the kings had sorcerers and magicians in their retinue.

The state-sanctioned worship of Marduk, Ishtar, and the rest of the gods was an inherent part of Babylonian life. Temple priests, priestesses, exorcists, and other personnel dealt with worship and organized ceremonies. They dressed the gods and goddesses, served their meals, made sacrifices, recited prayers, and sang hymns. They exorcized evil spirits and purified the temple grounds and sanctuaries. Only certain people could enter the temple: the priests/priestesses, artisans and carpenters (who made the idols and built the temples), and staff who prepared the food offerings.

Care of the idols was a sacred duty because Babylonians believed their gods literally inhabited them. For instance, Adad, the storm god, lived within his temple idol but also floated around in the clouds, shooting out flashes of lightning and pouring rain down on the fields. Stealing or destroying an idol could incur that god's wrath; if enemies stole a city's patron god, the city would lose its divine protection. When Sennacherib attacked Babylon, Prince Marduk-apla-iddina II gathered up the city's idols and fled to the marshlands to protect them from being stolen or demolished by the Assyrians.

The New Year was the Babylonians' most important festival. The first month of the Babylonian calendar was Nisannu, which would fall in April or May in our Gregorian calendar. The New Year celebrations took place over several days. Reading the Babylonian creation myth *Enuma Elish* was an essential New Year ritual, along with taking Marduk's idol out of his temple and parading him through the streets. The people rejoiced and danced as they watched the idol travel to a small "vacation house." It would stay there for the festival's duration.

Babylonia's creation myth was the *Enuma Elish* or *The Seven Tablets of Creation*. It told the story of the god Marduk's victory over the older gods, how the world and humans were created, and how Marduk appointed the gods to their positions and duties. Multiple tablets containing the story have been found throughout central Mesopotamia, dating to around 1200 BCE, when Assyria conquered the older Babylonian empire. However, the colophons, or information about the tablets' publication written on the back of the tablets, stipulate that the newer tablets were copies or translations of older versions that dated to or before the First Babylonian Dynasty's establishment in the mid-18th century BCE.

The *Enuma Elish* includes many Sumerian gods, such as Anu (An) and Ea (Enki), who play leading roles in the story. However, the myth introduces a strictly Babylonian god, Marduk, as its main protagonist. Like the Sumerian *Eridu Genesis*, the oldest god is annoyed by the noise and clamor of the youngsters keeping him awake, except in the Sumerian version, it's the first humans who are noisy. In the *Enuma Elish*, it's the younger gods.

Enki was a popular god and a friend of mankind for all of Mesopotamia.
https://commons.wikimedia.org/wiki/File:Enki(Ea).jpg

In both stories, the older god decided to eradicate the irritating humans/younger gods, but the Sumerian version has Enki warning Ziusudra to build an ark to preserve human and animal life from the Great Flood. The Babylonian version descends into the macabre, as the younger gods save themselves by killing the older gods and creating the heavens, earth, and humans from their grisly remains.

The *Enuma Elish* story begins in the time before the heavens and the earth were created, with water churning in chaos. Only two beings existed: Apsu, the first, the progenitor, and his partner Tiamat, who gave birth to all. None of the other gods had been formed. Apsu and Tiamat mingled their waters together. Apsu's sweet water and Tiamat's chaotic, bitter ocean swirled together, creating the gods.

However, the young gods were extremely loud! Their clamor threw Tiamat into turmoil, jarring her nerves. Their dancing kept Apsu awake at night; however, he did nothing to quiet them. Tiamat was displeased with their behavior, but she kept silent; she didn't confront their tumultuous behavior. Finally, Apsu called his vizier Mummu, saying, "Let's discuss this with Tiamat!"

Apsu and Tiamat sat facing each other, discussing their noisy sons. "Their behavior is maddening! I can't rest day or night," Apsu raged. "I'm going to break up their way of life! I'm going to destroy them! Then, we can have peace and be able to sleep."

When Tiamat heard this, she fumed against Apsu's evil plot, raging, cursing, and wailing in grief. "How can we destroy what we've given birth to? Yes, their behavior is distressing, but let's extend grace. Let's tighten up our discipline and give them a chance to reform."

But Mummu the vizier spoke up. "My father, you should eradicate this lawless lifestyle so you can get some rest!"

Apsu's face beamed; he was pleased with Mummu, who backed up his plot to murder his sons. Mummu sat on Apsu's lap and put his arms around his neck, kissing him. Meanwhile, the younger gods heard about their father's plot and were frantic. Their knees buckled underneath them, and they collapsed, howling and moaning.

Enki decided to do something. He spoke an incantation over his father, pouring sleep over him until Apsu was in a deep slumber. Mummu wheezed in agitation, but Enki tied him up with a rope through his nose; he could do nothing to rescue Apsu now. Enki ripped off Apsu's crown and put it on his own head. He then tied Apsu up and killed him. He built his house in Apsu's body, holding on to Mummu's nose rope while doing so.

In his house, the Chamber of the Destinies, he sat with his wife, Damkina, in splendor. They conceived, and Damkina gave birth to Bel (Marduk), who had four eyes, four ears, and flames shooting forth from his mouth. His grandfather Anu created the four winds and gave them to Marduk, saying, "Let them whirl, son!"

Marduk created dust and drove it along with a hurricane. He sent a tidal wave crashing over Tiamat. Some gods chastised Tiamat; she had remained passive and did not interfere when the younger gods killed her partner. They insisted she must avenge Apsu. With the older god Qingu, her champion and new spouse, Tiamat called up the forces of chaos, creating eleven horrendous demons with sharp teeth and poison instead of blood. She sent them with weapons to slaughter her children.

Enki, who had killed Apsu and provoked the war, went to Tiamat to try to sedate her with magic spells and then trample her neck under his feet. But he couldn't resist her devious maneuvers; his incantations were unequal to hers. He fell silent at her fearful howls and slunk away. Then Anu went to Tiamat to appease her rage, but she was too terrible and struck fear into his heart.

None of the other gods wanted to confront Tiamat; they sat tight-lipped, staring at the ground. What were they to do? Then, the champion Marduk emerged, charging out in his chariot with its four steeds: the Trampler, the Destroyer, the Merciless, and the Fleet. He sent out the seven winds to harass Tiamat's entrails. When he saw Qingu's sorcery, he faltered at first, losing his nerve. But then he challenged Tiamat, angrily shouting, "You! Mother of the gods. Have you no pity for your children? Have you only contempt?"

Hearing these words, Tiamat lost all reason. Insane and trembling with rage, she spat out incantations and spells against Marduk, but he caught her in his net. As she shrieked loud, piercing cries, Marduk sent a hurricane into her gaping mouth, inflating her body. He then plunged a spear into her heart, tore open her entrails, and smashed her skull. He bound the eleven demons, trampling them under his feet, and bound Qingu.

Marduk then returned to Tiamat's corpse, resting as he surveyed her body. His father Enki had crafted a home out of Apsu's body, and Marduk would make a home from her body. He sliced her in two, like filleting a fish, and stretched out one half to make the sky while the other half became the earth. From her tears flowed the Tigris and Euphrates. Then he fixed the stars of the Zodiac in the sky to mark the twelve months and created Nanna, the moon, the god of the night. He appointed all the gods to their specific roles: three hundred in the heavens and three hundred in the underworld.

The other gods gathered around, cheering, kissing his feet, and giving kingship to Marduk. Marduk then consulted with his father Ea (Enki), and they decided to kill Qingu, "the one who instigated warfare." They created humans from his body. Ea created the first man, Lullu, from Qingu's blood to serve the gods, which freed the gods from mundane tasks and allowed them to better maintain order and keep chaos away.

The exhilarated gods proposed building Babylon as a home for the great gods and Marduk's resting place. They built Babylon's walls, constructed the temple of Esagil for Marduk, and created their own shrines. When they completed their building project, beer mugs were set out, and they all sat down to a festive banquet, toasting Marduk as king over the gods.

Curiously, the preeminent goddess Ishtar was not named in the *Enuma Elish*. However, she has several myths of her own, including her famous visit to the underworld. Ishtar's sister Ereshkigal was the queen of the underworld, and Ishtar's pretext for visiting the underworld was to mourn with her sister, whose husband had died. But the other gods suspected she was attempting a hostile takeover of the underworld.

Before making her descent, Ishtar carefully applied kohl around her eyes and draped herself in resplendent royal robes. She marched to the entrance of the underworld, banging on its gates, and ordered the gatekeeper to let her in. If he refused, she swore she would tear the gates off their hinges. He let her through the first gate but informed her she must remove a symbol of power as she passed through each gate. By the time she passed through the seventh gate, she was naked.

This "Queen of the Night" relief may depict Ishtar arriving naked in the underworld.
British Museum, CC0, via Wikimedia Commons;
https://commons.wikimedia.org/wiki/File:British_Museum_Queen_of_the_Night.jpg

Ishtar swiftly stole her sister's throne, but the seven judges of the underworld found her guilty of usurpation. They sentenced her to death and hung her body on a hook. Ishtar's death created pandemonium on earth, as Ishtar was the goddess of sexual love and fertility. Now, no one was making love and conceiving children. After Ishtar failed to return, her handmaiden Ninshubur went to the temples of the gods, pleading with them to rescue her mistress from the underworld.

Enlil, Nanna, and Anu refused to help, saying Ishtar brought her fate upon herself. But Enki realized that humans would die if Ishtar was not restored. He scraped the dirt under his fingernails and created two androgynous creatures to ask Queen Ereshkigal for Ishtar's body. They sprinkled Ishtar with the water of life, and she revived. But she couldn't leave the underworld unless someone took her place. From the underworld, Ishtar looked up to see her husband Tammuz (Dumuzi) *not* mourning her death! She picked him to replace her for half the year, and the demons would drag him to the underworld every year for six months.

Another Babylonian myth concerned Adapa, son of Enki, the first man to be created. Adapa was fishing when his boat overturned. In anger, he broke the South Wind's wings, and he had to go to heaven to apologize to Anu. Before he left for heaven, Enki warned him not to eat or drink anything while there, or he would die. Adapa apologized to Anu, who forgave him and offered him food and drink. Adapa refused the food, thinking it would kill him, but in reality, it would have made him immortal. He was tricked out of living forever.

A third myth was about Nergal, the god of war, who got into the underworld, slept with Ereshkigal, then tried to sneak away. She caught him and tried to kill him. He attempted to kill her, but they decided to get married and jumped back in bed! Before all this happened, Nergal was bored, so he decided to start a war. After all, the humans wouldn't respect the god of war if no fighting happened.

Nergal targeted Babylon for his war. Using sorcery, he tricked Marduk into leaving town for a while. The world descended into temporary chaos in Marduk's absence. However, Marduk returned from vacation before Nergal got his campaign off the ground. Nergal kept plotting, and eventually, Marduk left again. This time, Nergal plunged the world into horrible warfare and suffering and threatened to destroy the cosmic order. His vizier distracted him by starting a war on Mount Sharshar, which somehow quenched Nergal's rage. He came back to his senses, grateful that he hadn't destroyed the heavens and the earth. Marduk's absence in this myth may reference the times when the Hittites, Assyrians, and Elamites stole his statue.

Even when Babylon wasn't ruling much of the known world, it was still a place of religious pilgrimage, as it was considered a holy city. The Babylonians regarded their city as the center of the world, a sort of idyllic Eden, symbolizing cosmic harmony through Marduk's defeat of chaos.

SECTION THREE:
AGE OF INNOVATION

Chapter 9: The Epic of Gilgamesh

Over four thousand years old, the *Epic of Gilgamesh* may be the world's oldest written story. It is more than one thousand years older than Homer's *Iliad* and *Odyssey*. Partially written versions of the epic date to 2100 BCE, but its oral history undoubtedly traces back further. Tablet fragments with the story include Sumerian, Babylonian, and Akkadian gods, indicating that the epic originated in Sumer, with other Mesopotamian civilizations later adopting it. This chapter will unwrap the story itself and analyze its background and significance.

Archaeological and literary evidence places Gilgamesh as a real king in Uruk's history. As far as heroes go, Gilgamesh was a bit of an anomaly. He was two-thirds divine and one-third human, but his subjects were unhappy with their cruel, arrogant king. The most glaring reason was he felt entitled to rape the virgins in Uruk on their wedding night.

His subjects got a prostitute to partially tame a wild man named Enkidu, who possessed unnatural strength. They wanted him to challenge Gilgamesh and change the order of things. Instead, the two men hit it off and set off on adventures together. Enkidu's death forced Gilgamesh to recognize his mortality. And that's what made him a true hero; not his brilliant feats with grotesque monsters, or at least not *just* his brilliant feats, but acknowledging and accepting his humanity.

This stone carving from the Shara Temple depicts Gilgamesh wrestling two lions.
Osama Shukir Muhammed Amin FRCP(Glasg), CC BY-SA 4.0
https://creativecommons.org/licenses/by-sa/4.0 via Wikimedia Commons;
https://commons.wikimedia.org/wiki/File:Gilgamesh_in_a_Sculptured_Vase,_Shara_T
emple,_Tell_Agrab,_Iraq.jpg

The *Sumerian King List* records Gilgamesh as the fourth king of Uruk. The *Sumerian King List* mentions Gilgamesh's father as "invisible" or supernatural, and the epic says his father was Uruk's second king, the "divine Lugalbanda." His mother was the goddess Rimat-Ninsun, so for Gilgamesh to be "one-third" human, his father must have been half-god. But that still doesn't work mathematically—maybe in myths, it doesn't matter.

The *Epic of Gilgamesh* has multiple ancient sources in several languages, and five Sumerian poems dating to 2100 BCE contain portions of the story. The oldest version of the entire epic is the Old Babylonian Tablets, which date to 1800 BCE; however, some tablets are missing or damaged. The Akkadian scholar-priest Sîn-lēqi-unninni compiled the best-preserved version between 1300 to 1000 BCE in twelve tablets, which were uncovered in Nineveh's Library of Ashurbanipal.

The themes in the *Epic of Gilgamesh* are enlightening in regard to Mesopotamian culture. They take us beyond grand inscriptions and bas-reliefs to the story of a flawed king, who was also strikingly handsome and unassailably strong. Although most of the story is a fantastical myth, it reflects real-life struggles. We gain insight into the people's frustration with their political leader, the depths of friendship between two men, and beliefs about death and immortality.

The *Epic of Gilgamesh* opens with a description of Gilgamesh, who crossed the ocean, explored the world, and sought eternal life. "He brought information of the time before the Flood. He went on a distant journey, pushing himself to exhaustion, but then was brought to peace."

Gilgamesh was the most beautiful and perfect of men. But he had a dark side, and the people of Uruk implored the gods for justice for the brides he had raped. So, the gods created a man who was Gilgamesh's equal in strength: Enkidu, the hairy man of the forest! He ate grass with the gazelles and jostled with the wild animals at the watering hole. One day, a trapper saw him at the watering hole and went rigid with fear. His heart pounded, and his face drained of color. He told his father of the wild man who had been destroying his traps and setting the wild animals free. His father told him to go to Uruk and get Shamhat, the prostitute; she would tame this mighty man.

So, the trapper brought Shamhat to the watering hole. When Enkidu saw her voluptuousness, he groaned with lust, and for seven days, he had intercourse with her. But afterward, the gazelles darted off when they saw him, and the wild animals distanced themselves. Shamhat asked him, "Enkidu, why do you gallop around with these wild beasts? Come to Uruk with me and meet Gilgamesh, who struts his power like a wild bull."

This terracotta wall panel from Ur, circa 2027–1763, depicts Enkidu.
Osama Shukir Muhammed Amin FRCP(Glasg), CC BY-SA 4.0
https://creativecommons.org/licenses/by-sa/4.0 via Wikimedia Commons;
https://commons.wikimedia.org/wiki/File:Enkidu,_Gilgamesh%27s_friend._From_Ur,_Iraq._2027-1763_BCE._Iraq_Museum.jpg

Enkidu agreed to accompany Shamhat to Uruk to challenge Gilgamesh and change the order of things. Meanwhile, Gilgamesh dreamed that a meteorite fell from the sky and landed next to him. His goddess mother told him the meteorite represented the most rugged man in the land who would be his comrade.

On their way to Uruk, Shamhat took Enkidu to some shepherds, who put food and beer in front of him. Shamhat showed him how to eat human food. Enkidu drank seven mugs of beer until his face glowed, and he sang with joy! Then he bathed, rubbed oil on himself, and became human.

One shepherd told Enkidu of Gilgamesh's dastardly habit of raping the brides before their husbands could make love to them. This enraged Enkidu, and he stormed to Uruk, where a wedding had just taken place. He blocked the door to the bridal chamber, keeping Gilgamesh out. The two fought fiercely. The doorposts trembled, and the walls shook. After they wore each other out fighting, they kissed and became friends.

Forgetting the bride, they started talking about the ferocious monster Humbaba, the guardian of the cedars of Lebanon. With their joint strength, they determined to kill Humbaba. Hand in hand, they went to the forge to have weapons made. The Uruk elders counseled Gilgamesh not to be too foolhardy and told Enkidu to protect him. They then went to Gilgamesh's goddess mother, Ninsun, asking her to intercede with the sun god Shamash on their behalf.

The two men strode off, walking fifty leagues a day until they reached Lebanon. That night, Gilgamesh had a frightening dream that a mountain had fallen on him. Enkidu interpreted the dream to mean the mountain represented Humbaba, the monster, and that they would capture and kill him. For the next three nights, Gilgamesh had disturbing nightmares: a wild bull, a bolt of lightning, a tall, fearful creature. Each time, Enkidu assured him the dreams meant they would triumph over Humbaba.

On the fifth night, Gilgamesh had another disturbing dream. Tears were streaming down his face, but before he told the dream to Enkidu, the sun god Shamash warned them it was time to fight Humbaba. "Hurry! Don't let him enter the forest and hide in the thickets. He's only wearing one coat of armor, not all seven!"

Gilgamesh and Enkidu lunged at the Humbaba monster. Humbaba scoffed at them. "An idiot and a moron! Enkidu, you son of a fish! You don't even know your own father! I saw you when you were young but didn't bother you. Now you've brought Gilgamesh, an enemy! A stranger! I will feed your flesh to the screeching vultures!"

Just then, the ground shook, and they whirled around to see Mount Hermon split open. The clouds suddenly darkened, and the sun god Shamash sent thirteen winds against Humbaba. Locked in place by the winds, the monster begged Gilgamesh for his life. "Let me go! I'll be your servant! I'll cut down trees for you."

Enkidu warned Gilgamesh, "Don't listen to Humbaba!"

Humbaba turned to Enkidu. "You know the rules of the forest. I should have killed you when you were young. But I spared you! Now, clemency is up to you. Speak to Gilgamesh to spare my life!"

But Enkidu urged Gilgamesh on. "Kill Humbaba! Grind him up! Pulverize him!"

Gilgamesh killed Humbaba, and they cut off his head. They made a raft and sailed home. Enkidu steered while Gilgamesh held Humbaba's head. Before arriving in Uruk, Gilgamesh bathed, washed his hair, and cleaned his weapons. He shook out his long locks of hair, put on clean regal garments, tied his sash, and put his crown on his head.

His beauty captivated Princess Ishtar (Inanna, the patron goddess of Uruk). "Gilgamesh! Come, be my husband! You will have a chariot of lapis lazuli and gold harnessed to storming mountain mules! Kings, lords, and princes will bow before you and bring you tribute."

But Gilgamesh snorted. "What about all your previous bridegrooms? Where is your little shepherd Tammuz; you send him to the underworld for six months every year!"

One by one, he listed Ishtar's husbands, who had suffered terribly at her hands. Enraged, Ishtar flew to heaven to see her father, Anu. "Father! Gilgamesh has insulted me over and over!"

Anu replied, "What's the matter? Did you provoke King Gilgamesh?"

But Ishtar screeched, "Give me the Bull of Heaven so he can kill Gilgamesh! If you don't, I'll knock down the gates of the underworld, and the dead will come up to eat the living!"

Anu warned Ishtar, "If I give you the Bull of Heaven, Uruk will have seven years of famine. Have you stored enough food for your people?"

Ishtar nodded. "I have stored seven years of grain for the people and grass for the animals."

Anu handed Ishtar the nose rope of the Bull of Heaven. She led it down to Uruk. Once there, he snorted, and a pit opened up. One hundred men fell in. The bull snorted again. Another hole opened up, and two hundred men fell in. The third time he snorted, Enkidu fell in, up to his waist, but he jumped out and grabbed the bull by his horns. The massive bull snorted, lifted his tail, and flung out his dung behind him. Enkidu called to Gilgamesh, "I'll hold his tail, and you thrust your sword between his horns!"

Together, they killed the Bull of Heaven, ripped out his heart, and offered it to Shamash, the sun god. From the top of Uruk's wall, Ishtar hurled curses at Gilgamesh, but Enkidu wrenched off the bull's hindquarter and flung it at her. Enkidu and Gilgamesh washed their hands in the Euphrates and strode through Uruk, hand in hand.

Gilgamesh slays the Bull of Heaven in this Mesopotamian terracotta relief, circa 2255 BCE.

But the gods were holding a conference in heaven, and Anu decreed that because Gilgamesh and Enkidu had killed the Bull of Heaven and slew Humbaba, one of them must die.

Enlil snorted, "Let Enkidu die, not Gilgamesh!"

But Shamash, the sun god, replied, "Wasn't it at my command that they killed Humbaba and the Bull of Heaven? Should innocent Enkidu die?"

Enlil angrily retorted, "You're responsible! You enabled them!"

The verdict fell on Enkidu, and as he lay dying, Gilgamesh's tears flowed like rivers. "Oh, my dear brother, why are they absolving me instead of you?"

Enkidu turned to Gilgamesh and told him about the horrible dream he had. It involved a gruesome demon overpowering him and dragging him down to the House of Darkness on the road of no return. "Remember me and all we went through!"

As the day dawned, Gilgamesh promised Enkidu all the creatures would mourn him: the gazelles, the four wild asses who raised him on their milk, the herds who taught him where to graze. The people would mourn him: the elders of Uruk, the shepherds, and the harlot. Even the land would mourn him; the pasturelands would shriek like a mother who had lost her child. Gilgamesh touched his friend's heart, but it beat no longer. "And I mourn you in anguish. You were my sword and my shield. What is this sleep that has seized you?"

Gilgamesh cried bitterly over his friend; deep sadness penetrated his core. He mourned over Enkidu for six days and seven nights. Gilgamesh would not allow his friend to be buried until a maggot fell out of his nose.

He then considered his own mortality, realizing that, like Enkidu, he, too, would die. He decided to travel to Utnapishtim for counsel. Who was Utnapishtim? He was the Noah-like figure from the Great Flood; the Sumerians called him Ziusudra in the *Eridu Genesis*. He was the man who built the ark and saved humanity and the animals. After all these years, Utnapishtim was still alive. Perhaps he held the key to immortality.

Gilgamesh traveled to Mount Mashu, the highest mountain in the sky, whose roots reach the netherworld. Scorpion beings guarded the gate. Although petrified with fear, Gilgamesh pulled himself together and approached them. The male scorpion-being called out to Gilgamesh, "Why have you traveled such a long journey?"

Gilgamesh answered, "I have come to see my ancestor, Utnapishtim, who was given eternal life. I must ask him about death and life!"

The scorpion-being said, "No mortal man has ever crossed through the mountain; for twelve leagues, it is dense darkness."

Gilgamesh convinced the scorpion-being to allow him through. After passing through the twelve leagues of horrifying darkness, Gilgamesh finally came to a beautiful land by the sea with cedars, agates, and fruit like lapis lazuli, carnelian, rubies, and emeralds. He sailed across the sea to the Waters of Death until he finally arrived in Utnapishtim's land.

Utnapishtim asked Gilgamesh why he looked so haggard and emaciated. Gilgamesh told him, "Should I not have such deep sadness within me? My friend Enkidu has died. Together we destroyed Humbaba and killed the Bull of Heaven. Now the fate of mankind has overtaken him. How can I be silent? How can I be still? Am I not like him? Will I lie down, never to get up again? How have you found eternal life?"

Utnapishtim replied, "I will reveal a secret of the gods. When the father god Anu decided to flood the earth, the clever god Ea came to my reed house and spoke through the wall, saying, 'Build a boat! Make all living things go inside.' So, I built the boat and coated it with bitumen. Then it started raining, submerging the mountains in water, overwhelming the people. The storm and flood flattened the land for six days and seven nights.

Then the rain stopped, and the wind calmed. I opened a vent, and fresh air came in. I fell to my knees, weeping. The boat lodged on Mount Nimush. On the seventh day, I released a dove; it flew around but couldn't find a perch, so it returned. I sent out a swallow, but it returned. Then I sent out a raven, and it did not return. So, I sent the animals out in all directions and sacrificed a sheep. The god Enlil told my wife and me to kneel, and he proclaimed us immortal."

As Utnapishtim spoke, the exhausted Gilgamesh struggled to keep his eyes open. "Wait!" Utnapishtim exclaimed. You've got to stay awake six days and seven nights!"

Apparently, staying awake was a key to immortality. But by that time, Gilgamesh was so deeply asleep that he did not awaken for days. Kindly, Utnapishtim gave him a second chance. He told Gilgamesh about a plant growing under the sea with thorns like a rose that would provide him with immortality. Gilgamesh attached stones to his feet and sank to the bottom of the sea. He found the plant, cut it, then cut off the rocks tied to his feet, and rose to the surface.

Unfortunately, as Gilgamesh traveled home with the plant of immortality, he stopped by a cool spring to bathe. A snake came along and carried off the plant, leaving its sloughed-off skin behind. Gilgamesh sat down weeping, tears streaming down his face. He returned home to Uruk, realizing the city was his destiny. Although his mortal body would die, he would live on through the city's people.

Gilgamesh achieved astounding successes but also dismal failures. He was courageous or at least had a daring disrespect for what would terrify most people. But his brazen overconfidence ended up getting his best friend killed. Gilgamesh's epic portrayed his attempt to escape his mortal constraints, answer inexplicable questions, and conquer mortality. But despite his extraordinary strength, he still had limitations. He was not omniscient, and one day, he would die just as his friend Enkidu died. Once he came to grips with these truths, he was genuinely heroic.

Realizing and accepting his true identity empowered Gilgamesh to live a wise and virtuous life. Well, at least virtuous in contrast to his former dishonorable ways; he most likely was not a stellar role model. But in whatever time he had left, he strived to grow and learn from his mistakes and be a better king. Perhaps he could even be an admired king, not for his extraordinary adventures but for what he could do for his kingdom.

Chapter 10: Innovations and Inventions

Many technologies, scientific advances, and items we use every day without even thinking about originated in Mesopotamia. After all, it was the land of many firsts! Ancient Mesopotamia gave birth to a plethora of ingenious inventions and brilliant developments. Let's examine how the various Mesopotamian civilizations came to invent and use things like the wheel, the chariot, cuneiform writing, maps, mathematics, and even medicine.

Did you know that the first wheels weren't used for transportation? Archaeologists believe that a slow hand-turned pottery wheel called a tournette came first. An excavation at Tepe Pardis in Iran uncovered a tournette dating between 5200 and 4700 BCE. The fast, freely spinning pottery wheels with an axle emerged in Mesopotamia later; archaeologists found one in Ur dating to 3100 BCE.

The Sumerians invented the transportation wheel in the 4th century BCE. They inserted rotating axles into disks made from horizontal slices of tree trunks. The first wheels were solid pieces of wood; after about a thousand years, they developed a hollow wheel with spokes. This was much faster and lighter! Once the Mesopotamians developed the transportation wheel, they surged ahead in utilizing carts for hauling big loads and chariots for fast transportation or battle.

Onagers draw this early wheeled cart in the "Battle Standard of Ur" (circa 2600 BCE).
https://commons.wikimedia.org/wiki/File:Ur_chariot.jpg

Once the wheel was invented, carts were used, pushed, or pulled by people or animals. Of course, this meant the people had to domesticate animals and train them to do things like pulling a cart. The first animals they used were oxen, donkeys, and a larger ass called an onager (which are almost extinct today). Mesopotamia did not have horses until the Akkadian Empire, and they were probably imported from the northern steppes. They had to figure out the technology of attaching the animals to the cart with a harness, breeching straps, collar, and pole.

Once the Sumerians succeeded in basic cart technology, they quickly developed chariots. Four-wheeled war chariots with solid wood wheels pulled by onagers are depicted in the Standard of Ur, dating to 2600 BCE. They were definitely meant for warfare, as some of the pictures show them running over the bodies of fallen warriors. They would have been slower and less maneuverable than spoked two-wheeled chariots, which Mesopotamians began using around the 2nd millennium BCE.

Horses were domesticated in Turkey's Caucasus region in the late 4th century BCE, but Mesopotamians didn't start using them until around 2400 BCE. Using horses to pull spoke-wheeled chariots brought about unprecedented speed. Around 1700 BCE, the Hittites developed an even faster chariot using wheels with only four spokes instead of six or eight. The Hittite chariot carried three men: the charioteer, the archer, and the shield-bearer.

Located between the Tigris and the Euphrates, with the Persian Gulf at its southern borders, water transportation in Mesopotamia offered an excellent opportunity for trade. Fish was an important food source, and boats made fishing more productive. Boats predated wheeled vehicles and provided another vital means of transportation in Mesopotamia. Southern Sumer's topography changed since river silting caused the Persian Gulf to shrink, but it once lay on the Persian Gulf's shores, near the Euphrates.

The Ubaid culture of the ancient coastal cities of Sumer invented the world's first sailboats, or at least the first for which we have physical evidence. Archaeologists uncovered several clay models of sailboats in Eridu, Mashnaqa, Oueili, Uruk, and Uqair, dating to the earlier Ubaid period (6250–4000 BCE). The sailboats facilitated long-distance trade on the Tigris and Euphrates Rivers and even 280 miles down the Persian Gulf coast to places like Bahrain, Qatar, and Saudi Arabia. Archaeologists have discovered Ubaid-period pottery in coastal settlements of the Persian Gulf.

The earliest sailboat had an uncomplicated design with a hull made initially from bundled reeds roped together and water-proofed by a thick layer of bitumen. Later, they used wood planks. They made square sails from linen, wool, or papyrus. The early sailors didn't have a way to control the sails' direction. The boaters had to wait until the wind was blowing in the direction they wanted to go. Although ancient Sumerian sailboats couldn't hold many people or much cargo, they were the prototype for future vessels that had a grander design and size.

The Sumerians developed the world's first writing system—cuneiform—early in their history. They needed a way to record business transactions, keep track of trade, and record events like astronomical anomalies. The first cuneiform, developed at the end of the 4th millennium BCE, used pictogram symbols representing words and objects. For instance, the word for fish looked like a simple drawing of a fish.

Thousands of tablets using these prototype pictograms and cuneiform still exist today, five thousand years later! They give us outstanding insight into the history and culture of ancient

Mesopotamia. The first writers used the sharp end of a reed to draw in wet clay, which would then harden and preserve the writing. Pictogram writing was suitable for most nouns and some verbs, but it was difficult for more abstract words, like success, freedom, or good. Expressing past, present, and future tenses was also challenging.

The prototype pictograms evolved into cuneiform, which was easier to write. They still used wet clay tablets, but now, instead of drawing the word, they pushed the end of a cut reed into the clay to make wedge-shaped marks. The symbols were more stylized and abstract than the original pictures. Gradually, they began using symbols representing phonetics (sounds) for more abstract words.

Fortunately, for those who speak the English language, we only have to learn twenty-six letters of the alphabet. But one had to memorize over a thousand symbols to read and write in cuneiform; it took about twelve years for a scribe to be trained. The Mesopotamians reduced symbols to about six hundred by 2900 BCE to make writing easier. By comparison, if you learn the five hundred most basic Chinese characters, you can read about 75 percent of a newspaper in simplified Chinese. However, our modern language is more complex, as we have advanced technology and global concepts. The ancient Mesopotamians didn't require as many words.

About fifteen distinct languages, including Sumerian, Akkadian, Assyrian, Babylonian, Elamite, and Hittite, used cuneiform writing over a period of about three thousand years before the Aramaic and Phoenician alphabets gradually replaced it. In addition to clay tablets, the Mesopotamians carved cuneiform inscriptions into stone and began writing on parchment or papyrus.

	Line Character. (Vertical)	Line Character. (Rotated)	Old Babylonian.	Assyrian.	New Babylonian.
FISH					
REED					
DRINKING POT					
HOUSE					
RAIN					
CIRCLE, SUN					
KING (with his crown)					
MAN					
EAR OF WHEAT					
HEAD OF A MAN					
STAR					

This chart shows how cuneiform evolved from pictographs to abstract symbols.
https://commons.wikimedia.org/wiki/File:Evolution_of_cuneiform.jpg

The Babylonians innovated maps; the oldest that has survived dates to about 2300 BCE. Ancient Babylonian cartography used drawings on wet clay tablets, which reflect accurate surveying techniques. These ancient clay maps depicted hills and valleys and had labeled features; most maps were of small areas and used for city planning or hunting. More extensive maps were used for military campaigns and trading. The *Imago Mundi*, a Babylonian map of their world, dates to the 6th century BCE. It depicts Babylon on the Euphrates surrounded by Assyria, Armenia, and several cities. These locations are encompassed by the sea ("bitter river"). Eight outlying regions in triangular shapes form a star.

The ancient Mesopotamians had plenty of clay and mud available. They not only made clay bricks and wrote cuneiform in damp clay, but they also used it for their exquisite cylinder seals beginning in the 4th millennium BCE. They rolled these cylinders in soft clay to form impressions, which were often intricate pictures. Today, the ancient cylinders can be rolled in clay to obtain pristine examples of ancient Mesopotamian art. Scholars believe the Sumerians in Uruk invented the first cylinder seals around 3500 BCE, although they were used throughout the Near East.

People from royalty to commoners used cylinder seals when transacting business and sending mail. Made from marble, lapis lazuli, or metal, the owners wore them around their necks on leather lanyards or pinned to their clothing. Cylinder seals were like personal signatures that authenticated correspondence and important documents. Cylinder seals usually measure about three to four inches. Before developing cylinder seals, Mesopotamians used stamp seals, which measure less than one inch across.

A lapis lazuli cylinder seal circa 2800–2450 BCE is on the left. On the right is the impression the seal leaves on moist clay in this representation of the Myth of Etana.
https://commons.wikimedia.org/wiki/File:Sceau-cylindre_avec_la_repr%C3%A9sentation_du_mythe_d%27Etana.jpg

Many people say that math was not their favorite subject in school; nevertheless, we depend on math daily. Just think of how many times in the day we use basic counting, which was developed by the Sumerians. They used the twelve knuckles on one hand (not counting thumb joints) for counting by one, and each finger on the opposite hand represented twelve. So, they counted up to twelve on one hand and held up one finger on the other. They could do this up to sixty, using all five fingers (including the thumb).

We base our present-day counting on tens (ten, twenty, thirty, etc.), but Mesopotamians based their counting on sixty: the sexagesimal system (60, 120, 180, etc.) They divided the sky into 360 degrees and invented the 60-second minute and the 60-minute hour. Beginning in the 4th millennium BCE, Sumerians used objects to represent numbers: a tiny clay cone for the number one, a small ball for ten, a bigger cone for sixty. Gradually, they began using these objects to write numbers in cuneiform. Using the sexagesimal system, Sumerians started using an abacus prototype between 2700 and 2300 BCE.

The Babylonians developed the concept of zero. They were the first to use place values, with left-column digits representing larger values and right-column digits representing ones. Like the Sumerians, they used base sixty rather than ten. The number one in the left column represented sixty, so if you saw 2 / 7, it stood for (2 x 60) + 7 = 127.

The Sumerians quickly forged on from simple counting to advanced mathematics. By 3000 BCE, they began using basic measurements, and by 2600 BCE, they were using multiplication, division, square roots, cubic roots, and geometry. The Babylonians built on this knowledge. Beginning in 1800 BCE, they learned to use algebra and fractions; solve linear, quadratic, and cubic equations; and calculate reciprocal pairs, which multiply together to equal sixty. One Babylonian tablet, circa 1900–1680 BCE, calculated pi (π) to a value of 3.125.

The Plimpton 322 clay tablet, circa 1800 BCE, is a trigonometric table demonstrating that the Babylonians used sophisticated geometry and understood the Pythagorean theorem twelve centuries before Pythagoras was born. The tablet contains numbers in columns. Careful analysis of the numbers shows Pythagorean triples, where the longest side squared is equal to the sum of the squares of the two shorter sides.

One especially remarkable early Mesopotamian development was mathematical and scientific astronomy. The early Mesopotamians observed the movements of the celestial bodies—the sun, moon, planets, and stars—and reduced these observations to mathematical order. The Chaldeans in Mesopotamia probably initiated the study of astronomy in the 4th millennium BCE. Astronomy blended with religious elements, mainly astrology: the belief that the positions of the stars and planets affect people and events on Earth.

Through their study of the skies, the Chaldeans could accurately predict planets' motion, even apparent retrograde or backward motions (an illusion caused by Earth passing the outer planets in their orbits). They could also predict helical rising (when a star or planet becomes visible on the eastern horizon just before sunrise) and when planets or principal stars would come into alignment. The Chaldeans also calculated when the moon would go through its phases and when solar and lunar eclipses would occur.

The Babylonians began predicting eclipses in 721 BCE during the Neo-Babylonian Empire. Today, astronomers studying long-term variations in the lunar orbit consult the Chaldean and Babylonian eclipse records. The Babylonian months followed the lunar cycle, but the seasons followed the sun. So, they developed a lunisolar calendar of twelve months with four weeks of seven days. Every so often, they would throw in a thirteenth month to keep the calendar consistent with solar activity. An accurate calendar was intrinsic in an agricultural society, as it allowed farmers to plant and harvest at favorable times.

During the Neo-Babylonian Empire, Babylonians studied astronomy as a science disconnected from astrology. One contribution of Babylonian astronomers was dividing a circle into 360 degrees. They divided the day into twelve divisions; each division was a *kaspu*, the distance the sun travels in two hours (corresponding to thirty degrees). They split time into four-minute increments.

Over one thousand years before Hippocrates, medicine and doctoring were well-developed professions in Mesopotamia. Mesopotamians continued to refine their knowledge of pharmaceuticals and techniques in surgery and wound care through the coming centuries. Cuneiform tablets dating as far back as 3000 BCE document the evolution of medicine. Although Mesopotamian medicines involved religious rituals combined with physical treatments, doctors' facilities did exist independently of temples.

The Code of Hammurabi (1755–1750 BCE) had specific rules for doctors. Their fees had to be on a sliding scale depending on their patients' social class. The government could inspect a doctor's work, and doctors could be punished if they omitted necessary treatment or caused further harm to a patient. Although large-scale hospitals did not exist, physicians did have small clinics with beds for patients who needed round-the-clock care.

A Sumerian cuneiform tablet circa 3000 BCE lists fifteen medicines used to treat illnesses or for wound care, including potassium nitrate, cassia (cinnamon), myrtle, thyme, honey, and beer. They used all parts of plants—roots, seeds, bark, and sap—for wound care, laxatives, antiseptics, and to treat diseases. Doctors also treated pain using cannabis, mandrake, and opium. They used alcohol, myrrh, and honey as antiseptics. Inventory tablets in a Babylonian pharmacy, circa 1000 BCE, enumerated over 250 medicinal plants, 120 minerals, and 180 other medicines, which doctors mixed with alcohol, bouillon, honey, and oil.

Doctors performed surgeries in ancient Mesopotamia, including setting bones and excising wounds with bronze lancets. They castrated boys destined to become eunuchs. They used scalpels for surgeries, including cutting between the third and fourth ribs to relieve pleural effusion (fluid build-up in the membranes lining the lungs). They also operated on abscesses beneath the scalp, scraping away the affected bone.

The Mesopotamian shekel, which emerged over four thousand years ago, is the first known metal currency. In Semitic languages, the word shekel carried the idea of "weighing." The shekel was first documented about 2150 BCE during Naram-Sin's reign over the Akkadian Empire. In the Third Dynasty of Ur, Ur-Nammu's law code, written between 2048 and 2030 BCE, charged fines of shekels. These early shekels were not coins; they weren't round and flat with some sort of picture on them. They were simply a piece of metal (usually silver) that weighed about one-third of an ounce.

Many scholars believe the first stamped coins (flat and round with a picture on them) were minted in Lydia (in western Turkey) around 650 BCE. However, Neo-Assyrian King Sennacherib may have minted the first half-shekel coins decades before Lydia. One of his inscriptions mentions building a form of clay and pouring bronze into it to make half-shekel pieces. However, no one has yet found minted coins from Sennacherib's era.

Mesopotamians were also responsible for developing the first plow, called an ard, which a farmer would harness to an ox. The earliest "scratch plows," dating to around 5000 BCE, were wooden and heavy. The Assyrians began using iron plows around 2300 BCE. The plow's invention revolutionized civilization, enabling large-scale agriculture and allowing hunter-gatherer populations to remain in the same place. With a reliable food source, populations grew. People began building towns and cities, and they enhanced agriculture even more through irrigation.

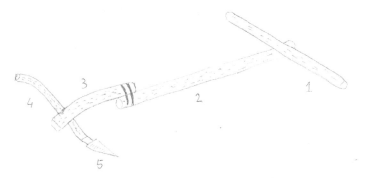

This drawing depicts a primitive ard: a type of ancient plow.
https://commons.wikimedia.org/wiki/File:AncientPlough.jpg

The Mesopotamians gifted us with many things that we consider basic necessities today. Their innovations and inventions have served the world for millennia. Their ingenious developments thousands of years ago intrigue and fascinate us, giving a glimpse of how people lived so long ago and what they did to organize and improve so many aspects of their lives. They must have constantly been brainstorming ways to do things more efficiently and effectively.

Chapter 11: King Hammurabi and His Code

Among the numerous brilliant innovations birthed in Mesopotamia, written legal codes stand out for establishing law, order, and justice in society. King Hammurabi, who ruled Babylon from 1792 to 1750 BCE, was a sensational leader on many fronts. He was a relentless and ruthless conqueror and a canny administrator. But he is most remembered for his detailed legal codes that provided stability and unity for his expanding empire.

Hammurabi's stated goal in writing his law code was "to prevent the strong from oppressing the weak and to see that justice is done to widows and orphans, so that I should enlighten the land, to further the well-being of mankind." His legal treatise wasn't the first; the earliest known law code was Ur-Nammu's, which had been written three centuries earlier. The Assyrians also had a law code. But Hammurabi's was much more extensive; it had a total of 282 laws!

Who was Hammurabi? He was the sixth Amorite king in the First Babylonian Dynasty (1894–1595 BCE). The Amorites were nomadic shepherds, probably from Syria, who swept into Mesopotamia in massive hordes during the Bronze Age Collapse. Hammurabi's predecessors established the modest city-state of Babylon in central Mesopotamia, not far from today's

Baghdad. Babylon only consisted of a small town with surrounding agricultural lands in its early days. But Hammurabi's father, Sin-Muballit, had started consolidating several city-states under Babylonian hegemony.

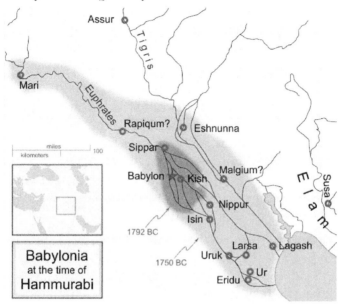

This map shows Babylon in relation to other central and southern Mesopotamian cities.

MapMaster, CC BY-SA 4.0 https://creativecommons.org/licenses/by-sa/4.0 via Wikimedia Commons; https://commons.wikimedia.org/wiki/File:Hammurabi%27s_Babylonia_1.svg

When Hammurabi was crowned king of Babylon, he had to contend with the complex politics of powerful rivals surrounding his minor kingdom. The Sumerian city-state of Eshnunna dominated the northern Tigris region. To the south, the Sumerian city-state of Larsa held supremacy over the Lower Euphrates. The Elamites in the east repeatedly invaded the small southern Mesopotamian city-states, exacting tribute. Although it was beginning to fragment, the formidable Old Assyrian Empire reigned in the north.

What did Hammurabi achieve as king of Babylon? Hammurabi took advantage of the relative peace in his early reign to focus on Babylon's infrastructure. He dug canals to improve the irrigation system, built the city walls higher for more substantial protection, and built and restored temples, championing the worship of Babylon's ancestral god Marduk.

The power-hungry Elamites broke the region's tranquility by invading Mesopotamia's eastern plains and demolishing Eshnunna. The Elamites then attempted to instigate a war between Babylon and Larsa. Their objective was to conquer one or the other or both while the cities were distracted and weakened from fighting each other. However, the two cities didn't fall for the ploy. Instead, they allied and pulverized the Elamites.

The Babylonians were the ones who carried the victory. To Hammurabi's annoyance, Larsa didn't help much, leaving most of the fighting to the Babylonians. Once he settled affairs with Elam, Hammurabi punished his ally for failing to keep their end of the treaty. He annexed Larsa, which controlled most of southern Sumer. The fall of Elam and Larsa began Hammurabi's explosion of expansion, and most of Mesopotamia was brought under Babylon's sway by 1763 BCE.

Hammurabi proceeded to add Eshnunna and Mari to Babylonia's territory. After a protracted war with Assyria, he ousted King Ishme-Dagan I, making his son, Mut-Ashkur, a vassal king who paid tribute to Babylon. As Hammurabi grew his empire, he built Babylon up as a cultural and religious center: the premier "holy city" of Mesopotamia. Many civilizations coexisted in Mesopotamia, but Babylon's prominence as a cultural and spiritual center outlasted the Amorite dynasty.

This portrayal of Babylon shows how the city may have appeared.
https://en.wikipedia.org/wiki/Babylon#/media/File:The_walls_of_Babylon_and_the_te
mple_of_Bel.png

What was Hammurabi's significance in history? His quest to unify and promote peace in all his newly acquired city-states produced the legal treatise for which he is most famous: the Code of Hammurabi. Like the Code of Ur-Nammu, earlier law codes had given attention to compensating victims of crimes. Hammurabi focused on the corporal punishment of criminals and those who disenfranchised the poor and weak. Each crime had a specific penalty. These penalties are harsh by today's standards, but it is important to keep in mind that Hammurabi was actually limiting the harm inflicted when people took matters into their own hands. His law code was among the first to acknowledge the presumption of innocence.

What was Hammurabi's legacy? He was the most honored of the 2nd-millennium BCE Mesopotamian kings, and his subjects perceived him as an earthly representation of a god in his lifetime. After he died, the Babylonians and people from other civilizations revered him as a spectacular conqueror, admiring him for bringing peace, stability, and justice to Mesopotamia. The Babylonians championed his military campaigns as a sacred mission to "force evil into submission" and for spreading civilization and the worship of Babylon's patron god Marduk.

The paramount aspect of Hammurabi's legacy was his role as the consummate lawgiver for Babylon and all of Mesopotamia. Even after the Babylonian Empire faltered under his son, Samsu-iluna, not to mention that the Amorite dynasty completely collapsed 155 years after his death, the Mesopotamians continued to idolize Hammurabi as the paradigm for leadership and justice. When archaeologists discovered this remarkable king in the late 1800s, he rose to preeminence again for his contributions to the history of law.

The Code of Hammurabi contains 282 laws, which set standards for property legislation, trade and commerce, marriage and family, agriculture, employment wages, and regulation of slavery. It stipulated punishment for crimes such as false charges, false testimony, stealing, kidnapping, adultery, incest, and assault. It regulated the work of doctors, veterinarians, barbers, construction workers, and shipbuilders.

Hammurabi had his law code etched onto a black stone pillar that was over seven feet tall. The finger-shaped stele carved from durable diorite weighed four tons! Its surface held up well for four thousand years, but diorite is so hard that it must have been an arduous task to etch the cuneiform script. When archaeologists discovered this massive stele, it was over 250 miles from Babylon in Susa, the capital of the Elamites. How did it get there?

Jean-Jacques de Morgan, a mining engineer from France, headed up an expedition to Iran in 1901 to conduct archaeological excavations in Susa. That's when they dug up Hammurabi's black stele in three pieces. It must have been stolen in the mid-12th century BCE when the Elamites, under their king Shutruk-Nahhunte, raided and plundered Babylon. They took the stele back to Susa as booty, with Marduk's idol and the Kassite king Enlil-nadin-ahi.

The carving on the stele shows Hammurabi and Shamash.
Hammurabi, CC BY 3.0 https://creativecommons.org/licenses/by/3.0 via Wikimedia Commons; https://commons.wikimedia.org/w/index.php?curid=59794940

At the top of the towering stele was a two-and-a-half-foot tall relief carving of Hammurabi with Shamash, the Babylonian god of the sun, justice, and morality. One of the figures is standing, and the other is seated; opinions differ on who is who. The standing figure is probably Hammurabi, lifting his right arm in reverence to Shamash on his throne.

The bottom five feet of the finger-shaped stele have the 282 laws chiseled into the black stone with a cuneiform script. The text is interspersed with statements lauding Hammurabi as a devout and fair-minded king. The inscriptions don't explain the principles behind the laws; they seem to be based on legal precedent. The regulations provide several examples of "an eye for an eye" retribution; for instance, if a man puts out another man's eye, he must have his own eye gouged out. If he breaks another man's bone, his own bone must be broken. If a man knocks out the teeth of his equal, his teeth shall be knocked out in return.

Hammurabi wrote most of the laws in an "if-then" format. For instance, "If anyone steals the minor son of another, he shall be put to death." "If anyone finds runaway male or female slaves in the open country and brings them to their masters, the master of the slaves shall pay him two shekels of silver." "If he puts out the eye of a man's slave or breaks the bone of a man's slave, he shall pay one-half of the slave's value."

You'll notice from that last one that the standard of justice depended on whether the victim was someone higher in rank, a social equal, or an enslaved person. Sometimes the inequity was for the benefit of the slaves and freemen (landless citizens who usually did manual labor for others). For instance, Hammurabi set up a sliding scale for doctor's fees. If the doctor treated a severe wound, his fee would be ten silver shekels for a higher-class citizen, five for a freeman, and two for an enslaved person.

At the top of the stele is the carving of Hammurabi and Shamash.
The law code etched into the stone covers the entire bottom of the monument.

The same scheme applied to malpractice. If a doctor's treatment killed an upper-class citizen, the doctor's hands would be cut off. But if an enslaved person died under his care, he only needed to pay the owner for a new slave. The level of punishment also depended on the social status of the offender. Wealthy, high-ranking citizens only had to pay a fine if they injured commoners, not give up an eye or a tooth.

Although women's rights were closely tied to their fathers or husbands, they did have some protection. For instance, if a man accused a woman of adultery but could not prove it, his "brow shall be marked" (apparently a cut or tattoo). If a man raped a virgin betrothed to another man, he would be executed, and the woman would be blameless. If a man wanted to separate from his wife and mother of his children, he had to give back her dowry (money given by her family when they married) and give her the use of his fields and garden to support her children. When the children were grown, they and their mother would each get a financial portion. Then, the woman could "marry the man of her heart."

Hammurabi took false accusations and false testimonies quite seriously. For instance, if a man accused another of murder but couldn't prove it, the accuser must die. If someone falsely accused you of something, you could prove your innocence by jumping in the river. If you drowned, you were guilty, but if you escaped the waters, you were innocent. Your accuser would have to give his house to you.

Hammurabi held judges to a high standard as well. If a judge heard a case and charged someone a fine, but it was discovered later that the defendant was innocent, the judge would be deemed to have not done due diligence on the case. The judge would have to pay the defendant twelve times the fine he charged. The judge would also be publicly and permanently removed from the judge's bench.

Hammurabi felt the temples should be considered sacred. If anyone stole from the temple, they would be executed, and anyone receiving stolen goods from a temple would likewise die. Anyone dealing in stolen goods of any kind got the death sentence. For instance, what if your favorite earrings went missing, and you saw someone else wearing them, but they swore they honestly bought them from a merchant? Hammurabi said you should bring witnesses to the judge attesting the earrings were yours, and the person who bought the earrings would bring witnesses saying they had paid for them honestly. The merchant would die for being a thief if proven. You would get your earrings back, and the one who bought them would get their money back from the dead merchant's estate.

Hammurabi's laws about husbands divorcing their wives or taking a second wife were fairly strict. The husband had to provide financial support to a divorced wife in most cases. If his first wife became sick with an incurable disease or became disabled, he could not divorce her unless she wanted to leave him. In that case, he had to return her dowry. If she wanted to stay, he could take a second wife, but he had to continue caring for his first wife in his home for the rest of her life.

How was Hammurabi's law code significant? Well, first, let's see what Hammurabi had to say about the implications and relevance of his law code; it's etched on the stele with the laws:

"I have guaranteed security to the inhabitants in their homes; a disturber was not permitted. In Babylon, I have the temple to speak justice in the land, settle all disputes, and heal all injuries. Let the oppressed, who has a case at law, come and stand before this my image as king of righteousness; let him read the inscription and understand my precious words: the inscription will explain his case to him; he will find out what is just, and his heart will be glad."

Did Hammurabi's law code influence the Law of Moses as some scholars contend? Let's consider the logistics. The Israelites lived one thousand miles away in Egypt during Hammurabi's reign, and, according to tradition, Moses wrote the Torah three hundred years after Hammurabi's death. As part of Egypt's royal family, Moses was trained in Egypt's legal system, although the Egyptians may have been aware of Hammurabi's law code. Moses did spend forty years living in Midian (today's Jordan and northwestern Saudi Arabia), but we don't know whether the Bedouins knew or followed Hammurabi's law code.

How similar is Hammurabi's code to the Torah's law? How are they different? They both have the law of restitution; they even mention injury to the eye, bone, and tooth almost word for word. "Anyone who injures their neighbor is to be injured in the same manner: fracture for fracture, eye for eye, tooth for tooth" (Torah, Leviticus 24:19).

In Hammurabi's law code, if a man could not pay a debt, he could sell himself, his wife, his son, or his daughter. They had to work for three years in the house of the man who bought them, and in the fourth year, they would be set free. In the Law of Moses, the same arrangement stood, except they would be set free in the Year of Jubilee, which came every seven years. Moses was adamant that Israelites were *not* to be treated as slaves; in this situation, their master should treat them as hired workers (Torah, Leviticus 25:39-43).

Some laws were similar yet different. For instance, what was the judgment if two men were fighting and one struck a pregnant woman? Hammurabi said that if the woman lost her unborn child, the man who hurt her had to pay ten shekels. But if she died, her assaulter's daughter would be killed. Moses said if the woman had a miscarriage, the man had to pay a fine; if the woman died, her assaulter, *not* his daughter, had to die. Moses was clear that everyone was responsible for their own sin. "Fathers shall not be put to death for their children, nor children for their fathers; each is to die for his own sin" (Torah, Deuteronomy 24:16).

Despite the striking similarities of several secular laws, many of the Torah's laws deal with sacred ceremonies, festivals, and regulations regarding God, such as "Don't worship idols" and "Don't worship any other gods." Hammurabi included nothing of this in his law code, but he had large sections regulating doctors, barbers, housebuilders, and shipbuilders that were not in the Law of Moses.

Interestingly, although Hammurabi said he wrote his laws to defend the orphans and widows, he had no rules expressly offering them protection. But the Torah certainly did, and it provided protection to aliens and the poor in multiple laws, such as, "Do not mistreat or oppress a foreigner, for you were foreigners in Egypt. Do not take advantage of the widow or the fatherless" (Torah, Exodus 22:21-22).

As we consider the historical significance of Hammurabi's laws, some are cringe-worthy by today's standards. Most of the punishments in the Code of Hammurabi were brutally harsh, such as cutting off someone's breast, ears, hands, or tongue. On the other hand, Hammurabi was a forerunner in promoting legal concepts like considering an accused person innocent until proven guilty. His laws recognized a defendant's intentions: was the crime willful or accidental? Today, most legal codes consider premeditation, the intent to cause harm, and mitigating circumstances. In this regard, Hammurabi's law code served as a prototype for modern laws.

Chapter 12: Zoroastrianism

Zoroastrianism, one of the world's oldest religions still practiced today, emerged as Mesopotamia's primary religious school of thought during the Persian dynasties, beginning in the 5th century BCE. An especially notable aspect of Zoroastrianism was something approaching monotheism: the belief in one god. The other ancient Mesopotamians were polytheistic, except for the Jews. This means they worshiped many gods. Let's explore the origins of Zoroastrianism, their beliefs, and their core values.

Zoroastrianism's origins are somewhat obscure because no written documentation of this religion existed before 440 BCE. When the Greek historian Herodotus wrote about the Persians in general, he mentioned some customs that probably were Zoroastrian, although he didn't name them. He said they had no idols or temples but offered animal sacrifices to Zeus on the highest mountains. (He likely meant Ahura Mazda when he said Zeus.) He said they also offered sacrifices to the sun, moon, earth, fire, water, and winds. Herodotus said they worshiped the god they called Mithra. (Mithra was a Vedic god who became a Zoroastrian *yazata*, a lesser deity). Herodotus mentioned "sky burials," which means they left corpses exposed after death, a Zoroastrian custom. Other Mesopotamian civilizations buried their dead.

The Zoroastrians passed down their religious heritage orally. They did not write it down until they produced a master copy of the Avesta (their original scripture) in the 5th century CE during the Sasanian Empire. They didn't record any founding dates, but most scholars believe the religion probably emerged between 1500 to 600 BCE in northeastern Iran. It then spread south and west, infiltrating Mesopotamia.

Some scholars believe the Gonur Depe archaeological site in Turkmenistan (which dates from 2400 to 1600 BCE) suggests an earlier existence of Zoroastrianism because archaeologists found temples with fire altars and a preparation area for the *soma* (*haoma*) drink that is part of Zoroastrian worship. But the Vedic religion, which gave birth to Zoroastrianism, existed in that region during that period; fire sacrifices and the intoxicating soma drink were intrinsic to Vedic worship as well.

In 550 BCE, Persia's Achaemenid Empire rose to dominance over the Middle East and beyond, and Zoroastrianism surged in popularity during this era. It quickly spread east to modern-day India, Pakistan, Afghanistan, Tajikistan, Kyrgyzstan, Uzbekistan, and Turkmenistan. It spread west around the Black Sea to Turkey, Macedonia, and Greece, down the Mediterranean to Syria, Lebanon, and Israel, and south to Egypt and Libya.

What were the other major religions of ancient Mesopotamia when Zoroastrianism emerged? Most ancient Mesopotamians were polytheistic, worshiping a similar pantheon of gods, which included Anu, Ea, Shamash, and Ishtar, with some local deities rising to prominence like Marduk and Ashur. Abraham of Ur abandoned his father Terah's polytheism to become the monotheistic patriarch of the Israelites around 2100 BCE. Moses established Judaism as a monotheistic religion at Mount Sinai in 1446 BCE.

Did Judaism influence Zoroastrianism or vice versa? Both religions share core theology but also have differences. For instance, the Jews practiced circumcision, and the Zoroastrians did not. The Zoroastrians prayed to Azura Mazda and lesser deities like Anahita and Mithra. In contrast, Jews prayed only to YHWH (Jehovah) and believed angels were God's messengers but were not meant to be worshiped.

The Assyrians and Babylonians had exiled most of the Jewish population to Babylon or other places in Mesopotamia, beginning with Tiglath-Pileser III of Assyria in 733 BCE and ending with Nebuchadnezzar of Babylonia in 597 BCE. The Jews would have interacted with the Persian Zoroastrians even before Cyrus conquered Babylon and certainly after.

Who founded Zoroastrianism? Around 1500 to 1200 BCE, perhaps even more recently, a man named Zarathustra (later called Zoroaster by the Greeks) lived in the region bordering today's Iran and Afghanistan. He belonged to the Spitama clan: an Indo-Iranian nomadic herding tribe that practiced the polytheistic Vedic religion. The Vedic worshipers had no temples or idols but offered animal sacrifices to a sacred fire and consumed a mind-altering drink from the soma plant.

The Dakmeh (Tower of Silence) in Yazd, Iran, is where Zoroastrians left bodies for vultures to eat. They believed this prevented decaying bodies from polluting the soil.

Fars Media Corporation, CC BY 4.0 https://creativecommons.org/licenses/by/4.0 via Wikimedia Commons;

https://commons.wikimedia.org/wiki/File:Zoroastrians%27_Dakhmeh_of_Yazd_20190316_02.jpg

Zarathustra was a married Vedic priest with three sons and three daughters. While engaging in a Vedic purification rite at the age of thirty, he had a vision of a supreme being: Ahura Mazda ("Wise Lord"). After this epiphany, Zarathustra repudiated Vedic polytheism and began teaching his disciples to worship Ahura Mazda. He wrote hymns (the Gathas) to this god, helping the people to understand Ahura Mazda's nature. His followers called themselves Zartoshtis or Zoroastrians.

Some believe Cyrus the Great (Cyrus II), King of Persia, was a Zoroastrian. Zarathustra's teachings may have influenced him, but we have no evidence that Cyrus practiced Zoroastrianism, although it became popular under his reign. Cyrus never mentioned the god Ahura Mazda in any of his inscriptions. He did have an inscription legitimizing his rule that said the Babylonian god Marduk appointed him as king. The Ketuvim records that in his first year as king, Cyrus sent a proclamation saying the God of heaven had appointed him to rebuild the Jewish temple at Jerusalem. Cyrus returned the items Nebuchadnezzar had looted from the Temple in Jerusalem to the Jewish exiles returning to Jerusalem (Ketuvim, Ezra 1).

At any rate, within several decades, Zoroastrianism became the de facto religion of the Achaemenid Empire. Darius I (r. 522-486 BCE) was the first Persian king known to worship Ahura Mazda. The Persian kings were highly tolerant of other religions and did not force conversions of conquered people. However, as the Persian Empire spread, Zoroastrianism spread with it.

What do Zoroastrians believe? They worship Ahura Mazda: the completely good, uncreated, universal god who created the world. However, they also worship the Amesha Spenta and *yazatas*. These beings are hard to explain; they are created yet immortal. They seem to be "divine sparks" or lesser divine entities. They are sometimes compared to the angels and archangels of Judeo-Christianity. However, the Zoroastrian priests invoke them by name in their hymns and prayers as if they were deities, and some Persian kings built temples to these lesser divinities.

Most of the seven Amesha Spentas and dozens of *yazatas* were gods and goddesses in the ancient Vedic religion or Iranian pantheon, and some are deities in today's Hinduism. During Artaxerxes II's' reign, he invoked the deities Mithra, god of the sun, and Anahita, goddess of water, alongside Ahura Mazda. He built temples and statues to Anahita in Babylon, Ecbatana, and Susa. The Sasanian dynasty repaired and maintained Anahita's temple in Istakhr.

It is not entirely accurate to define Zoroastrianism as a monotheistic religion, although it was closer to monotheism than the polytheistic pantheons of Mesopotamia and surrounding civilizations. Clearly, Ahura Mazda is the chief divinity who created these other deities, and Zoroastrianism teaches they are under him as emanations of his divine power.

Zoroastrianism is a dualistic religion, meaning the world has two competing forces. The first force is goodness and light, represented by the Amesha Spenta: the "Bountiful Immortals who are good rulers and possessing good sense." Goodness and light struggle against darkness and evil, represented by Ahriman, who is something like Satan. Goodness and evil both exist but separately and in opposition. The goal is to incapacitate Ahriman and the evil and darkness accompanying him. This dualism involves both cosmic forces of the universe and moral forces of the mind.

The dualism of cosmic forces encompasses the continuing antagonism between good and evil in the universe. While the good god Ahura Mazda is at war against the evil Ahriman (Angra Mainyu), they are not opposites in the sense of being equal, similar to how YHWH (Jehovah) of Judeo-Christian theology is not equal to Satan but above him. Angra Mainyu (Ahriman) is the toxic evil energy combating Ahura Mazda's perfect creative energy.

Cosmic dualism means day and night, good and evil, and life and death. Ahriman persistently attacks the pure and perfect world Ahura Mazda created, polluting it with sickness, death, drought, famine, and other calamities. The *daevas* (demons) assist in his evil quest as the adversary of all that is good and true. The *daevas* were ancient Vedic deities of war and violence that became evil spirits in Zoroastrianism.

Moral dualism goes on in a person's mind and spirit in the battle between good and evil. Zoroastrians believe in free will; each person chooses to either follow *Asha* (truth and righteousness) or *Drui* (deceit and evil). One's choice determines their destiny: misery in life and hell after death for those who choose Drui or peace in life and heaven for those who select Asha. A person's choices bring either joy or distress, truth or falsehoods, peace or anxiety. The choices one makes determine whether they are helping Ahura Mazda or Angra Mainyu.

All mankind must choose Asha over Drui to conquer evil and bring paradise to Earth. Zoroastrianism holds a firm belief in heaven and hell and a day of judgment. At the end of the world, everything will return to its pristine and perfect state. Even people who made the wrong choices in life, the damned ones, will, in the fullness of time, reunite with Ahura Mazda in heaven as he ultimately prevails over evil.

Zoroastrianism's core teachings include following the path of good thoughts, good words, and virtuous deeds. One does not practice goodness to earn any reward; rather, one should be good for the sake of goodness. Zoroastrianism teaches that practicing charity spreads happiness and aligns one's soul with Asha. Men and women are spiritually equal and share spiritual duties.

For some reason, the Zoroastrians apparently did not have written scriptures for hundreds of years. The religion arose in a nomadic tribe, so the people were perhaps more accustomed to singing and telling their traditions. But even when they assimilated into the literate Persian culture, they still didn't write down any scriptures, or at least any that were preserved. There may have been some scrolls that Alexander the Great destroyed when he burned down Persepolis (a religious center in Iran) around 330 BCE. It seems that the mobeds, the Zoroastrian priestly caste, memorized and transmitted their teachings orally for at least one thousand years until the late Sassanian Empire, around 550 CE.

This sacred flame in the Yazd temple in Iran has reportedly burned since 470 CE.
David Stanley from Nanaimo, Canada, CC BY 2.0 https://creativecommons.org/licenses/by/2.0
via Wikimedia Commons; Photo modified: zoomed in;
https://commons.wikimedia.org/wiki/File:Sacred_Eternal_Flame_(8906006775).jpg

When the Zoroastrians finally wrote their scriptures down, they developed an alphabet expressly for their holy book. They used letters from Persia's old Pahlavi script, a descendent of the Aramaic alphabet, which, like Hebrew and Arabic, was read from right to left and contained only consonants. The Zoroastrians added in Greek vowel sounds.

The oldest Zoroastrian scripture is the Avesta, named after the ancient Iranian language Avestan. The oldest section of the Avesta is the Gathas, which means "a divine song, a song of praise, a sacred hymn." These were five metrical compositions of the Prophet Zarathustra to worship Ahura Mazda, the Amesha Spenta (or Spenta Mainyu, the seven created immortal gods or archangels), and the *yazatas* (lesser gods or angels). The priests sang these scriptures or chanted them from memory.

When they were finally written down, these five hymns filled seventeen chapters. The Gathas also included several sacred prayers used in the Zoroastrian worship liturgy, and they were considered the source of spiritual nourishment and protection for the soul. Zarathustra's disciples composed the rest of the Avesta, the core teachings. Then, priests memorized these scriptures, recited them in worship, and passed them down through the centuries.

The Khordeh Avesta (meaning the little, minor, or younger Avesta) is the second part of Zoroastrianism's sacred scriptures, and it is much longer than the first. It contains a confession of faith, commentaries, short readings on the earlier Avesta, prayers for various times of the day, and details for observing rituals. It's something like the Book of Common Prayer. These scriptures aren't nearly as ancient as the Avesta, and there isn't even a standard text; different publications vary concerning the contents. They were likely composed in the late Sassanian period or even later. The Khordeh Avesta was probably memorized along with the Avesta, although the "Zand" section on exegesis was more of a work in progress. It tended to be changed and lengthened.

The two most important symbols of Zoroastrianism are water and fire, which represent purity. Purification is an essential concept of Zoroastrian daily life and religious rituals. As part of the quest to overcome evil, they endeavor to keep their minds and bodies clean and clear and strive for a pristine environment. Fire represents the zenith of purity. Water is a living element protected by Anahita (the ancient Iranian goddess of water, fertility, wisdom, and healing who became a *yazata* in Zoroastrianism).

Zoroastrian ceremonies and rituals are always performed in the presence of sacred fire. They sometimes worship in "fire temples" or Agiaries, which have an altar with a continuously burning eternal flame. They believe that three of their ancient temples, the "great fires," came from Ahura Mazda when the world was created. The fires represent Ahura Mazda's light, which illuminates the mind; thus, the fires must burn perpetually.

Zoroastrians practice the prayer ritual of Yasna daily, which honors creation. It begins by drawing water from the Agiary for purification. The Yasna service is directed toward Anahita, displaying the reverence for water. Yasna also involves rituals of preparing the sacred beverage (soma or haoma), which they drink with a bread offering. Yasna is meant to maintain the cosmic integrity of Ahura Mazda's perfect creation.

The Yasna includes devotional texts from the Khordeh Avesta, which are recited by priests and lay members. Twenty-one hymns are chanted to the *yazatas* or lesser deities under Ahura Mazda. In the ceremony, the priests ask theoretical questions of Ahura Mazda, such as the creation of the world and who set the sun and stars on their paths. Each day of the month in the Zoroastrian calendar is devoted to a *yazata*, and a hymn is recited to the deity of the day. Various short prayers and blessings are also recited. Attending the Yasna service helps maintain good actions, thoughts, and words and ward off the forces of evil. Zoroastrians pray facing the fire or sun, which represents Ahura Mazda.

In ancient times, Zoroastrians practiced "sky burials" in their *dakhmas* or "towers of silence." These were tall, flat-topped structures where they placed dead bodies, which vultures would eat. In their minds, burying a dead person meant defiling the pristine earth with a decaying corpse. Once the bones were clean and bleached by the sun, the people gathered and placed them in ossuaries (lime pits). Today, the Parsi Zoroastrians of Mumbai,

India, still practice this sky burial custom.

Sky burial is also practiced today by the Tibetan tantric Buddhists and was practiced by Mongolian Vajrayāna Buddhists before communist rule. The ancient Vedic religion that gave birth to Zoroastrianism also practiced sky burials. The Vedic religion shaped Hinduism and prescribed sky burials in the *Paingala Upanishad,* an Indian Vedic scripture, although feeding dead loved ones to vultures never really took off in India. But Hinduism gave birth to Buddhism, and the tantric-Vajrayāna division of Buddhism carried the practice of sky burials to Tibet and Mongolia.

The Faravahar became a Zoroastrian symbol in the Achaemenid Dynasty.

An ancient symbol of Zoroastrianism is the Faravahar: a bearded man reaching one hand forward and holding a ring in the other. He stands or sits in front of a pair of wings outstretched from another circle. The symbol of the wings and wheel goes back to ancient Egypt, predating Zoroastrianism, but the wheel and wings with the man appeared in Zoroastrian art around 550 BCE. No one is quite sure what it symbolized in ancient times, but the circles may represent eternal life. Today, it is the national symbol of Iran.

As with most religions, festivals and holy days play a vital role in the Zoroastrian faith. Six festivals relate to the seasons and predate Zoroastrianism. Nowruz celebrates the New Year on the day of the spring equinox. Other festivals relate to the *yazatas*, the lesser gods or angels in Zoroastrianism who were Vedic deities, like Mithra, Anahita, Atar, Rashnu, Sraosha, and Verethraghna.

The Navjote or *Sedreh-Pushi* is an initiation ceremony that receives children into the Zoroastrian faith. This occurs sometime between their seventh to twelfth birthday. Each child receives their first kusti and sudreh (a sacred cord and shirt) and engages in the "kusti ritual," where they tie the kusti cord three times around the sudreh shirt. This ceremony represents the Zoroastrian ideals of "good words, good thoughts, and good actions" and is led by a priest called a *mobed*.

Whatever happened to Zoroastrianism? For about one thousand years, Zoroastrianism was the de facto religion of three Persian empires: the Achaemenid (550–330 BCE), Parthian (247 BCE–224 CE), and Sasanian (224–651 CE). The Muslim-Arab conquest of Persia defeated the Sasanian Empire in 651 CE and broke Zoroastrianism's dominant influence over the Middle East. The Islamic Arabs forced the Zoroastrians to pay extra taxes for continuing their religion.

Islam had a three-fold effect on Iranian Zoroastrians. Some converted to Islam, and others continued to practice Zoroastrianism in remote, rural areas; they still do in the desert communities of Yazd and Kerman in Iran. A mass exodus of Zoroastrians, especially the priests and their families, sailed over the Arabian Sea to Gujarat in western India between 785 to 936 CE. The Indians called them Parsis, and they were influential during the British rule over India.

How widespread is Zoroastrianism today? They continue as a religious minority of up to thirty thousand devotees in Iran. About 60,000 Parsi in India and 1,400 in Pakistan continue as Zoroastrians. Worldwide Zoroastrian diaspora communities are especially prevalent in North America, Australia, and Britain, with up to 200,000 worshipers. Freddie Mercury, the lead singer of the rock band Queen, was of Parsi descent. He practiced Zoroastrianism and was buried with rites by a Zoroastrian priest.

Do you wonder if there's a connection between the god Ahura Mazda and the Japanese car? Yes, there is! It was a play on words. The pronunciation of the car company's founder Matsuda was similar to the god Mazda. But how would the Japanese know about Mazda? In Uzbekistan and Afghanistan, the worship of Buddha and Ahura Mazda syncretized in the 1st century CE; they had a Buddha-Mazda. Esoteric Buddhists took the worship of Buddha-Mazda, the god of light, to China and Japan, where it's still practiced. The Japanese were familiar with Mazda, the god of light, so the new company adopted Mazda's name as a "light" in the car industry.

SECTION FOUR: HERE COME THE PERSIANS (550 BCE–330 BCE)

Chapter 13: The Achaemenid Empire Rises

The spectacular Achaemenid Empire, founded in 550 BCE by Cyrus the Great, ranks as the world's first superpower; it had been the most extensive empire at this time. It brought three major global regions—Mesopotamia, India, and North Africa—under one central government. This cultural intermingling created a dynamic surge in science, technology, and culture that persisted for over two centuries before the empire fell to Alexander the Great in 330 BCE.

From Egypt and Libya to the south, the colossal empire stretched up and around the Mediterranean, west to northern Greece and Macedonia. It spread north, encircled most of the Black Sea, then east to the southern Caspian Sea, then northeast to present-day Kazakhstan, down to India, and back west along the Arabian Sea, around the Persian Gulf, and across the Arabian Peninsula.

Valuable knowledge about the awe-inspiring Persian Empire comes from several sources, including Herodotus's *Histories*. He was born into a Greek family in Anatolia around 484 BCE, when it was part of the Achaemenid Empire. His family participated in the Greek insurrection against Persia, so he wrote about the Greco-Persian Wars from the opposition's perspective. He focused on the Persian court's immorality, extravagant luxury, and political intrigues.

In the Tanakh (Old Testament), we have insider information from two Jews within the Persian palace. The first was Daniel (Belteshazzar), one of three administrators for the satraps (Persian governors) under Cyrus the Great. The other was Nehemiah, cupbearer to King Artaxerxes I. Another valuable source is Xenophon, who was born around 430 BCE. He was a Greek who fought as a mercenary for the Persians and wrote *Cyropaedia*, a biography of Cyrus the Great.

The First Persian Empire is often called the Achaemenid Empire after Achaemenes: an obscure ancestor of some, if not all, of the kings of the First Persian Empire. The Persians were nomadic Indo-Iranian herders from the north and east of Iran who settled in southwestern Iran's Persis region by the 9th century BCE. The Assyrians dominated them initially and then Babylon, but the Persians allied with the Medes around 612 BCE to get out from under Babylonian hegemony.

Cyrus II created the largest empire yet seen in the ancient world.
Arya.Go, CC BY-SA 4.0 https://creativecommons.org/licenses/by-sa/4.0 via Wikimedia Commons; https://commons.wikimedia.org/wiki/File:Cyrus_the_Great_II.jpg

Xenophon recorded that Cyrus II (Cyrus the Great) was the son of King Cambyses of Anshan (Persia) and the grandson of King Astyages of Media, his mother's father. His parent's marriage represented the alliance of the Medes and Persians against Babylonian control; however, the Medes originally held overlordship. Cyrus married his beloved Cassandane, who was also of the Achaemenid dynasty, and became king of Persia in 559 BCE upon his father's death. He took the throne name Cyrus II after his paternal grandfather, Cyrus I; his birth name was Agradates.

The Babylonian Nabonidus Chronicle records that his grandfather King Astyages attacked the Persian kingdom because his grandson Cyrus refused to submit to Median overlordship. However, Astyages's army and some nobility defected to Cyrus during the three-year struggle. Finally, Cyrus captured his grandfather, but he spared his life. The Medes and Persians renewed their alliance, but the Persians now held overlordship.

Although Herodotus said that Cyrus became king of both the Medes and Persians after the war with his grandfather, the historian Xenophon recorded in *Cyropaedia* that Astyages's son, Cyaxares II, became king of the Medes at this point. Perhaps both accounts are correct; Cyaxares was likely a vassal king under his nephew Cyrus. Inscriptions on the Harran Stele, depictions on the Persepolis reliefs, and the Greek Aeschylus's *The Persians* support Xenophon on this.

Xenophon said that after conquering Babylon, Cyrus gave his uncle Cyaxares, King of Media, a palace in Babylon. Cyaxares II gave his daughter to Cyrus in marriage (Cyrus's first wife Cassandane had died shortly before Babylon fell, according to the Nabonidus Chronicle). Some scholars believe that Cyaxares II's throne name was Darius and that he was the Darius the Mede who Daniel said conquered Babylon at the age of sixty-two and then briefly administered Babylon (Ketuvim: Daniel 5-6).

Cyrus is mentioned twenty-three times in the Tanakh (Old Testament). Isaiah, a prophet in Jerusalem when the Assyrian king Sennacherib besieged it, wrote this prophecy about Cyrus 150 years before Cyrus ascended Persia's throne:

"This is what the LORD says to Cyrus His anointed,

whose right hand I have grasped to subdue nations before him, to disarm kings,

to open the doors before him, so that the gates will not be shut:

'I will go before you and level the mountains;

I will break down the gates of bronze and cut through the bars of iron.

I will give you the treasures of darkness and the riches hidden in secret places,

so that you may know that I am the LORD, the God of Israel, who calls you by name.

For the sake of Jacob, My servant, and Israel, My chosen one, I call you by name;

I have given you a title of honor, though you have not known Me.

I am the LORD, and there is no other; there is no god but Me.

I will equip you for battle, though you have not known Me,

so that all may know, from where the sun rises to where it sets,

that there is none but Me; I am the LORD, and there is no other.'"

(Nevi'im, Isaiah 45)

Once Cyrus II gained dominance over both Persia and Media, what were his next empire-building moves? The Medes had vassal governments under their control, which became part of the Persian Empire. These included Bactria (modern-day Tajikistan and Uzbekistan), Parthia (northeastern Iran), and the nomadic Saka, who roamed the Eurasian Steppe and China's Xinjiang region. Cyrus assigned satraps (governors) to rule these provinces; some were the governors already in place, while others were Cyrus's relatives.

King Croesus of Lydia in western Asia Minor tried to take advantage of the power shift by attempting to conquer Asia

Minor's former Median territory. Cyrus counterattacked in a drawn-out, indecisive battle in Cappadocia. Croesus withdrew for the winter but planned to renew the war in the spring with new allies. He didn't expect Cyrus to lead his forces in a lightning strike through Lydia. Cyrus reached the capital of Sardis before Croesus had any inkling he was coming.

Croesus mustered 420,000 men and met Cyrus's forces of 196,000 Medes and Persians. Cyrus ingeniously put his three hundred camels in front; the Lydian horses had not seen or smelled camels and charged off in a panic. After a cataclysmic loss, Croesus fled inside the city, but Cyrus had six siege towers! Sardis fell in two weeks, making Lydia part of the Persian Empire. Cyrus ordered Croesus to be burned to death, but he had a change of heart and ordered the flames to be extinguished. Croesus became an advisor.

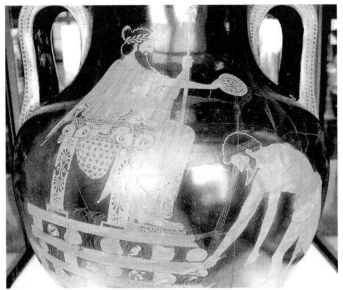

This Attica pottery depicts Croesus' execution, from which he was rescued!

Once Lydia was conquered, the Greek colony of Ionia on the Aegean coast lay wide open to Cyrus. In 547 BCE, Cyrus's powerful empire embarked on the beginnings of its clash with Greece's far-flung city-states. The shattering collapse of the Ionian League's twelve Greek city-states sent shockwaves through the Greek world. As with other lands conquered by Cyrus, the

Ionians paid tribute and supplied men for the Achaemenid army but maintained some local autonomy for the next three centuries.

From 547 to 539 BCE, Cyrus campaigned against the Sogdian nomads, who roamed the lands north of Bactria, where modern-day Uzbekistan, Tajikistan, Kazakhstan, and Kyrgyzstan meet. Once Sogdiana was conquered, it remained under Persian control until around 400 BCE. It paid a tribute of semi-precious stones, namely lapis lazuli and carnelian. Meanwhile, Cyrus's general Harpagus conquered the rest of Asia Minor, taking Lycia and Cilicia on the Mediterranean coast.

The ancient Phoenicians, whose territory stretched down the Mediterranean coast from Syria through Lebanon to Galilee, pragmatically surrendered to the Persians. Other than paying an annual tribute of 350 talents, their kings remained in power. Their maritime technology and ships proved to be an asset to the Achaemenids in the Greco-Persian Wars. The Persians annexed Elam, which had been weakened by the Assyrians and Medes, around 542 BCE.

Cyrus now turned his focus to the great Neo-Babylonian Empire, which controlled Mesopotamia, Arabia, and the Levant. In 539 BCE, his army forded the Tigris in autumn when the river was at its lowest ebb. They crossed at Opis at the northern end of the Median Wall, which had been built by Nebuchadnezzar II to keep the Medes out. The Babylonians met the Medes and Persians at the riverbank, and the ensuing battle was a brutal loss for the Babylonians.

Cyrus's troops then marched into Babylon with hardly any resistance. The army carefully protected the temples and sacred sites of the holy city, ensuring that rituals continued as usual. By taking Babylon, Cyrus was taking all of Mesopotamia, which was mainly under Babylonian control. He proclaimed himself "King of Babylon, King of Sumer and Akkad, King of the four corners of the world."

The Jewish historian Josephus wrote in the *Antiquities of the Jews* that the exiled Jews in Babylon, from at least two population-relocation programs, showed Isaiah's prophecy to Cyrus. This motivated him to allow the Jews to return to Israel and rebuild their temple.

"In the first year of King Cyrus, he issued a decree concerning the house of God in Jerusalem:

'Let the house be rebuilt as a place for offering sacrifices, and let its foundations be firmly laid. It is to be sixty cubits high and sixty cubits wide, with three layers of cut stones and one of timbers. The costs are to be paid from the royal treasury.

Furthermore, the gold and silver articles of the house of God, which Nebuchadnezzar took from the temple in Jerusalem and carried to Babylon, must also be returned to the temple in Jerusalem and deposited in the house of God.'"

(Ketuvim, Ezra 6:3-5)

Once Cyrus had control of Mesopotamia, he quickly took possession of Israel, Syria, and northern Arabia. Cyrus died at the age of seventy. He was killed in a battle against Queen Tomyris of the Massagetae, a people of the lower Eurasian Steppe. When he died in 530 BCE, his mighty Achaemenid Empire stretched from the Indus River to Asia Minor. Cyrus won the admiration of the people he conquered by respecting their religions and customs, permitting broad autonomy, and governing for his subjects' profit and advantage. He established a successful centralized administrative model through satraps (governors) of the provinces.

When Cyrus's son Cambyses ascended the throne, he set out to achieve one of his father's unfulfilled goals: conquering Egypt. In 525 BCE, he besieged the Egyptian capital of Memphis in the Nile Delta, achieving victory in ten days. He next conquered the Cyrenaica region of Libya. While consolidating Persia's new African territories, an attempted coup in Persia demanded his attention. As Cambyses hurried home, one of his injuries became gangrenous. He died of sepsis in 522 BCE.

Cambyses was childless, so his younger brother should have succeeded him; however, he died mysteriously just before or after Cambyses's death; he was likely murdered. Rising from obscurity, Darius I (also known as Darius the Great) usurped the throne. Darius was supposedly a descendant of Achaemenes from a different line than Cyrus. He stabilized the empire, built infrastructure, and conquered northwestern India, expanding the empire to its greatest size.

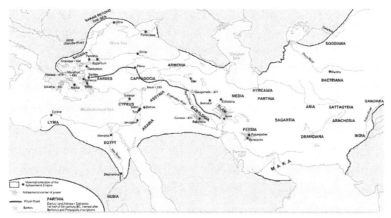

The Achaemenid Empire reached its most extensive size under Darius I.

Fabienkhan, CC BY-SA 2.5 <https://creativecommons.org/licenses/by-sa/2.5>, via Wikimedia Commons https://commons.wikimedia.org/wiki/File:Map_achaemenid_empire_en.png

In 499 BCE, Ionia allied with the Greek city-states of Athens and Eretria, sacking and burning Sardis in a rebellion against the Persians. King Darius's troops massacred most of the Greek forces outside of Ephesus, and the Ionian insurrection imploded. But Darius seethed with rage against Greece's Eretria and Athens for intruding in his empire's affairs, and he vowed revenge. In 492 BCE, he invaded Thrace and Macedonia, adding them to the Persian Empire, then set sail for Greece. But a brutal storm obliterated most of his ships, forcing him to limp home to Persia.

While rebuilding his fleet, Darius sent his delegates to all the Greek city-states, demanding they submit to the Achaemenid Empire. All the city-states capitulated, except Sparta and Athens. Infuriated, Darius sailed across the Aegean in 490 BCE. He flattened Eritrea, then landed in Marathon, twenty-five miles from Athens. The Athenians marched across the Attica Peninsula to meet Darius in Marathon, knowing its mountainous, swampy terrain would render Darius's cavalry useless, as they would be unable to easily maneuver. Sinking in the quagmire and unnerved by the Greek hoplite battle formation, the Persians panicked and fled, losing 6,400 soldiers to the Greek's 203 casualties.

Darius's son, Xerxes I, vowed to avenge his father's humiliating loss to Athens. While preparing for his campaign, his Phoenician engineers accomplished an astonishing feat. They built a one-mile bridge over the Hellespont (the Dardanelles Strait), which allowed Xerxes's massive army to march overland to Greece. The engineers constructed a two-span bridge over the 180-foot-deep waterway by lashing 674 ships together, then building a wooden-plank bridge over the ships' decks.

Xerxes's bridge over the Dardanelles spanned one mile over stormy, churning water.
https://commons.wikimedia.org/wiki/File:Construction_of_Xerxes_Bridge_of_boats_b y_Phoenician_sailors.jpg

But then a fierce storm hit, breaking the bridge into pieces. Xerxes was furious; he ordered the engineers to be decapitated, then punished the recalcitrant waterway itself, branding it with red-hot irons and beating it with three hundred lashes! The Phoenicians reassembled the bridge, and the enormous army crossed over to Europe, heading toward Greece. Meanwhile, a Persian fleet of 1,200 ships sailed across the Aegean.

No Greek city-states offered opposition until Xerxes came to the Thermopylae Pass, where seven thousand men from Sparta, Thespiae, and Thebes blocked the narrow fifty-foot-wide mountain pass guarding southern Greece. The Greek coalition held off the large Persian army for two days, fighting to the last man. After getting through the pass, Xerxes swiftly gained control of mainland Greece but received the troubling news that two savage storms had sunk two-thirds of his fleet.

Meanwhile, the Athenians abandoned their city, fleeing to the island of Salamis, where they joined up with the Greek fleet that had withdrawn to the island. Xerxes commanded what was left of his fleet, four hundred ships, to sail to Salamis. Queen Artemisia of Halicarnassus, one of Xerxes's naval commanders, warned him against fighting in the straits. Xerxes was confident that his ships would win the day and ignored her concerns.

Xerxes didn't know that three hundred Greek ships were hiding out of sight behind an island. Once his fleet entered the strait, the Greek ships surrounded him. Singing a triumphant hymn to Apollo, they crushed the Persian ships with their battering rams. Corpses and the remains of wrecked ships floated in the water as the Greeks plowed into one Persian vessel after another. The Salamis victory was a watershed moment. The Persians had been the aggressors up to this point, and now they switched to the defensive.

With winter approaching and trouble stirring back home, a demoralized Xerxes returned to Persia, never to return to Greece. He hurried back to crush a revolt in Babylon. Several years later, Xerxes was dead, assassinated by his bodyguard commander in 465 BCE. His son Artaxerxes made no more attempts to expand Persia's hegemony over Greece. His cupbearer Nehemiah and the Jewish priest Ezra both recorded Artaxerxes's generous and kind demeanor toward his subjects. Artaxerxes consolidated and organized the massive Persian Empire throughout his long reign.

What was the significance of Persia's monumental rise in the ancient world? The Achaemenid Empire's surging ascent under Cyrus's rule profoundly impacted world history. Iran's literature, philosophy, and religions played a commanding role in global affairs for the next thousand years. The Achaemenid Empire and the two Persian dynasties that followed revered Cyrus as their father and a role model in leadership.

This brilliant founder of a soaring empire deeply impressed the Greeks. Xenophon praised Cyrus's keen administrative abilities and heroism in war. After reading Xenophon's *Cyropaedia* as a child, Alexander the Great was entranced by Cyrus and Persia. Even though Alexander conquered Persia, he set himself up as the next Cyrus, wearing Persian clothing, adopting Persian customs, and setting up his center of operations in Persia. He never returned home to Macedonia.

The Achaemenid Empire greatly impacted the cultural identity and heritage of the Middle East, Asia, and Europe. At its zenith, the empire reigned over an unprecedented 44 percent of the global population, influencing future empires' structure and development. The genius administrative model of the Achaemenid Empire served as a prototype for the Greek and Roman empires.

Chapter 14: Everyday Life in Persia

Everyday life in the Persian Empire depended on where one lived; after all, it spanned three continents and encompassed hundreds of civilizations and languages. Even the ethnic Persians practiced different customs depending on their ancestral background and assimilation with neighboring cultures. This chapter will look at empire-wide factors and others indigenous to Persia on a journey of life in the Persian Empire.

Cyrus the Great had not just one but four capitals serving as administrative centers of his massive empire. Cyrus built Pasargadae, located ninety kilometers (fifty-six miles) northeast of modern-day Shiraz, Iran. The other capital cities were Babylon, Susa (the ancient Elamite capital), and Ecbatana in western Iran. He likely moved from city to city depending on the seasons and which regions demanded his attention. The Tanakh mentions his successors living in Susa.

How did life change for people in the countries conquered by Persia? When the Persians conquered a region, the Persian king or his general might stay long enough to organize a local government and assign leaders; after that, he would generally leave the day-to-day administration to the satraps (governors). The people living in a newly conquered region would not experience much change in their daily lives, and they continued in their religious practices and customs.

The main change was their governments now had to pay tribute (a sort of tax) to Persia. Tribute could be in the form of money or in goods that were a specialty of the area: gemstones, metal, cloth, leather, or any number of items. Unlike the Assyrian Empire, which bled the provinces dry, the Persians' tribute system was sustainable, or at least it was until the Greco-Persian Wars drained the treasury.

This gold daric coin represented the universal currency Darius I instituted. *Classical Numismatic Group, Inc.* http://www.cngcoins.com *CC BY-SA 2.5* https://creativecommons.org/licenses/by-sa/2.5 *via Wikimedia Commons;* https://commons.wikimedia.org/wiki/File:Daric_coin_of_the_Achaemenid_Empire_(D arius_I_to_Xerxes_II).jpg

Darius the Great initiated a coordinated tax system based on each province's economy, assets, and productivity. Wealthy Babylon paid the highest tribute. It had to provide enough food to feed the army for four months and pay one thousand silver talents. India paid its tribute in gold. Egypt's vast farms in the Nile River Delta provided 120,000 measures of grain for the empire (and later served as Athens's and Rome's granaries). Egypt also paid 700 silver talents. If a conquered region proved too ungovernable, the population could be enslaved. The Persian Empire registered and charged a sales tax on the slave markets. Other tariffs on trade provided valuable income for the empire.

Life in the Persian Empire sometimes meant heavy taxes, especially after the disastrous Greco-Persian Wars decimated the Persian fleet multiple times. The military campaign also required mammoth resources and food for its large army. The territories around the empire would occasionally attempt to overthrow their Persian overlords, especially toward the end of the Achaemenid

Empire when taxes were higher and the kings less benevolent. Revolts happened with increasing frequency, making the empire vulnerable to Alexander the Great's invasion.

The Persians' centralized government permitted regional autonomy by entrusting the day-to-day government of satrapies (provinces) to governors called satraps. The satraps were not necessarily Persian; they could be chosen from the local leaders. For instance, the Jewish Daniel had served as an advisor to the Babylonian kings. When Babylon fell, the Persians appointed 120 satraps to rule throughout the kingdom. Three administrators who were accountable to the king oversaw these satraps, and Daniel was one of the three (Ketuvim, Daniel 6).

Within a satrapy (province or region), the satrap (governor) was the administrator. Under him, a military general recruited, trained, and organized a local army, and a state secretary maintained records. The general and secretary reported to both the satrap and central government. Each satrap had a measure of independence; however, royal inspectors would travel around the empire as the king's eyes and ears to learn of local situations. The main concern was ensuring the satrap's loyalty to the central government and tax compliance.

With an empire stretching across three continents and holding almost half the world's population, transportation and communication were crucial for keeping the central government abreast of what was happening around the empire. Darius I (Darius the Great) linked the satrapies with a 1,553-mile (2,500-kilometer) highway with roadside inns for merchant caravans and other travelers. It also had relay stations for the Persian postal service. The switch from clay tablets to parchment scrolls made for a much lighter load for the Persian postmen.

By changing out horses and riders, a message could travel the 1,553 miles of highway in just seven days! Chiseled in gray granite over the doors of today's Eighth Avenue New York City Post Office is Herodotus's praise of the Persian postal service: "Neither snow, nor rain, nor heat, nor gloom of night stays these courageous couriers from the swift completion of their appointed rounds."

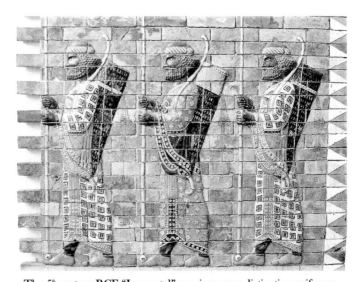

The 5th-century BCE "Immortal" warriors wore distinctive uniforms.

Cyrus realized his vast empire needed a professional army to maintain order over internal power struggles, protect the people from external threats, and conquer new lands. His powerful full-time land army of over 100,000 men was the first to wear standard uniforms of bright colors. He recruited men to serve in his military as he conquered new lands. Various regions produced an array of exceptional soldiers with specialized military skills, such as archers, swordsmen, cavalrymen, camel-riders, elephant mahouts, and javelin throwers.

The empire had an elite military unit. Striking fear into their opponents, the elite Immortals were a specially-trained band of exactly ten thousand heavy infantrymen. A trained replacement would immediately step in if a soldier were sick, seriously wounded, or killed in battle. Under their tunics, the Immortals wore scale armor—small plates or scales (of metal, leather, or horn) sewn to leather or cloth shirts (and sometimes pants) in overlapping rows. They carried wicker shields and wielded daggers, swords, and short spears. They strapped a quiver of arrows on their back and carried a bow hooked over their shoulder.

The *sparabara* warriors were Persians trained in war from childhood. These men usually fought during the military season instead of in the year-round standing army. When not fighting, they were herdsmen and farmers. They wore quilted linen armor and carried two-meter-long spears and wicker shields. The shields effectively fended off arrows but were no match for the Greek hoplites' eighteen-foot sarissas (5.5-meter pikes). However, the *sparabara* effectively fought non-Greek forces.

The Persian military was renowned for its astonishing archers. The Elamites, Medes, Persians, and Scythians were skilled in the deadly three-bladed, socketed, copper alloy arrowheads. Their invincible charioteers, lethal cavalry, camels, and war elephants terrified their opponents. And let's not forget the incredible Phoenician maritime engineers. Xerxes's boat bridge across the Dardanelles Strait wasn't a one-off; Darius had built a similar bridge across the Bosporus.

The Persians were accustomed to fighting on land, but as their empire stretched into Europe and Africa, they realized they needed a navy. Darius the Great recruited seasoned sea warriors from Sidon and other Phoenician cities, as well as Egypt and Greece. The Phoenicians were master shipbuilders and skilled in naval war maneuvers. They built forty-meter-long ships that could carry three hundred troops. The Persians also used smaller ships to patrol large rivers like the Indus, Nile, and Tigris. The vessels had miniature siege engines to launch missiles at their opponents.

Did Xerxes really have a million men in his army when he invaded Greece? Various Greek sources, including Herodotus and Simonides the poet, reported one to three million, including the navy and non-combatants like drivers and cooks. Was this possible? Let's remember that the Achaemenid Empire held 49.4 million of about 112.4 million people globally. With such a vast population, one million military men is a possibility. But the logistics of feeding and moving that many men from Asia to Europe are almost inconceivable. They did say it took a week to cross the boat bridge over the Dardanelles.

By 400 BCE, Persians began using yakhchāls to cool food and ice.

Pastaitaken, CC BY-SA 3.0 https://creativecommons.org/licenses/by-sa/3.0, via Wikimedia Commons; https://commons.wikimedia.org/wiki/File:Yakhchal_of_Yazd_province.jpg

An essential part of daily life is eating and drinking, and the Persians reveled in both. They built underground chambers insulated with mud and bricks to keep their food cool in the hot desert climate. Their diet was similar to the Mesopotamian civilizations; they ate mutton, fish, yogurt, bread, and a vast array of fruits and vegetables. But the Persians insisted on desserts! They scoffed at the Greeks for not eating sweets at the end of the meal, saying they were leaving the table hungry.

The Persian court was infamous for its absurdly lavish lifestyle. King Darius III traveled with an entourage of three hundred cooks and seventy wine-filterers. Birthdays were occasions for elaborate feasts. The Persians were fond of their wine and scandalized the Greeks by drinking it full strength (the Greeks watered theirs down). Herodotus wrote about Persian rulers:

"If a crucial decision is to be made, they discuss the question when they are drunk, and the following day, the master of the house where the discussion was held submits their decision for reconsideration when they are sober. It is adopted if they still approve it; if not, it is abandoned. Conversely, any decision they make when sober is reconsidered afterward when they are drunk."

What was the Persian social structure like? They followed a hierarchal system, with the king and his extensive royal family at the top, priests and magi next, then the satraps and other nobles, military commanders and the Immortals, merchants, artisans and craftspeople, peasants, and enslaved people. The color of clothing labeled some social classes. For instance, warriors wore red, priests wore white, and shepherds wore blue. The magi were a priestly caste in Persia and Babylon, known as astrologers, seers, and exceptional scholars.

The Persians honored those of higher status by bowing to them. They didn't just bow their heads or go down on one knee; they went flat on their faces before the king and other superiors and would kiss the earth or their superior's sandals. When Alexander the Great conquered Persia, he had a bout of megalomania and began demanding his Greek military officers and others to prostrate themselves before him. The Greeks were used to democracy and thought Alexander was deranged.

Women's status in the Persian Empire seemed higher than in the Assyrian and Babylonian cultures. They were active in public life, worked alongside men for the same wages, and occasionally held supervisory positions. Some queens were even warriors. One example was Queen Artemisia of Halicarnassus, which was a Greek colony in present-day Turkey that had come under Persian rule. Herodotus, who was also from Halicarnassus, noted the respect that the Persian king Xerxes had for her advice when she commanded five ships in Xerxes's fleet against Greece. Xerxes praised her for excelling over the other naval officers.

The Persians were notable for their tolerance of minorities. Cyrus the Great proclaimed the lack of prejudice for all ethnicities, religions, and languages throughout the empire on the clay Cyrus Cylinder. The Achaemenid Empire's ethnic and religious minorities continued practicing their faiths and cultures without interference. Cyrus even helped fund the Jews' return to Jerusalem from the Babylonian exile to rebuild their temple.

What did Persians wear? The men were vain about their appearance. They wore kohl eyeliner, used hot irons to curl their hair and beards, and anointed their hair and skin with scented oils. Cyrus's Jewish administrator Daniel mentioned going on a three-week religious fast, which included not anointing himself with oil.

While most men in Mesopotamia and nearby civilizations wore knee-length or ankle-length tunics, the Persian men started wearing pants and leggings, especially in the military, where tunics could be restricting. A typical male outfit might have included a tall cylindrical cap, close-fitting trousers and jacket, a long-sleeved coat, and leather shoes or boots tied with laces. Other men's headgear included a turban or a long scarf draped around the head.

Persian men wore a variety of headgear, clothing, and shoes.
https://commons.wikimedia.org/wiki/File:Ancient_Times,_Persian._-_007_-_Costumes_of_All_Nations_(1882).JPG

Women wore ankle-length tunics or pleated dresses. They wore a single braid and something like today's chador: a large scarf covering the head and neck but leaving their face uncovered. Cotton was cultivated in Mesopotamia during this era, and Persians liked to dye their material in bright colors and wear luxurious scarves, multiple layers, and eye-catching earrings and pendants. Silk from China was a prized trade item and a favorite fabric of the nobility.

What languages did the Persians speak? Up through Darius the Great's reign, Elamite, with an Old Persian language influence, was the spoken and written language for the chancellery and the empire's administration. Elam was located in western Iran on the Persian Gulf and had previously dominated Iran and northern Mesopotamia. Carved inscriptions on monuments and seals were usually trilingual, containing the Old Persian, Elamite, and Akkadian languages. Akkadian was the commonly spoken language in Persia. Persian cuneiform developed under Darius the Great, mixing alphabetic, logogram, and syllabic symbols. Aramaic continued as the lingua franca (common language) for reading and writing in Mesopotamia and the Levant.

When considering the religious beliefs of Persia, we cannot forget how the Persians valued the virtue of truth. Regardless of which gods they worshiped, integrity and honesty shone through as the epitome of a righteous individual. Herodotus recorded that Persian boys concentrated on learning three things: horse-riding, archery, and speaking the truth. He said the Persians believed the biggest disgrace was lying. Next in line was being in debt, which caused problems on many fronts, but the biggest issue was that a debtor tended to lie. The Achaemenid Persians considered lying a cardinal sin, sometimes even punishable by death. This concept predated the Persians, as Hammurabi's code included the death penalty for false witnesses and false accusers.

In the Achaemenid period, Zoroastrianism spread to southwestern Iran, influencing the Persian leadership and becoming a defining cultural element. Along with the ancient Vedic deities from the east, Zoroastrianism encompassed the concepts and gods of the ancient Iranian pantheon; they became minor deities or something like angels. This syncretism helped spur the broad acceptance of Zoroastrianism throughout Iran, allowing it to gain the patronage of Persian kings.

The Achaemenid-era relief pictures the struggle between good (the king) and evil (the lion-griffin creature), representing Zoroastrian dualism.

Bernard Gagnon, CC BY-SA 4.0 https://creativecommons.org/licenses/by-sa/4.0 via Wikimedia Commons; https://commons.wikimedia.org/wiki/File:Zoroastrian_Fire_Temple,_Yazd_03.jpg

Beginning with Darius the Great, perhaps earlier, the imperial patronage of Zoroastrianism made it effectively the state religion throughout the empire. However, the Persian kings continued to exercise the broad tolerance of all faiths, something that Cyrus the Great had initiated. For instance, Cyrus directed Persia's treasurer, Mithredath, to count out all the articles Nebuchadnezzar had looted from the Jewish temple and placed in Marduk's Babylonian temple. Cyrus returned these to Sheshbazzar, Prince of Judah.

Even though Darius the Great was Zoroastrian, he intervened on behalf of the Jews who came into conflict with the Babylonians and other people. The Assyrians had relocated them to Israel over a hundred years earlier. The issue was rebuilding Jerusalem's temple, which had begun in Cyrus's reign, but the local non-Jewish leadership in Israel stopped the construction. Darius ordered the cost of rebuilding the Jewish temple to be paid for from the royal treasury of the provinces west of the Euphrates. He also mandated sacrificial animals and food for the priests so they could offer sacrifices and pray for Darius and his family.

In the later Achaemenid Empire, Zoroastrian worship became much less monotheistic. Berossus, a Chaldean priest of Marduk and a historian, wrote that Artaxerxes II Mnemon, who reigned from 405 to 358 BCE, began making cult statues of the Zoroastrian lesser deities. This was the first time that idols appeared in Persian temples. Both Herodotus and Berossus reported that the Persians had not previously prayed to images of the gods.

A trilingual inscription in Susa preserved Artaxerxes's prayers to Ahura Mazda, Anahita, and Mithra. He elevated the worship of Anahita, goddess of water, fertility, wisdom, and healing, by erecting temples and images of her in Babylon, Ecbatana, and Susa. The Persian Sasanian dynasty repaired and decorated these temples five hundred years later.

The daily lives of ancient Persians in the Achaemenid Empire included a rich and diverse culture that respected all religions and where multiple ethnicities lived together and learned from each other. Speaking the truth was a highly valued virtue; the Greeks and others outside the empire admired the Persians' honesty. Persian culture enriched the lives of people around the realm and beyond.

Chapter 15: Persian Art, Architecture, and Technology

Ancient Persia produced a rich heritage of art, architecture, and technological innovations that has captured the imagination and encouraged new techniques for thousands of years. Its intricate and enchanting architecture, ceramics, painting, metalworking, and sculptures graced palaces, temples, and even ordinary homes. By exploring Persian inventions, we get an insight into their way of life.

Before the nomadic Persians arrived on the Iranian Plateau, other civilizations lived there that had a rich and distinctive culture, which helped shape Persian art and architecture. Influences of the older cultures of Elam and Susiana and the neighboring civilizations of Sumer, Babylon, Assyria, and Akkad all blended into a novel milieu of creative beauty. Herodotus commented, "The Persians adopt more foreign customs than anyone else."

The Persians had a true knack for embracing and assimilating other cultures and concepts and then putting their stamp on them by improving and taking them to a higher level. When Cyrus the Great established the Achaemenid Empire, he appreciated the ancient cultures of his own land and those he conquered. He encouraged innovations in art, architecture, and technology, developing a brilliant and distinctive Persian style in the process.

This reproduction of the ornate pillars and roof of Persepolis's Apadana is an example of elaborate Persian architecture.

Before the Medes and Persians arrived in the Iranian Plateau, nomadic people had put down roots, establishing Susa in the lower Zagros Mountains. And before they came, the Elamites were already there, east of Sumer and down along the Persian Gulf. The people of Susa and Elam interacted with each other and with the Sumerians and the Zagros Mountain tribes. Eventually, the mountain tribes and the plateau tribes united to form a sophisticated urban state.

Eventually, King Eannatum (circa 2500–2400 BCE) and other Sumerian kings established hegemony over Elam, influencing Elamite art, such as statuettes of human worshipers representing communal devotion. Akkadian and Sumerian cylinder seals shaped Elamite depictions of gods and humans, which were motifs the Persians would later adopt and develop. The Persian

Empire's artists drew on these past artistic elements and refined them.

Sargon of Akkad conquered today's Iran in the late 3rd millennium and implemented further advances in syncretizing art and architectural motifs. Persian architecture was an eclectic blending of multiple cultures that had a distinctive Persian identity. The Akkadian influence was dramatically displayed in Chogha Zanbil: a massive complex built during the reign of Elamite King Untash-Napirisha, circa 1340 BCE. Its brick ziggurat with a temple on top is relatively well preserved over three thousand years later.

A stunning example of Achaemenid architecture and art is the Persepolis ruins near the southern Zagros Mountains, which date back to 515 BCE. Cyrus the Great selected the remote location for the Persian ceremonial capital or religious center and thoughtfully developed its stately design. But Darius the Great began the construction of Persepolis's terraces and palaces, and his son Xerxes completed most of Persepolis.

One of Persepolis's first structures was the Apadana: the opulent main hall of the kings, where they received tribute from the nations and bestowed gifts on their subjects. Twenty-meter-high columns supported the roof, with figures of bulls adorning the columns' capitals. Two colossal stairways rose to the hall on the north and east, decorated with reliefs depicting men in the costumes of the empire's nations. Magnificently landscaped gardens surrounded the Apadana.

Not only did Darius oversee the early construction of Persepolis, but the incredibly ambitious king also rebuilt his summer capital of Susa, following Cyrus's design of elaborate gardens and erecting a breathtaking palace complex. Both Persepolis and Susa featured animals, such as birds, bulls, and lions, at the tops of columns. They were also etched into the borders of the roofs. The slender columns drew the eye upward to the colorful and intricate designs around the ceiling, which was built with planks from the cedars of Lebanon.

This lamassu-like creature decorated the wall of Darius's palace.
https://commons.wikimedia.org/wiki/File:Sphinx_Darius_Louvre.jpg

Darius decorated his palace with enameled terracotta reliefs of lions, archers, unicorns, double bulls, palms, flowers, and bells. The reliefs' brightly colored dyes gave a lifelike quality to the images. Perhaps the most eye-catching is a relief of a creature with a man's head, a lion's body, and an eagle's wings, something like a *lamassu* or griffin.

Was the unicorn real or mythical?
*Mohammad.m.nazari, CC BY-SA 4.0 https://creativecommons.org/licenses/by-sa/4.0 via
Wikimedia Commons;
https://commons.wikimedia.org/wiki/File:Unicorn_in_Apadana,_Shush,_Iran–2017-10.jpg*

A spectacular image of a unicorn graced the wall of the Apadana in Susa. A relief set on blue-glazed tile portrayed the white, horse-like creature with a spiral horn, a tail like a lion, and wings of an eagle. Did the Persians consider the unicorn a mythical creature or a real animal? We do not have any written Persian accounts of unicorns, but Greek natural history authors believed they were real animals that lived in India. Many seals from Bronze-Age India show a single-horned animal looking more like a cow than a horse. Ctesias, a Greek physician living in Persia during the Achaemenid Empire, described unicorns as wild asses with black, red, or white coats and a horn that was a cubit and a half (twenty-eight inches).

An important example of Achaemenid art is the reliefs decorating the stairs of Persepolis's Apadana hall. On the northern panel, the king (probably Darius the Great) receives a distinguished official performing a greeting ritual of blowing a kiss. Typically, everyone was required to prostrate themselves before the king, face to the floor, and kiss his feet or kiss the ground (as in, "I worship the ground you stand on"). This official is standing and blowing a kiss to the king, indicating his high rank.

Along the other walls of the stairs, more sets of reliefs portray the people of the vast empire's regions lined up to offer tribute to the king. They can be identified by their clothing: Medes, Elamites, Armenians, Parthians, Babylonians, Lydians, Syrians, Cappadocians, Sacae, Greeks, Bactrians, Indians, and on and on. A hippopotamus is shown roaming around. He's with the Egyptians, so perhaps he was part of the tribute.

The relief's history is intriguing. At some point, the reliefs on the northern stairs with the king were removed and placed in the treasury, where they stayed until archaeologists dug them up over two thousand years later.

This section of the enormous relief from the Apadana Hall in Persepolis shows Lydians offering tribute. The official (with the knife in his belt) leads the first man by the hand, implying an amicable relationship between the king and the conquered people.

Perhaps the best-known art collection of the Achaemenid Empire is the Oxus treasure, a hoard of crafted gold and silver treasures found near and in the Oxus River, where it separates modern-day Tajikistan and Afghanistan. The treasure dates to the Achaemenid period, when the region belonged to the First Persian Empire. In 1880, a Russian newspaper reported that locals had found treasure in the ruins of the ancient fort of Takht-i Kuwad and in the river itself. These priceless items had been scattered in the sand, exposed by the dry season.

The finds included exquisite bowls, coins, figurines, jewelry, jugs, and gold plaques. Scholars believe they may have once adorned a nearby temple, and the priests hid them for safekeeping during a tumultuous political period. The stunning and complex craftsmanship demonstrates tremendous metallurgy skill, especially in a miniature golden chariot and horses with riders. The fine detail required exceptional skill and reflected Egyptian influence.

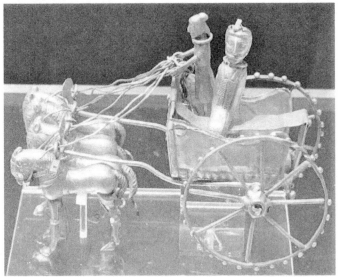

This Oxus golden chariot displays incredible craftsmanship.

These exquisite pieces may have been cut from sheet gold. The craftmanship is so realistic that the chariot wheels would have freely turned when created thousands of years ago. The chariot shows signs of repair in ancient times. Four horses pull the chariot, which carries two figures: a driver and a seated passenger. Handrails are attached to the chariot's rear to assist with stepping in and out. The front of the chariot has the image of Bes, the Egyptian dwarf god.

The Oxus treasure represents what must have been an enormous production of precious-metal work in the Achaemenid period. As the Persian Empire exploded in all directions, conquering regions from India to Greece to Egypt, it swallowed up the artistic hubs of the ancient world. As the Persians assimilated creative skills and techniques from these areas, they developed a unique Persian style, such as the griffin-headed gold bracelets from Oxus pictured in the 5th-century Persepolis reliefs and which Xenophon described as gifts of honor in the Achaemenid court.

The Oxus treasure trove included multiple silver and gold figurines. Some of them probably represent worshipers rather than deities. One silver and gold figure is wearing a headdress, suggesting he is a king. A larger silver statuette shows a nude young man wearing a gold conical hat. Scholars believe this figure has Greek influences, as nude art was not typical of Persia.

Entrancing armlets, bracelets, and neck torcs are adorned with animal heads: bulls, ducks, goats, ibex, lions, sheep, and mythical creatures like griffins. The griffin-headed bracelets required complex manufacturing since several elements are soldered together. Although most are now missing, their inlays held jewels in their original state. The jewelry hints at Assyrian and Egyptian influences. Other jewelry includes signet rings and cylinder seals.

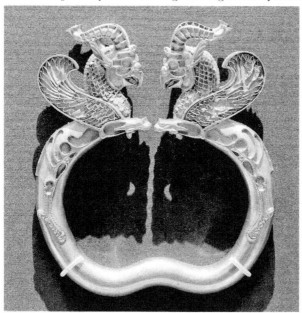

This griffin-headed armlet once held jewels or enamel in the inlay.
https://commons.wikimedia.org/wiki/File:Armlet_from_the_Oxus_Treasure_BM_189 7.12-31.116.jpg

The Oxus treasure includes a lion-griffin gold plaque with an ibex's body and a leaf-shaped tail. The position of the creature suggests a Scythian influence. Two prongs at the back of the piece imply it was an ornament worn on a cap or adorning someone's hair. Like tribute vessels pictured in the Persepolis reliefs, a leaping ibex carving probably once served as a vase handle.

Before the Persians arrived in Iran, the Elamites produced eye-catching pottery: bowls, cups, and pots in striking geometric shapes or depicting ibex and other animals. They also made numerous clay figurines of beguiling animals: rabbits, cows, and dogs—many dogs. The animals may have represented people in Aesop-like fables. One almost life-sized clay cow found at the entrance to the Chogha Zanbil ziggurat, circa 1250 BCE, was dedicated to the god Inshushinak.

This realistic piebald pottery cow exemplifies Elamite art.

Pottery from the Achaemenid period includes excavated pieces dating from Darius the Great's reign (521–486 BCE). This pottery is distinctly less ornate than Elamite ceramics. It featured eggshell, white, reddish, and yellow glazes on bowls, jars, and cylindrical amphorae, reflecting central and southern Mesopotamian influences. Painted pottery was rare; the few painted ceramics featured red paint on buff-colored pottery. Some of the Achaemenid-era pottery dating to the 6th to 5th centuries BCE appeared mass-produced for everyday utilitarian use.

Metal or ceramic festoon-ware was distinctive in Persia beginning in the Achaemenid era: drinking vessels of bronze, copper, gold, or silver or pottery with an animal head. They were probably used for special occasions like ceremonial court banquets. In their nomadic days, Persians drank wine from animal horns, which evolved into ornate drinking vessels resembling a horn with an animal head. These fascinating vessels spread throughout the empire and to Greece.

This mountain-goat drinking horn from Anatolia dates to 500–400 BCE.
Dosseman, CC BY-SA 4.0 https://creativecommons.org/licenses/by-sa/4.0 via Wikimedia Commons; https://commons.wikimedia.org/wiki/File:Ankara_Archaeology_and_art_museum_Rhy ton_Bronze_Achaemenid_Persian_500-400_BC_2019_3473.jpg

Another example of Achaemenid-era pottery is dotted Triangle Ware, which dates to the 5th and 4th centuries BCE and is found in northwestern Persia and central Anatolia. Potters produced them from local clays, and they have a well-smoothed surface. They feature vertical and horizontal bands forming panels decorated with animal, floral, or geometric motifs with ladder or chevron patterns on the vessel rims. Triangles were the dominant decoration, hence the name. They were painted bold orange, red, purple, and mahogany brown. They apparently formed table sets with bowls, jugs, and other ceramics.

Persians began working with glass starting in the Late Bronze Age. Archaeologists found glass beads in the Dinkha Tepe site in Iranian Azerbaijan. They found glass tubes from the Elamite period at Chogha Zanbil and Iron Age mosaic glass cups in northern Iran, reflecting Mesopotamian influences. Glassware from the Achaemenid period includes glass tubes holding kohl in Azerbaijan and Kurdistan.

In addition to delightful art and architecture, the Persians produced intriguing innovations in technology and other fields. Water sources are always a concern in arid and semi-arid regions. This led to the development of the qanat irrigation system, which brought water from an aquifer or well up to the surface using an underground aqueduct. This ancient qanat irrigation system permitted water transport over long distances without losing much water to evaporation in the hot, dry climate. Another advantage was its resistance to earthquakes, floods, or wartime destruction by enemies.

Unlike the Mesopotamian irrigation systems, which were fed from rivers, the qanat system used underground water. Thus, it did not depend on rainfall levels and delivered a relatively reliable flow even during times of drought. It was built with vertical shafts at intervals, similar to shaft wells, and connected to a sloping tunnel, drawing the water up from the aquafers. The qanat system turned deserts into farmland and provided a water source for the Persians' lush gardens in their cities and palaces.

The Persians invented the world's first known windmill as early as 134 BCE and perhaps even earlier. They used this used to pump water or grind grain. They used wicker paddles woven from reeds or fabric sails. They attached four to eight wicker paddles or cloth sails to a central axis in a panemone design (with a vertical rotating axis and the sails or paddles moving parallel to the wind). As the wind blew the sails, this turned the axle, which was connected to a water-transportation device or grain grinders.

Using ancient Persian technology, these towers are windcatchers in today's Yazd, Iran. An "ab anbar" (water reservoir) is in the middle.

Persia had cool or cold winters (depending on the location), but the summer heat could be brutal: over 100°F (38°C) on some scorching days. This propelled the enterprising Persians to devise ways of staying cool. They developed windcatchers or wind towers, which are still used today. These provided natural ventilation and passive cooling. The windcatchers drew the cooler air down and pushed the stifling air up and out, maintaining a somewhat comfortable indoor temperature.

Egypt had established hospitals in the Old Kingdom (2613–2181 BCE), and the Babylonians had a well-developed medical system. But the Persians developed the world's first teaching hospital. Even before that happened, the Persians had a deep respect for medical science; for instance, Darius the Great restored the medical books and equipment at the Sais medical school in Egypt.

But the innovators of the Persian Sassanian Empire took the medical concepts in place and developed a teaching hospital with a library and medical school. Azadokht Shahbanu, the wife of King Shapur (r. 240–270 CE), brought Greek physicians to the royal court to establish a teaching hospital where experienced physicians could train new doctors. The Academy of Gundeshapur became the region's premier intellectual center. One of the requirements for graduation was to cure three patients. Doctors' fees were on a sliding scale depending on the patient's income.

Ancient Persians worked hard and fought hard, but they enjoyed taking time to unwind with friends and family, which is an essential part of any culture. They loved throwing banquets and birthday parties. They developed animation for amusement at these gatherings; they would have a cup painted with successive scenes around it, so it looked like the picture on the cup was moving when they turned it. One example is a ram jumping into the air to catch leaves from a tree in his mouth. The Persians also enjoyed singing to stringed instruments like the *tar*, the prototype for today's guitar.

Ancient Persia brought multiple cultures from three continents under its dominion; it was the most expansive empire at that time. Through respecting and encouraging individual cultures and blending them, the distinctive Persian culture emerged as a driving force in art, architecture, and technical innovations. Although Islamic Arabs initially suppressed Persian culture, it endured and later became a decisive influence on Islamic culture. Today, we enjoy and appreciate the vibrant Persian contributions to art, architecture, and technology as people continue to rework ancient customs and innovations with a unique Persian spin.

Chapter 16: Persia's Great Enemy: Alexander the Great

Everything was ready! Philip II of Macedon had spent years fighting the Greeks, ending their incessant internecine conflicts and molding them into one united front, something no one thought possible. Philip was now poised to launch his stupendous Greek coalition forces against Persia. An advance force of ten thousand men was already in Asia Minor, preparing to free the Greek city-states from Persian hegemony.

Nothing could stop him now. Nothing that was except murder. While Philip was celebrating his daughter's wedding, Philip's bodyguard and former lover Pausanias suddenly pulled out his dagger and plunged it into Philip's ribs.

It was 336 BCE. Over two hundred years had passed since Cyrus formed the mighty Achaemenid Empire. The Persian Empire's control over multiple Greek city-states along Asia Minor's Ionian coast was a bone of contention for the Ionian Greeks and the mainland Greeks, who were accustomed to freely trading with their ancient relatives. The Persians impeded their seafaring trade.

The Persians had invaded Thrace, Macedonia, and Greece under Darius the Great. But Darius and his son Xerxes I were defeated multiple times by storms at sea, by the Spartans' intransigence, and by the Athenians' cunning naval strategies.

When the southern Greek states stopped fighting each other and formed a united front against Xerxes's large army, they won!

The loss was catastrophic for the Achaemenid Empire. The costly Greco-Persian Wars had depleted Persia's treasury. And the Ionian-Greek city-states revolted again. When Xerxes's son Artaxerxes I ascended the throne, he initiated a new strategy. Instead of military action against Greece, he endeavored to weaken the Athens-led southern Greek coalition by funding their rival Greek city-states.

Artaxerxes's ploy worked. The Greek coalition began unraveling, and the southern Greek states started fighting each other again in the Peloponnesian Wars. While fighting Sparta, Athens sent two hundred ships to aid Egypt and Libya in a revolt against their Persian overlords. Although Athens fared well against Sparta, it received appalling news from Egypt: the Persians had crushed the Athenian fleet. Athens forgot all about Sparta and focused on Persia, strengthening its Delian League coalition.

After several years, Athens and Sparta were back at war, which didn't go well for Athens. First, a horrible plague decimated the population. Next, the city suffered devastating losses from Sparta. Then, a coup overthrew Athens's democracy. But the commander of the Athenian fleet, Alcibiades, refused to submit to the new Athenian government. Instead, in 410 BCE, he sailed the fleet to the Hellespont, engaging Sparta and Persia and winning an astounding victory in the Battle of Cyzicus.

This triumph spurred the Athenians to restore democracy and take back the Ionian Greek city-states from Persia. But the Athenian victory was short-lived. Darius II was now ruling the Persian-Achaemenid Empire, and he supported Sparta in the struggle with Athens. With Persia's support, Sparta rebuilt its fleet and ultimately crushed Athens. In 404 BCE, Athens and its allies surrendered to Sparta, handed over their naval fleets, and gave up their tributary cities.

Meanwhile, the Persian Empire enjoyed 45 years of relative stability under Artaxerxes II, who was notable for having over 300 wives and 115 sons. Artaxerxes II invested energy and funds to improve the Persian Empire's infrastructure and build temples. But he also inserted himself into Greece's affairs. Hoping to destabilize Greece, Persia subsidized Athens, Corinth, and Thebes against Sparta. Then, in 387 BCE, Artaxerxes abandoned the Athenian coalition, took back the Greek city-states in Ionia, and gave Sparta hegemony over all of Greece. Artaxerxes prevailed over Greece, but Egypt had revolted early in his reign, and his attempt to retake Egypt in 373 BCE failed.

The year before Artaxerxes III became ruler of the Persian Empire, Philip II ascended the throne of Macedonia. This was a large but obscure and weak state north of Greece; at this time, it was on the brink of obliteration by its neighbors. But Philip II was ambitious and well-schooled in military tactics after spending his teen years in Thebes. He would soon reform his army and transform Macedonia into an empire. In his first year as king, he trounced the states surrounding Macedonia, which had been threatening to annihilate Macedonia just months earlier. He then fought his way through northern, central, and southern Greece, conquering states and forming a coalition of all of Greece except Sparta. His goal was to rid Greece of its perpetual threat by swallowing up the Persian Empire.

Meanwhile, Artaxerxes III had been busy retaking Egypt, savagely squelching a revolt in Sidon, and dealing with rebellions in Asia Minor and Cyprus. He finally got the entire Persian Empire under control and enjoyed the last six years of his reign in relative peace. But Bagoas, his favorite eunuch and commander, poisoned him. Bagoas then poisoned the next king, Artaxerxes IV, and killed all of his children. Finally, a distant relative, Darius III, ascended the throne and poisoned Bagoas out of self-preservation.

And that brings us to 336 BCE. Poison had exterminated the Persian royal family, and Philip II lay bleeding out in Macedonia. While his body was still warm, Philip's military and nobles proclaimed his son, twenty-year-old Alexander, as the next king of Macedonia. Alexander had spent his childhood being tutored by Aristotle, and he had joined his father in war for several years. Although he was young, he was an astute general and well-trained in statesmanship. Alexander was ready to step into his father's shoes and continue his mission to take on the Persian Empire.

But first, he had to quell some revolts. His father Philip had the Greek city-states all lined up to invade Persia, but with his death, Athens, Thebes, Thessaly, and Thrace began backing out. Alexander marched south with three thousand men. The Thessalian army waited for him at the pass at Mount Olympus. But Alexander circumnavigated the pass by night, climbing up and over nearby Mount Ossa. When the Thessalians woke up, he was at their rear! Shaken, the Thessalians surrendered.

This 3rd-century BCE statue of Alexander is signed "Menas."
https://commons.wikimedia.org/wiki/File:Alexander_The_Great_statue_-estatua_de_Alejandro_Magno.jpg

The rest of the city-states in southern Greece quickly bowed to his leadership, apologizing for revolting. Alexander forgave them; he needed their military strength for his quest against Persia. But now, the northern states were openly revolting, so Alexander headed north, brilliantly reining them in. However, Athens and Thebes rebelled—again! Enraged, Alexander marched back south, flattened Thebes, and sold the citizens into slavery. Aghast, Athens promptly surrendered.

Alexander now had his unified Greek coalition ready to campaign against the Achaemenid superpower in what would rank among the most spectacular military expeditions in history. Alexander's audacious Asian invasion established a vast and powerful, albeit brief, empire within ten years. The Greeks called him Alexander the Great, but he was Alexander the Accursed to the Persians.

With a forty-thousand-man army, Alexander and his proficient general, Parmenion, crossed into Asia Minor in 334 BCE. As the Persian generals tracked his approach, they discussed their strategies. One Persian general, Memnon of Rhodes, was a Greek mercenary. He advised the Persians to pursue a scorched earth strategy, in which the men would withdraw to the interior and destroy the fields and fruit trees on the way. "He'll leave if he can't feed his army!"

But the Persian generals thought it cowardly to retreat, and they weren't keen on destroying their own food sources. They decided to engage Alexander in battle at the River Granicus. The Persians lined up along the shallow river's steep banks, forcing the Greeks to wade across and climb up to meet them. Alexander's formation had the Thessalian-Thracian cavalry at the left flank and his phalanx (the soldier formation carrying shields and spears) in the middle. He joined the right flank with his specialized Macedonian cavalry, elite infantry, expert archers, and Bulgarian javelin-throwers.

The Persians looked at the setting sun and assumed the Greeks would cross the river at sunrise. But Alexander surprised them, suddenly charging his forces swiftly across the river. Under a hail of Persian arrows, Alexander's cavalry plunged through the water, then raced up the steep bank. The Persians tried to push them down the bank and back into the river, but the Greeks came at them too fast.

Alexander impaled Mithridates, Darius's son-in-law. Before he could retrieve his spear, a Persian horseman struck Alexander with his scimitar, cutting his helmet in two. Alexander jerked his javelin out of Mithridates, swung around, and plunged it into his attacker. At that moment, another Persian on horseback had his sword poised to stab Alexander in the back. But Alexander's good friend, Cleitus the Black, sliced off the Persian's arm.

Finally, the infantry waded through the river and formed a wall of formidable eighteen-foot sarissas (long pikes). The Persians had never been met by spears three times as long as they were! Panicked, they whirled around in full retreat. Alexander's first battle of the great war was a sensational victory, and Asia Minor's Greek states were now emancipated from Persia. When Alexander marched toward Lydia's capital city of Sardis, its satrap immediately surrendered.

Alexander knew he needed to shut down the Persian navy so they couldn't transport food, supplies, and men or attack his navy. Instead of attacking their ships by sea, he stormed Miletus and Halicarnassus, two important naval bases, rendering Persia's navy impotent.

Alexander then marched to Lycia and Phrygia. Gordium, Phrygia's capital, had the Gordian Knot. An oracle said that the man who untied it would be Asia's ruler. Alexander took one look at the tangle, drew his sword, and hacked it in two. He had undone the knot: Asia was his! This is, of course, a legend, so it might not have actually occurred, but it is an interesting story nonetheless.

Meanwhile, King Darius mustered a massive army and approached Alexander near Cilicia, spreading his men across the coastal plain and trapping Alexander's men against the Nur Mountains. Unperturbed, Alexander swiftly ordered his men into formation, using the same lineup at Granicus. General Parmenion was on the left with the Greek allies, the indomitable Macedonian phalanx was in the middle, and Alexander and his elite cavalry and infantry were at the right end.

The two armies lined up facing each other on opposite banks of the Pinarus River. Suddenly, Alexander charged at full speed. His horses galloped through the water, but the foot soldiers' armor and long spears slowed their crossing in the swift river. Alexander charged straight into the Persian foot soldiers with his cavalry, creating pandemonium, while the Macedonian infantry waded the river and regrouped into position.

Darius III from a Pompeii mosaic that probably copied a 3rd-century BCE painting.
Carole Raddato from Frankfurt, Germany, CC BY-SA 2.0
https://creativecommons.org/licenses/by-sa/2.0 via Wikimedia Commons;
https://commons.wikimedia.org/wiki/File:Darius_III_mosaic.jpg

King Darius intently scanned the battle and paled as he watched Alexander. Despite his thigh running with blood from a stab wound, Alexander heedlessly and relentlessly charged, cutting down anyone in his way. "He's insane!" Darius likely said, trembling as he watched Alexander approach.

Suddenly, the Persian king swung his chariot around and charged off the battlefield, leaving his men to fend for themselves. Word swiftly shot through the Persian ranks that Darius had abandoned the field. They looked at each other, then at the Macedonians' bristling sarissas. Why should they be impaled by eighteen-foot pikes? They swirled around and ran! Alexander's victory at the Battle of Issus was swift and sensational. Darius didn't just leave his army behind. His mother, wife, and two daughters were at the Persian camp. Alexander took the queen-mother, the queen, and the princesses as hostages but gave them profound respect and care. He later married Princess Stateira.

One by one, the Phoenician cities on the Mediterranean coast surrendered to Alexander, further breaking Persia's Mediterranean naval power. Only the ancient city of Tyre on an island off Lebanon's shores, the fierce ruler of the sea for two thousand years, refused to concede. Alexander's engineers built a causeway to the island, and he rolled his siege engines across as the Phoenicians attacked with their fire ships. After seven months of horrendous battle, Tyre fell. At this point, King Darius sent Alexander a letter offering his friendship, his daughter in marriage, a hefty ransom to return his family, and all the territory west of the Halys River in Turkey (where the Greek colonies of Asia Minor lay). Alexander refused.

Passing out of Phoenicia on their way to Egypt, the Macedonian army approached the seemingly invincible Gaza. Alexander's engineers shook their heads. The city stood on a high hill; the siege engines couldn't reach the walls. But Alexander insisted there was a way to take the city. Finally, the engineers devised a plan of building hills alongside Gaza's hill, bringing their missile launchers high enough. While constructing the hills, an arrow shot from Gaza. It penetrated Alexander's shield, impaling his shoulder. In the end, though, Gaza fell.

The Egyptians welcomed Alexander as their deliverer from Persian rule, against which they had been revolting for decades. Their satrap handed him the keys to the treasury, and the Memphis priest crowned him as their new pharaoh. At the mouth of the Nile, Alexander founded Alexandria, a city that would soon become a brilliant Hellenistic center. Alexander visited the Oracle of Amun-Ra, who pronounced Alexander as the son of Amun, the Egyptians' chief god. Hearing this, Alexander seemed to really believe he was divine, and he expected everyone to acknowledge his celestial standing.

King Darius wrote Alexander again, thanking him for kindly caring for his mother and offering him all the territory west of the

Euphrates (essentially half the empire), co-rulership, his daughter's hand in marriage, and thirty thousand talents in silver. Alexander roared in laughter. Darius's two daughters were his captives, and he wasn't settling for just half of the empire; he wanted it all! Alexander messaged Darius that Asia could only have one king. He should surrender now or prepare to fight to see who the one king would be.

Alexander fighting Darius in the Battle of Issus in a mosaic from Pompeii.
https://commons.wikimedia.org/wiki/File:Alexander_and_Bucephalus_-_Battle_of_Issus_mosaic_-_Museo_Archeologico_Nazionale_-_Naples_BW.jpg

Darius marched out to meet Alexander at Gaugamela in northern Mesopotamia with almost twice as many men, war elephants, and chariots; the Greeks were unaccustomed to fighting elephants and men in chariots. But Alexander's forces lined up in their usual formation, and Alexander raced his cavalry toward the Persians, outflanking them. In the middle of his line with his infantry, Darius moved over to block Alexander, but Alexander's horses charged right through Darius's infantry. Darius's chariots came rumbling out, but Alexander's Bulgarian javelin-throwers massacred the men and horses.

Horrified, Darius broke and ran. Before Alexander could chase him down, he received word that the Indian and Scythian cavalries had trapped General Parmenion's left flank. Alexander raced to his aid in a lethal conflict that killed sixty elite Macedonian cavalrymen. Finally, the Persian army heard Darius had left the battle and likewise fled. Alexander marched into

Babylon with no resistance, and the people announced him as the new ruler of Persia.

Darius fled with a small remnant of his army to Media, but his Bactrian satrap Bessus murdered him; Bessus then proclaimed himself king. After ordering his rival's royal burial, Alexander began organizing his empire. He appointed leaders to his provinces, keeping all the Persian satraps who swore loyalty to him. His next task was to hunt Bessus down in the east and execute him for assassinating King Darius. But the Bactrian chieftains betrayed Bessus; Alexander found him chained to a stake and ordered him sent to Persia for trial and execution.

Alexander's soldiers were weary and ready to go home to their wives and children. But Alexander wanted to keep going to the empire's eastern borders, to the Ganges River, the "end of the world." Alexander reached the Jaxartes River, the empire's eastern boundary. Then, the Scythians attacked, and an arrow pierced Alexander's shin, breaking his calf bone.

Nevertheless, Alexander pummeled the nomadic Scythians but could not thwart the Bactrian and Sogdian guerilla attacks. A rock struck his head in the 329 BCE Siege of Cyropolis (in present-day Tajikistan). The violent head injury (on top of multiple previous head injuries) caused transient blindness and a temporary inability to speak or walk.

Alexander's troops were increasingly edgy and demoralized; they just wanted to go home, but Alexander wanted to press farther east. Alexander annoyed his troops further by wearing Persian clothing and expecting everyone to prostrate themselves before him in the Persian fashion. His erratic behavior turned lethal when he got drunk and murdered Cleitus the Black, his close friend who had once saved his life.

While fighting the Sogdians in 327 BCE, Alexander captured Roxana, the lovely daughter of the Bactrian Lord Oxyartes. Oxyartes surrendered immediately to save his daughter and other family members, but Alexander was captivated by his captive! Alexander married her, overriding the objections of his appalled generals. He appointed Oxyartes as the satrap of the Hindu Kush mountain region. Hopefully, his father-in-law would rein in the rest of the Bactrians and Sogdians.

Alexander forged on, scaling the lofty, snow-encrusted Hindu Kush mountains at the 3,500-foot Khyber Pass between Afghanistan and Pakistan. During his descent into the Indian subcontinent, he fought the vicious Assaceni and Aspasii tribes. On the swollen banks of the Jhelum River, he faced the Pauravas' king Porus. It was monsoon season, and crossing the churning river was impossible. Alexander camped across the river from Porus, keeping most of his troops out of sight. By doing this, he was able to trick Porus into thinking his army was smaller.

During the nights, his cavalry searched for a place to cross the river and found one seventeen miles upstream. While General Craterus and part of the Greek forces created a distraction across the river from Porus, Alexander and the rest of the men crept upstream, out of sight. His forces crossed the river in small boats or held onto inflated skins. Then they moved downstream toward Porus's forces, who moved into ranks to face Alexander.

Alexander positioned his cavalry on both flanks using a pincer maneuver in what is now known as the Battle of the Hydaspes. A wall of bristling eighteen-foot-sarissas broke the Indian war elephants' charge. The elephants killed many of Alexander's men, but the long pikes panicked the beasts into turning around and charging back, crushing as many of Porus's men as they had Alexander's. Alexander then implemented a hammer and anvil maneuver: one force encircling the enemy while the other attacked frontally, bringing a stunning victory that won control of Punjab.

Alexander's quest to reach the "edge of the world," the great river of India, dissipated when his soldiers mutinied. After years of fighting in the Persian Empire, the men were battle-weary, and they heard India was assembling giant armies. A peeved Alexander led the men down the Indus River to the coast. He sent half his army by the Arabian Sea and the Persian Gulf to Persia. Alexander marched back with the rest of his men over the harsh Makran desert, where the extreme heat and thirst killed one-third of his army. After arriving in Persia, Alexander paid off the debts of his remaining soldiers.

And then Alexander threw a massive, multi-couple wedding. At a lavish feast, he married eighty Persian princesses to his

Macedonian nobility, intermingling the leading families to cement the takeover of the empire. Alexander married two princesses: King Darius's daughter Stateira, who had been his captive for a decade, and Parysatis II, daughter of King Artaxerxes III. Alexander was thrilled to learn his beloved wife Roxana had conceived, but he would never hold his son in his arms.

Alexander fell ill with a fever in 323 BCE and died within two weeks. The indomitable warrior who had never lost a battle and created a new empire stretching from Greece to the Indus Valley lost his final struggle at only thirty-two. Alexander's fellow Macedonians carried his body in a honey-filled sarcophagus back to Macedon for burial. But on their journey, Alexander's general, Ptolemy (Egypt's new pharaoh), stole the coffin! It remained a prized possession in Alexandria for centuries; Roman emperors even made pilgrimages to view the sarcophagus. Historians are not quite sure where his tomb is today, but there are several theories. Perhaps one day, it will be unearthed.

What happened to Persia? Alexander's unexpected death created chaos in the empire. Roxana, who gave birth to their son after his death, killed his Persian wives. One of Alexander's generals, Cassander, later poisoned Roxana and her son. Alexander's generals contended over the vast territory that spanned three continents. They finally divided the empire into three: Macedon to the Antigonus dynasty, Egypt to the Ptolemy dynasty, and the remnants of the Persian Empire to the Seleucus dynasty.

The new Seleucid Empire, founded by Alexander's general Seleucus I Nicator, lasted from 312 to 63 BCE as a center of Hellenistic culture. At its zenith, the Persian-Seleucid Empire stretched from Anatolia (Turkey) down through the Levant on the Mediterranean and west through Mesopotamia and Iran to today's Kuwait, Afghanistan, and Turkmenistan. As other kingdoms rose to power over the centuries, the Persian-Seleucid Empire gradually declined until it was reduced to an area encompassing Syria. General Pompey of Rome ultimately overthrew the remnants of the empire in 63 BCE.

Conclusion

Ancient Mesopotamia's legacy was truly revolutionary. The "cradle of civilization" fostered innovations that transformed the world through its many inventions, law codes, and political organizations that integrated numerous cultures under one central government. The story of civilization—the inception of the wheel, the concept of time, writing, schools, measurements, basic counting, higher math, and hydraulic engineering—all began in ancient Mesopotamia.

Development and innovation thrived in this semi-arid land that was fed by two great rivers flowing from the Taurus Mountains into the Persian Gulf. Farming settlements blossomed into the world's first urban centers, where people built sophisticated buildings and infrastructure like roads, sewer drains, defensive walls, and irrigation. They gazed at the sky and mapped it, dividing the year into twelve months named after the constellations. They observed the retrograde motion of the planets, predicted helical rising, and knew when lunar and solar eclipses would happen.

Childlike pictures scratched into wet clay morphed into the complex cuneiform script used to record over a dozen spoken languages. The Mesopotamians used cuneiform to write the first epic poems, the first hymns, the first histories, and the first law codes. They developed the wheel to speed the task of pottery-making, then realized it could be utilized for transportation.

Simple carts hauling bricks or farm produce evolved into chariots that could race along at thirty-five miles per hour.

For over a millennium, the incipient city-states were independent and self-contained. Gradually, one city would rise to "kingship" over the others, becoming the regional center of power, trade, and religion. These eventually developed into multi-ethnic empires covering hundreds of miles, then thousands, and then multiple continents. They developed highways and postal systems to travel and communicate over massive distances.

Mesopotamia's inventions and firsts continue to be relevant, and we still use many of them in some form today. Think of all the ways we use the wheel today! Trains, planes, trucks, cars, motorcycles, and bicycles: almost all our transportation modes use the wheel, which was invented in ancient Sumer. Even boats and ships use them with the ship's wheel, rudder, and pulley systems. Let's not forget other modern ways we use the wheel like the cogwheel, the propeller, the gyroscope, and the turbine.

Mesopotamia instituted the first schools to teach students to read and write the first written language. Try to imagine a world without schools today. Everyone needs basic literacy and math to function at the lowest level, but we live in a constantly changing world. Education, in some form, enables us to keep up with all the recent technologies. Our schooling helps us understand the world around us, like what's going on with disease control, government, and economics.

How many times throughout the day does the ordinary person use basic counting, math, and even higher math? We give little thought to measuring ingredients or doubling recipes. We calculate how much weight we've gained or lost when we step on the scale. We use basic math to pay bills, balance the checkbook, and make a budget. When we do home renovation projects, we calculate how much tile, carpet, or fabric to buy, which requires basic geometry. The simple math that all of us use every day was developed over four thousand years ago in Mesopotamia.

How did ancient Mesopotamia's innovations and explosions of knowledge in various fields pave the way for modern technologies that have molded society as we know it today? For one thing, the ancient Mesopotamians didn't stop with developing basic counting and measurements. They progressed with higher mathematical sciences that contribute to the technology base underlying a multitude of functions in our world.

The ancient Mesopotamians' higher mathematics are implemented in manufacturing new or improved products and in weather forecasts that use computer simulations and mathematical modeling. Geometry contributes to fuel economy by designing advanced wing foils on aircraft. Math is applied to technological topics such as structural mechanics, optics, building construction, and engineering thermodynamics.

Mathematics forms the groundwork for computer technology that implements abstract language, logical deductions, and algorithms. Healthcare technology and research use math to draw up statistical graphs of pandemic infections, hospitalizations, and deaths or track vaccine rates and efficacy. Medical laboratories use math in converting grams to micrograms and mass to molar conversions. Higher math is used in the statistical analysis of standard deviations and standard curves.

The ancient Mesopotamians also developed technology in irrigation systems and hydraulic engineering. They created levees and dams to channel river water and later invented the qanat irrigation system to pull water up from underground aquifers. Even the oldest Sumerian cities had sewer drains for their houses. The basic hydraulic engineering innovated by ancient Mesopotamians has continued to develop, and its applications in the modern world are widespread. We still have dams, levees, and water distribution networks, but we also have automated sprinkler systems, sewage collection, and stormwater management. Fluid dynamic principles are utilized in aeronautical, mechanical, and even traffic engineering.

The ancient Mesopotamian law codes and their political and organizational practices are still relevant and applied in some form today. We all need concepts of basic morality, an understanding of right and wrong, that lifts us out of chaos and into true civilization. When Ur-Nammu and Hammurabi wrote their law codes, they first had to consider the underlying morality, and they had to decide what was good for society and what was disruptive. Their law codes sought to protect all citizens, especially the weak and disenfranchised, from harmful behaviors by others. Our legislative branches today still struggle with writing laws that stop detrimental behaviors and protect the safety and rights of all citizens.

The writers of ancient law codes and the political leaders of ancient Mesopotamia also had to contemplate the concepts of fairness to all, regardless of social standing. They had to consider how to stop immorality and crime in society. They had to ponder justice so that the strong didn't prevail over the weak or the wicked over the innocent. Cyrus the Great *was* great because he seemed to genuinely champion protection and opportunities for all, regardless of ethnicity, religion, or ideology. Today's legislative and judicial branches worldwide still struggle to ensure that fairness extends to everyone and that justice prevails against corruptness and exploitation.

Although the once-spectacular cities have sunk into the desert sands, the ideas of the ancient Mesopotamians continue to persevere and evolve in virtually all knowledge we have regarding astronomy, math, literacy, law, transportation, communication, engineering, architecture, and government. Although the once-magnificent ancient civilizations have faded into the mist of history, the ideals of the ancient Mesopotamians continue to guide us today: our understanding of the spiritual world, our appreciation of art and beauty, and our concepts of morality, tenacity, truth, justice, fairness, and friendship. Ancient Mesopotamia lives on through us all.

Here's another book by Enthralling History that you might like

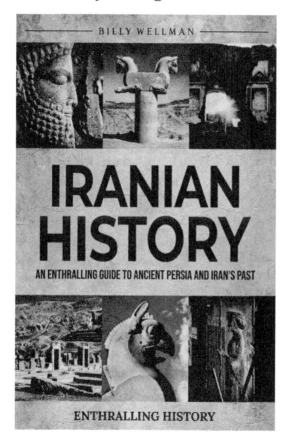

Free limited time bonus

Stop for a moment. We have a free bonus set up for you. The problem is this: we forget 90% of everything that we read after 7 days. Crazy fact, right? Here's the solution: we've created a printable, 1-page pdf summary for this book that you're reading now. All you have to do to get your free pdf summary is to go to the following website:

https://livetolearn.lpages.co/enthrallinghistory/

Once you do, it will be intuitive. Enjoy, and thank you!

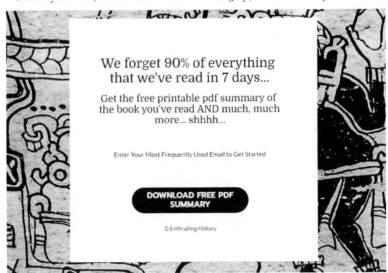

Bibliography

Calvert, A. (n.d.). Old Kingdom and First Intermediate Period, an introduction – Smarthistory. https://smarthistory.org/old-kingdom-first-intermediate-period-introduction/

Edfu Temple - Greco-Roman Period Monuments. (n.d.). https://egyptianmuseum.org/explore/greco-and-roman-period-monuments-edfu-temple

Egypt, Egyptian art during the Ptolemaic Period of Egyptian history | Antiquities Experts. (n.d.). https://www.antiquitiesexperts.com/egypt_ptol.html

Egypt: Piye and the 25th Dynasty. (n.d.). http://www.touregypt.net/featurestories/piye.htm

Egyptian Mummies. (n.d.). Smithsonian Institution. https://www.si.edu/spotlight/ancient-egypt/mummies

Freed, Rita E. *Egypt's Golden Age: The Art of Living in the New Kingdom, 1558-1085 B.C.* Boston: Museum of Fine Arts; 1981.

Heart Scarab | Ancient Egypt Online. (n.d.). https://ancientegyptonline.co.uk/heartscarab/

Herodotus. *The Histories (Penguin Classics Deluxe Edition).* New York: Penguin Classics; May 19, 2015.

History.com Editors. (2020, November 24). Alexander the Great. HISTORY. https://www.history.com/.amp/topics/ancient-history/alexander-the-great

Ian Shaw. *The Oxford History of Ancient Egypt (Oxford Illustrated History).* New York: Oxford University Press; October 23, 2003.

J. G. Manning. *The Last Pharaohs: Egypt Under the Ptolemies, 305–30 BC.* Princeton: Princeton University Press; 2009.

King Snefru (Sneferu). (n.d.). https://www.ancient-egypt-online.com/snefru.html

Kinnaer, J. (2014, August 11). Menes | The Ancient Egypt Site. http://www.ancient-egypt.org/who-is-who/m/menes.html

Kitchen, Kenneth Anderson. The Third Intermediate Period in Egypt (1100–650 BC). Warminster: Aris & Phillips Limited; 1996.

Mark, J. J. (2022, November 22). The Great Sphinx of Giza. World History Encyclopedia. https://www.worldhistory.org/Great_Sphinx_of_Giza/

Mark, J. J. (2022, November 23). Djoser. World History Encyclopedia. https://www.worldhistory.org/Djoser/

Mark, J. J. (2022, November 23). Hyksos. World History Encyclopedia. https://www.worldhistory.org/Hyksos/

Mark, J. J. (2022, November 23). The Temple of Hatshepsut. World History Encyclopedia. https://www.worldhistory.org/article/1100/the-temple-of-hatshepsut/

Mark, J. J. (2022, November 24). The Battle of Pelusium: A Victory Decided by Cats. World History Encyclopedia. https://www.worldhistory.org/article/43/the-battle-of-pelusium-a-victory-decided-by-cats/

Mark, J. J. (2022, November 25). Conflict Between the Temple and the Crown in Ancient Egypt. World History Encyclopedia. https://www.worldhistory.org/article/1027/conflict-between-the-temple-and-the-crown-in-ancie/

Mark, J. J. (2022, October 3). Narmer. World History Encyclopedia. https://www.worldhistory.org/Narmer/

Mark, J. J. (2022, September 26). Fayum. World History Encyclopedia. https://www.worldhistory.org/Fayum/

Memphis Tours. (n.d.). Abu Simbel Temples. https://www.memphistours.com/Egypt/Egypt-Wikis/aswan-attractions/wiki/Abu-Simbel-Temples

Merimde in Egypt. (n.d.). https://www.nemo.nu/ibisportal/0egyptintro/2aegypt/merimde.htm

Miroslav Bárta. *Analyzing Collapse: The Rise and Fall of the Old Kingdom (The AUC History of Ancient Egypt).* The American University in Cairo Press; 30 May 2019.

Nijssen, D. (2022, November 21). Cambyses II. World History Encyclopedia. https://www.worldhistory.org/Cambyses_II/

Old Kingdom Monuments Abu Ghurab. (n.d.). https://egyptianmuseum.org/explore/old-kingdom-monuments-abu-ghurab

Oren, Eliezer D. *The Hyksos: New Historical and Archaeological Perspectives.* University of Pennsylvania Museum of Archaeology and Anthropology Philadelphia; 1997.

R.B. Parkinson. *Poetry and Culture in Middle Kingdom Egypt: A Dark Side to Perfection (Studies in Egyptology & the Ancient Near East).* Equinox Publishing Ltd; 1 Nov. 2010.

Rattini, K. B. (2021, May 3). Pharaoh Ahmose I—facts and information. Culture. https://www.nationalgeographic.com/culture/article/ahmose-i

Rattini, K. B. (2021, May 4). Cyrus the Great: History's most merciful conqueror? Culture. https://www.nationalgeographic.com/culture/article/cyrus-the-great

Roberto B. Gozzoli. *The Writing of History in Ancient Egypt During the First Millennium BCE (ca. 1070–180 BCE): Trends and Perspectives.* London: Golden House Publications; 2006.

Ryan, D. P. (2021). *24 Hours in Ancient Egypt: A Day in the Life of the People Who Lived There.* Adfo Books.

Ryholt, Kim. *The Political Situation in Egypt during the Second Intermediate Period c. 1800–1550 B.C.* Museum Tuscalanum Press; 1997.

Sculpture of the Old Kingdom. (n.d.). http://kolibri.teacherinabox.org.au/modules/en-boundless/

The Pyramids of the Middle Empire. (n.d.). https://www.wonders-of-the-world.net/Pyramids-of-Egypt/Pyramids-of-the-middle-empire.php

Thomas, Angela P. Akhenaten's Egypt. Shire Egyptology 10. Princes Risborough, UK Shire; 1988.

Bingen, Jean. Hellenistic Egypt: Monarchy, Society, Economy, Culture. Berkeley University of California Press; 2007.

Toby Wilkinson. *The Rise and Fall of Ancient Egypt.* United States: Random House; January 8, 2013.

Wasson, D. L. (2022, August 31). Ptolemy I. World History Encyclopedia. https://www.worldhistory.org/Ptolemy_I/

Wasson, D. L. (2022, November 22). Battle of Issus. World History Encyclopedia. https://www.worldhistory.org/Battle_of_Issus/

Wikipedia contributors. (2022, May 19). Ka statue. Wikipedia. https://en.wikipedia.org/wiki/Ka_statue

Wikipedia contributors. (2022, November 10). Book of the Dead. Wikipedia. https://en.wikipedia.org/wiki/Book_of_the_Dead

Wikipedia contributors. (2022, November 15). Prehistoric Egypt. Wikipedia. https://en.wikipedia.org/wiki/Prehistoric_Egypt

Wikipedia contributors. (2022, September 10). Achaemenid conquest of Egypt. Wikipedia. https://en.wikipedia.org/wiki/Achaemenid_conquest_of_Egypt

Wolfram Grajetzki. *The Middle Kingdom of Ancient Egypt: History, Archaeology and Society (Duckworth Egyptology Illustrated Edition).* London: Bristol Classical Press; 24 Feb. 2006.

Bertman, Stephen. *Handbook to Life in Ancient Mesopotamia.* Oxford: Oxford University Press, 2005.

Clark, Peter. *Zoroastrianism: An Introduction to an Ancient Faith (Beliefs & Practices).* East Sussex: Sussex Academic Press, 1998.

Dalley, Stephanie. *Myths from Mesopotamia Creation, the Flood, Gilgamesh, and Others.* Oxford: Oxford University Press, 2008.

Dalley, Stephanie. "Old Babylonian Tablets from Nineveh; And Possible Pieces of Early Gilgamesh Epic." In *Iraq* 63 (2001): 155–67. https://doi.org/10.2307/4200507

Editors. "The World's Oldest Writing." In *Archaeology*, May/June 2016. https://www.archaeology.org/issues/213-features/4326-cuneiform-the-world-s-oldest-writing

Enuma Elish: The Seven Tablets of Creation. Translated by Leonard William King. Sacred

Texts.com. Accessed November 20, 2021.

https://www.sacred-texts.com/ane/stc/index.htm

Eppihimer, Melissa. "Assembling King and State: The Statues of Manishtushu and the Consolidation of Akkadian Kingship." In *American Journal of Archaeology* 114, no. 3 (2010): 365–80. http://www.jstor.org/stable/25684286

Frymer-Kensky, Tikva. "The Tribulations of Marduk: The So-Called 'Marduk Ordeal Text." *Journal of the American Oriental Society* 103, no. 1 (1983): 131–41. https://doi.org/10.2307/601866

Hritz, Carrie, Jennifer Pournelle, Jennifer Smith, and سميثجنيفر. *Revisiting the Sealands: Report of Preliminary Ground Reconnaissance in the Hammar District, Dhi Qar and Basra Governorates, Iraq.* Iraq 74 (2012): 37–49. http://www.jstor.org/stable/23349778

Jacobsen, Thorkild. "The Assumed Conflict between Sumerians and Semites in Early Mesopotamian History." In *Journal of the American Oriental Society* 59, no. 4 (1939): 485-95. https://doi.org/10.2307/594482

Kramer, Samuel Noah. *The Sumerians: Their History, Culture, and Character*. Chicago: University of Chicago Press, 1971.

Marriage of Martu. Translated by J. A. Black, G. Cunningham, E. Robson, and G. Zólyomi. The Electronic Text Corpus of Sumerian Literature, Oxford 1998. Accessed November 17, 2021. https://www.gatewaystobabylon.com/myths/texts/classic/martu.htm

Mesopotamia: A Captivating Guide to Ancient Mesopotamian History and Civilizations, Hammurabi, and the Persian Empire. Captivating History, 2019.

Moorey, P. R. S. "The 'Plano-Convex Building' at Kish and Early Mesopotamian Palaces." *Iraq* 26, no. 2 (1964): 83-98. https://doi.org/10.2307/4199767

Oppenheim, Leo. *Ancient Mesopotamia: Portrait of a Dead Civilization*. Chicago: University of Chicago Press, 1977.

Petrovich, Douglas. "Identifying Nimrod of Genesis 10 with Sargon of Akkad by Exegetical and Archaeological Means." In *Journal of the Evangelical Theological Society* 56, no. 2 (2013): 273-305. https://www.etsjets.org/files/JETS-PDFs/56/56-2/JETS_56-2_273-305_Petrovich.pdf

Pollock, Susan. *Ancient Mesopotamia*. Cambridge: Cambridge University Press, 1999.

Ponchia, Simonetta, Saana Svärd, and Kazuko Watanabe. "Slaves, Serfs, and Prisoners in Imperial Assyria (IX-VII Cent. BC). A Review of Written Sources." In *State Archives of Assyria Bulletin* 23 (2017): 157-179. https://www.academia.edu/36199877/Slaves_Serfs_and_Prisoners_in_Imperial_Assyria_IX_VII_Cent_BC_A_Review_of_written_sources?auto=download

Postgate, Nicholas. *Early Mesopotamia: Society and Economy at the Dawn of History*. Oxfordshire: Routledge, 1994.

Sackrider, Scott. "The History of Astronomy in Ancient Mesopotamia." In *The NEKAAL Observer* 234. https://nekaal.org/observer/ar/ObserverArticle234.pdf

Speiser, E. A. "Some Factors in the Collapse of Akkad." In *Journal of the American Oriental Society* 72, no. 3 (1952): 97-101. https://doi.org/10.2307/594938

Sumerian King List. Translated by Jean-Vincent Scheil, Stephen Langdon, and Thorkild Jacobsen. Livius, accessed October 20, 2021. https://www.livius.org/sources/content/anet/266-the-sumerian-king-list/#Translation

Teall, Emily K. (2014) "Medicine and Doctoring in Ancient Mesopotamia." In *Grand Valley Journal of History* 3:1, Article 2. https://scholarworks.gvsu.edu/gvjh/vol3/iss1/2

The *Assyrian King List.* Translated by Jean-Jacques Glassner. Livius, accessed November 12, 2021. https://www.livius.org/sources/content/anet/564-566-the-assyrian-king-list

"The Code of Hammurabi." Translated by L.W. King. In *The Avalon Project: Documents in Law, History, and Diplomacy.* Yale Law School: Lillian Goldman Law Library. Accessed November 27, 2001. https://avalon.law.yale.edu/ancient/hamframe.asp

The *Epic of Atrahasis.* Translated by B. R. Foster. Livius, accessed October 18, 2021. https://www.livius.org/sources/content/anet/104-106-the-epic-of-atrahasis

The *Epic of Gilgamesh.* Translated by N. K. Sandars. London: Penguin Classics, 1960.

The Tanakh: Full Text. Jewish Virtual Library: A Project of AICE. 1997. https://www.jewishvirtuallibrary.org/the-tanakh-full-text

Van De Mieroop, Marc. *A History of the Ancient Near East ca. 3000 - 323 BC.* Hoboken: Blackwell Publishing, 2006.

Van De Mieroop, Marc. *King Hammurabi of Babylon: A Biography.* Hoboken: Blackwell Publishing, 2004.

Vargyas, Péter. "Sennacherib's Alleged Half-Shekel Coins." In *Journal of Near Eastern Studies,* 61, no. 2 (2002): 111–15. http://www.jstor.org/stable/545291